Fungi: Their Nature, Influence, and Uses

Fungi: Their Nature, Influence, and Uses

By

M. C. COOKE, M.A. LL.D.

EDITED BY THE

REV. M.J. BERKELEY, M.A., F.L.S.

GYAN

Published by

Gyan Publishing House
5, Ansari Road
Daryaganj, New Delhi-110002
Phone: 011-47034999, 9811692060
E-mail: books@gyanbooks.com

Distribution Network
gyanbooks.com
India, USA, Canada, UK, Australia, France

ISBN : 978-81-212-6689-5 (PB)
First Published, 1875

2nd Impression 2022

Printed at: Gyan Press, Delhi.

FUNGI: THEIR NATURE, INFLUENCE, AND USES
Author: M. C. COOKE

THE INTERNATIONAL SCIENTIFIC SERIES

VOLUME XIV.

List of Volumes already Published in

THE INTERNATIONAL SCIENTIFIC SERIES.

FUNGI: THEIR NATURE, INFLUENCE, AND USES

BY

M. C. COOKE, M.A., LL.D.

EDITED BY THE

Rev. M. J. BERKELEY, M.A., F.L.S.

SECOND EDITION

1875

PREFACE BY THE EDITOR.

As my name appears on the title-page of this volume, it is necessary that I should exactly state what part I had in its preparation. I had no doubt originally engaged to undertake the work myself; but finding, from multiplicity of engagements and my uncertain health, that I could not accomplish it satisfactorily, I thought the best course I could take was to recommend Mr. Cooke to the publishers; a gentleman well known, not only in this country, but in the United States. The whole of the work has therefore been prepared by himself, the manuscript and proof sheets being submitted to me from time to time, in which I merely suggested such additions as seemed needful, subjoining occasionally a few notes. As the work is intended for students, the author has had no hesitation in repeating what has been stated in former chapters where it has been thought to prove useful. I have no doubt that the same high character will justly apply to this as to Mr. Cooke's former publications, and especially to his "Handbook of British Fungi."

M. J. BERKELEY.

SIBBERTOFT,

November 23, 1874.

CONTENTS.

LIST OF ILLUSTRATIONS.

FUNGI

THEIR NATURE, USES, INFLUENCES, ETC.

I.

NATURE OF FUNGI.

THE most casual observer of Nature recognizes in almost every instance that comes under his notice in every-day life, without the aid of logical definition, the broad distinctions between an animal, a plant, and a stone. To him, the old definition that an animal is possessed of life and locomotion, a plant of life without locomotion, and a mineral deficient in both, seems to be sufficient, until some day he travels beyond the circuit of diurnal routine, and encounters a sponge or a zoophyte, which possesses only one of his supposed attributes of animal life, but which he is assured is nevertheless a member of the animal kingdom. Such an encounter usually perplexes the neophyte at first, but rather than confess his generalizations to have been too gross, he will tenaciously contend that the sponge must be a plant, until the evidence produced is so strong that he is compelled to desert his position, and seek refuge in the declaration that one kingdom runs into the other so imperceptibly that no line of demarcation can be drawn between them. Between these two extremes of broad distinction, and no distinction, lies the ground occupied by the scientific student, who, whilst admitting that logical definition fails in assigning briefly and tersely the bounds of the three kingdoms, contends that such limits exist so positively, that the universal scientific mind accepts the recognized limit without controversy or contradiction.

In like manner, if one kingdom be made the subject of inquiry, the same difficulties will arise. A flowering plant, as represented by a rose or a lily, will be recognized as distinct from a fern, a seaweed, or a fungus. Yet there are some flowering plants which, at first sight, and without examination, simulate cryptogams, as, for example, many *Balanophoræ*, which the unscientific would at once class with fungi. It is nevertheless true that even the incipient botanist will accurately separate the phanerogams from the cryptogams, and by means of a little more, but still elementary knowledge, distribute the latter amongst ferns, mosses, fungi, lichens, and algæ, with comparatively few exceptions. It is true that between fungi and lichens there exists so close an affinity that difficulties arise, and doubts, and disputations, regarding certain small groups or a few species; but these are the exception, and not the rule. Botanists generally are agreed in recognizing the five principal groups of Cryptogamia, as natural and distinct. In proportion as we advance from comparison of members of the three kingdoms, through that of the primary groups in one kingdom, to a comparison of tribes, alliances, and orders, we shall require closer observation, and more and more education of the eye to see, and the mind to appreciate, relationships and distinctions.

We have already assumed that fungi are duly and universally admitted, as plants, into the vegetable kingdom. But of this fact some have even ventured to doubt. This doubt, however, has been confined to one order of fungi, except, perhaps, amongst the most illiterate, although now the animal nature of the *Myxogastres* has scarcely a serious advocate left. In this order the early condition of the plant is pulpy and gelatinous, and consists of a substance more allied to sarcode than cellulose. De Bary insinuated affinities with *Amœba*,* whilst Tulasne

* De Bary, "Des Myxomycètes," in "Ann. des Sci. Nat." 4 sér. xi. p. 153; "Bot. Zeit." xvi. p. 357. De Bary's views are controverted by M. Wigand in "Ann. des Sci. Nat." 4 sér. (Bot.) xvi. p. 255, &c.

affirmed that the outer coat in some of these productions contained so much carbonate of lime that strong effervescence took place on the application of sulphuric acid. Dr. Henry Carter is well known as an old and experienced worker amongst amœboid forms of animal life, and, when in Bombay, he devoted himself to the examination of the *Myxogastres* in their early stage, and the result of his examinations has been a firm conviction that there is no relationship whatever between the *Myxogastres* and the lower forms of animal life. De Bary has himself very much modified, if not wholly abandoned, the views once propounded by him on this subject. When mature, and the dusty spores, mixed with threads, sometimes spiral, are produced, the *Myxogastres* are so evidently close allies of the *Lycoperdons*, or Puffballs, as to leave no doubt of their affinities. It is scarcely necessary to remark that the presence of zoospores is no proof of animal nature, for not only do they occur in the white rust (*Cystopus*), and in such moulds as *Peronospora*,* but are common in algæ, the vegetable nature of which has never been disputed.

There is another equally important, but more complicated subject to which we must allude in this connection. This is the probability of minute fungi being developed without the intervention of germs, from certain solutions. The observations of M. Trécul, in a paper laid before the French Academy, have thus been summarized:—1. Yeast cells may be formed in the must of beer without spores being previously sown. 2. Cells of the same form as those of yeast, but with different contents, arise spontaneously in simple solution of sugar, or to which a little tartrate of ammonia has been added, and these cells are capable of producing fermentation in certain liquids under favourable conditions. 3. The cells thus formed produce *Penicillium* like the cells of yeast. 4. On the other hand, the spores of *Penicillium* are capable of being transformed into yeast.† The interpretation of this is, that the mould *Penicillium* may be

* De Bary, "Recherches sur le Developpement de quelques Champignons Parasites," in "Ann. des Sci. Nat." 4 sér. (Bot.) xx. p. 5.

† "Popular Science Review," vol. viii. p. 96.

produced from a sugar solution by "spontaneous generation," and without spore or germ of any kind. The theory is, that a molecular mass which is developed in certain solutions or infusions, may, under the influence of different circumstances, produce either animalcules or fungi. "In all these cases, no kind of animalcule or fungus is ever seen to originate from preexisting cells or larger bodies, but always from molecules."* The molecules are said to form small masses, which soon melt together to constitute a globular body, from which a process juts out on one side. These are the so-called *Torulæ*,† which give off buds which are soon transformed into jointed tubes of various diameters, terminating in rows of sporules, *Penicillium*, or capsules containing numerous globular seeds, *Aspergillus* (*sic*).

This is but another mode of stating the same thing as above referred to by M. Trécul, that certain cells, resembling yeast cells (*Torula*), are developed spontaneously, and that these ultimately pass through the form of mould called *Penicillium* to the more complex *Mucor* (which the writer evidently has confounded with *Aspergillus*, unless he alludes to the ascigerous form of *Aspergillus*, long known as *Eurotium*). From what is now known of the polymorphism of fungi, there would be little difficulty in believing that cells resembling yeast cells would develop into *Penicillium*, as they do in *fact* in what is called the "vinegar plant," and that the capsuliferous, or higher condition of this mould may be a *Mucor*, in which the sporules are produced in capsules. The difficulty arises earlier, in the supposed spontaneous origination of yeast cells from molecules, which result from the peculiar conditions of light, temperature, &c., in which certain solutions are placed. It would be impossible to review all the arguments, or tabulate all the experiments, which have been employed for and against this theory. It could not be passed over in silence, since it has been one of the stirring questions of the day. The great problem how to exclude all germs

* Dr. J. H. Bennett "On the Molecular Origin of Infusoria," p. 56.

† They have, however, no close relation with real *Torulæ*, such as *T. monilioides*, &c.—COOKE's *Handbook*, p. 477.

from the solutions experimented upon, and to keep them excluded, lies at the foundation of the theory. It must ever, as we think, be matter of doubt that all germs were not excluded or destroyed, rather than one of belief that forms known to be developed day by day from germs should under other conditions originate spontaneously.

Fungi are veritably and unmistakably plants, of a low organization, it is true, but still plants, developed from germs, somewhat analogous, but not wholly homologous, to the seeds of higher orders. The process of fertilization is still obscure, but facts are slowly and gradually accumulating, so that we may hope at some not very distant period to comprehend what as yet are little removed from hypotheses. Admitting that fungi are independent plants, much more complex in their relations and development than was formerly supposed, it will be expected that certain forms should be comparatively permanent, that is, that they should constitute good species. Here, also, efforts have been made to develop a theory that there are no legitimate species amongst fungi, accepting the terms as hitherto applied to flowering plants. In this, as in allied instances, too hasty generalizations have been based on a few isolated facts, without due comprehension of the true interpretation of such facts and phenomena. Polymorphism will hereafter receive special illustration, but meantime it may be well to state that, because some forms of fungi which have been described, and which have borne distinct names as autonomous species, are now proved to be only stages or conditions of other species, there is no reason for concluding that no forms are autonomous, or that fungi which appear and are developed in successive stages are not, in their entirety, good species. Instead, therefore, of insinuating that there are no good species, modern investigation tends rather to the establishment of good species, and the elimination of those that are spurious. It is chiefly amongst the microscopic species that polymorphism has been determined. In the larger and fleshy fungi nothing has been discovered which can shake our faith in the species described half a century, or more, ago. In the Agarics, for instance, the forms seem to be as permanent and as distinct as in the flowering plants. In fact, there is still no reason to dissent, except to a very limited extent, from what was written before polymorphism was accredited, that, "with a few exceptions only, it may without doubt be asserted that more certain species do not exist in any part of the organized world than amongst fungi. The same species constantly recur in the same places, and if kinds not hitherto detected present themselves, they are either such as are well known in other districts, or species which have been overlooked, and which are found on better experience to be widely diffused. There is nothing like chance about their characters or growth." *

The parasitism of numerous minute species on living and growing plants has its parallel even amongst phanerogams in the mistletoe and broom-rape and similar species. Amongst fungi a large number are thus parasitic, distorting, and in many cases ultimately destroying, their host, burrowing within the tissues, and causing rust and smut in corn and grasses, or even more destructive and injurious in such moulds as those of the potato disease and its allies. A still larger number of fungi are developed from decayed or decaying vegetable matter. These are found in winter on dead leaves, twigs, branches, rotten wood, the remains of herbaceous plants, and soil largely charged with disintegrated vegetables. As soon as a plant begins to decay it becomes the source of a new vegetation, which hastens its destruction, and a new cycle of life commences. In these instances, whether parasitic on living plants or developed on dead ones, the source is still vegetable. But this is not always the case, so that it cannot be predicated that fungi are wholly epiphytal. Some species are always found on animal matter, leather, horn, bone, &c., and some affect such unpromising substances as minerals, from which it would be supposed that no nourishment could be obtained, not only hard gravel stones, fragments of rock, but also metals, such as iron and lead, of which more may be said when we come to treat of the habitats of fungi. Although in general terms fungi may be described as "hysterophytal or epiphytal mycetals deriving

* Berkeley's "Outlines of British Fungology," p. 24.

nourishment by means of a mycelium from the matrix,"* there are exceptions to this rule with which the majority accord.

Of the fungi found on animal substances, none are more extraordinary than those species which attack insects. The white mould which in autumn proves so destructive to the common house-fly may for the present be omitted, as it is probably a condition of one of the *Saprolegniei*, which some authors include with fungi, and others with algæ. Wasps, spiders, moths, and butterflies become enveloped in a kind of mould named *Isaria*, which constitutes the conidia of *Torrubia*, a genus of club-shaped *Sphæriæ* afterwards developed. Some species of *Isaria* and *Torrubia* also affect the larvæ and pupæ of moths and butterflies, converting the whole interior into a mass of mycelium, and fructifying in a clavate head. It has been subject for discussion whether in such instances the fungus commenced its development during the life of the insect, and thus hastened its death, or whether it resulted after death, and was subsequent to the commencement of decay.† The position in which certain large moths are found standing on leaves when infested with *Isaria* resembles so closely that of the house-fly when succumbing to *Sporendonema Muscæ*, would lead to the conclusion that certainly in some cases the insect was attacked by the fungus whilst still living; whilst in the case of buried caterpillars, such as the New Zealand or British *Hepialus*, it is difficult to decide. Whether in life or death in these instances, it is clear that the silk-worm disease *Muscardine* attacks the living insect, and causes death. In the case of the *Guêpes végétantes*, the wasp is said to fly about with the fungus partially developed.

In all fungi we may recognize a vegetative and a reproductive system: sometimes the first only becomes developed, and then the fungus is imperfect, and sometimes the latter is far more prominent than the former. There is usually an agglomeration of delicate threads, either jointed or not, which are somewhat analogous to the roots of higher plants. These delicate threads

* Berkeley's "Introduction to Cryptogamic Botany," p. 235.

† Gray, "Notices of Insects which form the Basis of Fungoid Parasites."

permeate the tissues of plants attacked by parasitic fungi, or they run over dead leaves forming whitened patches, formerly bearing the name of *Himantia*, but really the mycelium of some species of *Marasmius*. If checked or disturbed, the process stops here, and only a mycelium of interwoven threads is produced. In this condition the mycelium of one species so much resembles that of another, that no accurate determination can be made. If the process goes on, this mycelium gives rise to the stem and cap of an agaricoid fungus, completing the vegetative system. This in turn gives origin to a spore-bearing surface, and ultimately the fruit is formed, and then the fungus is complete; no fungus can be regarded as perfect or complete without its reproductive system being developed. In some this is very simple, in others it is as complex. In many of the moulds we have miniature representatives of higher plants in the mycelium. or roots, stem, branches, and at length capsules bearing sporidia, which correspond to seeds. It is true that leaves are absent, but these are sometimes compensated by lateral processes or abortive branchlets. A tuft of mould is in miniature a forest of trees. Although such a definition may be deemed more poetic than accurate, more figurative than literal, yet few could believe in the marvellous beauty of a tuft of mould if they never saw it as exhibited under the microscope. In such a condition no doubt could be entertained of its vegetable character. But there is a lower phase in which these plants are sometimes encountered; they may consist only of single cells, or strings of cells, or threads of simple structure floating in fluids. In such conditions only the vegetative system is probably developed, and that imperfectly, yet some have ventured to give names to isolated cells, or strings of cells, or threads of mycelium, which really in themselves possess none of the elements of correct classification—the vegetative system, even, being imperfect, and consequently the reproductive is absent. As already observed, no fungus is perfect without fruit of some kind, and the peculiarities of structure and development of fruit form one of the most important elements in classification. To attempt, therefore, to give names to such imperfect fragments of undeveloped plants is almost as absurd as to name a flowering plant from a stray fragment of a root-fibril accidentally cast out of the ground—nay, even worse, for identification would probably be easier. It is well to protest at all times against attempts to push science to the verge of absurdity; and such must be the verdict upon endeavours to determine positively such incomplete organisms as floating cells, or hyaline threads which may belong to any one of fifty species of moulds, or after all to an alga. This leads us to remark, in passing, that there are forms and conditions under which fungi may be found when, fructification being absent—that is, the vegetative system alone developed—they approximate so closely to algæ that it is almost impossible to say to which group the organisms belong.

Finally, it is a great characteristic of fungi in general that they are very rapid in growth, and rapid in decay. In a night a puffball will grow prodigiously, and in the same short period a mass of paste may be covered with mould. In a few hours a gelatinous mass of *Reticularia* will pass into a bladder of dust, or a *Coprinus* will be dripping into decay. Remembering this, mycophagists will take note that a fleshy fungus which may be good eating at noon may undergo such changes in a few hours as to be anything but good eating at night. Many instances have been recorded of the rapidity of growth in fungi; it may also be accepted as an axiom that they are, in many instances, equally as rapid in decay.

The affinity between lichens and fungi has long been recognized to its full and legitimate extent by lichenologists and mycologists.* In the "Introduction to Cryptogamic Botany," it

* On the relation or connection between fungi and lichens, H. C. Sorby has some pertinent remarks in his communication to the Royal Society on "Comparative Vegetable Chromatology" (Proceedings Royal Society, vol. xxi. 1873, p. 479), as one result of his spectroscopic examinations. He says, "Such being the relations between the organs of reproduction and the foliage, it is to some extent possible to understand the connection between parasitic plants like fungi, which do not derive their support from the constructive energy of their fronds, and those which are self-supporting and possess true fronds. In the highest classes of plants the flowers are connected with the leaves, more especially by means of xanthophyll and yellow xanthophyll,

was proposed to unite them in one alliance, under the name of *Mycetales*, in the same manner as the late Dr. Lindley had united allied orders under alliances in his "Vegetable Kingdom;" but, beyond this, there was no predisposition towards the theory since propounded, and which, like all new theories, has collected a small but zealous circle of adherents. It will be necessary briefly to summarize this theory and the arguments by which it is supported and opposed, inasmuch as it is intimately connected with our subject.

As recently as 1868, Professor Schwendener first propounded his views,* and then briefly and vaguely, that all and every individual lichen was but an algal, which had collected about it a parasitic fungal growth, and that those peculiar bodies which, under the name of *gonidia*, were considered as special organs of lichens, were only imprisoned algæ. In language which the Rev. J. M. Crombie † describes as "pictorial," this author gave the general conclusion at which he had arrived, as follows:— "As the result of my researches, all these growths are not simple plants, not individuals in the usual sense of the term; they are rather colonies, which consist of hundreds and thousands of individuals, of which, however, only one acts as master, while the others, in perpetual captivity, provide nourishment for themselves and their master. This master is a fungus of the order *Ascomycetes*, a parasite which is accustomed to live upon the work of others; its slaves are green algæ, which it has sought out, or indeed caught hold of, and forced into its service. It surrounds

whereas in the case of lichens the apothecia contain very little, if any, of those substances, but a large amount of the lichenoxanthines so characteristic of the class. Looking upon fungi from this chromatological point of view, they bear something like the same relation to lichens that the petals of a leafless parasitic plant would bear to the foliage of one of normal character—that is to say, they are, as it were, the coloured organs of reproduction of parasitic plants of a type closely approaching that of lichens, which, of course, is in very close, if not in absolute agreement with the conclusions drawn by botanists from entirely different data."

* Schwendener, "Untersuchungen über den Flechtenthallus."

† Crombie (J. M.) "On the Lichen-Gonidia Question," in "Popular Science Review" for July, 1874.

them, as a spider does its prey, with a fibrous net of narrow meshes, which is gradually converted into an impenetrable covering. While, however, the spider sucks its prey and leaves it lying dead, the fungus incites the algæ taken in its net to more rapid activity; nay, to more vigorous increase." This hypothesis, ushered upon the world with all the prestige of the Professor's name, was not long in meeting with adherents, and the cardinal points insisted upon were—1st. That the generic relationship of the coloured "gonidia" to the colourless filaments which compose the lichen thallus, had only been assumed, and not proved; 2nd. That the membrane of the gonidia was chemically different from the membrane of the other tissues, inasmuch as the first had a reaction corresponding to that of algæ, whilst the second had that of fungi; 3rd. That the different forms and varieties of gonidia corresponded with parallel types of algæ; 4th. That as the germination of the spore had not been followed further than the development of a hypothallus, it might be accounted for by the absence of the essential algal on which the new organism should become parasitic; 5th. That there is a striking correspondence between the development of the fruit in lichens and in some of the sporidiiferous fungi (*Pyrenomycetes*).

These five points have been combated incessantly by lichenologists, who would really be supposed by ordinary minds to be the most practically acquainted with the structure and development of these plants, in opposition to the theorists. It is a fact which should have some weight, that no lichenologist of repute has as yet accepted the theory. In 1873 Dr. E. Bornet* came to the aid of Schwendener, and almost exhausted the subject, but failed to convince either the practised lichenologist or mycologist. The two great points sought to be established are these, that what we call lichens are compound organisms, not simple, independent vegetable entities; and that this compound organism consists of unicellular algæ, with a fungus parasitic upon them. The coloured gonidia which are found in the

* Bornet, (E.), "Recherches sur les Gonidies des Lichens," in "Ann. des Sci. Nat." 1873, 5 sér. vol. xvii.

substance, or thallus of lichens, are the supposed algæ; and the cellular structure which surrounds, encloses, and imprisons the gonidia is the parasitic fungus, which is parasitic on something infinitely smaller than itself, and which it entirely and absolutely isolates from all external influences.

Dr. Bornet believed himself to have established that every gonidium of a lichen may be referred to a species of algæ, and that the connection between the hypha and gonidia is of such a nature as to exclude all possibility of the one organ being produced by the other. This he thinks is the only way in which it can be accounted for that the gonidia of diverse lichens should be almost identical.

Dr. Nylander, in referring to this hypothesis of an imprisoned algal,* writes: "The absurdity of such an hypothesis is evident from the very consideration that it cannot be the case that an organ (gonidia) should at the same time be a parasite on the body of which it exercises vital functions; for with equal propriety it might be contended that the liver or the spleen constitutes parasites of the mammiferæ. Parasite existence is autonomous, living upon a foreign body, of which nature prohibits it from being at the same time an organ. This is an elementary axiom of general physiology. But observation directly made teaches that the green matter originally arises within the primary chlorophyll- or phycochrom-bearing cellule, and consequently is not intruded from any external quarter, nor arises in any way from any parasitism of any kind. The cellule at first is observed to be empty, and then, by the aid of secretion, green matter is gradually produced in the cavity and assumes a definite form. It can, therefore, be very easily and evidently demonstrated that the origin of green matter in lichens is entirely the same as in other plants." On another occasion, and in another place, the same eminent lichenologist remarks,† as to the supposed algoid nature of gonidia—"that such an unnatural existence as they would thus pass, enclosed in a prison and

* Nylander, "On the Algo-Lichen Hypothesis," &c., in "Grevillea," vol. ii. (1874), No. 22, p. 146.

† In Regensburg "Flora," 1870, p. 92.

deprived of all autonomous liberty, is not at all consonant with the manner of existence of the other algæ, and that it has no parallel in nature, for nothing physiologically analogous occurs anywhere else. Krempelhuber has argued that there are no conclusive reasons against the assumption that the lichen-gonidia may be self-developed organs of the lichen proper rather than algæ, and that these gonidia can continue to vegetate separately, and so be mistaken for unicellular algæ." In this Th. Fries seems substantially to concur. But there is one strong argument, or rather a repetition of an argument already cited, placed in a much stronger light, which is employed by Nylander in the following words:—" So far are what are called algæ, according to the turbid hypothesis of Schwendener, from constituting true algæ, that on the contrary it may be affirmed that they have a lichenose nature, whence it follows that these pseudo-algæ are in a systematic arrangement to be referred rather to the lichens, and that the class of algæ hitherto so vaguely limited should be circumscribed by new and truer limits.

As to another phase in this question, there are, as Krempelhuber remarks, species of lichens which in many countries do not fructify, and whose propagation can only be carried on by means of the soredia, and the hyphæ of such could in themselves alone no more serve for propagation than the hyphæ from the pileus or stalk of an Agaric, while it is highly improbable that they could acquire this faculty by interposition of a foreign algal. On the other hand he argues: "It is much more conformable to nature that the gonidia, as self-developed organs of the lichens, should, like the spores, enable the hyphæ proceeding from them to propagate the individual.*

A case in point has been adduced† in which gonidia were produced by the hypha, and the genus *Emericella*,‡ which is allied to *Husseia* in the *Trichogastres*, shows a structure in the stem exactly resembling *Palmella botryoides* of Greville, and to what occurs in *Synalyssa*. *Emericella*, with one or two other

* Rev. J. M. Crombie, in "Popular Science Review," July, 1874.

† Berkeley's "Introduction to Cryptogamic Botany," p. 373, fig. 78*a*.

‡ Berkeley's "Introduction," p. 341, fig. 76.

genera, must, however, be considered as connecting *Trichogastres* with lichens, and the question cannot be considered as satisfactorily decided till a series of experiments has been made on the germination of lichen spores and their relation to free algæ considered identical with gonidia. Mr. Thwaites was the first to point out* the relation of the gonidia in the different sections of lichens to different types of supposed algæ. The question cannot be settled by mere *à priori* notions. It is, perhaps, worthy of remark that in *Chionyphe Carteri* the threads grow over the cysts exactly as the hypha of lichens is represented as growing over the gonidia.

Recently, Dr. Thwaites has communicated his views on one phase of this controversy,† which will serve to illustrate the question as seen from the mycological side. As is well known, this writer has had considerable experience in the study of the anatomy and physiology of all the lower cryptogamia, and any suggestion of his on such a subject will at least commend itself to a patient consideration.

"According to our experience," he writes, "I think parasitic fungi invariably produce a sad effect upon the tissues they fix themselves upon or in. These tissues become pale in colour, and in every respect sickly in appearance. But who has ever seen the gonidia of lichens the worse for having the 'hypha' growing amongst them? These gonidia are always in the plumpest state, and with the freshest, healthiest colour possible. Cannot it enter into the heads of these most patient and excellent observers, that a cryptogamic plant may have two kinds of tissue growing side by side, without the necessity of one being parasitic upon the other, just as one of the higher plants may have half a dozen kinds of tissue making up its organization? The beautifully symmetrical growth of the same lichens has seemed to me a sufficient argument against one portion being parasitic upon another, but when we see all harmony and robust health, the idea that one portion is subsisting parasitically upon another appears to me to be a perfect absurdity."

* "Annals and Magazine of Natural History," April, 1849.

† In "Gardener's Chronicle" for 1873, p. 1341.

It appears to us that a great deal of confusion and a large number of errors which creep into our modern generalizations and hypotheses, may be traced to the acceptance of analogies for identities. How many cases of mistaken identity has the improvement of microscopes revealed during the past quarter of a century. This should at least serve as a caution for the future.

Apart, however, from the "gonidia," whatever they may be, is the remainder of the lichen a genuine fungus? Nylander writes, "The anatomical filamentose elements of lichens are distinguished by various characters from the hyphæ of fungi. They are firmer, elastic, and at once present themselves in the texture of lichens. On the other hand, the hyphæ of fungi are very soft, they possess a thin wall, and are not at all gelatinous, while they are immediately dissolved by the application of hydrate of potash, &c.*

Our own experience is somewhat to the effect, that there are some few lichens which are doubtful as to whether they are fungi or lichens, but, in by far the majority of cases, there is not the slightest difficulty in determining, from the peculiar firmness and elasticity of the tissues, minute peculiarities which the practised hand can detect rather than describe, and even the general character of the fruit that they differ materially from, though closely allied to fungi. We have only experience to guide us in these matters, but that is something, and we have no experience in fungi of anything like a *Cladonia*, however much it may resemble a *Torrubia* or *Clavaria*. We have *Pezizæ* with a subiculum in the section *Tapesia*, but the veriest tyro would not confound them with species of *Parmelia*. It is true that a great number of lichens, at first sight, and casually, resemble species of the *Hysteriacei*, but it is no less strange than true, that lichenologists and mycologists know their own sufficiently not to commit depredations on each other.

Contributions are daily being made to this controversy, and already the principal arguments on both sides have appeared in

* "Grevillea," vol. ii. p. 147, in note.

an English dress,* hence it will be unnecessary to repeat those which are modifications only of the views already stated, our own conclusions being capable of a very brief summary: that lichens and fungi are closely related the one to the other, but that they are not identical; that the "gonidia" of lichens are part of the lichen-organization, and consequently are not algæ, or any introduced bodies; that there is no parasitism; and that the lichen thallus, exclusive of gonidia, is wholly unknown amongst fungi.

The Rev. J. M. Crombie has therefore our sympathies in the remark with which his summary of the gonidia controversy closes, in which he characterizes it as a "sensational romance of lichenology," of the "unnatural union between a captive algal damsel and a tyrant fungal master."

* W. Archer, in "Quart. Journ. Micr. Sci." vol. xiii. p. 217; vol. xiv. p. 115. Translation of Schwendener's "Nature of the Gonidia of Lichens," in same journal, vol. xiii. p. 235.

II.

STRUCTURE.

Without some knowledge of the structure of fungi, it is scarcely possible to comprehend the principles of classification, or to appreciate the curious phenomena of polymorphism. Yet there is so great a variety in the structure of the different groups, that this subject cannot be compressed within a few paragraphs, neither do we think that this would be desired if practicable, seeing that the anatomy and physiology of plants is, in itself, sufficiently important and interesting to warrant a rather extended and explicit survey. In order to impart as much practical utility as possible to this chapter, it seems advisable to treat some of the most important and typical orders and suborders separately, giving prominence to the features which are chiefly characteristic of those sections, following the order of systematists as much as possible, whilst endeavouring to render each section independent to a considerable extent, and complete in itself. Some groups naturally present more noteworthy features than others, and will consequently seem to receive more than their proportional share of attention, but this seeming inequality could scarcely have been avoided, inasmuch as hitherto some groups have been more closely investigated than others, are more intimately associated with other questions, or are more readily and satisfactorily examined under different aspects of their life-history.

Agaricini.—For the structure that prevails in the order to which the mushroom belongs, an examination of that species will be almost sufficient. Here we shall at once recognize three distinct parts requiring elucidation, viz. the rooting slender fibres that traverse the soil, and termed the *mycelium*, or spawn, the stem and cap or pileus, which together constitute what is called the *hymenophore*, and the plates or gills on the under surface of the cap, which bear the *hymenium*. The earliest condition in which the mushroom can be recognized as a vegetable entity is in that of the "spawn" or mycelium, which is essentially an agglomeration of vegetating spores. Its normal form is that of branched, slender, entangled, anastomosing, hyaline threads. At certain privileged points of the mycelium, the threads seem to be aggregated, and become centres of vertical extension. At first only a small nearly globose bud-

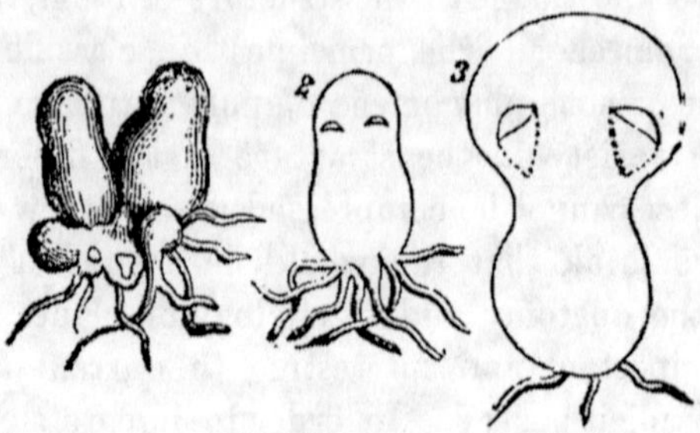

FIG. 1.—Agaric in Process of Growth.

ding, like a grain of mustard seed, is visible, but this afterwards increases rapidly, and other similar buddings or swellings appear at the base.* These are the young hymenophore. As

* A curious case occurred some years since at Bury St. Edmunds, which may be mentioned here in connection with the development of these nodules. Two children had died under suspicious circumstances, and an examination of the body of the latter after exhumation was made, a report having arisen that the child died after eating mushrooms. As certain white nodules appeared on the inner surface of the intestines, it was at once hastily concluded that the spores of the mushroom had germinated, and that the nodules were infant mushrooms. This appeared to one of us so strange, that application was made for specimens, which were kindly forwarded, and a cursory glance was enough to convince us that they were not fungoid. An examination under the microscope further confirmed the diagnosis, and the application of nitric acid showed that the nodules were merely due to chalk mixture, which had been given to the child for the diarrhetic symptoms under which he succumbed.

it pushes through the soil, it gradually loses its globose form, becomes more or less elongated, and in this condition a longitudinal section shows the position of the future gills in a pair of opposite crescent-shaped darker-coloured spots near the apex. The dermal membrane, or outer skin, seems to be continuous over the stem and the globose head. At present, there is no external evidence of an expanded pileus and gills; a longitudinal section at this stage shows that the gills are being developed, that the pileus is assuming its cap-like form, that the membrane stretching from the stem to the edge of the young pileus is separating from the edge of the gills, and forming a *veil*, which, in course of time, will separate below and leave the gills exposed. When, therefore, the mushroom has arrived almost at maturity, the pileus expands, and in this act the veil is torn away from the margin of the cap, and remains for a time like a collar around the stem. Fragments of the veil often remain attached to the margin of the pileus, and the collar adherent to the stem falls back, and thenceforth is known as the *annulus* or ring. We have in this stage the fully-developed hymenophore,—the stem with its ring, supporting an expanded cap or pileus, with gills on the under surface bearing the hymenium.* A longitudinal section cut through the pileus and down

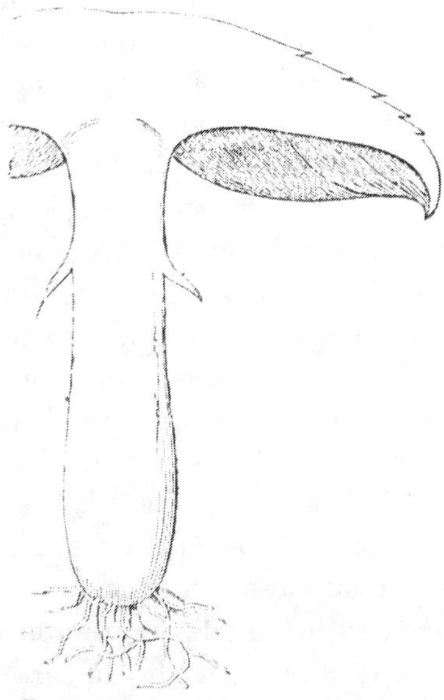

FIG. 2.—Section of Common Mushroom.

* Ehrenberg compared the whole structure of an Agaric with that of a mould, the mycelium corresponding with the hyphasma, the stem and pileus with the flocci, and the hymenium with the fructifying branchlets. The comparison is no less ingenious than true, and gives a lively idea of the connection of the more noble with the more humble fungi.—*Ehrb. de Mycetogenesi.*

the stem, gives the best notion of the arrangement of the parts, and their relation to the whole. By this means it will be seen that the pileus is continuous with the stem, that the substance of the pileus descends into the gills, and that relatively the substance of the stem is more fibrous than that of the pileus. In the common mushroom the ring is very distinct surrounding the stem, a little above the middle, like a collar. In some Agarics the ring is very fugacious, or absent altogether. The form of the gills, their mode of attachment to the stem, their colour, and more especially the colour of the spores, are all very important features to be attended to in the discrimination of species, since they vary in different species. The whole substance of the Agaric is cellular. A longitudinal slice from the stem will exhibit under the microscope delicate tubular cells, the general direction of which is lengthwise, with lateral branches, the whole interlacing so intimately that it is difficult to trace any individual thread very far in its course. It will be evident that the structure is less compact as it approaches the centre of the stem, which in many species is hollow. The *hymenium* is the spore-bearing surface, which is exposed or naked, and spread over the gills. These plates are covered on all sides with a delicate membrane, upon which the reproductive organs are developed. If it were possible to remove this membrane in one entire piece and spread it out flat, it would cover an immense surface, as compared with the size of the pileus, for it is plaited or folded like a lady's fan over the whole of the gill-plates, or lamellæ, of the fungus.* If the stem of a mushroom be cut off close to the gills, and the cap laid upon a sheet of paper, with the gills downwards, and left there for a few hours, when removed a number of dark radiating lines will be deposited upon the paper, each line corresponding with the interstices between one pair of gills. These lines are made up of spores which have fallen from the hymenium, and, if placed under the microscope, their character will at once be made evident. If a fragment of the hymenium be also submitted to a similar examination, it will be found that the whole surface is studded

* In *Paxillus involutus* the hymenium may be readily torn off and unfolded.

with spores. The first peculiarity which will be observed is, that these spores are almost uniformly in groups of four together. The next feature to be observed is, that each spore is borne upon a slender stalk or sterigma, and that four of these sterigmata proceed from the apex of a thicker projection, from the hymenium, called a *basidium*, each basidium being the supporter of four sterigmata, and each sterigma of a spore.* A closer examination of the hymenium will reveal the fact that the basidia are accompained by other bodies, often larger, but without sterigmata or spores; these have been termed *cystidia*, and their structure and functions have been the subject of much controversy.† Both kinds of bodies are produced on the hymenium of most, if not all, the Agaricini.

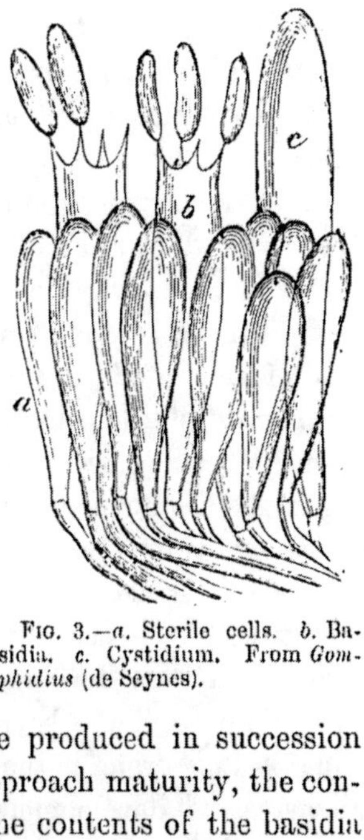

Fig. 3.—*a*. Sterile cells. *b*. Basidia. *c*. Cystidium. From *Gomphidius* (de Seynes).

The basidia are usually expanded upwards, so as to have more or less of a clavate form, surmounted by four slender points, or tubular processes, each supporting a spore; the contents of these cells are granular, mixed apparently with oleaginous particles, which communicate through the slender tubes of the spicules with the interior of the spores. Corda states that, although only one spore is produced at a time on each sporophore, when this falls away others are produced in succession for a limited period. As the spores approach maturity, the connection between their contents and the contents of the basidia diminishes and ultimately ceases. When the basidium which bears mature spores is still well charged with granular matter, it may be presumed that the production of a second or third

* This was well delineated in "Flora Danica," plate 834, as observed in *Coprinus comatus* as long ago as 1780.

† A. de Bary, "Morphologie und Physiologie der Pilze," in "Hofmeister's Handbuch," vol. ii. cap. 5, 1866, translated in "Grevillea," vol. i. p. 181.

series of spores is quite possible. Basidia exhausted entirely of their contents, and which have become quite hyaline, may often be observed.

The cystidia are usually larger than the basidia, varying in size and form in different species. They present the appearance of large sterile cells, attenuated upwards, sometimes into a slender neck. Corda was of opinion that these were male organs, and gave them the name of *pollinaires.* Hoffmann has also described* both these organs under the names of *pollinaria* and *spermatia*, but does not appear to recognize in them the sexual elements which those names would indicate; whilst de Seynes suggests that the cystidia are only organs returned to vegetative functions by a sort of hypertrophy of the basidia.† This view seems to be supported by the fact that, in the section *Pluteus* and some others, the cystidia are surmounted by short horns resembling sterigmata. Hoffmann has also indicated‡ the passage of cystidia into basidia. The evidence seems to be in favour of regarding the cystidia as barren conditions of basidia. There are to be found upon the hymenium of Agarics a third kind of elongated cells, called by Corda§ basilary cells, and by Hoffmann "sterile cells," which are either equal in size or smaller than the basidia, with which also their structure agrees, excepting in the development of spicules. These are the "proper cells of the hymenium" of Léveillé, and are simply the terminal cells of the gill structure—cells which, under vigorous conditions, might be developed into basidia, but which are commonly arrested in their development. As suggested by de Seynes, the hymenium seems to be reduced to great simplicity, "one sole and self-same organ is the basis of it; according as it experiences an arrest of development, as it grows and fructifies, or as it becomes hypertrophied, it gives us a paraphyse, a basidium, or a cystidium—in other terms, atrophied basidium, normal basi-

* "Die Pollinarien und Spermatien von *Agaricus*," in "Botanische Zeitung," Feb. 29 and March 7, 1856.

† "Essai d'une Flore mycologique de la Région de Montpellier." Paris, 1863.

‡ Hoffmann, "Botanische Zeitung," 1856, p. 139.

§ Corda, "Icones Fungorum hucusque cognitorum," iii. p. 41. Prague, 1839.

dium, and hypertrophied basidium; these are the three elements which form the hymenium."*

The only reproductive organs hitherto demonstrated in Agarics are the spores, or, as sometimes called, from their method of production, *basidiospores.*† These are at first colourless, but afterwards acquire the colour peculiar to the species. In size and form they are, within certain limits, exceedingly variable, although form and size are tolerably constant in the same species. At first all are globose; as they mature, the majority are ovoid or elliptic; some are fusiform, with regularly attenuated extremities. In *Hygrophorus* they are rather irregular, reniform, or compressed in the middle. Sometimes the external surface is rough with more or less projecting warts. Some mycologists are of opinion that the covering of the spore is double, consisting of an *exospore* and an *endospore*, the latter being very fine and delicate. In other orders the double coating of the spore has been demonstrated. When the spore is coloured, the external membrane alone appears to possess colour, the endospore being constantly hyaline. It may be added here, that in this order the spore is simple and unicellular. In *Lactarius* and *Russula* the trama, or inner substance, is vesicular. True latex vessels occur occasionally in *Agaricus*, though not filled with milk as in *Lactarius.*

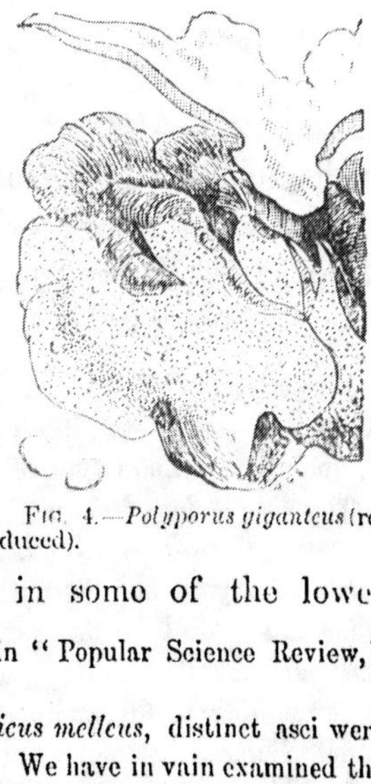

FIG. 4.—*Polyporus giganteus* (reduced).

POLYPOREI.—In this order the gill plates are replaced by tubes or pores, the interior of which is lined by the hymenium; indications of this structure having already been exhibited in some of the lower

* Cooke, M. C., "Anatomy of a Mushroom," in "Popular Science Review," vol. viii. p. 380.

† An attempt was made to show that, in *Agaricus melleus*, distinct asci were found, in a certain stage, on the gills or lamellæ. We have in vain examined the gills in various conditions, and could never detect anything of the kind. It is probable that the asci belonged to some species of *Hypomyces*, a genus of parasitic Sphæriaceous fungi.

Agaricini. In many cases the stem is suppressed. The substance is fleshy in *Boletus*, but in *Polyporus* the greater number of species are leathery or corky, and more persistent. The basidia, spicules, and quaternate spores agree with those of *Agaricini.** In fact there are no features of importance which relate to the hymenium in any order of *Hymenomycetes* (the *Tremellini* excepted) differing from the same organ in *Agaricini*, unless it be the absence of *cystidia.*

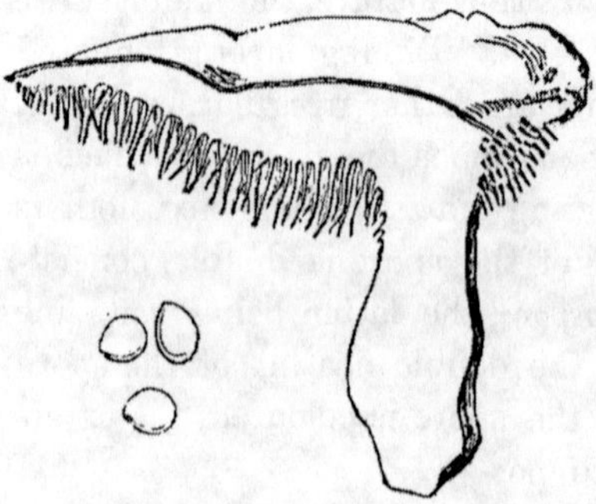

FIG. 5.—*Hydnum repandum.*

HYDNEI.—Instead of pores, in this order the hymenium is spread over the surface of spines, prickles, or warts.†

AURICULARINI.—The hymenium is more or less even, and in—

CLAVARIEI the whole fungus is club-shaped, or more or less intricately branched, with the hymenium covering the outer surface.

TREMELLINI.—In this order we have a great departure from the character of the substance, external appearance, and internal structure of the other orders in this family. Here we have a gelatinous substance, and the form is lobed, folded, convolute, often resembling the brain of some animal. The internal struc-

* It is not intended that the spores are always quaternate in *Agaricini*, though that number is constant in the more typical species. They sometimes exceed four, and are sometimes reduced to one.

† The species long known as *Hydnum gelatinosum* was examined by Mr. F. Currey in 1860 (*Journ. Linn. Soc.*), and he came to the conclusion that it was not a good *Hydnum.* Since then it has been made the type of a new genus (*Hydnoglœa B. and Br.* or, as called by Fries, in the new edition of "Epicrisis," *Tremellodon*, Pers. Myc. Eur.), and transferred to the *Tremellini.* Currey says, upon examining the fructification, he was surprised to find that, although in its external characters it was a perfect *Hydnum*, it bore the fruit of a *Tremella.* If one of the teeth be examined with the microscope, it will be seen to consist of threads bearing four-lobed sporophores, and spores exactly similar to *Tremella.* It will thus be seen, he adds, that the plant is exactly intermediate between *Hydnei* and *Tremellini*, forming, as it were, a stepping-stone from one to the other.

ture has been specially illustrated by M. Tulasne,* through the common species, *Tremella mesenterica*. This latter is of a fine golden yellow colour, and rather large size. It is uniformly composed throughout of a colourless mucilage, with no appreciable texture, in which are distributed very fine, diversely branched and anastomosing filaments. Towards the surface, the ultimate branches of this filamentous network give birth, both at their summits and laterally, to globular cells, which acquire a comparatively large size.

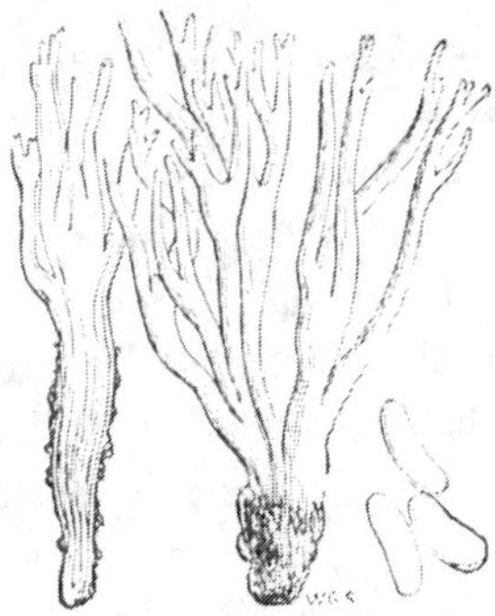

FIG. 6.—*Calocera viscosa.*

These cells are filled with a protoplasm, to which the plant owes its orange colour. When they have attained their normal dimensions, they elongate at the summit into two, three, or four distinct, thick, obtuse tubes, into which the protoplasm gradually passes. The development of these tubes is unequal and not simultaneous, so that one will often attain its full dimensions, equal, perhaps, to three or four times the diameter of the generative cell, whilst the others are only just appearing. By degrees, as each tube attains its full size, it is attenuated into a fine point, the extremity of which swells into a spheroidal cell, which ultimately becomes a spore.

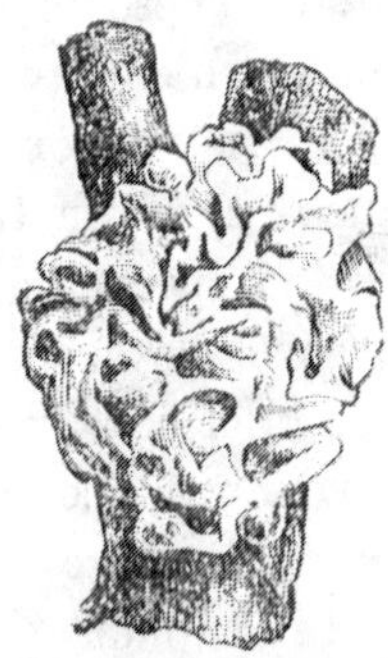

FIG. 7.—*Tremella mesenterica.*

Sometimes these tubes, or spicules, send out one or two lateral branches, each terminated by a spore. These spores (about ·006 to ·008 *mm.* diameter) are smooth, and deposit themselves, like a fine white dust, on the surface of the *Tremella* and on its matrix. M. Léveillé † was of opinion that

* Tulasne, L. R. and C., "Observations on the Organization of the Tremellini," in "Ann. des Sci. Nat." 3me sér. xix. (1853), pp. 193, &c.

† M. Léveillé, in "Ann. des Sci. Nat." 2me sér. viii. p. 328; 3me sér. ix. p. 127; also Bonorden, "Handbuch der Mycologie," p. 151.

the basidia of the Tremellini were monosporous, whilst M. Tulasne has demonstrated that they are habitually tetrasporous, as in other of the Hymenomycetes. Although agreeing in this, they differ in other features, especially in the globose form of the basidia, mode of production of the spicules, and, finally, the division of the basidia into two, three, or four cells by septa which cut each other in their axis. This division precedes the growth of the spicules. It is not rare to see these cells, formed at the expense of an unilocular basidium, become partly isolated from each other; in certain cases they seem to have separated very early, they then become larger than usual, and are grouped on the same filament so as to represent a kind of buds. This phenomenon usually takes place below the level of the fertile cells, at a certain depth in the mucous tissue of the *Tremella*.

Besides the reproductive system here described, Tulasne also made known the existence of a series of filaments which produce spermatia. These filaments are often scattered and confused with those which produce the basidia, and not distinguishable from them in size or any other apparent characteristic, except the manner in which their extremities are branched in order to produce the spermatia. At other times the spermatia-bearing surface covers exclusively certain portions of the fungus, especially the inferior lobes, imparting thereto a very bright orange colour, which is communicated by the layer of spermatia, unmixed with spores. These spots retain their bright colour, while the remainder of the plant becomes pale, or covered with a white dust. The spermatia are very small, spherical, and smooth, scarcely equalling ·002 *mm.* They are sessile, sometimes solitary, sometimes three or four together, on the slightly swollen extremities of certain filaments of the weft of the fungus.* Tulasne found it impossible to make these corpuscles germinate, and in all essential particulars they agreed with the spermatia found in ascomycetous fungi.

In the genus *Dacrymyces*, the same observer found the structure

* Tulasne, in "Ann. des Sci. Nat." (loc. cit.) xix. pl. x. fig. 29. Tulasne, "New Notes upon Tremellinous Fungi," in "Journ. Linn. Soc." vol. xiii. (1871), p. 31.

to have great affinity with that of *Tremella*. The spores in the species examined were of a different form, being oblong, very obtuse, slightly curved (·013—·019 × ·004—·006 *mm.*), at first unilocular, but afterwards triseptate. The basidia are cylindrical or clavate, filled with coloured granular matter; each of these bifurcates at the summit, and gradually elongates into two very open branches, which are attenuated above, and ultimately each is crowned by a spore. There are to be found also in the species of this genus globose bodies, designated "sporidioles" by M. Léveillé, which Tulasne took considerable care to trace to their source. He thus accounts for them:—Each of the cells or the spore emits exteriorly one or several of these corpuscles, supported on very short and very slender pedicels, which remain after the corpuscles are detached from them, new corpuscles succeeding the first as long as there remains any plastic matter within the spore. The pedicels are not all on the same plane; they are often implanted all on the same, and oftenest on the convex side of the reproductive body. These corpuscles, though placed under the most favourable conditions, never gave the least sign of vegetation, and Tulasne concludes that they are spermatia, analogous to those produced in *Tremella*. The spores which produce spermatia are not at all apt to germinate, whilst those which did not produce spermatia germinated freely. Hence it would appear that, although all spores seem to be perfectly identical, they have not all the same function. The same observer detected also amongst specimens of the *Dacrymyces* some of a darker and reddish tint, always bare of spores or spermatia on the surface, and these presented a somewhat different structure. Where the tissue had turned red it was sterile, the constituent filaments, ordinarily colourless, and almost empty of solid matter, were filled with a highly-coloured protoplasm; they were of less tenuity, more irregularly thick, and instead of only rarely presenting partitions, and remaining continuous, as in other parts of the plant, were parcelled out into an infinity of straight or curved pieces, angular and of irregular form, especially towards the surface of the fungus, where they compose a sort of pulp, varying in cohesion according to the dry or moist condition of the atmosphere. All parts of these reddish individuals seemed more or less infected with this disintegration, the basidia divided by transverse diaphragms into several cylindrical or oblong pieces, which finally become free. Transitional conditions were also observed in mixed individuals. This sterile condition is called by Tulasne "gemmiparous," and he believes that it has ere now given origin to one or more spurious species, and misled mycologists as to the real structure of perfect and fruitful *Dacrymyces*.

PHALLOIDEI.—In this order the hymenium is at first enclosed within a sort of peridium or universal volva, maintaining a somewhat globose or egg-shape. This envelope consists of an outer and inner coat of somewhat similar texture, and an intermediate gelatinous layer, often of considerable thickness. When a section is made of the fungus, whilst still enclosed in the volva, the hymenium is found to present numerous cavities, in which basidia are developed, each surmounted by spicules (four to six) bearing oval or oblong spores.* It is very difficult to observe the structure of the hymenium in this order, on account of its deliquescent nature. As the hymenium approaches maturity, the volva is ruptured, and the plant rapidly enlarges. In *Phallus*, a long erect cellular stem bears the cap, over which the hymenium is spread, and this expands enormously after escaping the restraint of the volva. Soon after exposure, the hymenium deliquesces into a dark mucilage, coloured by the minute spores, which drips from the pileus, often diffusing a most loathsome odour for a considerable distance. In *Clathrus*, the receptacle forms a kind of network. In *Aseröe*, the pileus is beautifully stellate. In many the attractive forms would be considered objects of beauty, were it not for their deliquescence, and often fœtid odour.†

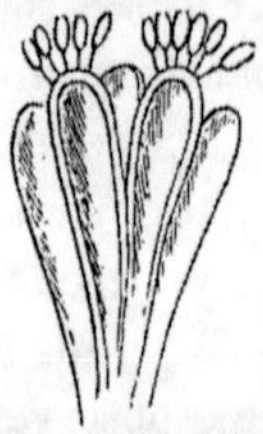

FIG. 8.—Basidia and spores of *Phallus*.

* Berkeley, M. J., "On the Fructification of Lycoperdon, Phallus, &c.," in "Ann. Nat. Hist." 1840, vol. iv. p. 158, pl. 5. Berkeley, M. J., "Introduction Crypt. Bot." p. 346.

† Tulasne, L. R. and C., "Fungi Hypogæi." Paris. Berkeley and Broome,

PODAXINEI.—This is a small but very curious group of fungi, in which the peridium resembles a volva, which is more or less confluent with the surface of the pileus. They assume hymenomycetal forms, some of them looking like Agarics, Boleti, or species of *Hydnum*, with deformed gills, pores, or spines; in *Montagnites*, in fact, the gill structure is very distinct. The spores are borne in definite clusters on short pedicels in such of the genera as have been examined.*

HYPOGŒI.—These are subterranean puff-balls, in which sometimes a distinct peridium is present; but in most cases it consists entirely of an external series of cells, continuous with the internal structure, and cannot be correctly estimated as a peridium. The hymenium is sinuous and convolute, bearing basidia with sterigmata and spores in the cavities. Sometimes the cavities are traversed by threads, as in the *Myxogastres*. The spores are in many instances beautifully echinulate, sometimes globose, at others elongated, and produced in such numbers as to lead to the belief that their development is successive on the spicules. When fully matured, the peridia are filled with a dusty mass of spores, so that it is scarcely possible in this condition to gain any notion of the structure. This is, indeed, the case with nearly all *Gasteromycetes*. The hypogœous fungi are curiously connected with *Phalloidei* by the genus *Hysterangium*.

TRICHOGASTRES.†—In their early stages the species contained in this group are not gelatinous, as in the *Myxogastres*, but are rather fleshy and firm. Very little has been added to our knowledge of structure in this group since 1839 and 1842, when one of us wrote to the following effect:—If a young plant of *Lycoperdon cœlatum* or *L. gemmatum* be cut through and examined with a common pocket lens, it will be found to consist of a fleshy mass,

"British Hypogœous Fungi," in "Ann. Nat. Hist." 1846, xviii. p. 74. Corda, "Icones Fungorum," vol. vi. pl. vii. viii.

* Tulasne, "Sur le Genre *Secotium*," in "Ann. des Sci. Nat." (1845), 3me sér. vol. iv. p. 169, plate 9.

† Tulasne, L. R. and C., "De la Fructification des *Scleroderma* comparée a celle des *Lycoperdon* et des *Bovista*," in "Ann. des Sci. Nat." 1842, xvii. p. 5. Tulasne, L. R. and C., "Sur les Genres Polysaccum et Geaster," in "Ann. des Sci. Nat." 1842, xviii. p. 129, pl. 5 and 6.

perforated in every direction with minute elongated, reticulated, anastomosing, labyrinthiform cavities. The resemblance of these to the tubes of *Boleti* in an early stage of growth, first led me to suspect that there must be some very close connection between them. If a very thin slice now be taken, while the mass is yet firm, and before there is the slightest indication of a change of colour, the outer stratum of the walls of these cavities is found to consist of pellucid obtuse cells, placed parallel to each other like the pile of velvet, exactly as in the young hymenium of an Agaric or Boletus. Occasionally one or two filaments cross from one wall to another, and once I have seen these anastomose. At a more advanced stage of growth, four little spicules are developed at the tips of the sporophores, all of which, as far as I have been able to observe, are fertile and of equal height, and on each of these spicules a globose spore is seated. It is clear that we have here a structure identical with that of the true Hymenomycetes, a circumstance which accords well with the fleshy habit and mode of growth. There is some difficulty in ascertaining the exact structure of the species just noticed, as the fruit-bearing cells, or sporophores, are very small, and when the spicules are developed the substance becomes so flaccid that it is difficult to cut a proper slice, even with the sharpest lancet. I have, however, satisfied myself as to the true structure by repeated observations. But should any difficulty arise in verifying it in the species in question, there will be none in doing so in *Lycoperdon giganteum*. In this species the fructifying mass consists of the same sinuous cavities, which are, however, smaller, so that the substance is more compact, and I have not seen them traversed by any filaments. In an early stage of growth, the surface of the hymenium, that is of the walls of the cavities, consists of short threads composed of two or three articulations, which are slightly constricted at the

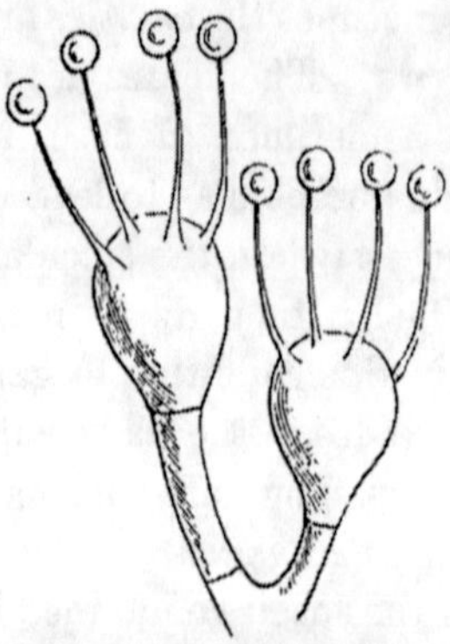

FIG. 9.—Basidia and spores of *Lycoperdon*.

joints, from which, especially from the last, spring short branchlets, often consisting of a single cell. Sometimes two or more branchlets spring from the same point. Occasionally the threads are constricted without any dissepiments, the terminal articulations are obtuse, and soon swell very much, so as greatly to exceed in diameter those on which they are seated. When arrived at their full growth, they are somewhat obovate, and produce four spicules, which at length are surmounted each with a globose spore. When the spores are fully developed, the sporophores wither, and if a solution of iodine be applied, which changes the spores to a rich brown, they will be seen still adhering by their spicules to the faded sporophores. The spores soon become free, but the spicule often still adheres to them; but they are not attached to the intermingled filaments. In *Bovista plumbea*, the spores have very long peduncles.* As in the *Hymenomycetes*, the prevailing type of reproductive organs consisted of quaternary spores borne on spicules ; so in *Gasteromycetes*, the prevailing type, in so far as it is yet known, is very similar, in some cases nearly identical, consisting of a definite number of minute spores borne on spicules seated on basidia. In a very large number of genera, the minute structure and development of the fructification (beyond the mature spores) is almost unknown, but from analogy it may be concluded that a method prevails in a large group like the *Myxogastres* which does not differ in essential particulars from that which is known to exist in other groups. The difficulties in the way of studying the development of the spores in this are far greater than in the previous order.

MYXOGASTRES.—At one time that celebrated mycologist, Professor De Bary, seemed disposed to exclude this group from the vegetable kingdom altogether, and relegate them to a companionship with amœboid forms. But in more recent works he seems to have reconsidered, and almost, if not entirely, abandoned, that disposition. These fungi, mostly minute, are characterized in their early stages by their gelatinous nature. The substance

* Berkeley, "On the Fructification of Lycoperdon, &c.," in "Annals of Natural History" (1840), iv. p. 155.

of which they are then composed bears considerable resemblance to sarcode, and, did they never change from this, there might be some excuse for doubting as to their vegetable nature; but as the species proceed towards maturity they lose their mucilaginous texture, and become a mass of spores, intermixed with threads, surrounded by a cellular peridium. Take, for instance, the genus *Trichia*, and we have in the matured specimens a somewhat globose peridium, not larger than a mustard seed, and sometimes nearly of the same colour; this ultimately ruptures and exposes a mass of minute yellow spherical spores, intermixed with threads of the same colour.* These threads, when highly magnified, exhibit in themselves a spiral arrangement, which has been the basis of some controversy, and in some species these threads are externally spinulose. The chief controversy

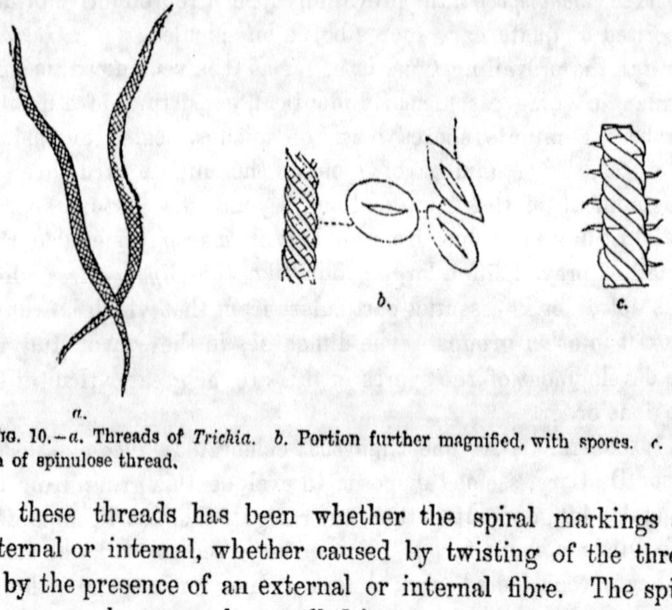

FIG. 10.—*a*. Threads of *Trichia*. *b*. Portion further magnified, with spores. *c*. Portion of spinulose thread.

on these threads has been whether the spiral markings are external or internal, whether caused by twisting of the thread or by the presence of an external or internal fibre. The spiral appearance has never been called in question, only the structure from whence it arises, and this, like the striæ of diatoms, is very much an open question. Mr. Currey held that the spiral

* Wigand, "Morphologie des Genres Trichia et Arcyria," in "Ann. des Sci. Nat." 4me sér. xvi. p. 223.

appearance may be accounted for by supposing the existence of an accurate elevation in the wall of the cell, following a spiral direction from one end of the thread to the other. This supposition would, he thinks, accord well with the optical appearances, and it would account exactly for the undulations of outline to which he alludes. He states that he had in his possession a thread of *Trichia chrysosperma*, in which the spiral appearance was so manifestly caused by an elevation of this nature, in which it is so clear that no internal spiral fibre exists, that he did not think there could be a doubt in the mind of any person carefully examining it with a power of 500 diameters that the cause of the spiral appearance was not a spiral fibre. In *Arcyria*, threads of a different kind are present;

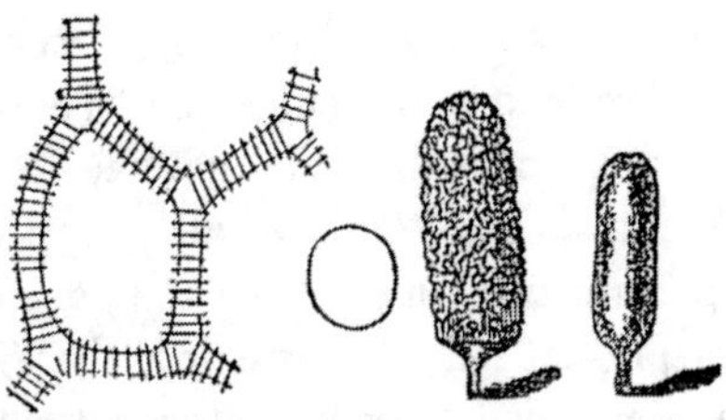

FIG. 11.—*Arcyria incarnata*, with portion of threads and spore, magnified.

they mostly branch and anastomose, and are externally furnished with prominent warts or spines, which Mr. Currey * holds are also arranged in a spiral manner around the threads. In other Myxogastres, threads are also present without any appreciable spiral markings or spines. In the mature condition of these fungi, they so clearly resemble, and have such close affinities with, the Trichogastres that one is led almost to doubt whether it was not on hasty grounds, without due examination or consideration, that proposals were made to remove them from the society of their kindred.

Very little is known of the development of the spores in this group; in the early stages the whole substance is so pulpy, and in the latter so dusty, whilst the transition from one to

* Currey, "On Spiral Threads of Trichia," in "Quart. Journ. Micr. Science" (1855), iii. p. 17.

the other is so rapid, that the relation between the spores and threads, and their mode of attachment, has never been definitely made out. It has been supposed that the spinulose projections from the capillitium in some species are the remains of pedicels from which the spores have fallen, but there is no evidence beyond this supposition in its favour, whilst on the other hand, in *Stemonitis*, for instance, there is a profuse interlacing capillitium, and no spines have been detected. In order to strengthen the supposition, spines should be more commonly present. The threads, or capillitium, form a beautiful reticulated network in *Stemonitis*, *Cribraria*, *Diachæa*, *Dictydium*, &c. In *Spumaria*, *Reticularia*, *Lycogala*, &c., they are almost obsolete.* In no group is the examination of the development of structure more difficult, for the reasons already alleged, than in the Myxogastres.

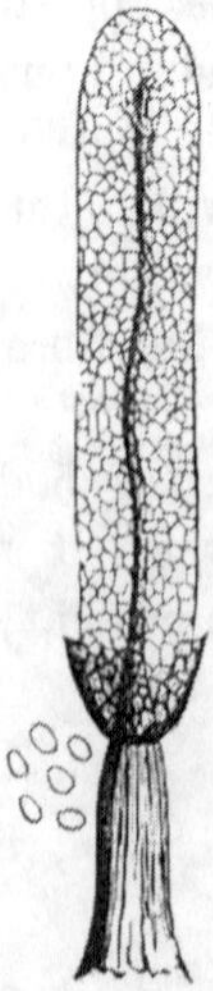

FIG. 12.—*Diachæa elegans.*

NIDULARIACEI.—This small group departs in some important particulars from the general type of structure present in the rest of the Gasteromycetes.† The plants here included may be described under three parts, the mycelium, the peridium, and the sporangia. The mycelium is often plentiful, stout, rigid, interlacing, and coloured, running over the surface of the soil, or amongst the vegetable débris on which the fungi establish themselves. The peridia are seated upon this mycelium, and in most instances are at length open above, taking the form of cups, or beakers. These organs consist of three strata of tissue varying in structure, the external being fibrous, and sometimes hairy, the interior cellular and delicate, the intermediate thick and at length tough, coriaceous, and resistant.

FIG. 13.—*Cyathus vernicosus.*

* In some of the genera, as, for instance, in *Badhamia*, *Enerthenema*, and *Reticularia*, the spores are produced within delicate cells or cysts, which are afterwards absorbed.

† Tulasne, "Essai d'une Monographie des Nidulariées," in "Ann. des Sci. Nat." (1844), i. 41 and 64.

When first formed, the peridia are spherical, they then elongate and expand, the mouth being for some time closed by a veil, or diaphragm, which ultimately disappears. Within the cups lentil-shaped bodies are attached to the base and sides by elastic cords. These are the sporangia. Each of these has a complicated structure; externally there is a filamentous tunic, composed of interlaced fibres, sometimes called the peridiole; beneath this is the cortex, of compact homogenous structure, then follows a cellular thicker stratum, bearing, towards the centre of the sporangia, delicate branched threads, or sporophores, on which, at their extremities, the ovate spores are generated, sometimes in pairs, but normally, it would seem that they are quaternary on spicules, the threads being true basidia. The whole structure is exceedingly interesting and peculiar, and may be studied in detail in Tulasne's memoir on this group.

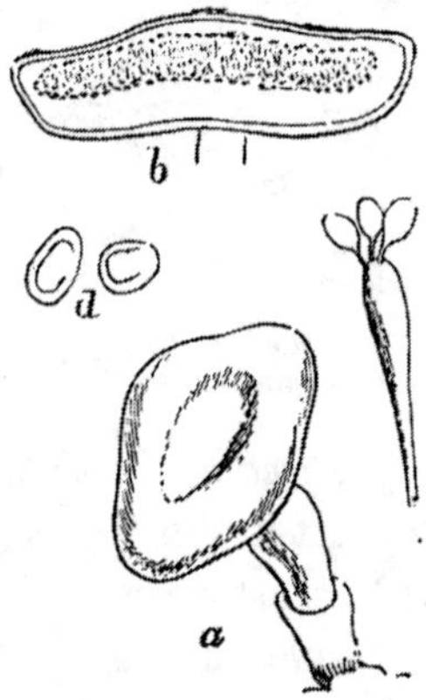

FIG. 14.—*Cyathus*. *a*. Sporangium. *b*. Section. *c*. Sporophore. *d*. Spores.

SPHÆRONEMEI.—In this very large and, within certain limits, variable order, there is but little of interest as regards structure, which is not better illustrated elsewhere; as, for instance, some sort of perithecium is always present, but this can be better studied in the *Sphæriacei*. The spores are mostly very minute, borne on delicate sporophores, which originate from the inner surface of the perithecia, but the majority of so-called species are undoubtedly conditions of sphæriaceous fungi, either spermatogonia or pycnidia, and are of much more interest when studied in connection with the higher forms to which they belong.* Probably the number of complete and autonomous species are very few.

MELANCONIEI.—Here, again, are associated together a great number of what formerly were considered good species of fungi, but which are now known to be but conditions of other forms.

* Berkeley, M. J., "Introduction, Crypt. Bot." p. 330.

One great point of distinction between these and the preceding is the absence of any true perithecium, the spores being produced in a kind of spurious receptacle, or from a sort of stroma. The spores are, as a rule, larger and much more attractive than in *Sphæronemei*, and, in some instances, are either very fine, or very curious. Under this head we may mention the multi-septate spores of *Coryneum;* the tri-radiate spores of *Asterosporium;* the curious crested spores of *Pestalozzia;* the doubly crested spores of *Dilophospora;* and the scarcely less singular gelatinous coated spores of *Cheirospora.* In all cases the fructification is abundant, and the spores frequently ooze out in tendrils, or form a black mass above the spurious receptacle from which they issue.*

FIG. 15.—*Asterosporium Hoffmanni.*

TORULACEI.—In this order there seems at first to be a considerable resemblance to the *Dematiei*, except that the threads are almost obsolete, and the plant is reduced to chains of spores, without trace of perithecium, investing cuticle, or definite stroma. Sometimes the spores are simple, in other cases septate, and in *Sporochisma* are at first produced in an investing cell. In most cases simple threads at length become septate, and are ultimately differentiated into spores, which separate at the joints when fully mature.

CÆOMACEI.—Of far greater interest are the Coniomycetous parasites on living plants. The present order includes those in which the spore † is reduced to a single cell; and here we may observe that, although many of them are now proved to be imperfect in themselves, and only forms or conditions of other fungals, we shall write of them here without regard to their duality. These originate, for the most part, within the tissues of living plants, and are developed outwards in pustules, which burst through the cuticle. The mycelium penetrates the inter-

* Berkeley, M. J., "Introduction, Crypt. Bot." p. 329.

† In the *Cœomacei* and *Pucciniæi* the term "pseudospore' would be much more accurate.

cellular passages, and may sometimes be found in parts of the plants where the fungus does not develop itself. There is no proper excipulum or peridium, and the spores spring direct from a more compacted portion of the mycelium, or from a cushion-like stroma of small cells. In *Lecythea*, the sub-globose spores are at first generated at the tips of short pedicels, from which they are ultimately separated; surrounding these spores arise a series of barren cells, or cysts, which are considerably larger than the true spores, and colourless, while the spores are of some shade of yellow or orange.* In *Trichobasis*, the spores are of a similar character, sub-globose, and at first pedicellate; but there are no surrounding cysts, and the colour is more usually brown, although sometimes yellow. In *Uredo*, the spores are at first generated singly, within a mother cell; they are globose, and either yellow or brown, without any pedicel. In *Coleosporium*, there are two kinds of spores, those of a pulverulent nature, globose, which are sometimes produced alone at the commencement of the season, and others which originate as an elongated cell; this becomes septate, and ultimately separates at the joints. During the greater part of the year, both kinds of spores are to be found in the same pustule. In *Melampsora*, the winter spores are elongated and wedge-shaped, compacted together closely, and are only matured during winter on dead leaves; the summer spores are pulverulent and globose, being, in fact, what were until recently regarded

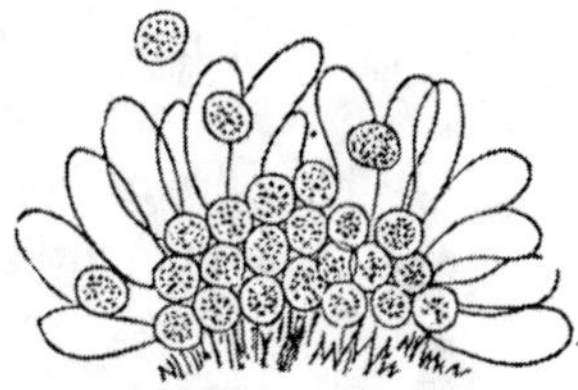

Fig. 16.—Barren Cysts and Pseudospores of *Lecythea*.

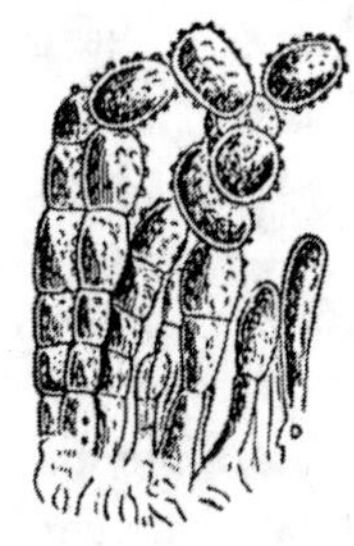

Fig. 17.—*Coleosporium Tussilaginis*, Lev.

Fig. 16.—*Melampsora salicina*.

* Léveillé, "Sur la Disposition Méthodique des Urédinées," in "Ann. des Sci. Nat." (1847), vol. viii. p. 369.

as species of *Lecythea*. In *Cystopus*, the spores are sub-globose, or somewhat angular, generated in a moniliform manner, and afterwards separating at the joints. The upper spore is always the oldest, continuous production of spores going on for some time at the base of the chain. Under favourable conditions of moisture, each of these spores, or conidia, as De Bary terms them, is capable of producing within itself a number of zoospores; * these ultimately burst the vesicle, move about by the aid of vibratile cilia, and at last settle down to germinate. Besides these, other reproductive bodies are generated upon the mycelium, within the tissues of the plant, in the form of globose oogonia, or resting spores, which, when mature, also enclose great numbers of zoospores. Similar oogonia are produced amongst the *Mucedines* in the genus *Peronospora*, to which De Bary considers *Cystopus* to be closely allied. At all events, this is a peculiarity of structure and development not as yet met with in any other of the *Cæomacei*.

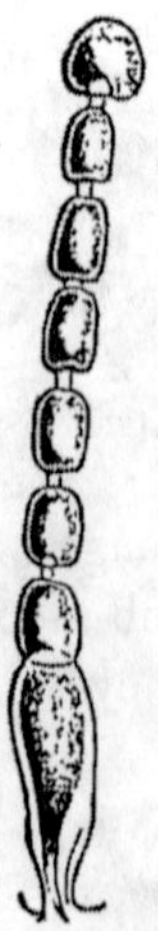

FIG. 19.—*Cystopus candidus.*

In *Uromyces* is the nearest approach to the *Pucciniæi;* in fact, it is *Puccinia* reduced to a single cell. The form of spore is usually more angular and irregular than in *Trichobasis*, and the pedicel is permanent. It may be remarked here, that of the foregoing genera, many of the species are not autonomous that have hitherto been included amongst them. This is especially true of *Lecythea*, *Trichobasis*, and, as it now appears, of *Uromyces*.†

PUCCINIÆI.—This group differs from the foregoing chiefly in having septate spores. The pustules, or sori, break through the cuticle in a similar manner, and here also no true peridium is present. In *Xenodochus*, the highest development of joints is reached, each spore being composed of an indefinite number, from ten to twenty cells. With it is associated an unicellular

* De Bary, "Champignons Parasites," in "Ann. des Sci. Nat." 4me sér. vol. xx.

† Tulasne, "Mémoire sur les Urédinées, &c.," in "Ann. des Sci. Nat." (1854), vol. ii. p. 78.

yellow Uredine, of which it is a condition. Probably, in every species of the *Pucciniæi*, it may hereafter be proved, as it is now suspected, that an unicellular Uredine precedes or is associated with it, forming a condition, or secondary form of fruit of that species. Many instances of that kind have already been traced by De Bary,* Tulasne, and others, and some have been a little too rashly surmised by their followers. In *Phragmidium*, the pedicel is much more elongated than in *Xenodochus*, and the spore is shorter, with fewer and a more definite number of cells for each species; Mr. Currey is of opinion that each cell of the spore in *Phragmidium* has an inner globose cell, which he caused to escape by rupture of the outer cell wall as a sphæroid nucleus,† leading to the inference that each cell has its own individual power of germination and reproduction. In *Triphragmium*, there are three cells for each spore, two being placed side by side, and one superimposed. In one species, however, *Triphragmium deglubens* (North American), the cells are arranged as in *Phragmidium*, so that this represents really a tricellular *Phragmidium*, linking the present with the latter genus. In *Puccinia* the number of species is by far the most numerous; in this genus the spores are uniseptate, and, as in all the *Pucciniæi*, the peduncles are permanent. There is great variability in the compactness of the spores in the sori, or pulvinules. In some species, the sori are so pulverulent that the spores are as readily dispersed as in the Uredines, in others they are so compact as to be separated from each

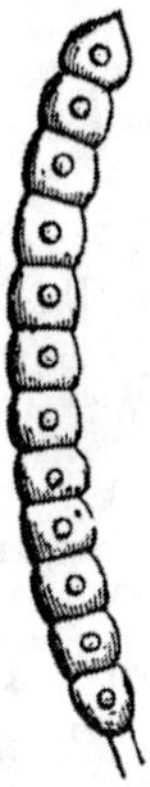

FIG. 20.—*Xenodochus carbonarius.*

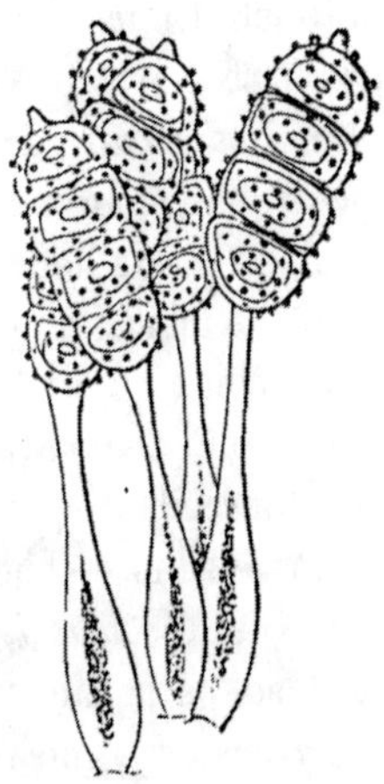

FIG. 21.—*Phragmidium bulbosum.*

* De Bary, "Ueber die Brandpilze," Berlin, 1853.

† Currey, in "Quart. Journ. Micr. Sci." (1857), vol. v. p. 119, pl. 8, fig. 13.

other with great difficulty. As might be anticipated, this has considerable effect on the contour of the spores, which in pulverulent species are shorter, broader, and more ovate than in the compact species. If a section of one of the more compact sori be made, it will be seen that the majority of the spores are side by side, nearly at the same level, their apices forming the external surface of the sori, but it will not be unusual to observe smaller and younger spores pushing up from the hymenial cells, between the peduncles of the elder spores, leading to the inference that there is a succession of spores produced in the same pulvinule. In *Podisoma*, a rather anomalous genus, the septate spores are immersed in a gelatinous stratum, and some authors have imagined that they have an affinity with the Tremellini, but this affinity is more apparent than real. The phenomena of germination, and their relations to *Rœstelia*, if substantiated, establish their claim to a position amongst the *Pucciniæi*.* It seems to us that *Gymnosporangium* does not differ generically from *Podisoma*. In a recently-characterized species, *Podisoma Ellisii*, the spores are bi-triseptate. This is, moreover, peculiar from the great deficiency in the gelatinous element. In another North American species, called *Gymnosporangium biseptatum*, Ellis, which is distinctly gelatinous, there are similar biseptate spores, but they are considerably broader and more obtuse. In other described species they are uniseptate.

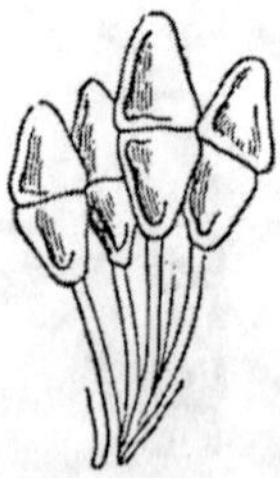

FIG. 22.—Pseudospores of *Puccinia*.

USTILAGINEI.—These fungi are now usually treated as distinct from the *Cæomacei*, to which they are closely related.† They are also parasitic on growing plants, but the spores are usually black or sooty, and never yellow or orange; on an average much smaller than in the *Cæomacei*. In *Tilletia*, the spores are spherical and reticulated, mixed with delicate threads, from

* Cooke, "On Podisoma," in "Journal of Quekett Microscopical Club," vol. ii. p. 255.

† Tulasne, "Mémoire sur les Ustilaginées," in "Ann. des Sci. Nat." (1847), vii. pp. 12 and 73.

whence they spring. In the best known species, *Tilletia caries*, they constitute the "bunt" of wheat. The peculiarities of germination will be alluded to hereafter. In *Ustilago*, the minute sooty spores are developed either on delicate threads or in compacted cells, arising first from a sort of semi-gelatinous, grumous stroma. It is very difficult to detect any threads associated with the spores. The species attack the flowers and anthers of composite and polygonaceous plants, the leaves, culms, and germen of grasses, &c., and are popularly known as "smuts." In *Urocystis* and *Thecaphora*, the spores are united together into sub-globose bodies, forming a kind of compound spore. In some species of *Urocystis*, the union which subsists between them is comparatively slight. In *Thecaphora*, on the contrary, the complex spore, or agglomeration of spores, is compact, being at first apparently enclosed in a delicate cyst. In *Tuburcinia*, the minute cells are compacted into a hollow sphere, having lacunæ communicating with the interior, and often exhibiting the remains of a pedicel.

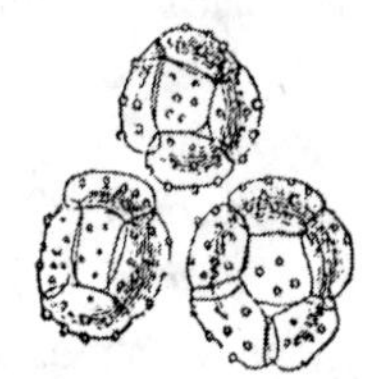

FIG. 23.—*Thecaphora hyalina.*

ÆCIDIACEI.—This group differs from the foregoing three groups prominently in the presence of a cellular peridium, which encloses the spores; hence some mycologists have not hesitated to propose their association with the Gasteromycetes, although every other feature in their structure seems to indicate a close affinity with the *Cæomacei.* The pretty cups in the genus *Æcidium* are sometimes scattered and sometimes collected in clusters, either with spermogonia in the centre or on the opposite surface. The cups are usually white, composed of regularly arranged bordered cells at length bursting at the apex, with the margins turned back and split into radiating teeth. The spores are commonly of a bright orange or golden yellow, sometimes white or brownish, and are produced in chains, or moniliform

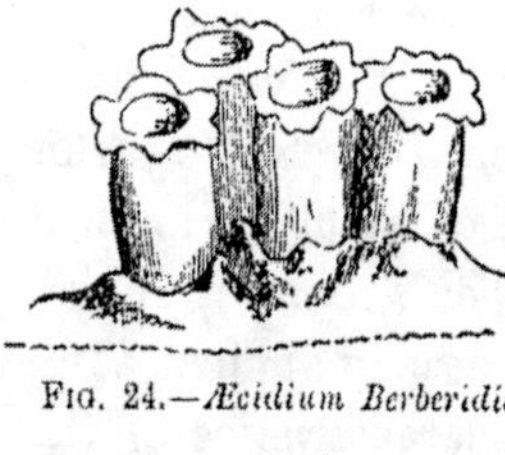

FIG. 24.—*Æcidium Berberidis.*

strings, slightly attached to each other,* and breaking off at the summit at the same time that they continue to be produced at the base, so that for some time there is a successive production of spores. The spermogonia are not always readily detected, as they are much smaller than the peridia, and sometimes precede them. The spermatia are expelled from the lacerated and fringed apices, and are very minute and colourless. In *Rœstelia* the peridia are large, growing in company, and splitting longitudinally in many cases, or by a lacerated mouth. In most instances, the spores are brownish, but in a splendid species from North America (*Rœstelia aurantiaca*, Peck), recently characterized, they are of a bright orange. If Œrsted is correct in his observations, which await confirmation, these species are all related to species of *Podisoma* as a secondary form of fruit.† In the *Rœstelia* of the pear-tree, as well as in that of the mountain ash, the spermogonia will be found either in separate tufts on discoloured spots, or associated with the *Rœstelia*. In *Peridermium* there is very little structural difference from *Rœstelia*, and the species are all found on coniferous trees. In *Endophyllum*, the peridia are immersed in the succulent substance of the matrix; whilst in *Graphiola*, there is a tougher and withal double peridium, the inner of which form a tuft of erect threads resembling a small brush.‡

HYPHOMYCETES.—The predominant feature in the structure of this order has already been intimated to consist in the development of the vegetative system under the form of simple or branched threads, on which the fruit is generated. The common name of mould is applied to them perhaps more generally than to other groups, although the term is too vague, and has been too vaguely applied to be of much service in giving an idea of the characteristics of this order. Leaving the smaller groups, and confining ourselves to the *Dematiei* and the *Mucedines*, we

* Corda, "Icones Fungorum," vol. iii. fig. 45.

† Cooke, "On Podisoma," in "Quekett Journal," vol. ii. p. 255.

‡ It may be a question whether *Graphiola* is not more nearly allied to *Trichocoma* (Jungh Fl. Crypt. Javæ, p. 10, f. 7) than to the genera with which it is usually associated.—M. J. B.

shall obtain some notion of the prevalent structure. In the former the threads are more or less carbonized, in the latter nearly colourless. One of the largest genera in *Dematiei* is *Helminthosporium*. It appears on decaying herbaceous plants, and on old wood, forming effused black velvety patches. The mycelium, of coloured jointed threads, overlays and penetrates the matrix; from this arise erect, rigid, and usually jointed threads, of a dark brown, nearly black colour at the base, but paler towards the apex. In most cases these threads have an externally cortical layer, which imparts rigidity; usually from the apex, but sometimes laterally, the spores are produced. Although sometimes colourless, these are most commonly of some shade of brown, more or less elongated, and divided transversely by few or many septa. In *Helminthosporium Smithii*, the spores much exceed the dimensions of the threads;* in other species they are smaller. In *Dendryphium*, the threads and spores are very similar, except that the threads are branched at their apex, and the spores are often produced one at the end of another in a short chain.† In *Septosporium* again, the threads and spores are similar, but the spores are pedicellate, and attached at or near the base; whilst in *Acrothecium*, with similar threads and spores, the latter are clustered together at the apex of the threads. In *Triposporium*, the threads are similar, but the spores are tri-radiate; and in *Helicoma*, the spores are twisted spirally. Thus, we might pass

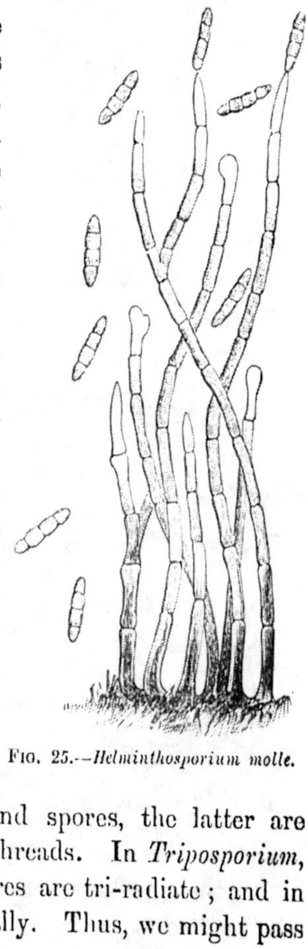

FIG. 25.—*Helminthosporium molle.*

* Cooke, "On Microscopic Moulds," in "Quekett Journal," vol. ii. plate 7.

† *See* "Dendryphium Fumosum," in "Quekett Journal," vol. ii. plate 8; or, "Corda Prachtflora," plate 22.

through all the genera to illustrate this chief feature of coloured, septate, rather rigid, and mostly erect threads, bearing at some point spores, which in most instances are elongated, coloured, and septate.

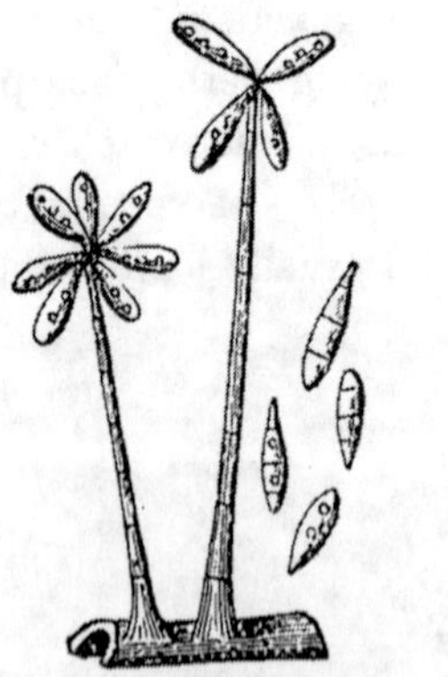

FIG. 26.—*Acrothecium simplex.*

MUCEDINES.—Here, on the other hand, the threads, if coloured at all, are still delicate, more flexuous, with much thinner walls, and never invested with an external cortical layer. One of the most important and highly developed genera is *Peronospora*, the members of which are parasitic upon and destructive of living vegetables. It is to this genus that the mould of the too famous potato disease belongs. Professor De Bary has done more than any other mycologist in the investigation and elucidation of this genus; and his monograph is a masterpiece in its way.* He was, however, preceded by Mr. Berkeley, and more especially by Dr. Montagne, by many years in elucidation of the structure of the flocci and conidia in a number of species.† In this genus, there is a delicate mycelium, which penetrates the intercellular passages of living plants, giving rise to erect branched threads, which bear at the tips of their ultimate ramuli, sub-globose, ovate, or elliptic spores, or, as De Bary terms them—conidia. Deeply seated on the mycelium, within the substance of the foster plant, other reproductive bodies, called oogonia, originate. These are spherical, more or

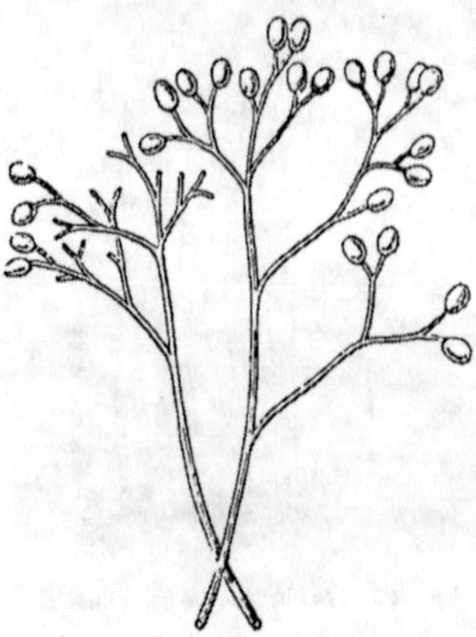

FIG. 27.—*Peronospora Arenariæ.*

* De Bary, "Champignons Parasites," in "Ann. des Sci. Nat." 4me sér. vol. xx.

† Berkeley, "On the Potato Murrain," in "Journ. of Hort. Soc. of London," vol. i. (1846), p. 9.

less warted and brownish, the contents of which become differentiated into vivacious zoospores, capable, when expelled, of moving in water by the aid of vibratile cilia. A similar structure has already been indicated in *Cystopus*, otherwise it is rare in fungi, if the *Saprolegniei* be excluded. In *Botrytis* and in *Polyactis*, the flocci and spores are similar, but the branches of the threads are shorter and more compact, and the septa are more common and numerous; the oogonia also are absent. De Bary has selected *Polyactis cinerea*, as it occurs on dead vine leaves, to illustrate his views of the dualism which he believes himself to have discovered in this species. "It spreads its mycelium in the tissue which is becoming brown," he writes, "and this shows at first essentially the same construction and growth as that of the mycelium filaments of *Aspergillus*." On the mycelium soon appear, besides those which are spread over the tissue of the leaves, strong, thick, mostly fasciculate branches, which stand close to one another, breaking forth from the leaf and rising up perpendicularly, the conidia-bearers. They grow about 1 *mm.* long, divide themselves, by successively rising partitions, into some prominent cylindrical linked cells, and then their growth is ended, and the upper cell produces near its point three to six branches almost standing rectangularly. Of these the under ones are the longest, and they again shoot forth from under their ends one or more still shorter little branches. The nearer they are to the top, the shorter are the branches, and less divided; the upper ones are quite branchless, and their length scarcely exceeds the breadth of the principal stem. Thus a system of branches appears, upon which, on a small scale, a bunch of grapes is represented. All the twigs soon end their

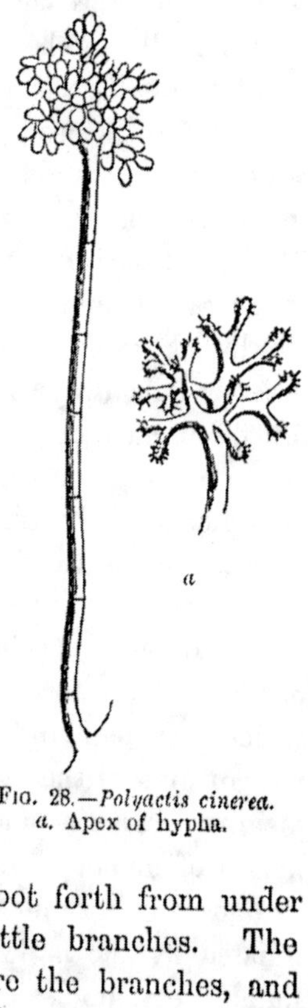

FIG. 28.—*Polyactis cinerea.*
a. Apex of hypha.

growth; they all separate their inner space from the principal stem, by means of a cross partition placed close to it. All the ends, and also that of the principal stem, swell about the same time something like a bladder, and on the upper free half of each swelling appear again, simultaneously, several fine protuberances, close together, which quickly grow to little oval bladders filled with protoplasm, and resting on their bearers with a sub-sessile, pedicellate, narrow basis, and which at length separate themselves through a partition as in *Aspergillus*. The detached cells are the conidia of our fungus; only one is formed on each stalk. When the formation is completed in the whole of the panicle, the little branches which compose it are deprived of their protoplasm in favour of the conidia; it is the same with the under end of the principal stem, the limits of which are marked by a cross partition. The delicate wall of these parts shrinks up until it is unrecognizable; all the conidia of the panicle approach one another to form an irregular grape-like bunch, which rests loosely on the bearer, and from which it easily falls away as dust. If they be brought into water they fall off immediately; only the empty, shrivelled, delicate skins are to be found on the branch which bore them, and the places on which they are fixed to the principal stem clearly appear as round circumscribed hilums, generally rather arched towards the exterior. The development of the main stem is not ended here. It remains solid and filled with protoplasm as far as the portion which forms the end through its conidia. Its end, which is to be found among these pieces, becomes pointed after the ripening of the first panicle, pushes the end of the shrivelled member on one side, and grows to the same length as the height of one or two panicles, and then remains still, to form a second panicle similar to the first. This is later equally perfoliated as the first, then a third follows, and thus a large number of panicles are produced after and over one another on the same stem. In perfect specimens, every perfoliated panicle hangs loosely to its original place on the surface of the stem, until by shaking or the access of water to it, it falls immediately into the single conidia, or the remains of branches, and the already-mentioned oval hilums are left behind. Naturally, the stem becomes longer by every perfoliation; in luxuriant specimens the length can reach that of some lines. Its partition is already, by the ripening of the first panicle from the beginning of its foundation, strong and brown; it is only colourless at the end which is extending, and in all new formations. During all these changes the filament remains either unbranched, except as regards the transient panicles, or it sends out here and there, at the perfoliated spots, especially from the lower ones, one or two strong branches, standing opposite one another and resembling the principal stem.

The mycelium, which grows so exuberantly in the leaf, often brings forth many other productions, which are called *sclerotia*, and are, according to their nature, a thick bulbous tissue of mycelium filaments. Their formation begins with the profuse ramification of the mycelium threads in some place or other; generally, but not always, in the veins of the leaf; the intertwining twigs form an uninterrupted cavity, in which is often enclosed the shrivelling tissue of the leaf. The whole body swells to a greater thickness than that of the leaf, and protrudes on the surface like a thickened spot. Its form varies from circular to fusiform; its size is also very unequal, ranging between a few lines and about half a millimetre in its largest diameter. At first it is colourless, but afterwards its outer layers of cells become round, of a brown or black colour, and it is surrounded by a black rind, consisting of round cells, which separate it from the neighbouring tissue. The tissue within the rind remains colourless; it is an entangled uninterrupted tissue of fungus filaments, which gradually obtain very solid, hard, cartilaginous coats. The sclerotium, which ripens as the rind becomes black, loosens itself easily from the place of its formation, and remains preserved after the latter is decayed.

The sclerotia are, here as in many other fungi, biennial organs, designed to begin a new vegetation after a state of apparent quietude, and to send forth special fruit-bearers. They may in this respect be compared to the bulbs and perennial roots of under shrubs. The usual time for the development of the sclerotia is late in the autumn, after the fall of the vine leaves. As long as the frost does not set in, new ones continually spring up, and each one attains to ripeness in a few days. If frost appears, it can lie dry a whole year, without losing its power of development. This latter commences when the sclerotium is brought into contact with damp ground during the usual temperature of our warmer seasons. If this occur soon, at the latest some weeks after it is ripe, new vegetation grows very quickly, generally after a few days; in several parts the colourless filaments of the inner tissue begin to send out clusters of strong branches, which, breaking through the black rind, stretch themselves up perpendicularly towards the surface, separate from one another, and then take all the characteristics of the conidia-bearers. Many such clusters can be produced on one sclerotium, so that soon the greater part of the surface is covered by filamentous conidia-bearers with their panicles. The colourless tissue of the sclerotium disappears in the same degree as the conidia-bearers grow, and at last the black rind remains behind empty and shrivelled. If we bring, after many months, for the first time, the ripe sclerotium, in damp ground, in summer or autumn, after it has ripened, the further development takes place more slowly, and in an essentially different form. It is true that from the inner tissue numerous filamentous branches shoot forth at the cost of this growing fascicle, and break through the black rind, but its filaments remain strongly bound, in an almost parallel situation, to a cylindrical cord, which for a time lengthens itself and spreads out its free end to a flat plate-like disc. This is always formed of strongly united threads, ramifications of the cylindrical cord. On the free upper surface of the disc, the filaments shoot forth innumerable branches, which, growing to the same height, thick and parallel with one another, cover the before-named disc.

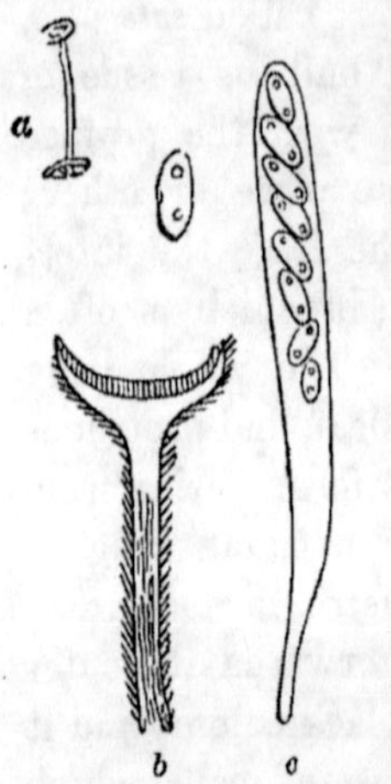

FIG. 29.—*Peziza Fuckeliana.* *a.* Natural size. *b.* Section enlarged. *c.* Ascus and sporidia.

Some remain narrow and cylindrical, are very numerous, and produce fine hairs (paraphyses); others, also very numerous, take the form of club-like ampulla cells, and each one forms in its interior eight free swimming oval spores. Those ampulla cells are sporidiiferous asci. After the spores have become ripe, the free point of the utricle bursts, and the spores are scattered to a great distance by a mechanism which we will not here further describe. New ampullas push themselves between those which are ripening and withering; a disc can, under favourable circumstances, always form new asci for weeks at a time. The number of the already described utricle-bearers is different, according to the size of the sclerotium; smaller specimens usually produce only one, larger two to four. The size is regulated by that of the sclerotia, and ranges, in full-grown specimens, between one and more millimetres for the length of the stalk, and a half to three (seldom more) millimetres for the breadth of the disc.* For some time the conidia form, belonging to the *Mucedines*, has been known as *Botrytis cinerea* (or *Polyactis cinerea*). The compact mycelium, or sclerotium, as an imperfect fungus, bore the name of *Sclerotium echinatum*, whilst to the perfect and cup-like form has been given the name of *Peziza Fuckeliana*. We have reproduced De Bary's life-history of this mould here, as an illustration of structure in the *Mucedines*, but hereafter we shall have to write of similar transformations when treating of polymorphism.

The form of the threads, and the form and disposition of the spores, vary according to the genera of which this order is composed. In *Oidium* the mostly simple threads break up into joints. Many of the former species are now recognized as conditions of *Erysiphe*. In *Aspergillus*, the threads are simple and erect, with a globose head, around which are clustered chains of simple spores. In *Penicillium*, the lower portion of the threads is simple, but they are shortly branched at the apex, the branches being terminated by necklaces of minute spores. In *Dactylium*,

* De Bary, "On Mildew and Fermentation," p. 25, reprinted from "German Quarterly Magazine," 1872; De Bary, "Morphologie und Physiologie der Pilze," (1866), 201

the threads are branched, but the spores are collected in clusters usually, and are moreover septate. In other genera similar distinctions prevail. These two groups of black moulds and white moulds are the noblest, and contain the largest number of genera and species amongst the *Hyphomycetes*. There is, however, the small group of *Isariacei*, in which the threads are compacted, and a semblance of such hymenomycetal forms as *Clavaria* and *Pterula* is the result, but it is doubtful if this group contains many autonomous species. In another small group, the *Stilbacei*, there is a composite character in the head, or receptacle,* and in the stem when the latter is present. Many of these, again, as *Tubercularia*, *Volutella*, *Fusarium*, &c., contain doubtful species. In *Sepedoniei* and *Trichodermacei*, the threads are reduced to a minimum, and the spores are such a distinctive element that through these groups the *Hyphomycetes* are linked with the *Coniomycetes*. These groups, however, are not of sufficient size or importance to demand from us, in a work of this character, anything more than the passing allusion which we have given to them.

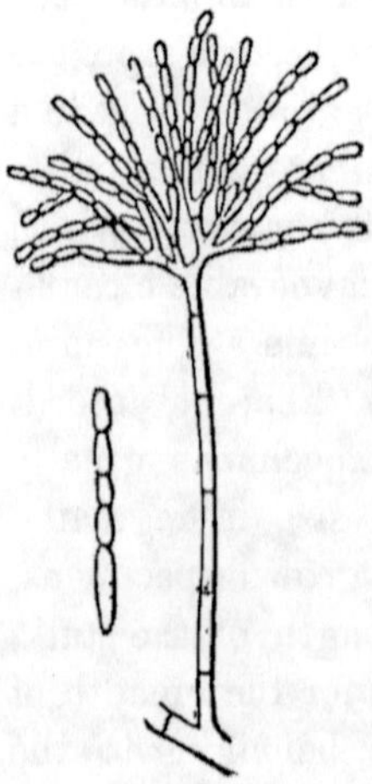

FIG. 30.—*Penicillium chartarum*, Cooke.

We come now to consider the structure in the Sporidiifera, in which the fructifying corpuscles or germs, whether called spores or sporidia, are generated within certain privileged cysts, usually in definite numbers. In systematic works, these are included under two orders, the *Physomycetes* and the *Ascomycetes*. The former of these consists of cyst-bearing moulds, and from their nearest affinity to the foregoing will occupy the first place.

PHYSOMYCETES include, especially amongst the *Mucorini*, many most interesting and instructive species for study, which even very lately have occupied the attention of continental mycologists. Most of these phenomena are associated more or less with reproduction, and as such will have to be adverted to again,

* Cooke, "Handbook of British Fungi," vol. ii. p. 552.

but there are points in the structure which can best be alluded to here. Again taking Professor de Bary's researches as our guide,* we will illustrate this by the common *Mucor mucedo:* If we bring quite fresh horse-dung into a damp confined atmosphere, for example, under a bell-glass, there appears on its surface, after a few days, an immense white mildew. Upright strong filaments of the breadth of a hair raise themselves over the surface, each of them soon shows at its point a round little head, which gradually becomes black, and a closer examination shows us that in all principal points it perfectly agrees with the sporangia of other species. Each of these white filaments is a sporangia-bearer. They spring from a mycelium which is spread in the dung, and appear singly upon it. Certain peculiarities in the form of the sporangium, and the little long cylindrical spores, which, when examined separately, are quite flat and colourless, are characteristic of the species. If the latter be sown in a suitable medium, for example, in a solution of sugar, they swell, and shoot forth germinating utricles, which quickly grow to mycelia, which bear sporangia. This is easily produced on the most various organic bodies, and *Mucor mucedo* is therefore found spontaneously on every substratum which is capable of nourishing mildew, but on the above-named the most perfect and exuberant specimens are generally to be found. The sporangia-bearers are at first always branchless and without partitions. After the sporangium is ripe, cross partitions in irregular order and number often appear in the inner space, and on the upper

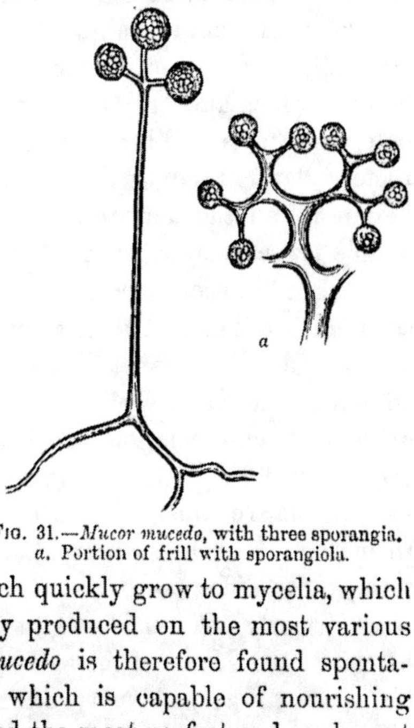

FIG. 31.—*Mucor mucedo*, with three sporangia. *a.* Portion of frill with sporangiola.

* De Bary, "On Mildew and Fermentation," in "Quarterly German Magazine," or 1872.

surface branches of different number and size, each of which forms a sporangium at its point. The sporangia which are formed later are often very similar, but sometimes very different, to those which first appeared, because their partition is very thick and does not fall to pieces when it is ripe, but irregularly breaks off, or remains entire, enclosing the spores, and at last falls to the ground, when the fungus withers. The cross partition which separates the sporangia from its bearers is in those which are first formed (which are always relatively thicker sporangia) very strongly convex, while those which follow later are often smaller, and in little weak specimens much less arched, and sometimes quite straight. After a few days, similar filaments generally show themselves on the dung between the sporangia-bearers, which appear to the naked eye to be provided with delicate white frills. Where such an one is to be found, two to four rectangular expanding little branches spring up to the same height round the filament. Each of these, after a short and simple process, branch out into a furcated form; the furcations being made in such a manner that the ends of the branch at last so stand together that their surface forms a ball. Finally, each of the ends of a branch swells to a little round sporangium, which is limited by a partition (called sporangiolum, to distinguish it from the larger ones), in which some, generally four, spores are formed in the manner already known. When the sporangiola are alone, they have such a peculiar appearance, with their richly-branched bearers, that they can be taken for something quite different to the organs of the *Mucor mucedo*, and were formerly not considered to belong to it. That they really belong to the *Mucor* is shown by the principal filament which it bears, not always, but very often, ending with a large sporangium, which is characteristic of the *Mucor mucedo*; it is still more evident if we sow the spores of the sporangiolum, for, as it germinates, a mycelium is developed, which, near a simple bearer, can form large sporangia, and those form sporangiola, the first always considerably preponderating in number, and very often exclusively. If we examine a large number of specimens, we find every possible middle form between the simple or less branched sporangia-bearers and the typical sporangiola frills; and we arrive at last at the conclusion simply to place the latter among the varieties of form which the sporangia-bearer of the *Mucor mucedo* shows, like every other typical organic form within certain limits. On the other hand, propagation organs, differing from those of the sporangia and their products, belong to *Mucor mucedo*, which may be termed conidia. On the dung (they are rare on any other substance) these appear at the same time, or generally somewhat later, than the sporangia-bearers, and are not unlike those to the naked eye. In a more accurate examination, they appear different; a thicker, partitionless filament rises up and divides itself, generally three-forked, at the length of one millimetre, into several series of branchlets. The forked branches of the last series bear under their points, which are mostly capillary, short erect little ramuli, and these, with which the ends of the principal branches articulate on their somewhat broad tops, several spores and conidia, near one another; about fifteen to twenty are formed at the end of each little ramulus. The peculiarities and variations which so often appear in the ramification need not be discussed here. After the articulation of the conidia, their bearers sink together by degrees, and are quite destroyed. The ripe conidia are round like a ball, their surface is scarcely coloured, and almost wholly smooth. These conidioid forms were at first described as a separate species under the name of *Botrytis Jonesii*. How, then, do they belong to the *Mucor?* * That they appear gregariously is as little proof of an original relation to one another, here as elsewhere. Attempts to prove that the conidia and sporangia-bearers originate on one and the same mycelium filament may possibly hereafter succeed. Till now this has not been the case,

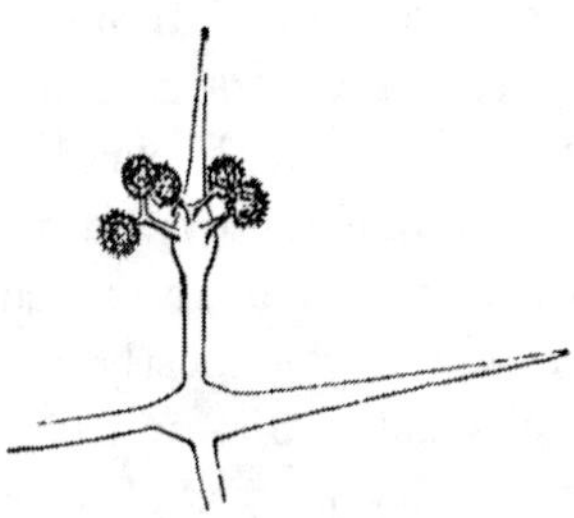

Fig. 32.—Small portion of *Botrytis Jonesii.*

* We are quite aware that Von Tieghem and Le Monnier, in "Ann. des Sci. Nat." 1873, p. 335, dispute that this belongs to *Mucor mucedo*, and assert that *Chætocladium Jonesii* is itself a true *Mucor*, with monosporous sporangia.

and he who has ever tried to disentangle the mass of filaments which exuberantly covers the substratum of a *Mucor* vegetation, which has reached so far as to form conidia, will not be surprised that all attempts have hitherto proved abortive. The suspicion of the connection founded on the gregariously springing up, and external resemblance, is fully justified, if we sow the conidia in a suitable medium, for example, in a solution of sugar. They here germinate and produce a mycelium which exactly resembles that of the *Mucor mucedo*, and, above all, they produce in profusion the typical sporangia of the same on its bearers. The latter are till now alone reproductions of conidia-bearers, and have never been observed on mycelia which have grown out of conidia.

These phenomena of development appear in the *Mucor* when it dwells on a damp substance, which must naturally contain the necessary nourishment for it, and is exposed to the atmospheric air. Its mycelium represents at first strong branched utricles without partitions; the branches are of the higher order, mostly divided into rich and very fine-pointed ramuli. In old mycelium, and also in the sporangia-bearers, the contents of which are mostly used for the formation of spores, and the substratum of which is exhausted for our fungus, short stationary pieces, filled with protoplasm, are very often formed into cells through partitions in order to produce spores, that is, grow to a new fruitful mycelium. These cells are called gemmules, brooding cells, and resemble such vegetable buds and sprouts of foliaceous plants which remain capable of development after the organs of vegetation are dead, in order to grow, under suitable circumstances, to new vegetating plants, as, for example, the bulbs of onions, &c.

If we bring a vegetating mycelium of *Mucor mucedo* into a medium which contains the necessary nourishment for it, but excluded from the free air, the formation of sporangia takes place very sparingly or not at all, but that of gemmules is very abundant. Single interstitial pieces of the ramuli, or even whole systems of branches, are quite filled with a rich greasy protoplasm; the short pieces and ends are bound by partitions which form particular, often tun-like or globular cells; the longer ones are changed, through the formation of cross partitions, into chains of similar cells; the latter often attain by degrees strong, thick walls, and their greasy contents often pass into innumerable drops of a very regular globular form and of equal size. Similar appearances show themselves after the sowing of spores, which are capable of germinating in the medium already described, from which the air is excluded. Either short germinating utricles shoot forth, which soon form themselves into rows of gemmules, or the spores swell to large round bladders filled with protoplasm, and shoot forth on various parts of their surface innumerable protuberances, which, fixing themselves with a narrow basis, soon become round vesiculate cells, and on which the same sprouts which caused their production are repeated, formations which remind us of the fungus of fermentation called globular yeast. Among all the known forms of gemmules we find a variety which are intermediate, all of which show, when brought into a normal condition of development, the same proportion, and the same germination, as those we first described.

We have detailed rather at length the structure and development of one of the most common of the Mucors, which will serve as an illustration of the order. Other distinctions there may be which are of more interest as defining the limits of genera, except such as may be noticed when we come to write more specially of reproduction.

ASCOMYCETES.—Passing now to the *Ascomycetes*, which are especially rich in genera and species, we must first, and but superficially, allude to *Tuberacei*, an order of sporidiiferous fungi of subterranean habit, and rather peculiar structure.* In this order an external stratum of cells forms a kind of perithecium, which is more or less developed in different genera. This encloses the hymenium, which is sinuous, contorted, and twisted, often forming lacunæ. The hymenium in some genera consists of elongated, nearly cylindrical asci, enclosing a definite number of sporidia; in the true truffles and their immediate allies, the asci are broad

* Vittadini, "Monographia Tuberacearum," 1831.

sacs, containing very large and beautiful, often coloured, sporidia. These latter have either a smooth, warted, spinulose, or lacunose epispore, and, as will be seen from the figures in Tulasne's Monograph,* or those in the last volume of Corda's great work,† are attractive microscopical objects. In some cases, it is not difficult to detect paraphyses, but in others they would seem to be entirely absent. A comparatively large number have been discovered and recorded in Great Britain,‡ but of these none are more suitable for study of general structure than the ordinary truffle of the markets.

The structure of the remaining Ascomycetes can be studied under two groups, *i.e.*, the fleshy Ascomycetes, or, as they have been termed, the Discomycetes, and the hard, or carbonaceous Ascomycetes, sometimes called the Pyrenomycetes. Neither of these names gives an accurate idea of the distinctions between the two groups, in the former of which the discoid form is not universal, and the latter contains somewhat fleshy forms. But in the Discomycetes the hymenium soon becomes more or less exposed, and in the latter it is enclosed in a perithecium. The Discomycetes are of two kinds, the pileate and the cup-shaped. Of the pileate such a genus as *Gyromitra* or *Helvella* is, in a certain sense, analogous to the Agarics amongst *Hymenomycetes*, with a superior instead of an inferior hymenium, and enclosed, not naked, spores. Again, *Geoglossum* is somewhat analogous to *Clavaria.* Amongst the cup-shaped, *Peziza* is an Ascomycetous *Cyphella.* But these are perhaps more fanciful than real analogies.

Recently Boudier has examined one group of the cup-shaped Discomycetes, the *Ascobolei*, and, by making a somewhat free use of his Memoir,§ we may arrive at a general idea of the structure in the cupulate Discomycetes. They present themselves at

* Tulasne, "Fungi Hypogæi," 1851.

† Corda, "Icones Fungorum," vol. vi.

‡ Berkeley and Broome, in "Ann. of Nat. Hist." 1st ser. vol. xviii. (1846), p. 73; Cooke, in "Seem. Journ. Bot."

§ Boudier (E.), "Mémoire sur les Ascobolés," in "Ann. des Sci. Nat." 5me sér. vol. x. (1869).

first under the form of a small rounded globule, and almost entirely cellular. This small globule, the commencement of the receptacle, is not long in increasing, preserving its rounded form up to the development of the asci. At this period, under the influence of the rapid growth of these organs, it soon produces at its summit a fissure of the external membrane, which becomes a more marked depression in the marginate species. The receptacle thus formed increases rapidly, becomes plane, more convex, or more or less undulated at the margin, if at all of large size. Fixed to the place where it is generated by some more or less abundant mycelioid filaments, the receptacle becomes somewhat cup-shaped and either stipitate or sessile, composed of the receptacle proper and the hymenium.

The receptacle proper comprehends the subhymenial tissue, the parenchyma, and the external membrane. The subhymenial

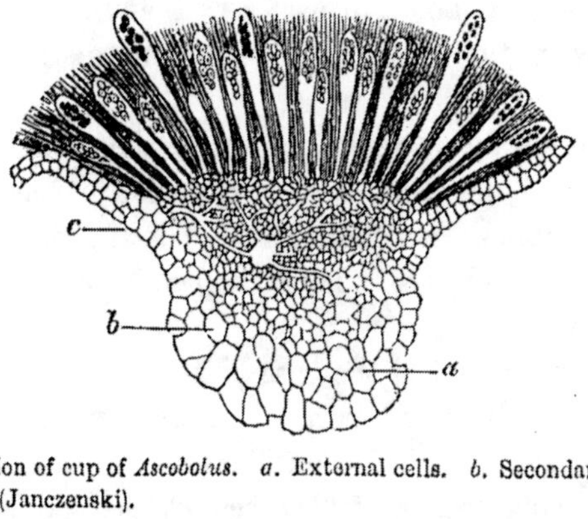

FIG. 33.—Section of cup of *Ascobolus*. *a*. External cells. *b*. Secondary layer. *c*. Subhymenial tissue (Janczenski).

tissue is composed of small compact cells, forming generally a more coloured and dense stratum, the superior cells of which give rise to the asci and paraphyses. The parenchyma is seated beneath this, and is generally of interlaced filaments, of a looser consistency than the preceding, united by intermediate cellules. The external membrane, which envelopes the parenchyma, and limits the hymenium, differs from the preceding by the cells often being polyhedric, sometimes transverse, and united together, and sometimes separable. Externally it is sometimes smooth, and sometimes granular or hairy.

The hymenium is, however, the most important part, consisting of (1) the paraphyses, (2) the asci, and sometimes (3) an investing mucilage. The asci are always present, the paraphyses are sometimes rare, and the mucilage in many cases seems to be entirely wanting.

The paraphyses, which are formed at the first commencement of the receptacle, are at first very short, but soon elongate, and become wholly developed before the appearance of the asci. They are linear, sometimes branched and sometimes simple, often more or less thickened at their tips; almost always they contain within them some oleaginous granules, either coloured or colourless. Their special function seems still somewhat obscure, and Boudier suggests that they may be excitatory organs for the dehiscence of the asci. However this may be, some mycologists are of opinion that, at least in some of the Ascomycetes, the paraphyses are abortive asci, or, at any rate, that abortive asci mixed with the paraphyses cannot be distinguished from them.

The mucilage forms itself almost at the same time as the paraphyses, and previous to the formation of the asci. This substance appears as a colourless or yellowish mucilage, which envelopes the paraphyses and asci, and so covers the hymenium with a shining coat.

The asci appear first at the base of the paraphyses, under the form of oblong cells, filled with colourless protoplasm. By rapid growth, they soon attain a considerable size and fulness, the protoplasm being gradually absorbed by the sporidia, the first indication of which is always the central nucleus. The mucilage also partly disappears, and the asci, attaining their maturity, become quite distinct, each enclosing its sporidia. But before they take their complete growth they detach themselves from the subhymenial tissue, and being attenuated towards their base, are forced upwards by pressure of the younger asci, to, and in some instances beyond, the upper surface of the disc. This phenomenon commences during the night, and continues during the night and all the morning. It attains its height at mid-day, and it is then that the slightest breath of air, the slightest movement, suffices to cause dehiscence, which is generally followed by a scarcely perceptible contractile motion of the receptacle.

There is manifestly a succession in formation and maturity of the asci in a receptacle. In the true *Ascobolei*, in which the sporidia are coloured, this may be more distinctly seen. At first some thin projecting points appear upon the disc, the next day they are more numerous, and become more and more so on following days, so as to render the disc almost covered with raised black or crystalline points;* these afterwards diminish day by day, until they ultimately cease. The asci, after separation from the subhymenial tissue, continue to lengthen, or it may be that their elasticity permits of extension during expulsion. Boudier considers that an amount of elasticity is certain, because he has seen an ascus arrive at maturity, eject its spores, and then make a sharp and considerable movement of retraction, then the ascus returned again immediately towards its previous limits, always with a reduction in the number of its contained sporidia.

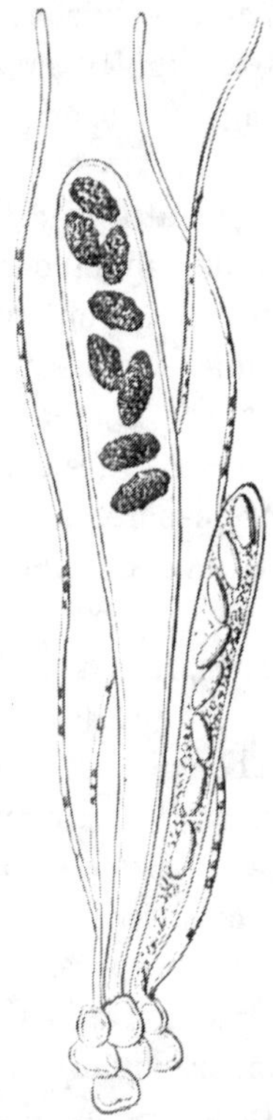

FIG. 34.—Asci, sporidia, and paraphyses of *Ascobolus* (Boudier).

The dehiscence of the asci takes place in the *Ascobolei*, in some species of *Peziza*, *Morchella*, *Helvella*, and *Verpa*, by means of an apical operculum, and in other *Pezizæ*, *Helotium*, *Geoglossum*, *Leotia*, *Mitrula*, &c., by a fissure of the ascus. This operculum may be the more readily seen when the ascus is coloured by a drop of tincture of iodine.

The sporidia are usually four or eight, or some multiple of that number, in each ascus, rarely four, most commonly eight. At a fixed time the protoplasm, which at first filled the asci, dis-

* Only in some of the Discomycetes are the asci exserted.

appears or is absorbed in a mucilaginous matter, which occupies its place, in the midst of which is a small nucleus, which is the rudiment of the first spore; other spores are formed consecutively, and then the substance separates into as many sections as there are sporidia. From this period each sporidium seems to have a separate existence. All have a nucleus, which is scarcely visible, often slightly granular, but which is quite distinct from the oleaginous sporidioles so frequent amongst the Discomycetes, and which are sometimes called by the same name. The sporidia are at first a little smaller than when mature, and are surrounded by mucilage. After this period the sporidia lose their nebulous granulations, whilst still preserving their nucleus; their outlines are distinct, and, amongst the true *Ascobolei*, commence acquiring a rosy colour, the first intimation of maturity. This colour manifests itself rapidly, accumulating exclusively upon the epispore, which becomes of a deep rose, then violet, and finally violet blue, so deep as sometimes to appear quite black. There are some modifications in this coloration, since, in some species, it passes from a vinous red to grey, then to black, or from rose-violet to brown.

The epispore acquires a waxy consistence by this pigmentation, so that it may be detached in granules. It is to this particular consistency of the epispore that the cracks so frequent in the coloured sporidia of *Ascobolus* are due, through contraction of the epispore. As they approach maturity, the sporidia accumulate towards the apex of the asci, and finally escape in the manner already indicated.

In all essential particulars there is a great similarity in the structure of the other Discomycetes, especially in their reproductive system. In most of them coloured sporidia are rare. In some the receptacle is pileate, clavate, or inflated, whilst in *Stictis* it is very much reduced, and in the lowest form of all, *Ascomyces*, it is entirely absent. In the *Phacidiacei*, the structure is very similar to that of the *Elvellacei*, whilst the *Hysteriacei*, with greater affinities with the latter, still tend towards the *Pyrenomycetes* by the more horny nature of the receptacle, and the greater tendency of the hymenium to remain closed, at least when dry. In some species of *Hysterium*, the sporidia are remarkably fine. M. Duby* has subjected this group to examination, and M. Tulasne partly so.†

SPHÆRIACEI.—In this group there is considerable variation, within certain limits. It contains an immense number oi species, and these are daily being augmented. The general feature in all is the presence of a perithecium, which contains and encloses the hymenium, and at length opening by a pore or ostiolum at the apex. In some the perithecia are simple, in others compound; in some immersed in a stroma, in others free; in some fleshy or waxy, in others carbonaceous, and in others membranaceous. But in all there is this important difference from the Ascomycetes we have already had under consideration, that the hymenium is never exposed. The perithecium consists usually of an external layer of cellular structure, which is either smooth or hairy, usually blackish, and an internal stratum of less compact cells, which give rise to the hymenium.

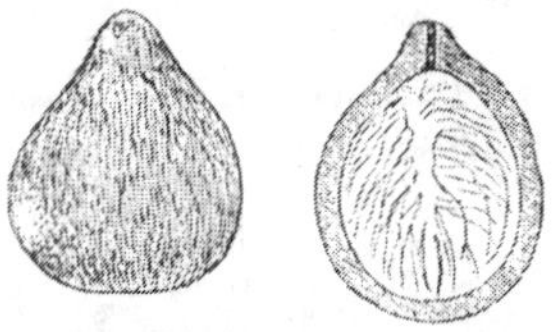

FIG. 35.—Perithecium of *Sphæria* and Section.

As in the *Discomycetes*, the hymenium consists of asci, paraphyses, and mucilage, but the whole forms a less compact and more gelatinous mass within the perithecium. The formation and growth of the asci and sporidia differ little from what we have described, and when mature the asci dehisce, and the sporidia alone are ejected from the ostiolum. We are not aware that operculate asci have yet been detected. It has been shown in some instances, and suspected in others, that certain moulds, formerly classed with *Mucedines* and *Dematiei*, especially in the genus *Helminthosporium*, bear the conidia of species of *Sphæria*, so that this may be regarded as one form of fruit.

Perithecia, very similar externally to those of *Sphæria*, but containing spores borne on slender pedicels and not enclosed in asci, have had their relations to certain species of *Sphæria* indi-

* Duby, "Mémoire sur la Tribu des Hysterinées," 1861.

† Tulasne, "Selecta Fungorum Carpologia," vol. iii.

cated, and these are no longer regarded so much as species of *Hendersonia* or *Diplodia* as the pycnidia of *Sphæria.* Other and more minute perithecia, containing minute, slender stylospores in great numbers, formerly classed with *Aposphæria*, *Phoma*, &c., but are now recognized as spermogonia containing the spermatia of *Sphæriæ.* How these influence each other, when and under what circumstances the spermatia are instrumental in impregnation of the sporidia, is still matter of mystery. It is clear, however, that in all these conidia, macrospores, microspores, and some spermatia, or by whatever names they may be called, there exists a power of germination. Tulasne has indicated in some instances five or six forms of fruit as belonging to one fungus, of which the highest and most perfect condition is a species of *Sphæria.*

PERISPORIACEI.—Except in the perithecia rupturing irregularly, and not dehiscing by a pore, some of the genera in this group differ little in structure from the *Sphæriacei.* On the other hand, the *Erysiphei* present important and very interesting features. They occur chiefly on the green parts of growing plants. At first there is a more or less profuse white mycelium.* This gives rise to chains of conidia (*Oidium*), and afterwards small sphæroid projections appear at certain points on the mycelium. These enlarge, take an orange colour, ultimately passing into brown, and then nearly black. Externally these perithecia are usually furnished with long, spreading, intertwined, or branching appendages, sometimes beautifully branched or hooked at their tips. In the interior of the receptacles, pear-shaped or ovate asci are formed in clusters, attached together at the base, and containing two or more hyaline sporidia. Other forms of fruit have also been observed on the same mycelium. In an exotic genus, *Meliola*, the fulcra, or appendages, as well as the mycelium, are black, otherwise it

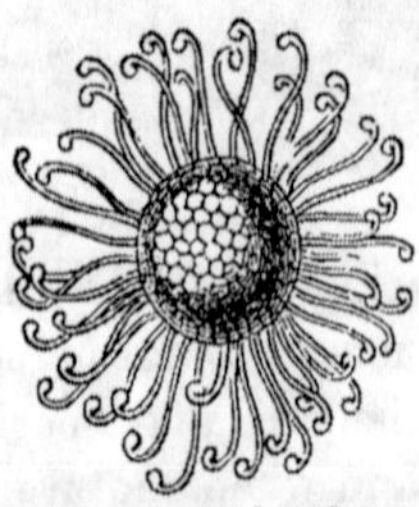

FIG. 36.—*Uncinula adunca.*

* Tulasne, "Selecta Fungorum Carpologia," vol. i. Léveillé, "Organisation, &c., sur l'Érysiphé," in "Ann. des Sci. Nat." (1851), vol. xv. p. 109.

is very analogous to such a genus of *Erysiphei* as *Microsphæria*. In *Chætomium*, the perithecia bristle with rigid, dark-coloured hairs, and the sporidia are coloured. Our limits, however, will not permit of further elucidation of the complex and varied structure to be found amongst fungi.*

---

* Other works besides those already cited, which may be consulted with advantage on structure, are—

Tulasne, L. R. and C., various articles in "Annales des Sciences Naturelles," série iii. and iv.

Hoffmann, "Icones Analyticæ Fungorum."

De Bary, "Der Ascomyceten." Leipzic, 1863.

Berkeley, M. J., "Introduction to Cryptogamic Botany."

Seynes, J. de, "Recherches, &c., des Fistulines." Paris, 1874.

Winter, G., "Die Deutschen Sordarien." 1874.

Corda, J., "Prachtflora." Prague, 1840.

De Bary, "Über der Brandpilze." 1853.

Brefeld, O., "Botan. Untersuch. ü Schimmelpilze."

Fresenius, G., "Beiträge zur Mykologie." 1850.

Von Tieghem and Le Monnier, in "Annales des Sciences Naturelles" (1873), p. 335.

Cornu, M., "Sur les Saprolegniées," in "Ann. des Sci. Nat." 5me sér. xv. p. 5.

Janczenski, "Sur l'Ascobolus furfuraceus," in "Ann. des Sci. Nat." 5me sér. xv. p. 200.

De Bary and Woronin, "Beiträge zur Morphologie und Physiologie der Pilze." 1870.

Bonorden, H. F., "Abhandlungen ans dem Gebiete der Mykologie." 1864.

Coemans, E., "Spicilége Mycologique." 1862, etc.

III.

CLASSIFICATION.

A WORK of this kind could not be considered complete without some account of the systematic arrangement or classification which these plants receive at the hands of botanists. It would hardly avail to enter too minutely into details, yet sufficient should be attempted to enable the reader to comprehend the value and relations of the different groups into which fungi are divided. The arrangement generally adopted is based upon the "Systema Mycologicum" of Fries, as modified to meet the requirements of more recent microscopical researches by Berkeley in his "Introduction,"* and adopted in Lindley's "Vegetable Kingdom." Another arrangement was proposed by Professor de Bary,† but it has never met with general acceptance.

In the arrangement to which we have alluded, all fungi are divided into two primary sections, having reference to the mode in which the fructification is produced. In one section, the spores (which occupy nearly the same position, and perform similar functions, to the seeds of higher plants) are naked; that is, they are produced on spicules, and are not enclosed in cysts or capsules. This section is called SPORIFERA, or spore-bearing, because, by general consent, the term *spore* is limited in fungi to such germ-cells as are not produced in cysts. The second section is termed SPORIDIIFERA, or sporidia-bearing, because in like manner the term *sporidia* is limited to such germ-cells as

* Rev. M. J. Berkeley, "Introduction to Cryptogamic Botany" (1857), London, pp. 235 to 372.

† De Bary, in "Streinz Nomenclator Fungorum," p. 722.

are produced in cells or cysts. These cysts are respectively known as *sporangia*, and *asci* or *thecæ*. The true meaning and value of these divisions will be better comprehended when we have detailed the characters of the families composing these two divisions.

First, then, the section Sporifera contains four families, in two of which a hymenium is present, and in two there is no proper hymenium. The term *hymenium* is employed to represent a more or less expanded surface, on which the fructification is produced, and is, in fact, the fruit-bearing surface. When no such surface is present, the fruit is borne on threads, proceeding direct from the root-like filaments of the mycelium, or an intermediate kind of cushion or stroma. The two families in which an hymenium is present are called *Hymenomycetes* and *Gasteromycetes*. In the former, the hymenium is exposed; in the latter, it is at first enclosed. We must examine each of these separately.

The common mushroom may be accepted, by way of illustration, as a type of the family *Hymenomycetes*, in which the hymenium is exposed, and is, in fact, the most noticeable feature in the family from which its name is derived. The pileus or cap bears on its under surface radiating plates or gills, consisting of the hymenium, over which are thickly scattered the basidia, each surmounted by four spicules, and on each spicule a spore. When mature, these spores fall freely upon the ground beneath, imparting to it the general colour of the spores. But it must be observed that the hymenium takes the form of gill-plates in only one order of *Hymenomycetes*, namely, the *Agaricini;* and here, as in *Cantharellus*, the hymenium is sometimes spread over prominent veins rather than gills. Still further divergence is manifest in the *Polyporei*, in which order the hymenium lines the inner surface of pores or tubes, which are normally on the under side of the pileus. Both these orders include an immense number of species, the former more or less fleshy, the latter more or less tough and leathery. There are still other forms and orders in this family, as the *Hydnei*, in which the hymenium clothes the surface of prickles or spines, and the *Auricularini*, in which the hymenium is entirely or almost even. In the two remaining orders, there is a still further divergence from the mushroom form. In the one called *Clavariei*, the entire fungus is either simply cylindrical or club-shaped, or it is very much branched and ramified. Whatever form the fungus assumes, the hymenium covers the whole exposed surface. In the *Tremellini*, a peculiar structure prevails, which at first seems to agree but little with the preceding. The whole plant is gelatinous when fresh, lobed and convolute, often brain-like, and varying in size, according to species, from that of a pin's head to that of a man's head. Threads and sporophores are imbedded in the gelatinous substance,* so that the fertile threads are in reality not compacted into a true hymenium. With this introduction we may state that the technical characters of the family are thus expressed:—

FIG. 37.—*Agaricus nudus.*

Hymenium free, mostly naked, or, if enclosed at first, soon exposed; spores naked, mostly quaternate, on distinct spicules = HYMENOMYCETES.

In this family some mycologists believe that fungi attain the highest form of development of which they are capable, whilst others contend that the fructification of the *Ascomycetes* is more perfect, and that some of the noblest species, such as the pileate forms, are entitled to the first rank. The morel is a familiar example. Whatever may be said on this point, it is incontrovertible that the noblest and most attractive, as well as the largest, forms are classed under the *Hymenomycetes*.

In *Gasteromycetes*, the second family, a true hymenium is also present, but instead of being exposed it is for a long time enclosed in an outer peridium or sac, until the spores are fully matured, or the fungus is beginning to decay. The common puff-ball (*Lycoperdon*) is well known, and will illustrate the principal feature of the family. Externally there is a tough

* Tulasne, L. and C. R., "Observations sur l'Organisation des Trémellinées," "Ann. des Sci. Nat." 1853, xix. p. 193.

coat or peridium, which is at first pale, but ultimately becomes brown. Internally is at first a cream-coloured, then greenish, cellular mass, consisting of the sinuated hymenium and young spores, which at length, and when the spores are fully matured, become brownish and dusty, the hymenium being broken up into threads, and the spores become free. In earlier stages, and before the hymenium is ruptured, the spores have been found to harmonize with those of *Hymenomycetes* in their mode of production, since basidia are present surmounted each by four spicules, and each spicule normally surmounted by a spore.* Here is, therefore, a cellular hymenium bearing quaternary spores, but, instead of being exposed, this hymenium is wholly enclosed within an external sac or peridium, which is not ruptured until the spores are fully matured, and the hymenium is resolved into threads, together forming a pulverulent mass. It must, however, be borne in mind, that in only some of the orders composing this family is the hymenium thus evanescent, in others being more or less permanent, and this has led naturally enough to the recognition of two sub-families, in one of which the hymenium is more or less permanent, thus following the Hymenomycetous type; and in the other, the hymenium is evanescent, and the dusty mass of spores tends more towards the *Coniomycetes*, this being characterized as the coniospermous (or dusty-spored) sub-family.

The first sub-family includes, first of all, the *Hypogæi*, or subterranean species. And here again it becomes necessary to remind the reader that all subterranean fungi are not included in this order, inasmuch as some, of which the truffle is an example, are sporidiiferous, developing their sporidia in asci. To these allusion must hereafter be made. In the *Hypogæi*, the hymenium is permanent and convoluted, leaving numerous minute irregular cavities, in which the spores are produced on

* Berkeley, M. J., "On the Fructification of *Lycoperdon*, *Phallus*, and their Allied Genera," in "Ann. of Nat. Hist." (1840), vol. iv. p. 155; "Ann. des Sci. Nat." (1839), xii. p. 163. Tulasne, L. R. and C., "De la Fructification des *Scléroderma* comparée à celle des *Lycoperdon* et des *Bovista*," in "Ann. des Sci. Nat." 2me sér. xvii. p. 5.

sporophores. When specimens are very old and decaying, the interior may become pulverulent or deliquescent. The structure of subterranean fungi attracted the attention of Messrs. Tulasne, and led to the production of a splendid monograph on the subject.* Another order belonging to this sub-family is the *Phalloidei*, in which the volva or peridium is ruptured whilst the plant is still immature, and the hymenium when mature becomes deliquescent. Not only are some members of this order most singular in appearance, but they possess an odour so fœtid as to be unapproached in this property by any other vegetable production.† In this order, the inner stratum of the investing volva is gelatinous. When still young, and previous to the rupture of the volva, the hymenium presents sinuous cavities in which the spores are produced on spicules, after the manner of *Hymenomycetes*.‡ *Nidulariacei* is a somewhat aberrant order, presenting a peculiar structure. The peridium consists of two or three coats, and bursts at the apex, either irregularly or in a stellate manner, or by the separation of a little lid. Within the cavity are contained one or more secondary receptacles, which are either free or attached by elastic threads to the common receptacle. Ultimately the secondary receptacles are hollow, and spores are produced in the interior, borne on spicules.§ The appearance in some genera as of a little bird's-nest containing eggs has furnished the name to the order.

The second sub-family contains the coniospermous puff-balls, and includes two orders, in which the most readily distinguishable feature is the cellular condition of the entire plant, in its earlier stages, in the *Trichogastres*, and the gelatinous condition of the early state of the *Myxogastres*. Both are ultimately resolved internally into a dusty mass of threads and spores.

* Tulasne, L. R. and C., "Fungi Hypogæi," Paris, 1851; "Observations sur le Genre Elaphomyces," in "Ann. des Sci. Nat." 1841, xvi. 5.

† *Stapeliæ* in this respect approach most closely to the *Phalloidei*.

‡ Berkeley, in "Ann. Nat. Hist." vol. iv. p. 155.

§ Tulasne, L. R. and C., "Recherches sur l'Organisation et le Mode de Fructification des Nidulariées," "Ann. des Sci. Nat." (1844), i. p. 41.

In the former, the peridium is either single or double, occasionally borne on a stem, but usually sessile. In *Geaster*, the "starry puff-balls," the outer peridium divides into several lobes, which fall back in a stellate manner, and expose the inner peridium, like a ball in the centre. In *Polysaccum*, the interior is divided into numerous cells, filled with secondary peridia. The mode of spore-production has already been alluded to in our remarks on *Lycoperdon*. All the species are large, as compared with those of the following sub-family, and one species of *Lycoperdon* attains an enormous size. One specimen recorded in the "Gardener's Chronicle" was three feet four inches in circumference, and weighed nearly ten pounds. In the *Myxogastres*, the early stage has been the subject of much controversy. The gelatinous condition presents phenomena so unlike anything previously recorded in plants, that one learned professor* did not hesitate to propose their exclusion from the vegetable, and recognition in the animal, kingdom as associates of the Gregarines. When mature, the spores and threads so much resemble those of the *Trichogastres*, and the little plants themselves are so veritably miniature puff-balls, that the theory of their animal nature did not meet with a ready acceptance, and is now virtually abandoned. The characters of the family we have thus briefly reviewed are tersely stated, as—

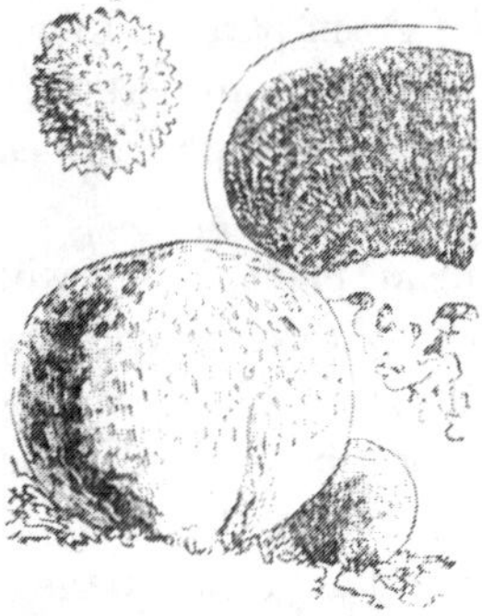

38.—*Scleroderma vulgare*, Fr.

Hymenium more or less permanently concealed, consisting in most cases of closely-packed cells, of which the fertile ones bear naked spores on distinct spicules, exposed only by the rupture or decay of the investing coat or peridium = GASTEROMYCETES.

We come now to the second section of the *Sporifera*, in which no definite hymenium is present. And here we find also two families, in one of which the dusty spores are the

* De Bary, A., "Des Myxomycètes," in "Ann. des Sci. Nat." 4me sér. xi. p. 153; "Bot. Zeit." xvi. p. 357.

prominent feature, and hence termed *Coniomycetes;* the other, in which the threads are most noticeable, is *Hyphomycetes.* In the former of these, the reproductive system seems to preponderate so much over the vegetative, that the fungus appears to be all spores. The mycelium is often nearly obsolete, and the short pedicels so evanescent, that a rusty or sooty powder represents the mature fungus, infesting the green parts of living plants. This is more especially true of one or two orders. It will be most convenient to recognize two artificial sub-families for the purpose of illustration, in one of which the species are developed on living, and in the other on dead, plants. We will commence with the latter, recognizing first those which are developed beneath the cuticle, and then those which are superficial. Of the sub-cuticular, two orders may be named as the representatives of this group in Britain, these are the *Sphæronemei,* in which the spores are contained in a more or less perfect perithecium, and the *Melanconiei,* in which there is manifestly none. The first of these is analogous to the *Sphæriacei* of *Ascomycetous* fungi, and probably consists largely of spermogonia of known species of *Sphæria,* the relations of which have not hitherto been traced. The spores are produced on slender threads springing from the inner wall of the perithecium, and, when mature, are expelled from an orifice at the apex. This is

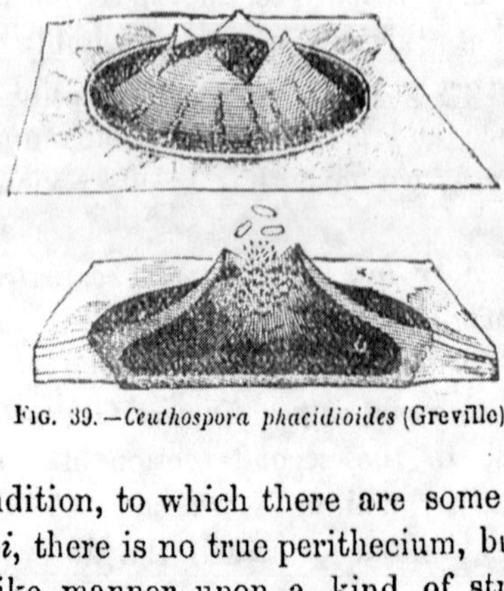

FIG. 39.—*Ceuthospora phacidioides* (Greville).

the normal condition, to which there are some exceptions. In the *Melanconiei,* there is no true perithecium, but the spores are produced in like manner upon a kind of stroma or cushion formed from the mycelium, and, when mature, are expelled through a rupture of the cuticle beneath which they are generated, often issuing in long gelatinous tendrils. Here, again, the majority of what were formerly regarded as distinct species have been found, or suspected, to be forms of higher fungi. The *Torulacei* represent the superficial fungi of this family, and these consist of a more or less developed mycelium, which gives rise to fertile threads, which, by constriction and division, mature into moniliform chains of spores. The species mostly appear as blackish velvety patches or stains on the stems of herbaceous plants and on old weathered wood.

Much interest attaches to the other sub-family of *Coniomycetes*, in which the species are produced for the most part on living plants. So much has been discovered during recent years of the polymorphism which subsists amongst the species in this section, that any detailed classification can only be regarded as provisional. Hence we shall proceed here upon the supposition that we are dealing with autonomous species. In the first place, we must recognize a small section in which a kind of cellular peridium is present. This is the *Æcidiacei*, or order of "cluster cups." The majority of species are very beautiful objects under the microscope; the peridia are distinctly cellular, and white or pallid, produced beneath the cuticle, through which they burst, and, rupturing at the apex, in one genus in a stellate manner, so that the teeth, becoming reflexed, resemble delicate fringed cups, with the orange, golden, brown, or whitish spores or pseudospores nestling in the interior.* These pseudospores are at first produced in chains, but ultimately separate. In many cases these cups are either accompanied or preceded by spermogonia. In two other orders there is no peridium. In the *Cæomacei*, the pseudospores are more or less globose or ovate, sometimes laterally compressed and simple; and in *Pucciniæi*, they are elongated, often subfusiform and septate. In both, the pseudospores are produced in tufts or clusters direct from the mycelium. The *Cæomacei* might again be sub-

* Corda, "Icones Fungorum," vol. iii. fig. 45.

divided into *Ustilagines* * and *Uredines.*† In the former, the pseudospores are mostly dingy brown or blackish, and in the latter more brightly coloured, often yellowish. The *Ustilagines* include the smuts and bunt of corn-plants, the *Uredines* include the red rusts of wheat and grasses. In some of the species included in the latter, two forms of fruit are found. In *Melampsora*, the summer pseudospores are yellow, globose, and were formerly classed as a species of *Lecythea*, whilst the winter pseudospores are brownish, elongated, wedge-shaped by compression, and compact. The *Pucciniæi* ‡ differ primarily in the septate pseudospores, which in one genus (*Puccinia*) are uniseptate; in *Triphragmium*, they are biseptate; in *Phragmidium*, multiseptate; and in *Xenodochus*, moniliform, breaking up into distinct articulations. It is probable that, in all of these, as is known to be the case in most, the septate pseudospores are preceded or accompanied by simple pseudospores, to which they are mysteriously related. There is still another, somewhat singular, group usually associated with the *Pucciniæi*, in which the septate pseudospores are immersed in gelatin, so that in many features the species seem to approach the *Tremellini.* This group includes two or three genera, the type of which will be found in *Podisoma.*§ These fungi are parasitic on living junipers in Britain and North America, appearing year after year upon the same gouty swellings of the branches, in clavate or horn-shaped gelatinous processes of a yellowish or orange colour. Anomalous as it may at first sight appear to include these tremelloid forms with the dust-like fungi, their relations will on closer examination be more fully appreciated, when the form of pseudospores, mode of germination, and other features are taken into consideration, especially when compared with *Podisoma Ellisii*, already alluded to. This family is technically characterized as,—

* Tulasne, "Mémoire sur les Ustilaginées," "Ann. des Sci. Nat." (1847), vii. 12–73.

† Tulasne, "Mémoire sur les Urédinées," "Ann. des Sci. Nat." (1854), ii. 78.

‡ Tulasne, "Sur les Urédinées," "Ann. des Sci. Nat." 1854, ii. pl. 9.

§ Cooke, M. C., "Notes on *Podisoma*," in "Journ. Quek. Micr. Club," No. 17 (1871), p. 255.

Distinct hymenium none. Pseudospores either solitary or concatenate, produced on the tips of generally short threads, which are either naked or contained in a perithecium, rarely compacted into a gelatinous mass, at length producing minute spores = CONIOMYCETES.

The last family of the sporifera is *Hyphomycetes*, in which the threads are conspicuously developed. These are what are more commonly called "moulds," including some of the most elegant and delicate of microscopic forms. It is true of many of these, as well as of the *Coniomycetes*, that they are only conidial forms of higher fungi; but there will remain a very large number of species which, as far as present knowledge extends, must be accepted as autonomous. In this family, we may again recognize three subdivisions, in one of which the threads are more or less compacted into a common stem, in another the threads are free, and in the third the threads can scarcely be distinguished from the mycelium. It is this latter group which unites the *Hyphomycetes* with the *Coniomycetes*, the affinities being increased by the great profusion with which the spores are developed. The first group, in which the fertile threads are united so as to form a compound stem, consists of two small orders, the *Isariacei* and the *Stilbacei*, in the former of which the spores are dry, and in the latter somewhat gelatinous. Many of the species closely imitate forms met with in the *Hymenomycetes*, such as *Clavaria;* and, in the genus *Isaria*, it is almost beyond doubt that the species found on dead insects, moths, spiders, flies, ants, &c., are merely the conidiophores of species of *Torrubia*.*

The second group is by far the largest, most typical, and attractive in this family. It contains the black moulds and white moulds, technically known as the *Dematiei* and the *Mucedines*. In the first, the threads are more or less corticated, that is, the stem has a distinct investing membrane, which peels off like a bark; and the threads, often also the spores, are dark-coloured, as if charred or scorched. In many cases, the spores are highly developed, large, multiseptate, and nucleate, and sel-

* Tulasne, L. R. and C., "Selecta Fungorum Carpologia," vol. iii. pp. 4–19.

dom are spores and threads colourless or of bright tints. In the *Mucedines*, on the contrary, the threads are never coated, seldom dingy, mostly white or of pure colours, and the spores have less a tendency to extra development or multiplex septation. In some genera, as in *Peronospora* for instance,* a secondary fruit is produced in the form of resting spores from the mycelium; and these generate zoospores as well as the primary spores, similar to those common in *Algæ*. This latter genus is very destructive to growing plants, one species being the chief agent in the potato disease, and another no less destructive to crops of onions. The vine disease is produced by a species of *Oidium*, which is also classed with *Mucedines*, but which is really the conidiiferous form of *Erysiphe*. In other genera, the majority of species are developed on decaying plants, so that, with the exception of the two genera mentioned, the *Hyphomycetes* exert a much less baneful influence on vegetation than the *Coniomycetes*. The last section, including the *Sepedoniei*, has been already cited as remarkable for the suppression of the threads, which are scarcely to be distinguished from the mycelium; the spores are profuse, nestling on the floccose mycelium; whilst in the *Trichodermacei*, the spores are invested by the threads, as if enclosed in a sort of false peridium. A summary of the characters of the family may therefore be thus briefly expressed:—

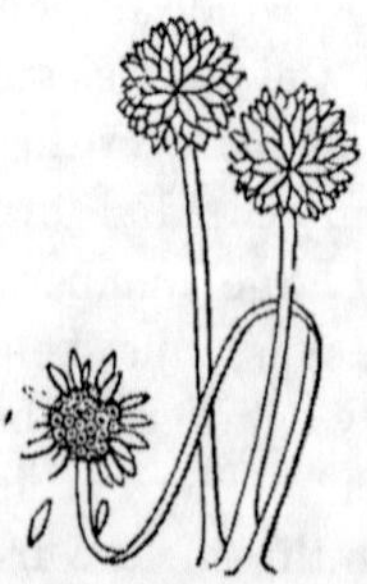

FIG. 40.—*Rhopalomyces candidus.*

Filamentous; fertile threads naked, for the most part free or loosely compacted, simple or branched, bearing the spores at their apices, rarely more closely packed, so as to form a distinct common stem = HYPHOMYCETES.

Having thus disposed of the *Sporifera*, we must advert to the two families of *Sporidiifera*. As more closely related to the *Hyphomycetes*, the first of these to be noticed is the

* De Bary, A., "Recherches sur les Champignons Parasites," in "Ann. des Sci. Nat." 4me sér. xx. p. 5; "Grevillea," vol. i. p. 150.

Physomycetes, in which there is no proper hymenium, and the threads proceeding from the mycelium bear vesicles containing an indefinite number of sporidia. The fertile threads are either free or only slightly felted. In the order *Antennariei*, the threads are black and moniliform, more or less felted, bearing irregular sporangia. A common fungus named *Zasmidium cellare*, found in cellars, and incrusting old wine bottles, as with a blackened felt, belongs to this order. The larger and more highly-developed order, *Mucorini*, differs in the threads, which are simple or branched, being free, erect, and bearing the sporangia at the tips of the thread, or branches. Some of the species bear great external resemblance to *Mucedines* until the fruit is examined, when the fructifying heads, commonly globose or ovate, are found to be delicate transparent vesicles, enclosing a large number of minute sporidia; when mature, the sporangia burst and the sporidia are set free. In some species, it has long been known that a sort of conjugation takes place between opposite threads, which results in the formation of a sporangium.* None of these species are destructive to vegetation, appearing only upon decaying, and not upon living, plants. A state approaching putrescence seems to be essential to their vigorous development. The following characters may be compared with those of the family preceding it:—

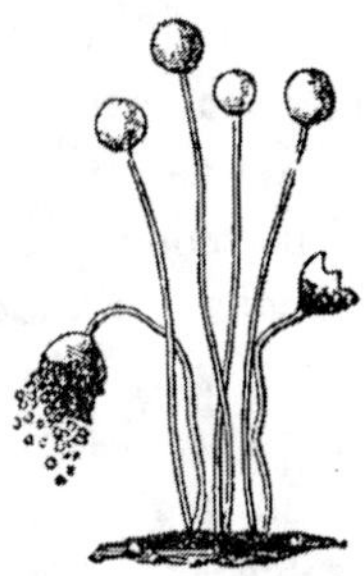

FIG. 41.—*Mucor caninus.*

Filamentous, threads free or only slightly felted, bearing vesicles, which contain indefinite sporidia = PHYSOMYCETES.

In the last family, the *Ascomycetes*, we shall meet with a very great variety of forms, all agreeing in producing sporidia contained in certain cells called asci, which are produced from the hymenium. In some of these, the asci are evanescent, but in the greater number are permanent. In *Onygenei*, the receptacle is either club-shaped or somewhat globose, and the

* A. de Bary, translated in "Grevillea," vol. i. p. 167; Tulasne, "Ann. des Sci. Nat." 5me sér. (1866), p. 211.

peridium is filled with branched threads, which produce asci of a very evanescent character, leaving the pulverulent sporidia to fill the central cavity. The species are all small, and singular for their habit of affecting animal substances, otherwise they are of little importance. The *Perisporiacei*, on the other hand, are very destructive of vegetation, being produced, in the majority of cases, on the green parts of growing plants. To this order the hop mildew, rose mildew, and pea mildew belong. The mycelium is often very much developed, and in the case of the maple, pea, hop, and some others, it covers the parts attacked with a thick white coating, so that from a distance the leaves appear to have been whitewashed. Seated on the mycelium, at the first as little orange points, are the perithecia, which enlarge and become nearly black. In some species, very elegant whitish appendages radiate from the sides of the perithecia, the variations in which aid in the discrimination of species. The perithecia contain pear-shaped asci, which spring from the base and enclose a definite number of sporidia.* The asci themselves are soon dissolved. Simultaneously with the development of sporidia, other reproductive bodies are produced direct from the mycelium, and in some species as many as five different kinds of reproductive bodies have been traced. The features to be remembered in *Perisporiacei*, as forming the basis of their classification, are, that the asci are saccate, springing from the base of the perithecia, and are soon absorbed. Also that the perithecia themselves are not perforated at the apex.

The four remaining orders, though large, can be easily characterized. In *Tuberacei*, all the species are subterranean, and the hymenium is mostly sinuated. In *Elvellacei*, the substance is more or less fleshy, and the hymenium is exposed. In *Phacidiacei*, the substance is hard or leathery, and the hymenium is soon exposed. And in *Sphæriacei*, although the substance is variable, the hymenium is never exposed, being enclosed in perithecia with a distinct opening at the apex, through which the mature spores escape. Each of these four orders must be

* Léveillé, J. H., "Organisation, &c., de l'Érysiphé," in "Ann. des Sci. Nat." (1851), xv. p. 109.

examined more in detail. The *Tuberacei*, or subterranean *Ascomycetes*, are analogous to the *Hypogæi* of the *Gasteromycetes*. The truffle is a familiar and highly prized example. There is a kind of outer peridium, and the interior consists of a fleshy hymenium, more or less convoluted, sometimes sinuous and confluent, so as to leave only minute elongated and irregular cavities, and sometimes none at all, the two opposing faces of the hymenium meeting and coalescing.* Certain privileged cells of the hymenium swell, and ultimately become asci, enclosing a definite number of sporidia. The sporidia in many cases are large, reticulated, echinulate or verrucose, and mostly somewhat globose. In the genus *Elaphomyces*, the asci are more than commonly diffluent.

The *Elvellacei* are fleshy in substance, or somewhat waxy, sometimes tremelloid. There is no peridium, but the hymenium is always exposed. There is a great variety of forms, some being pileate, and others cup-shaped, as there is also a great variation in size, from the minute *Peziza*, small as a grain of sand, to the large *Helvella gigas*, which equals in dimensions the head of a child. In the pileate forms, the stroma is fleshy and highly developed; in the cup-shaped, it is reduced to the external cells of the cup which enclose the hymenium. The hymenium itself consists of elongated fertile cells, or asci, mixed with linear thread-like barren cells, called paraphyses, which are regarded by some authors as barren asci. These are placed side by side in juxtaposition with the apex outwards. Each ascus contains a definite number of sporidia, which are sometimes coloured. When mature, the asci explode above, and the sporidia may be seen escaping like a miniature cloud of smoke in the light of the mid-day sun. The disc or surface of the hymenium is often brightly coloured in the genus *Peziza;* tints of orange, red, and brown having the predominance.

In *Phacidiacei*, the substance is hard and leathery, intermediate between the fleshy *Elvellacei* and the more horny of the *Sphæriacei*. The perithecia are either orbicular or elongated, and the

* Tulasne, L. R. and C., "Fungi Hypogæi," Paris; Vittadini, C., "Monographia Tuberacearum," Milan, 1831.

hymenium soon becomes exposed. In some instances, there is a close affinity with the *Elvellacei*, the exposed hymenium being similar in structure, but in all the disc is at first closed. In orbicular forms, the fissure takes place in a stellate manner from the centre, and the teeth are reflexed. In the *Hysteriacei*, where the perithecia are elongated, the fissure takes place throughout their length. As a rule, the sporidia are more elongated, more commonly septate, and more usually coloured, than in *Elvellacei*. Only a few solitary instances occur of individual species that are parasitic on living plants.

In the *Sphæriacei*, the substance of the stroma (when present) and of the perithecia is variable, being between fleshy and waxy in *Nectriei*, and tough, horny, sometimes brittle, in *Hypoxylon*. A perithecium, or cell excavated in the stroma which fulfils the functions of a perithecium, is always present. The hymenium lines the inner walls of the perithecium, and forms a gelatinous nucleus, consisting of asci and paraphyses. When fully mature, the asci are ruptured and the sporidia escape by a pore which occupies the apex of the perithecium. Sometimes the perithecia are solitary or scattered, and sometimes gregarious, whilst in other instances they are closely aggregated and immersed in a stroma of variable size and form. Conidia, spermatia, pycnidia, &c., have been traced to and associated with some species, but the history of others is still obscure. Many of the coniomycetous forms grouped under the *Sphæronemei* are probably conditions of the *Sphæriacei*, as are also the *Melanconiei*, and some of the *Hyphomycetes*. A very common fungus, for instance, which is abundant on sticks and twigs, forming rosy or reddish pustules the size of a millet seed, formerly named *Tubercularia vulgaris*, is known to be the conidia-bearing stroma of the sphæriaceous fungus, *Nectria cinnabarina*;* and so

FIG. 42.—*Sphæria aquila.*

* "A Currant Twig and Something on it," in "Gardener's Chronicle" for January 28, 1871.

with many others. The following are the technical characters of the family:—

Fruit consisting of sporidia, mostly definite, contained in asci, springing from a naked or enclosed stratum of fructifying cells and forming a hymenium or nucleus = ASCOMYCETES.

If the characters of the different families are borne in mind, there will be but little difficulty in assigning any fungus to the order to which it belongs by means of the foregoing remarks. For more minute information, and for analytical tables of the families, orders, and genera, we must refer the student to some special systematic work, which will present fewer difficulties, if he keeps in mind the distinctive features of the families.*

To assist in this we have given on the following page an analytical arrangement of the families and orders, according to the system recognized and adopted in the present volume. It is, in all essential particulars, the method adopted in our "Handbook," based on that of Berkeley's "Introduction" and "Outlines."

* Berkeley, M. J., "Introduction to Cryptogamic Botany," London, 1857; Cooke, M. C., "Handbook of British Fungi," London, 1871; Corda, A. C. J., "Anleitung zum Studium der Mycologie," Prag, 1842; Kickx, J., "Flore Cryptogamique des Flanders," Gand, 1867; Fries, E., "Systema Mycologicum," Lund, 1830; Fries, E., "Summa Vegetabilium Scandinaviæ," 1846; Secretan, L., "Mycographie Suisse," Geneva, 1833; Berkeley, M. J., "Outlines of British Fungology," London, 1860.

TABULAR ARRANGEMENT OF FAMILIES AND ORDERS.

DIVISION I. SPORIFERA. *Spores naked.*

I. Hymenium free, mostly naked, or soon exposed . . HYMENOMYCETES.
  Hymenium normally inferior—
    Fruit-bearing surface lamellose . . . *Agaricini.*
    Fruit-bearing surface porous or tubular . . *Polyporei.*
    Fruit-bearing surface clothed with prickles . *Hydnei.*
    Fruit-bearing surface even or rugose . . . *Auricularini.*
  Hymenium superior or encircling—
    Clavate, or branched, rarely lobed . . . *Clavariei.*
    Lobed, convolute, or disc-like, gelatinous . . *Tremellini.*

II. Hymenium enclosed in a peridium, ruptured when mature GASTEROMYCETES.
  Hymenomycetous—
    Subterranean, naked or enclosed . . . *Hypogæi.*
    Terrestrial, hymenium deliquescent . . . *Phalloidei.*
    Peridium enclosing sporangia, containing spores *Nidulariacei.*
  Coniospermous—
    Stipitate, hymenium convolute, drying into a dusty mass, enclosed in a volva . . . *Podaxinei.*
    Cellular at first, hymenium drying up into a dusty mass of threads and spores . . *Trichogastres.*
    Gelatinous at first, peridium containing at length a dusty mass of threads and spores . . *Myxogastres.*

III. Spores naked, mostly terminal, on inconspicuous threads, free or enclosed in a perithecium . . . CONIOMYCETES.
  Growing on dead or dying plants—
    Subcutaneous—
      Perithecium more or less distinct . . *Sphæronemei.*
      Perithecium obsolete or wanting . . *Melanconiei.*
    Superficial—
      Fructifying surface naked
        Spores compound or tomiparous . *Torulacei.*
  Parasitic on living plants—
    Peridium distinctly cellular . . . . *Æcidiacei.*
    Peridium none—
      Spores sub-globose, simple or deciduous . *Cæomacei.*
      Spores mostly oblong, usually septate . *Pucciniæi.*

IV. Spores naked, on conspicuous threads, rarely compacted, small . . . . HYPHOMYCETES.
Fertile threads compacted, sometimes cellular—
Stem or stroma compound—
Spores dry, volatile . . . . . *Isariacei.*
Mass of spores moist, diffluent . . . *Stilbacei.*
Fertile threads, free or anastomosing—
Fertile threads dark, carbonized—
Spores mostly compound . . . . *Dematiei.*
Fertile threads not carbonized—
Very distinct—
Spores mostly simple . . . . *Mucedines.*
Scarcely distinct from mycelium—
Spores profuse . . . . . *Sepedoniei.*

DIVISION II. SPORIDIIFERA. *Sporidia in Asci.*

V. Fertile cells seated on threads, not compacted into a hymenium . . . . PHYSOMYCETES.
Threads felted, moniliform—
Sporangia irregular . . . . . . *Antennariei.*
Threads free—
Sporangia terminal or lateral . . . . *Mucorini.*
Aquatic . . . . *Saprolegniei.*

VI. Asci formed from the fertile cells of a hymenium . ASCOMYCETES.
Asci often evanescent—
Receptacle clavæform—
Asci springing from threads . . . *Onygenei.*
Perithecia free—
Asci springing from the base . . . *Perisporiacei.*
Asci persistent—
Perithecia opening by a distinct ostiolum . . *Sphæriacei.*
Hard or coriaceous, hymenium at length exposed *Phacidiacei.*
Hypogæous; hymenium complicated . . . *Tuberacei.*
Fleshy, waxy, or tremelloid; hymenium mostly exposed . . . . *Elvellacei.*

IV.

USES.

THE rigid utilitarian will hardly be satisfied with the short catalogue which can be furnished of the uses of fungi. Excepting those which are employed more or less for human food, very few are of any practical value in arts or medicine. It is true that imperfect conditions of fungi exert a very important influence on fermentation, and thus become useful; but, unfortunately, fungi have the reputation of being more destructive and offensive than valuable or useful. Notwithstanding that a large number of species have from time to time been enumerated as edible, yet those commonly employed and recognized are very few in number, prejudice in many cases, and fear in others, militating strongly against additions to the number. In Great Britain this is especially the case, and however advisable it may be to exercise great care and caution in experimenting on untried or doubtful species, it can only be regarded as prejudice which prevents good, in fact, excellent, esculent species being more extensively used, instead of allowing them to rot by thousands on the spots where they have grown. Poisonous species are also plentiful, and no golden rule can be established by means of which any one may detect at a glance good from bad, without that kind of knowledge which is applied to the discrimination of species. Yet, after all, the characters of half a dozen good esculent fungi are acquired as easily as the distinctions between half a dozen birds such as any ploughboy can discriminate.

The common mushroom (*Agaricus campestris*) is the best

known esculent, whether in its uncultivated or in a cultivated state. In Britain many thousands of people, notably the lower classes, will not recognize any other as fit for food, whilst in Italy the same classes have a strong prejudice against this very species.* In Vienna, we found by personal experience that, although many others are eaten, it is this which has the most universal preference, yet it appears but sparingly in the markets as compared with others. In Hungary it does not enjoy by any means so good a reputation. In France and in Germany it is a common article of consumption. The different varieties found, as the results of cultivation, present some variation in colour, scaliness of pileus, and other minor features, whilst remaining true to the constituent characters of the species. Although it is not our intention to enumerate here the botanical distinctions of the species to which we may call attention, yet, as mistakes (sometimes fatal) are often being recorded, in which other fungi are confounded with this, we may be permitted a hint or two which should be remembered. The spores are purple, the gills are at first delicate pink, afterwards purple; there is a permanent ring or collar round the stem, and it must *not* be sought in woods. Many accidents might have been spared had these facts been remembered.

The meadow mushroom (*Agaricus arvensis*) is common in meadows and lowland pastures, and is usually of a larger size than the preceding, with which it agrees in many particulars, and is sent in enormous quantities to Covent Garden, where it frequently predominates over *Agaricus campestris*. Some persons prefer this, which has a stronger flavour, to the ordinary mushroom, and it is the species most commonly sold in the autumn in the streets of London and provincial towns. According to Persoon, it is preferred in France; and, in Hungary, it is considered as a special gift from St. George. It has acquired in England the name of horse mushroom, from the enormous size

* Badham, Dr. C. D., "A Treatise on the Esculent Funguses of England," 1st edition (1847), p. 81, pl. 4; 2nd edition, edited by F. Currey, M.A. (1863), p. 94, pl. 4; Cooke, M. C., "A Plain and Easy Account of British Fungi," 1st edition (1862), p. 44.

it sometimes attains. Withering mentions a specimen that weighed fourteen pounds.*

One of the commonest (in our experience the *most* common) of all edible fungi in the public markets of Vienna is the Hallimasche (*Agaricus melleus*), which in England enjoys no good reputation for flavour or quality; indeed, Dr. Badham calls it "nauseous and disagreeable," and adds that "not to be poisonous is its only recommendation." In Vienna it is employed chiefly for making sauce; but we must confess that even in this way, and with a prejudice in favour of Viennese cookery, our experience of it was not satisfactory. It is at best a sorry substitute for the mushroom. In the summer and autumn this is a very common species in large tufts on old stumps. In similar localities, and also in tufts, but neither so large, nor so common, *Agaricus fusipes* is found. It is preferable to the foregoing as an esculent, and is easily recognized by the spindle-shaped stem.

Agaricus rubescens, P., belongs to a very suspicious group of fungi, in which the cap or pileus is commonly studded or sprinkled with paler warts, the remains of an investing volva. To this group the poisonous but splendid fly-agaric (*Agaricus muscarius*) belongs. Notwithstanding its bad company, this agaric has a good reputation, especially for making ketchup; and Cordier reports it as one of the most delicate mushrooms of the Lorraine.† Its name is derived from its tendency to become red when bruised.

The white variety of an allied species (*Agaricus vaginatus*) has been commended, and Dr. Badham says that it will be found inferior to but few agarics in flavour.

A scaly-capped fungus (*Agaricus procerus*), with a slender stem, called sometimes the parasol mushroom, from its habit, is an esteemed esculent. In Italy and France it is in high request,

* Mr. Worthington Smith has published, on two sheets, coloured figures of the most common esculent and poisonous fungi (London, Hardwicke), which will be found more useful than mere description in the discrimination of the species.

† Roques, J., "Hist. des Champignons Comestibles et Vénéneux," Paris 1832), p. 130.

and is included in the majority of continental works on the edible fungi.* In Austria, Germany, and Spain, it has special "vulgar" names, and is eaten in all these countries. It is much more collected in England than formerly, but deserves to be still better known. When once seen it can scarcely be confounded with any other British species, save one of its nearest allies, which partakes of its own good qualities (*Agaricus rachodes*), though not quite so good.

Agaricus prunulus, Scop., and *Agaricus orcella*, Badh., if they be not forms of the same species (which Dr. Bull contends that they are not †), have also a good reputation as esculents. They are both neat, white agarics, with a mealy odour, growing respectively in woods and open glades. *Agaricus nebularis*, Batsch, is a much larger species, found in woods, often in large gregarious patches amongst dead leaves, with a smoky mouse-coloured pileus, and profuse white spores. It is sometimes as much as five or six inches in diameter, with rather a faint odour and mild taste. On the continent, as well as in Britain, this is included amongst edible fungi. Still larger and more imposing is the magnificent white species, *Agaricus maximus*, Fr.,‡ which is figured by Sowerby,§ under the name of *Agaricus giganteus*. It will attain a diameter of fourteen inches, with a stem two inches thick, and rather a strong odour.

A spring fungus, the true St. George's mushroom, *Agaricus gambosus*, Fr., makes its appearance in pastures, usually growing in rings, in May and June, and is welcome to mycophagists from its early growth, when esculent species are rare. It is highly esteemed in France and Italy, so that when dried it will realize as much as from twelve to fifteen shillings per pound. Guillarmod includes it amongst Swiss esculents.‖ Professor Buck-

* Lenz, Dr. H. O., "Die Nützlichen und Schädlichen Schwämme," Gotha (1831), p. 32, pl. 2.

† Bull, H. G., in "Transactions of Woolhope Club" (1869). Fries admits them as distinct species in the new edition of his "Epicrisis."

‡ Hussey's "Illustrations of Mycology," ser. i. pl. 79.

§ Sowerby's "British Fungi," pl. 244.

‖ Favre-Guillarmod, "Les Champignons Comestibles du Canton de Neuchatel" (1861), p. 27.

man says that it is one of the earliest and best of English mushrooms, and others have endorsed his opinions, and Dr. Badham in writing of it observes, that small baskets of them, when they first appear in the spring in Italy, are sent as "presents to lawyers and fees to medical men."

The closely allied species, *Agaricus albellus*,* D.C., has also the reputation of being edible, but it is so rare in England that this quality cannot be put to the test. The curious short-stemmed *Agaricus brevipes*, Bull,† has a similar reputation.

Two singularly fragrant species are also included amongst the esculent. These are *Agaricus fragrans*, Sow., and *Agaricus odorus*, Bull. Both have a sweet anise-like odour, which is persistent for a long time. The former is pale tawny-coloured, nearly white, the latter of a dirty pale green. Both are white-spored, and although somewhat local, sufficient specimens of *Ag. odorus* may be collected in the autumn for domestic use. We have the assurance of one who has often proved them that they constitute an exquisite dish.

A clear ivory-white fungus, *Agaricus dealbatus*, of which a crisped variety is occasionally found in great numbers, springing up on old mushroom beds in dense clusters, is very good eating, but rather deficient in the delicate aroma of some other species. The typical form is not uncommon on the ground in fir plantations. A more robust and larger species, *Agaricus geotrupes*, Bull, found on the borders of woods, often forming rings, both in this country and in the United States, as well as on the continent of Europe, is recognized as esculent.

We may add to these three or four other species, in which the stem is lateral, and sometimes nearly obsolete. The largest and most common is the oyster mushroom (*Agaricus ostreatus*, Jacq.‡), so universally eaten, that it is included in almost every list and book on edible fungi; it is the most common species in

* Sowerby, "English Fungi," pl. 122; Smith, in "Seemann's Journ. Bot." (1866), t. 46, f. 45.

† Klotsch, "Flora Borussica," t. 374; Smith, in "Seem. Journ. Bot." (1869), t. 95, f. 1–4.

‡ Krombholz, "Abbildungen der Schwämme," pl. 41, f. 1–7.

Transylvania, tons of it sometimes appearing in the markets. It does not possess that delicate flavour which is found in many species, and although extolled by some beyond its merits, it is nevertheless perfectly wholesome, and, when young and carefully cooked, not to be despised. It must not be confounded with a very similar species (*Agaricus euosmus*, B.), with rosy spores, which is unpleasant. *Agaricus tessellatus*, Bull, *Agaricus pometi*, Fr., *Agaricus glandulosus*, Bull, are all allies of the foregoing, and recorded as edible in the United States, although not one of the three has hitherto been recorded as occurring in Great Britain. To these may also be added the following:—*Agaricus salignus*,* Fr., which is rare in England, but not uncommon abroad and in the United States. In Austria it is commonly eaten. *Agaricus ulmarius*,† Bull, is common on elm trunks, not only in Britain but also in North America, and is by some preferred to the oyster mushroom. An allied species, *Agaricus fossulatus*, Cooke,‡ is found on the Cabul Hills, where it is collected, dried, and forms an article of commerce with the plains. Another, but smaller species, is dried in the air on strings passed through a hole in the short stem (*Agaricus subocreatus*, Cooke), and sent, it is believed, from China to Singapore.

The smallest species with which we have any acquaintance, that is edible, is the "nail fungus" (*Agaricus esculentus*,§ Jacq.), scarcely exceeding one inch in diameter of the pileus, with a thin rooting stem. The taste in British specimens when raw is bitter and unpleasant, but it is clearly eaten in Austria, as its name testifies, and elsewhere in Europe. It is found in fir plantations in the spring, at which season it is collected from the fir woods around and sent to Vienna, where it is only used for flavouring sauces under the name of "Nagelschwämme."

Before quitting the group of true agarics, to which all hitherto enumerated belong, we must mention a few others of less importance, but which are included amongst those good for

* Tratinnick, L., "Fungi Austriaci," p. 47, pl. 4, f. 8.

† Vittadini, "Fungi Mangerecci," pl. 23.

‡ Cooke, in "Journal of Botany," vol. viii. p. 352.

§ Cooke, M. C., "A Plain and Easy Guide," &c., p. 38, pl. 6, fig. 1.

food. Foremost of these is a really splendid orange species (*Agaricus cæsarius*, Scop.*), which belongs to the same subgenus as the very deleterious fly-agaric, and the scarcely less fatal *Agaricus vernus*, Bull. It is universally eaten on the continent, but has hitherto never been found in Great Britain. In the same subgenus, *Agaricus strobiliformis*,† Fr., which is rare in this country, and probably also *Agaricus Ceciliæ*, B. & Br.‡ Besides these, *Agaricus excoriatus*, Schæff., *Agaricus mastoideus*, Fr., *Agaricus gracilentus*, Kromb., and *Agaricus holosericeus*, Fr.,§ all belonging to the same subgenus as the parasol mushroom, more or less uncommon in England.

Although the larger number of esculent agarics are white-spored, some few, worthy of note, will be found in the other sections, and notably amongst these the common mushroom and its congener the meadow, or horse mushroom. In addition to those already enumerated, might be included also the *Agaricus pudicus*, Bull, which is certainly wholesome, as well as its ally, *Agaricus leochromus*, Cooke,‖ both of which have rusty spores.

The late Dr. Curtis,¶ in a letter to the Rev. M. J. Berkeley, enumerates several of the fungi which are edible amongst those found in the United States. Of these, he says, *Agaricus amygdalinus*, Curt., can scarcely be distinguished when cooked from the common mushroom. *Agaricus frumentaceus*, Bull, and three allied new species, peculiar to the United States, are commended. *Agaricus cæspitosus*, Curt., he says, is found in enormous quantities, a single cluster containing from fifty to one hundred stems, and might well be deemed a valuable species in times of scarcity. It would not be highly esteemed where other and better species can be had, but it is generally preferred to *Agaricus melleus*, Fr. It is suitable for drying for winter use. In the same communication, he observes that the imperial (*Agaricus cæsarius*, Scop.),

* Krombholz, "Schwämme," t. 8. Vittadini, "Mang." t. 1.

† Vittadini, "Mangerecci," t. 9.

‡ Berkeley, "Outlines," pl. 3, fig. 5.

§ Saunders and Smith, "Mycological Illustr." pl. 23.

‖ Cooke, M. C., "Handbook of British Fungi," vol. i. pl. 1, fig. 2.

¶ "Gardener's Chronicle" (1869), p. 1066.

grows in great quantities in oak forests, and may be obtained by the cart-load in its season; but to his taste, and that of his family, it is the most unpalatable of fungi, nor could he find any of the most passionate mycophagists who would avow that they liked it. There is a disagreeable saline flavour that they could not remove nor overlay. In addition to these, the same authority enumerates *Agaricus russula*, Schæff., *Agaricus hypopithyus*, Curt., and *Agaricus consociatus*, Curt., the latter two being confined to the United States; *Agaricus columbetta*, Fr., found in Britain, but not eaten, as well as *Agaricus radicatus*, Bull. *Agaricus bombycinus*, Schæff., and *Agaricus speciosus*, Fr., are found in Britain, but by no means common; *Agaricus squarrosus*, Mull., has always been regarded with great suspicion in this country, where it is by no means uncommon; *Agaricus cretaceus*, Fr., and *Agaricus sylvaticus*, Schæff., are close allies of the common mushroom.

Dr. Curtis says that hill and plain, mountain and valley, woods, fields, and pastures, swarm with a profusion of good nutritious fungi, which are allowed to decay where they spring up, because people do not know how, or are afraid, to use them. By those of us who know their use, their value was appreciated, as never before, during the late war, when other food, especially meat, was scarce and dear. Then such persons as I have heard express a preference for mushrooms over meat had generally no need to lack grateful food, as it was easily had for the gathering, and within easy distance of their homes if living in the country. Such was not always the case, however. I remember once, during the gloomy period when there had been a protracted drought, and fleshy fungi were to be found only in damp shaded woods, and but few even there, I was unable to find enough of any one species for a meal, so, gathering of every kind, I brought home thirteen different kinds, had them all cooked together in one grand *pot pourri*, and made an excellent supper.

One important use to which several species of fungi can be applied, is the manufacture of ketchup. For this purpose, not only is the mushroom, *Agaricus campestris*, and the horse mushroom, *Agaricus arvensis*, available, but also *Agaricus rubescens* is declared to be excellent for the purpose, and a delicious, but pale, extract is to be obtained from *Marasmius oreades.* Other species, as *Coprinus comatus*, and *Coprinus atramentarius*, are also available, together with *Fistulina hepatica*, and *Morchella esculenta.* In some districts, when mushrooms are scarce, it is stated that almost any species that will yield a dark juice is without scruple mixed with the common mushroom, and it should seem without any bad consequence except the deterioration of the ketchup.* There is an extensive manufacture of ketchup conducted at Lubbenham, near Market Harborough, but the great difficulty appears to be the prevention of decomposition. Messrs. Perkins receive tons of mushrooms from every part of the kingdom, and they find, even in the same species, an immense difference in the quality and quantity of the produce. The price of mushrooms varies greatly with the season, ranging between one penny and sixpence per pound. Messrs. Perkins are very careful in their selection, but little discrimination is used by country manufacturers on a small scale, who use such doubtful species as *Agaricus lacrymabundus*, with *Agaricus spadiceus*, and a host of allied species, which they characterize as nonpareils and champignons. In the eastern counties *Agaricus arvensis* has the preference for ketchup.

The generic distinctions between the genuine Agarics and some of the allied genera can hardly be appreciated by the non-botanical reader, but we have nevertheless preferred grouping the edible species together in a somewhat botanical order; and, pursuing this plan, the next species will be those of *Coprinus*, in which the gills are deliquescent after the plant has arrived at maturity. The maned mushroom (*Coprinus comatus*, Fr.)† is the best of edible species in this group. It is very common here by roadsides and other places, and whilst still young and cylindrical, and the gills still whitish or with a roseate tint, it is highly to be commended. Similar, but perhaps somewhat inferior, is *Coprinus atramentarius*, Fr.,‡ equally common about

* Berkeley, "Outlines of British Fungology," p. 64.

† Cooke, "Easy Guide to British Fungi," pl. 11.

‡ Ibid., pl. 12.

old stumps and on the naked soil. Both species are also found and eaten in the United States.

In *Cortinarius*, the veil is composed of arachnoid threads, and the spores are rusty. The number of edible species are few. Foremost is the really handsome *Cortinarius violaeus*, Fr.,* often nearly four inches in diameter, and of a beautiful violet colour; and the smaller *Cortinarius castaneus*, Fr.,† scarcely exceeding an inch in diameter, both being found in woods, and common alike to Britain and the United States. *Cortinarius cinnamomeus*, Fr., is also a lover of woods, and in northern latitudes is found inhabiting them everywhere. It has a cinnamon-coloured pileus, with yellowish flesh, and its odour and flavour is said to partake of the same spice. In Germany it is held in high esteem. *Cortinarius emodensis*, B., is eaten in Northern India.

The small genus *Lepista* of Smith (which, however, is not adopted by Fries in his new edition of the "Epicrisis") includes one esculent species in *Lepista personata*, the *Agaricus personatus* of Fries.‡ It is by no means uncommon in Northern Europe or America, frequently growing in large rings; the pileus is pallid, and the stem stained with lilac. Formerly it was said to be sold in Covent Garden Market under the name of "blewits," but we have failed to see or hear of it during many years in London.

Small fungi of ivory-whiteness are very common amongst grass on lawns in autumn. These are chiefly *Hygrophorus virgineus*, Fr.,§ and although not much exceeding an inch in diameter, with a short stem, and wide decurrent gills, they are so plentiful in season that quantity soon compensates for the small size. Except that it is occasionally eaten in France, it does not enjoy much reputation abroad. A larger species, varying from buff to orange, *Hygrophorus pratensis*, Fr.,‖ is scarcely less common in open pastures. This is very gregarious in habit,

* Hussey, "Mycol. Illust." pl. 12.

† Bulliard, "Champ." t. 268.

‡ Cooke, "Easy Guide," pl. 4, fig. 1; Hussey, "Illust." vol. ii. pl. 40.

§ Greville, "Scot. Crypt. Flora," t. 166.

‖ Ibid., t. 91.

often growing in tufts, or portions of rings. The pileus is fleshy in the centre, and the gills thick and decurrent. In France, Germany, Bohemia, and Denmark, it is included with esculent species. In addition may be mentioned *Hygrophorus eburneus*, Fr., another white species, as also *Hygrophorus niveus*, Fr., which grows in mossy pastures. *Paxillus involutus*, Fr.,* though very common in Europe, is not eaten, yet it is included by Dr. Curtis with the esculent species of the United States.

The milky agarics, belonging to the genus *Lactarius*, are distinguished by the milky juice which is exuded when they are wounded. The spores are more or less globose, and rough or echinulate, at least in many species. The most notable esculent is *Lactarius deliciosus*, Fr.,† in which the milk is at first saffron-red, and afterwards greenish, the plant assuming a lurid greenish hue wherever bruised or broken. Universal commendation seems to fall upon this species, writers vying with each other to say the best in its praise, and mycophagists everywhere endorsing the assumption of its name, declaring it to be delicious. It is found in the markets of Paris, Berlin, Prague, and Vienna, as we are informed, and in Sweden, Denmark, Switzerland, Russia, Belgium; in fact, in nearly all countries in Europe it is esteemed.

Another esculent species, *Lactarius volemum*, Fr.,‡ has white milk, which is mild to the taste, whilst in deleterious species with white milk it is pungent and acrid. This species has been celebrated from early times, and is said to resemble lamb's kidney.

Lactarius piperatus, Fr., is classed in England with dangerous, sometimes poisonous species, whereas the late Dr. Curtis, of North Carolina, has distinctly informed us that it is cooked and eaten in the United States, and that he has partaken of it. He includes *Lactarius insulsus*, Fr., and *Lactarius subdulcis*, Fr.,§ amongst esculent species; both are also found in this country,

* Sowerby, "Fungi," pl. 56; Schæffer, "Icones Bav." t. 72.

† Trattinnick, L., "Die Essbaren Schwämme" (1809), p. 82, pl. M; Barla, J. B., "Champignons de la Nice" (1859), p. 34, pl. 19.

‡ Smith, "Edible Mushrooms," fig. 26.

§ Barla, "Champ. Nice," t. 20, f. 4–10.

but not reputed as edible; and *Lactarius angustissimus*, Lasch, which is not British. Species of *Lactarius* seem to be eaten almost indiscriminately in Russia when preserved in vinegar and salt, in which condition they form an important item in the kinds of food allowed in their long fasts, some *Boleti* in the dried state entering into the same category.

The species of *Russula* in many respects resemble *Lactarii* without milk. Some of them are dangerous, and others esculent. Amongst the latter may be enumerated *Russula heterophylla*, Fr., which is very common in woods. Vittadini pronounces it unsurpassed for fineness of flavour by even the notable *Amanita cæsarea.** Roques gives also an account in its favour as consumed in France. Both these authors give favourable accounts of *Russula virescens*, P.,† which the peasants about Milan are in the habit of putting over wood embers to toast, and eating afterwards with a little salt. Unfortunately it is by no means common in England. A third species of *Russula*, with buff-yellow gills, is *Russula alutacea*, Fr., which is by no means to be despised, notwithstanding that Dr. Badham has placed it amongst species to be avoided. Three or four others have also the merit of being harmless, and these recorded as esculent by some one or more mycological authors: *Russula lactea*, Fr., a white species, found also in the United States; *Russula lepida*, Fr., a roseate species, found also in lower Carolina, U.S.; and another reddish species, *Russula vesca*, Fr., as well as *Russula decolorans*, Fr. Whilst writing of this genus, we may observe, by way of caution, that it includes also one very noxious red species, *Russula emetica*, Fr., with white gills, with which some of the foregoing might be confounded by inexperienced persons.

The chantarelle *Cantharellus cibarius*, Fr., has a most charming and enticing appearance and odour. In colour, it is of a bright golden yellow, and its smell has been compared to that of ripe apricots. It is almost universally eaten in all countries

* Vittadini, C., "Funghi Mangerecci" (1835), p. 209; Barla, "Champ. Nice," pl. i.

† Vittadini, C., "Funghi Mangerecci," p. 245; Roques, "Champ. Comest." p. 86.

where it is found, England excepted, where it is only to be met with at the "Freemason's Tavern" on state occasions, and at the tables of pertinacious mycophagists.* Trattinnick says: "Not only this same fungus never did any one harm, but might even restore the dead."†

The fairy-ring champignon *Marasmius oreades*, Fr., though small, is plentiful, and one of the most delicious of edible fungi. It grows in exposed pastures, forming rings, or parts of rings. This champignon possesses the advantage of drying readily, and preserving its aroma for a long time. We have often regretted that no persistent attempts and experiments have been made with the view of cultivating this excellent and useful species. *Marasmius scorodonius*, Fr.,‡ a small, strong-scented, and in all respects inferior species, found on heaths and dry pastures, extending even to the United States, is consumed in Germany, Austria, and other continental countries, where, perhaps its garlic odour has been one of its recommendations as an ingredient in sauces. In this enumeration we have not exhausted all the gill-bearing species which might be eaten, having included only those which have some reputation as esculents, and of these more particularly those found in Great Britain and the United States.

Amongst the *Polyporei*, in which the gill plates are represented by pores or tubes, fewer esculent species are to be met with than in the *Agaricini*, and the majority of these belong to the genus *Boletus*. Whilst in Vienna and Hanover, we were rather surprised to find *Boletus edulis*, Fr., cut into thin slices and dried, exposed for sale in almost every shop where meal, peas, and other farinaceous edibles were sold. This species is common enough in England, but as a rule it does not seem to please the English palate, whereas on the continent no fungus is more commonly eaten. This is believed to be the suillus eaten by the ancient Romans,§ who obtained it from Bithynia. The

* Badham, Dr, "Esculent Funguses of Britain," 2nd ed. p. 110; Hussey, "Illust. Brit. Mycol." 1st ser. pl. 4; Barla, "Champ." pl. 28, f. 7-15.

† Trattinnick, L., "Essbaren Schwämme," p. 98.

‡ Lenz, "Die Nützlichen und Schädlichen Schwämme," p. 49.

§ Badham, "Esculent Funguses of Great Britain," 2 ed. p. 91.

modern Italians dry them on strings for winter use, and in Hungary a soup is made from them when fresh. A more excellent species, according to our judgment, is *Boletus æstivalis*, Fr.,* which appears in early summer, and has a peculiar nutty flavour when raw, reminding one more of a fresh mushroom. *Boletus scaber*, Fr.,† is also common in Britain, as well as the continent, but does not enjoy so good a reputation as *B. edulis*. Krombholz says that *Boletus bovinus*, Fr., a gregarious species, found on heaths and in fir woods, is much sought after abroad as a dish, and is good when dried. *Boletus castaneus*, Fr.,‡ is a small species with a mild, pleasant taste when raw, and very good when properly cooked. It is not uncommonly eaten on the continent. *Boletus chrysenteron*, Fr.,§ and *Boletus subtomentosus*, Fr., are said to be very poor eating, and some authors have considered them injurious; but Mr. W. G. Smith states that he has on more than one occasion eaten the former, and Trattinnick states that the latter is eaten in Germany. The late Mr. Salter informed us that, when employed on the geological staff, he at one time lived almost entirely on different species of Boleti, without using much discrimination. Sir W. C. Trevelyan also informs us that he has eaten *Boletus lurdius* without any unpleasant consequences, but we confess that we should be sorry to repeat the experiment. Dr. Badham remarks that he has eaten *Boletus Grevillei*, B., *Boletus flavus*, With., and *Boletus granulatus*, L., the latter being recognized also as edible abroad. Dr. Curtis experimented, in the United States, on *Boletus collinitus*, and although he professes not to be particularly fond of the Boleti, he recognizes it as esculent, and adds that it had been pronounced delicious by some to whom he had sent it. He also enumerates as edible *Boletus luteus*, Fr., *Boletus elegans*, Fr., *Boletus flavidus*, Fr., *Boletus versipellis*, Fr., *Boletus leucomelas*, Tr., and *Boletus ovinus*, Sch. Two Italian species of *Polyporus* must not be forgotten. These are *Polyporus tuberaster*, Pers.,

* Hussey, "Myc. Illus." ii. pl. 25; Paulet, "Champ." t. 170.

† Barla, J. B., "Champ. de la Nice," p. 71, pl. 35, f. 1-5.

‡ Hussey, "Illustr." ii. t. 17; Barla, "Champ. Nice," t. 32, f. 11-15.

§ Hussey, "Illustr." i. t. 5; Krombholz, "Schwämme," t. 76.

which is procured by watering the *pietra funghaia*, or fungus stone, a kind of tufa, in which the mycelium is embedded. It is confined to Naples. The other species is *Polyporus corylinus*, Mauri., procured artificially in Rome from charred stumps of the cob-nut tree.*

Of true *Polyporus*, only two or three species have been regarded favourably as esculents. These are—*Polyporus intybaceus*, Fr., which is of very large size, sometimes attaining as much as forty pounds; *Polyporus giganteus*, Fr., also very large, and leathery when old. Both these species are natives of Britain. Only young and juicy specimens must be selected for cooking. *Polyporus umbellatus*, Fr., is stated by Fries to be esculent, but it is not found in Britain. *Polyporus squamosus*, Fr., has been also included; but Mrs. Hussey thinks that one might as well think of eating saddle-flaps. None of these receive very much commendation. Dr. Curtis enumerates, amongst North American species, the *Polyporus cristatus*, Fr., *Polyporus poripes*, Fr., which, when raw, tastes like the best chestnuts or filberts, but is rather too dry when cooked. *Polyporus Berkeleii*, Fr., is intensely pungent when raw, but when young, and before the pores are visible, it may be eaten with impunity, all its pungency being dissipated by cooking. *Polyporus confluens*, Fr., he considers superior, and, in fact, quite a favourite. *Polyporus sulfureus*, Fr., which is not eaten in Europe, he considers just tolerably safe, but not to be coveted. It is by no means to be recommended to persons with weak stomachs. In his catalogue, Dr. Curtis enumerates one hundred and eleven species of edible fungi found in Carolina.†

With *Fistulina hepatica*, Fr., it is different; for here we encounter a fleshy, juicy fungus, resembling beefsteak a little in appearance, and so much more in its uses, that the name of "beefsteak fungus" has been given to it. Some authors are rapturous in their praise of *Fistulina*. It sometimes attains a very large size, Dr. Badham quoting ‡ one found by himself

* Badham's "Esculent Funguses," 1st ed. pp. 116 and 120.

† Catalogue of Plants of Carolina, U.S.

‡ Badham, Dr., "Esculent Funguses," 2nd ed. p. 128; Hussey, "Illustra-

nearly five feet in circumference, and weighing eight pounds; whilst another found by Mr. Graves weighed nearly thirty pounds. In Vienna it is sliced and eaten with salad, like beet-root, which it then much resembles. On the continent it is everywhere included amongst the best of edible species.

The *Hydnei*, instead of pores or tubes, are characterized by spines or warts, over which the fructifying surface is expanded. The most common is *Hydnum repandum*, Fr., found in woods and woody places in England, and on the continent, extending into the United States. When raw, it is peppery to the taste, but when cooked is much esteemed. From its drier nature, it can readily be dried for winter use. Less common in England is *Hydnum imbricatum*, Fr., although not so uncommon on the continent. It is eaten in Germany, Austria, Switzerland, France, and elsewhere. *Hydnum lævigatum*, Swartz, is eaten in Alpine districts.* Of the branched species, *Hydnum coralloides*, Scop.,† and *Hydnum Caput Medusæ*, Bull,‡ are esculent, but very rare in England. The latter is not uncommon in Austria and Italy, the former in Germany, Switzerland, and France. *Hydnum erinaceum*, Bull, is eaten in Germany § and France.

The Clavarioid fungi are mostly small, but of these the majority of the white-spored are edible. *Clavaria rugosa*, Bull, is a common British species, as also is *Clavaria coralloides*, L., the former being found also in the United States. *Clavaria fastigiata*, D. C., is not uncommon; but *Clavaria amethystina*, Bull, a beautiful violet species, is rare. In France and Italy, *Clavaria cinerea*, Bull, is classed with esculents; and it is not uncommon in Britain. *Clavaria botrytis*, P., and *Clavaria aurea*, Schæff., are large and beautiful species, but rare with us; they extend also into the United States. Others might be named (Dr. Curtis enumerates thirteen species eaten in Carolina), which are

tions," 1st ser. pl. 65; Berkeley, in "Gard. Chron." (1861), p. 121; Bull, in "Trans. Woolhope Club" (1869).

* Barla, "Champ. Nice," p. 79, pl. 38, f. 5, 6.

† Roques, l. c. p. 48.

‡ Lenz, p. 93; Roques, l. c. p. 47, pl. 2, fig. 5.

§ Lenz, H. O., "Die Nützlichen und Schädlichen Schwämme," p. 93.

certainly wholesome, but they are of little importance as edible species. *Sparassis crispa*, Fr., is, on the contrary, very large, resembling in size,* and somewhat in appearance, a cauliflower; it has of late years been found several times in this country. In Austria it is fricasseed with butter and herbs.

Of the true Tremellæ, none merit insertion here. The curious Jew's ear (*Hirneola auricula-Judæ*, Fr.), with one or two other species of *Hirneola*, are collected in great quantities in Tahiti, and shipped in a dried state to China, where they are used for soup. Some of these find their way to Singapore.

The false truffles (*Hypogæi*) are of doubtful value, one species (*Melanogaster variegatus*, Tul.) having formerly been sold in the markets of Bath as a substitute for the genuine truffle.† Neither amongst the *Phalloidei* do we meet with species of any economic value. The gelatinous volva of a species of *Ileodictyon* is eaten by the New Zealanders, to whom it is known as thunder dirt; whilst that of *Phallus Mokusin* is applied to a like purpose in China;‡ but these examples would not lead us to recommend a similar use for *Phallus impudicus*, Fr., in Britain, or induce us to prove the assertion of a Scotch friend that the porous stem is very good eating.

One species of puff-ball, *Lycoperdon giganteum*, Fr.,§ has many staunch advocates, and whilst young and cream-like, it is, when well manipulated, an excellent addition to the breakfast-table. A decided advantage is possessed by this species, since one specimen is often found large enough to satisfy the appetites of ten or twelve persons. Other species of *Lycoperdon* have been eaten when young, and we have been assured by those who have made the experiment, that they are scarcely inferior to their larger congener. *Bovista nigrescens*, Fr., and *Bovista plumbea*, Fr., are also eaten in the United States. More than one species of *Lycoperdon* and *Bovista* appear in the bazaars of India, as at Secunderabad and Rangoon; while the white ant-

* Berkeley, M. J., in "Intellectual Observer," No. 25, pl. 1.

† Berkeley, M. J., "Outlines of British Fungology," p. 293.

‡ Berkeley, M. J., "Introduction to Crypt. Bot." p. 347.

§ Cooke, M. C., "A Plain and Easy Guide," &c., p. 96.

hills, together with an excellent Agaric, produce one or more species of *Podaxon* which are esculent when young. A species of *Scleroderma* which grows abundantly in sandy districts, is substituted for truffles in Perigord pies, of which, however, it does not possess any of the aroma.

Passing over the rest of the sporiferous fungi, we find amongst the *Ascomycetous* group several that are highly esteemed. Amongst these may first be named the species of morel, which are regarded as delicacies wherever they are found. *Morchella esculenta*, Pers., is the most common species, but we have also

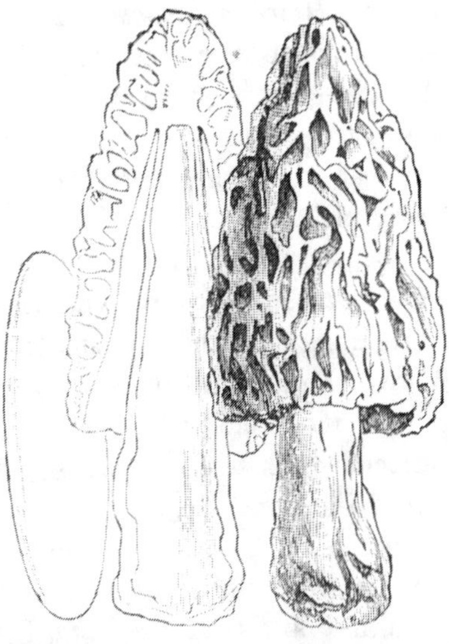

FIG. 43.—*Morchella gigaspora*, from Kashmir.

Morchella semilibera, D. C., and the much larger *Morchella crassipes*, Pers. Probably all the species of *Morchella* are esculent, and we know that many besides the above are eaten in Europe and other places; *Morchella deliciosa*, Fr., in Java; *Morchella bohemica*, Kromb., in Bohemia; *Morchella gigaspora*, Cooke, and *Morchella deliciosa*, Fr., in Kashmere.* *Morchella rimosipes*, D. C., occurs in France and Bohemia; *Morchella*

* Cooke, M. C., "On Kashmir Morels," in "Trans. Bot. Soc. Edin." vol. x. p. 439, with figs.

Caroliniana, Bosc., in the Southern United States of America. W. G. Smith records the occurrence in Britain of specimens of *Morchella crassipes*, P., ten inches in height, and one specimen was eleven inches high, with a diameter of seven and a half inches.*

Similar in uses, though differing in appearance, are the species of *Helvella*, of which several are edible. In both these genera, the individuals can be dried so readily that they are the more valuable on that account, as they can be used for flavouring in winter when fresh specimens of any kind of fungus are difficult to procure. The most common English species is *Helvella crispa*, Fr., but *Helvella lacunosa*, Fr., is declared to be equally good, though not so large and somewhat rare. *Helvella infula*, Fr., is also a large species, but is not British, although it extends to North America, as also does *Helvella sulcata*, Afz. Intermediate between the morel and *Helvella* is the species which was formerly included with the latter, but now known as *Gyromitra esculenta*, Fr.† It is rarely found in Great Britain, but is more common on the continent, where it is held in esteem. A curious stipitate fungus, with a pileus like a hood, called *Verpa digitaliformis*, Pers.,‡ is uncommon in England, but Vittadini states that it is sold in the Italian markets, although only to be recommended when no other esculent fungus offers, which is sometimes the case in spring.§

Two or three species of *Peziza* have the reputation of being esculent, but they are of very little value; one of these is *Peziza acetabulum*, L., another is *Peziza cochleata*, Huds., and a third is *Peziza venosa*, Pers.‖ The latter has the most decided nitrous odour, and also fungoid flavour, whilst the former seem to have but little to recommend them; we have seen whole baskets full of *Peziza cochleata* gathered in Northamptonshire as a substitute for morels.

A very interesting genus of edible fungi, growing on ever-

* Smith, "Journ. Bot." vol. ix. p. 214.

† Cooke, "Handbook," fig. 322.

‡ Cooke, "Handbook," fig. 324.

§ Vittadini, C., "Funghi Mangerecci," p. 117.

‖ Greville, "Sc. Crypt. Fl." pl. 156.

green beech trees in South America, has been named *Cyttaria.* One of these, *Cyttaria Darwinii*, B., occurs in Terra del Fuego, where it was found by Mr. C. Darwin* growing in vast numbers, and forming a very essential article of food for the natives. Another is *Cyttaria Berteroi*, B., also seen by Mr. Darwin in Chili, and eaten occasionally, but apparently not so good as the preceding.† Another species is *Cyttaria Gunnii*, B., which abounds in Tasmania, and is held in repute amongst the settlers for its esculent properties.‡

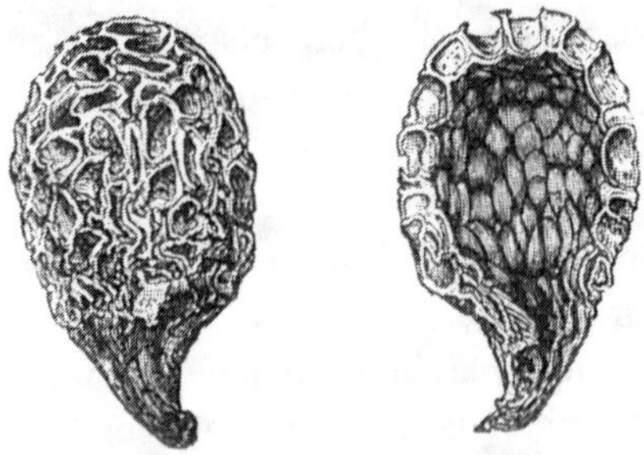

FIG. 44.—*Cyttaria Gunnii*, B.

It remains for us only to note the subterranean fungi, of which the truffle is the type, to complete our enumeration of esculent species. The truffle which is consumed in England is *Tuber æstivum*, Vitt.; but in France the more highly-flavoured *Tuber melanospermum*, Vitt.,§ and also *Tuber magnatum*, Pico, with some other species. In Italy they are very common, whilst some are found in Algeria. One species at least is recorded in the North-west of India, but in Northern Europe and North America they appear to be rare, and *Terfezia Leonis* is used as an esculent in Damascus. A large species of *Mylitta*, sometimes several inches in diameter, occurs plentifully in some parts of Australia. Although often included with fungi, the curious production known under the name of *Pachyma cocos*, Fr., is not

* Berkeley, in "Linn. Trans." xix. p. 37; Cooke, in "Technologist" (1864), p. 387.

† Berkeley, M. J., in "Linn. Trans." xix. p. 37.

‡ Berkeley, M. J., in "Hooker, Flora Antarctica," p. 147; in "Hooker's Journ. Bot." (1848), 576, t. 20, 21.

§ Vittadini, C., "Monographia Tuberacearum" (1831), pp. 36, &c.

a fungus, as proved by the examinations made by the Rev. M. J. Berkeley. It is eaten under the name of "Tuckahoe" in the United States, and as it consists almost entirely of pectic acid, it is sometimes used in the manufacture of jelly.

In the Neilgherries (S. India), a substance is occasionally found which is allied to the native bread of southern latitudes. It is found at an elevation of 5,000 feet. The natives call it "a little man's bread," in allusion to the tradition that the Neilgherries were once peopled by a race of dwarfs.* At first it was supposed that these were the bulbs of some orchid, but later another view was held of their character. Mr. Scott, who examined the specimens sent down to him, remarks that, instead of being the product of orchids, it is that of an underground fungus of the genus *Mylitta.* It indeed seems, he says, very closely allied to, if really distinct from, the so-called native bread of Tasmania.†

Of the fungi employed in medicine, the first place must be assigned to ergot, which is the sclerotioid condition of a species of *Claviceps.* It occurs not only on rye but on wheat, and many of the wild grasses. On account of its active principle, this fungus still holds its place in the Materia Medica. Others which formerly had a reputation are now discarded, as, for instance, the species of *Elaphomyces;* and *Polyporus officinalis*, Fr., which has been partly superseded as a styptic by other substances, was formerly employed as a purgative. The ripe spongy capillitium of the great puff-ball *Lycoperdon giganteum*, Fr., has been used for similar purposes, and also recommended as an anodyne; indeed formidable surgical operations have been performed under its influence, and it is frequently used as a narcotic in the taking of honey. Langsdorf gives a curious account of its employment as a narcotic; and in a recent work on Kamtschatka it is said to obtain a very high price in that country. Dr. Porter Smith writes of its employment medicinally by the Chinese, but from his own specimens it is clearly a species of *Polysaccum*, which he has mistaken for *Lycoperdon.* In China

* "Proceedings Agri. Hort. Soc. India" (Dec. 1871), p. lxxix.

† *Ibid.* (June, 1872), p. xxiii.

several species are supposed to possess great virtue, notably the *Torrubia sinensis*, Tul.,* which is developed on dead caterpillars; as it is, however, recommended to administer it as a stuffing to roast duck, we may be sceptical as to its own sanitary qualities. *Geaster hygrometricus*, Fr., we have also detected amongst Chinese drugs, as also a species of *Polysaccum*, and the small hard *Mylitta lapidescens*, Horn. In India, a large but imperfect fungus, named provisionally *Sclerotium stipitatum*, Curr., found in nests of the white ant, is supposed to possess great medicinal virtues.† A species of *Polyporus* (*P. anthelminticus*, B.), which grows at the root of old bamboos, is employed in Burmah as an anthelmintic.‡ In former times the Jew's ear (*Hirneola auricula Judæ*, Fr.) was supposed to possess great virtues, which are now discredited. Yeast is still included amongst pharmaceutical substances, but could doubtless be very well dispensed with. Truffles are no longer regarded as aphrodisiacs.

For other uses, we can only allude to amadou, or German tinder, which is prepared in Northern Europe from *Polyporus fomentarius*, Fr., cut in slices, dried, and beaten until it is soft. This substance, besides being used as tinder, is made into warm caps, chest protectors, and other articles. This same, or an allied species of *Polyporus*, probably *P. igniarius*, Fr., is dried and pounded as an ingredient in snuff by the Ostyacks on the Obi. In Bohemia some of the large Polyporei, such as *P. igniarius* and *P. fomentarius*, have the pores and part of the inner substance removed, and then the pileus is fastened in an inverted position to the wall, by the part where originally it adhered to the wood. The cavity is then filled with mould, and the fungus is used, with good effect, instead of flower-pots, for the cultivation of such creeping plants as require but little moisture.§

The barren mycelioid condition of *Penicillium crustaceum*,

* Lindley, "Vegetable Kingdom," fig. xxiv.

† Currey, F., in "Linn. Trans." vol. xxiii. p. 93.

‡ "Pharmacopœia of India," p. 258.

§ "Gard. Chron." (1862), p. 21.

Fr., is employed in country districts for the domestic manufacture of vinegar from saccharine liquor, under the name of the "vinegar plant." It is stated that *Polysaccum crassipes*, D. C.,* is employed in the South of Europe to produce a yellow dye; whilst recently *Polyporus sulfureus*, Fr., has been recommended for a similar purpose. *Agaricus muscarius*, Fr., the fly-agaric, known to be an active poison, is used in decoction in some parts of Europe for the destructiou of flies and bugs. Probably *Helotium æruginosum*, Fr.,† deserves mention here, because it stains the wood on which it grows, by means of its diffuse mycelium, of a beautiful green tint, and the wood thus stained is employed for its colour in the manufacture of Tonbridge ware.

This completes the list, certainly of the most important, of the fungi which are of any direct use to humanity as food, medicine, or in the arts. As compared with lichens, the advantage is certainly in favour of fungi; and even when compared with algæ, the balance appears in their favour. In fact, it may be questioned whether, after all, fungi do not present a larger proportion of really useful species than any other of the cryptogams; and without any desire to disparage the elegance of ferns, the delicacy of mosses, the brilliancy of some algæ, or the interest which attaches to lichens, it may be claimed for fungi that in real utility (not uncombined with injuries as real) they stand at the head of the cryptogams, and in closest alliance with the flowering plants.

* Barla, "Champ. de la Nice," p. 126, pl. 47, fig. 11.

† Greville, "Scott. Crypt. Flora," pl. 241.

V.

NOTABLE PHENOMENA.

THERE are no phenomena associated with fungi that are of greater interest than those which relate to luminosity. The fact that fungi under some conditions are luminous has long been known, since schoolboys in our juvenile days were in the habit of secreting fragments of rotten wood penetrated by mycelium, in order to exhibit their luminous properties in the dark, and thus astonish their more ignorant or incredulous fellows. Rumphius noted its appearance in Amboyna, and Fries, in his Observations, gives the name of *Thelephora phosphorea* to a species of *Corticium* now known as *Corticium cæruleum*, on account of its phosphorescence under certain conditions. The same species is the *Auricularia phosphorea* of Sowerby, but he makes no note of its phosphorescence. Luminosity in fungi "has been observed in various parts of the world, and where the species has been fully developed it has been generally a species of *Agaricus* which has yielded the phenomenon."* One of the best-known species is the *Agaricus olearius* of the South of Europe, which was examined by Tulasne with especial view to its luminosity.† In his introductory remarks, he says that four species only of Agaricus that are luminous appear at present to be known. One of them, *A. olearius*, D. C., is indigenous to Central Europe; another, *A. igneus*, Rumph., comes from Amboyna; the third, *A. noctileucus*, Lév., has been dis-

* M. J. Berkeley, "Introduction to Cryptogamic Botany," p. 265.

† Tulasne, "Sur la Phosphorescence des Champignons," in "Ann. des Sci. Nat." (1848), vol. ix p. 338.

covered at Manilla by Gaudichaud, in 1836; the last, *A. Gardneri*, Berk., is produced in the Brazilian province of Goyaz, upon dead leaves. As to the *Dematium violaceum*, Pers., the *Himantia candida*, Pers., cited once by Link, and the *Thelephora cærulea*, D. C. (*Corticium cæruleum*, Fr.), Tulasne is of opinion that their phosphorescent properties are still problematical; at least no recent observation confirms them.

The phosphorescence of *A. olearius*, D. C., appears to have been first made known by De Candolle, but it seems that he was in error in stating that these phosphorescent properties manifest themselves only at the time of its decomposition. Fries, describing the *Cladosporium umbrinum*, which lives upon the Agaric of the olive-tree, expressed the opinion that the Agaric only owes its phosphorescence to the presence of the mould. This, however, Tulasne denies, for he writes, "I have had the opportunity of observing that the Agaric of the olive is really phosphorescent of itself, and that it is not indebted to any foreign production for the light it emits." Like Delile, he considers that the fungus is only phosphorescent up to the time when it ceases to grow; thus the light which it projects, one might say, is a manifestation of its vegetation.

"It is an important fact," writes Tulasne, "which I can confirm, and which it is important to insist upon, that the phosphorescence is not exclusively confined to the hymenial surface. Numerous observations made by me prove that the whole of the substance of the fungus participates very frequently, if not always, in the faculty of shining in the dark. Among the first Agarics which I examined, I found many, the stipe of which shed here and there a light as brilliant as the hymenium, and led me to think that it was due to the spores which had fallen on the surface of the stipe. Therefore, being in the dark, I scraped with my scalpel the luminous parts of the stipe, but it did not sensibly diminish their brightness; then I split the stipe, bruised it, divided it into small fragments, and I found that the whole of this mass, even in its deepest parts, enjoyed, in a similar degree to its superficies, the property of light. I found, besides, a phosphorescence quite as brilliant in all the cap, for, having split it vertically in the form of plates, I found that the trama, when bruised, threw out a light equal to that of their fructiferous surfaces, and there is really only the superior surface of the pileus, or its cuticle, which I have never seen luminous.

"As I have said, the Agaric of the olive-tree, which is itself very yellow, reflects a strong brilliant light, and remains endowed with this remarkable faculty whilst it grows, or, at least, while it appears to preserve an active life, and remains fresh. The phosphorescence is at first, and more ordinarily, recognizable at the surface of the hymenium. I have seen a great number of young fungi which were very phosphorescent in the gills, but not in any other part. In another case, and amongst more aged fungi, the hymenium of which had ceased to give light, the stipe, on the contrary, threw out a brilliant glare. Habitually, the phosphorescence is distributed in an unequal manner upon the stipe, and the same upon the gills. Although the stipe is luminous at its surface, it is not always necessarily so in its interior substance, if one bruises it, but this substance frequently becomes phosphorescent after contact with the air. Thus, I had irregularly split and slit a large stipe in its length, and I found the whole flesh obscure, whilst on the exterior were some luminous places. I roughly joined the lacerated parts, and the following evening, on observing them anew, I found them all flashing a bright light. At another time, I had with a scalpel split vertically many fungi in order to hasten their dessication; the evening of the same day, the surface of all these cuts was phosphorescent, but in many of these pieces of fungi the luminosity was limited to the cut surface which remained exposed to the air; the flesh beneath was unchanged.

"I have seen a stipe opened and lacerated irregularly, the whole of the flesh of which remained phosphorescent during three consecutive evenings, but the brightness diminished in intensity from the exterior to the interior, so that on the third day it did not issue from the inner part of the stipe. The phosphorescence of the gills is in no way modified at first by immersing the fungus in water; when they have been immersed they are as bright as in the air, but the fungi which I left immersed until the next evening lost all their phosphorescence, and communicated to the water an already sensible yellow tint; alcohol put upon the phosphorescent gills did not at once completely obliterate the light, but visibly enfeebled it. As to the spores, which are white, I have found many times very dense coats of them thrown down on porcelain plates, but I have never seen them phosphorescent.

"As to the observation made by Delile that the Agaric of the olive does not shine during the day when placed in total darkness, I think that it could not have been repeated. From what I have said of the phosphorescence of *A. olearius*, one naturally concludes that there does not exist any necessary relation between this phenomenon and the fructification of the fungus; the luminous brightness of the hymenium shows, says Delile, 'the greater activity of the reproductive organs,' but it is not in consequence of its reproductive functions, which may be judged only as an accessory phenomenon, the cause of which is independent of, and more general than these functions, since all the parts of the fungus, its entire substance, throws forth at one time, or at successive times, light. From these experiments Tulasne infers that the same agents, oxygen, water, and warmth, are perfectly necessary to the production of phosphorescence as much in living organized beings as in those which have ceased to live. In either case, the luminous phenomena accompany a chemical reaction which consists principally in a combination of the organized matter with the oxygen of the air; that is to say, in its combustion, and in the discharge of carbonic acid which thus shows itself."

We have quoted at considerable length from these observations of Tulasne on the Agaric of the olive, as they serve very much to illustrate similar manifestations in other species, which doubtless resemble each other in their main features.

Mr. Gardner has graphically described his first acquaintance in Brazil with the phosphorescent species which now bears his name. It was encountered on a dark night of December, while passing through the streets of Villa de Natividate. Some boys were amusing themselves with some luminous object, which at first he supposed to be a kind of large fire-fly, but on making inquiry he found it to be a beautiful phosphorescent Agaric, which he was told grew abundantly in the neighbourhood on the decaying fronds of a dwarf palm. The whole plant gives out at night a bright light somewhat similar to that emitted by the larger fire-flies, having a pale greenish hue. From this circumstance, and from growing on a palm, it was called by the inhabitants "flor de coco."*

The number of recognized phosphorescent species of *Agaricus* is not large, although two or three others may be enumerated in addition to those cited by Tulasne. Of these, *Agaricus lampas*, and some others, are found in Australia.† In addition to the *Agaricus noctileucus*, discovered by Gaudichaud, and the *Agaricus igneus* of Rumphius, found in Amboyna, Dr. Hooker speaks of the phenomenon as common in Sikkim, but he seems never to have been able to ascertain with what species it was associated.

Dr. Cuthbert Collingwood has communicated some further information relative to the luminosity of a species of *Agaricus* in Borneo (supposed to be *A. Gardneri*), in which he says, "The night being dark, the fungi could be very distinctly seen, though not at any great distance, shining with a soft pale greenish light. Here and there spots of much more intense light were visible, and these proved to be very young and minute specimens. The older specimens may more properly be described as possessing a greenish luminous glow, like the glow of the electric discharge, which, however, was quite sufficient to define its shape, and, when closely examined, the chief details of its form and appearance. The luminosity did not impart itself to the hand, and did not appear to be affected by the separation from the root on which it grew, at least not for some hours. I think it probable that the mycelium of this fungus is also luminous, for, upon turning up the ground in search of small luminous worms, minute spots of light were

* In "Hooker's Journal of Botany" (1840), vol. ii. p. 426.

† Berkeley, "Introduction to Crypt. Bot." t. 265.

observed, which could not be referred to any particular object or body when brought to the light and examined, and were probably due to some minute portions of its mycelium."* The same writer also adds, "Mr. Hugh Low has assured me that he saw the jungle all in a blaze of light (by which he could see to read) as, some years ago, he was riding across the island by the jungle road; and that this luminosity was produced by an Agaric."

Similar experiences were detailed by Mr. James Drummond in a letter from Swan River, in which two species of Agaric are concerned. They grew on the stumps of trees, and had nothing remarkable in their appearance by day, but by night emitted a most curious light, such as the writer never saw described in any book. One species was found growing on the stump of a *Banksia* in Western Australia. The stump was at the time surrounded by water. It was on a dark night, when passing, that the curious light was first observed. When the fungus was laid on a newspaper, it emitted by night a phosphorescent light, enabling persons to read the words around it, and it continued to do so for several nights with gradually decreasing intensity as the plant dried up. In the other instance, which occurred some years after, the author, during one of his botanical trips, was struck by the appearance of a large Agaric, measuring sixteen inches in diameter, and weighing about five pounds. This specimen was hung up to dry in the sitting-room, and on passing through the apartment in the dark it was observed to give out the same remarkable light. The luminous property continued, though gradually diminishing, for four or five nights, when it ceased on the plant becoming dry. "We called some of the natives," he adds, "and showed them this fungus when emitting light, and the poor creatures cried out 'chinga,' their name for a spirit, and seemed much afraid of it."†

Although the examples already cited are those of species of Agaric, luminosity is not by any means wholly confined to that

* Dr. Collingwood, in "Journal of Linnæan Society (Botany)," vol. x. p. 469.

† In "Hooker's Journal of Botany" for April, 1842.

genus. Mr. Worthington Smith has recorded his experiences of some specimens of the common *Polyporus annosus* which were found on some timbers in the Cardiff coal mines. He remarks that the colliers are well acquainted with phosphorescent fungi, and the men state that sufficient light is given "to see their hands by." The specimens of *Polyporus* were so luminous that they could be seen in the dark at a distance of twenty yards. He observes further, that he has met with specimens of *Polyporus sulfureus* which were phosphorescent. Some of the fungi found in mines, which emit light familiar to the miners, belong to the incomplete genus *Rhizomorpha*, of which Humboldt amongst others gives a glowing account. Tulasne has also investigated this phenomenon in connection with the common *Rhizomorpha subterranea*, Pers. This species extends underneath the soil in long strings, in the neighbourhood of old tree stumps, those of the oak especially, which are becoming rotten, and upon these it is fixed by one of its branches. These are cylindrical, very flexible, branching, and clothed with a hard bark, encrusting and fragile, at first smooth and brown, becoming later very rough and black. The interior tissue, at first whitish, afterwards of a more or less deep brown colour, is formed of extremely long parallel filaments from ·0035 to ·015 *mm.* in diameter.

On the evening of the day when I received the specimens,* he writes, the temperature being about 22° Cent., all the young branches brightened with an uniform phosphoric light the whole of their length; it was the same with the surface of some of the older branches, the greater number of which were still brilliant in some parts, and only on their surface. I split and lacerated many of these twigs, but their internal substance remained dull. The next evening, on the contrary, this substance, having been exposed to contact with the air, exhibited at its surface the same brightness as the bark of the branches. I made this observation upon the old stalks as well as upon the young ones. Prolonged friction of the luminous surfaces reduced the brightness

* Tulasne, "Sur la Phosphorescence," in "Ann. des Sci. Nat." (1848), vol. ix. p. 340, &c.

and dried them to a certain degree, but did not leave on the fingers any phosphorescent matter. These parts continued with the same luminous intensity after holding them in the mouth so as to moisten them with saliva; plunged into water, held to the flame of a candle so that the heat they acquired was very appreciable to the touch, they still emitted in the dark a feeble light; it was the same after being held in water heated to 30° C.; but putting them in water bearing a temperature of 55° C. extinguished them entirely. They are equally extinguished if held in the mouth until they catch the temperature; perhaps, still, it might be attributed less to the heat which is communicated to them than to the deficiency of sufficient oxygen, because I have seen some stalks, having become dull in the mouth, recover after a few instants a little of their phosphorescence. A young stalk which had been split lengthwise, and the internal substance of which was very phosphorescent, could imbibe olive oil many times and yet continue for a long time to give a feeble light. By preserving these *Rhizomorphæ* in an adequate state of humidity, I have been able for many evenings to renew the examination of their phosphorescence; the commencement of dessication, long before they really perish, deprives them of the faculty of giving light. Those which had been dried for more than a month, when plunged into water, commenced to vegetate anew and send forth numerous branches in a few days; but I could only discover phosphorescence at the surface of these new formations, or very rarely in their immediate neighbourhood, the mother stalks appearing to have lost by dessication their luminous properties, and did not recover them on being recalled to life. These observations prove that what Schmitz has written was not true, that all parts of these fungi were seldom phosphorescent.

The luminous phenomenon in question is without doubt more complicated than it appears, and the causes to which we attribute it are certainly powerfully modified by the general character of the objects in which they reside. Most of the German botanists give this explanation, others suppose that it forms at first or during its continuance a special matter, in which the luminous property resides; this matter, which is said to be mucilaginous in the luminous wood, appears to be in the *Rhizomorpha* only a kind of chemical combination between the membrane and some gummy substance which they contain. Notwithstanding this opinion, I am assured that all external mucous matter was completely absent from the *Agaricus olearius*, and I neither discovered it upon the branches of *Rhizomorpha subterranea* nor upon the dead leaves which I have seen phosphorescent; in all these objects the luminous surfaces were nothing else than their proper tissue.

It may be remarked here that the so-called species of *Rhizomorpha* are imperfect fungi, being entirely devoid of fructification, consisting in fact only of a vegetative system—a sort of compact mycelium—(probably of species of *Xylaria*) with some affinity to *Sclerotium*.

Recently an extraordinary instance of luminosity was recorded as occurring in our own country.* "A quantity of wood had been purchased in a neighbouring parish, which was dragged up a very steep hill to its destination. Amongst them was a log of larch or spruce, it is not quite certain which, 24 feet long and a foot in diameter. Some young friends happened to pass up the hill at night, and were surprised to find the road scattered with luminous patches, which, when more closely examined, proved to be portions of bark or little fragments of wood. Following the track, they came to a blaze of white light which was perfectly surprising. On examination, it appeared that the whole of the inside of the bark of the log was covered with a white byssoid mycelium of a peculiarly strong smell, but unfortunately in such a state that the perfect form could not be ascertained. This was luminous, but the light was by no means so bright as in those parts of the wood where the spawn had penetrated more deeply, and where it was so intense that the roughest treatment scarcely seemed to check it. If any attempt was made to rub off the luminous matter it only shone the more brightly, and when wrapped up in five folds of paper the light penetrated through all the folds on either side as brightly as if the specimen was exposed; when,

* Rev. M. J. Berkeley, in "Gardener's Chronicle" for 1872, p. 1258.

again, the specimens were placed in the pocket, the pocket when opened was a mass of light. The luminosity had now been going on for three days. Unfortunately we did not see it ourselves till the third day, when it had, possibly from a change in the state of electricity, been somewhat impaired; but it was still most interesting, and we have merely recorded what we observed ourselves. It was almost possible to read the time on the face of a watch even in its less luminous condition. We do not for a moment suppose that the mycelium is essentially luminous, but are rather inclined to believe that a peculiar concurrence of climatic conditions is necessary for the production of the phenomenon, which is certainly one of great rarity. Observers as we have been of fungi in their native haunts for fifty years, it has never fallen to our lot to witness a similar case before, though Prof. Churchill Babington once sent us specimens of luminous wood, which had, however, lost their luminosity before they arrived. It should be observed that the parts of the wood which were most luminous were not only deeply penetrated by the more delicate parts of the mycelium, but were those which were most decomposed. It is probable, therefore, that this fact is an element in the case as well as the presence of fungoid matter."

In all cases of phosphorescence recorded, the light emitted is described as of the same character, varying only in intensity. It answers well to the name applied to it, as it seems remarkably similar to the light emitted by some living insects and other animal organisms, as well as to that evolved, under favourable conditions, by dead animal matter—a pale bluish light, resembling that emitted by phosphorus as seen in a dark room.

Another phenomenon worthy of note is the change of colour which the bruised or cut surface of some fungi undergo. Most prominent amongst these are certain poisonous species of *Boletus*, such, for instance, as *Boletus luridus*, and some others, which, on being bruised, cut, or divided, exhibit an intense, and in some cases vivid, blue. At times this change is so instantaneous that before the two freshly-cut portions of a *Boletus* can be separated, it has already commenced, and proceeds rapidly till the depth of intensity has been gained. This blue colour is so universally confined to dangerous species that it is given as a caution that all species which exhibit a blue colour when cut or bruised, should on no account be eaten. The degree of intensity varies considerably according to the condition of the species. For example, *Boletus cærulescens* is sometimes only very slightly, if at all, tinged with blue when cut, though, as the name implies, the peculiar phenomenon is generally highly developed. It cannot be said that this change of colour has as yet been fully investigated. One writer some time since suggested, if he did not affirm, that the colour was due to the presence of aniline, others have contented themselves with the affirmation that it was a rapid oxidization and chemical change, consequent upon exposure of the surfaces to the air. Archdeacon Robinson examined this phenomenon in different gases, and arrived at the conclusion that the change depends on an alteration of molecular arrangement.*

One of the best of the edible species of *Lactarius*, known as *Lactarius deliciosus*, changes, wherever cut or bruised, to a dull livid green. This fungus is filled with an orange milky fluid, which becomes green on exposure to the air, and it is consequently the juice which oxidizes on exposure. Some varieties more than others of the cultivated mushroom become brownish on being cut, and a similar change we have observed, though not recorded, in other species.

The presence of a milky juice in certain fungi has been alluded to. This is by no means confined to the genus *Lactarius*, in which such juice is universal, sometimes white, sometimes yellow, and sometimes colourless. In Agarics, especially in the subgenus *Mycena*, the gills and stem are replete with a milky juice. Also in some species of *Peziza*, as for instance in *Peziza succosa*, B., sometimes found growing on the ground in gardens, and in *Peziza saniosa*, Schrad., also a terrestrial species, the same phenomenon occurs. To this might be added such species as *Stereum spadiceum*, Fr., and *Stereum sanguinolentum*,

* Berkeley, "Introduction to Crypt. Bot." p. 266.

Fr., both of which become discoloured and bleeding when bruised, while *Corticium lactescens* distils a watery milk.

Fungi in general have not a good repute for pleasant odours, and yet it must be conceded that they are not by any means devoid of odour, sometimes peculiar, often strong, and occasionally very offensive. There is a peculiar odour common to a great many forms, which has come to be called a fungoid odour; it is the faint smell of a long-closed damp cellar, an odour of mouldiness and decay, which often arises from a process of eremocausis. But there are other, stronger, and equally distinct odours, which, when once inhaled, are never to be forgotten. Amongst these is the fetid odour of the common stinkhorn, which is intensified in the more beautiful and curious *Clathrus*. It is very probable that, after all, the odour of the *Phallus* would not be so unpleasant if it were not so strong. It is not difficult to imagine, when one encounters a slight sniff borne on a passing breeze, that there is the element of something not by any means unpleasant about the odour when so diluted; yet it must be confessed that when carried in a vasculum, in a close carriage, or railway car, or exposed in a close room, there is no scruple about pronouncing the odour intensely fetid. The experience of more than one artist, who has attempted the delineation of *Clathrus* from the life, is to the effect that the odour is unbearable even by an enthusiastic artist determined on making a sketch.

Perhaps one of the most fetid of fungi is *Thelephora palmata*. Some specimens were on one occasion taken by Mr. Berkeley into his bedroom at Aboyne, when, after an hour or two, he was horrified at finding the scent far worse than that of any dissecting room. He was anxious to save the specimens, but the scent was so powerful that it was quite intolerable till he had wrapped them in twelve thick folds of the strongest brown paper. The scent of *Thelephora fastidiosa* is bad enough, but, like that of *Coprinus picaceus*, it is probably derived from the imbibition of the ordure on which it is developed. There needs no stronger evidence that the scent must not only be powerful, but unpleasant, when an artist is compelled, before a rough sketch is more than half finished, to throw it away, and seek relief in the open air. A great number of edible Agarics have the peculiar odour of fresh meal, but two species, *Agaricus odorus* and *Agaricus fragrans*, have a pleasant anise-like odour. In two or three species of tough *Hydnum*, there is a strong persistent odour somewhat like melilot or woodruffe, which does not pass away after the specimen has been dried for years. In some species of *Marasmius*, there is a decidedly strong odour of garlic, and in one species of *Hygrophorus*, such a resemblance to that of the larva of the goat moth, that it bears the name of *Hygrophorus cossus*. Most of the fleshy forms exhale a strong nitrous odour during decay, but the most powerful we remember to have experienced was developed by a very large specimen of *Choiromyces meandriformis*, a gigantic subterranean species of the truffle kind, and this specimen was four inches in diameter when found, and then partially decayed. It was a most peculiar, but strong and unpleasantly pungent nitrous odour, such as we never remember to have met with in any other substance. *Peziza venosa* is remarkable when fresh for a strong scent like that of aquafortis.

Of colour, fungi exhibit an almost endless variety, from white, through ochraceous, to all tints of brown until nearly black, or through sulphury yellow to reds of all shades, deepening into crimson, or passing by vinous tints into purplish black. These are the predominating gradations, but there are occasional blues and mineral greens, passing into olive, but no pure or chlorophyllous green. The nearest approach to the latter is found in the hymenium of some *Boleti*. Some of the Agarics exhibit bright colours, but the larger number of bright-coloured species occur in the genus *Peziza*. Nothing can be more elegant than the orange cups of *Peziza aurantia*, the glowing crimson of *Peziza coccinea*, the bright scarlet of *Peziza rutilans*, the snowy whiteness of *Peziza nivea*, the delicate yellow of *Peziza theleboloides*, or the velvety brown of *Peziza repanda*. Amongst Agarics, the most noble *Agaricus muscarius*, with its warty crimson pileus, is scarcely eclipsed by the continental orange *Agaricus cæsarius*. The amethystine variety of *Agaricus laccatus* is so common and yet so attractive; whilst some forms and species *Russula* are gems of brilliant colouring. The golden tufts of more than one species of *Clavaria* are exceedingly attractive, and the delicate pink of immature *Lycogala epidendrum* is sure to command admiration. The minute forms which require the microscope, as much to exhibit their colour as their structure, are not wanting in rich and delicate tints, so that the colour-student would find much to charm him, and good practice for his pencil in these much despised examples of low life.

Amongst phenomena might be cursorily mentioned the peculiar sarcodioid mycelium of *Myxogastres*, the development of amœboid forms from their spores, and the extraordinary rapidity of growth, as the well-known instance of the *Reticularia* which Schweinitz observed running over iron a few hours after it had been red hot. Mr. Berkeley has observed that the creamy mycelium of *Lycogala* will not revive after it has become dry for a few hours, though so active before.

VI.

THE SPORE AND ITS DISSEMINATION.

A WORK of this character would hardly be deemed complete without some reference to the above subject, which has moreover a relation to some of the questions discussed, and particularly of spore diffusion in the atmosphere. The largest spore is microscopic, and the smallest known scarcely visible under a magnifying power of 360 diameters. Taking into account the large number of species of fungi, probably scarcely less numerous than all the flowering plants, and the immense number of spores which some of the individuals produce, they must be exceedingly plentiful and widely diffused, though from their minuteness not easy to be discerned. It has been attempted to estimate the number of spores which might be produced by one single plant of *Lycoperdon*, but the number so far exceeds that which the mind is accustomed to contemplate that it seems scarcely possible to realize their profusion. Recent microscopic examinations of the common atmosphere* show the large quantity of spores that are continually suspended. In these investigations it was found that spores and similar cells were of constant occurrence, and were generally present in considerable numbers. That the majority of the cells were living, and ready to undergo development on meeting with suitable conditions, was very manifest, as in those cases in which preparations were retained under observation for any length of time, germination rapidly took place in many of the cells. In few instances did any development take place,

* Cunningham, in "Ninth Annual Report of the Sanitary Commissioner with the Government of India." Calcutta, 1872.

beyond the formation of networks of mycelium, or masses of toruloid cells, but, in one or two, distinct sporules were developed on the filaments arising from some of the larger septate spores; and in a few others, *Penicillium* and *Aspergillus* produced their characteristic heads of fructification. With regard to the precise nature of the spores, and other cells present in various instances, little can be said, as, unless their development were to be carefully followed out through all its stages, it is impossible to refer them to their correct species or even genera. The greater number of them are apparently referable to the old orders of fungi, *Sphæronemei*, *Melanconei*, *Torulacei*, *Dematiei*, and *Mucedines*, while some probably belonged to the *Pucciniæi* and *Cæomacei.*

Hence it is demonstrated that a large number of the spores of fungi are constantly present in the atmosphere, which is confirmed by the fact that whenever a suitable pabulum is exposed it is taken possession of by floating spores, and soon converted into a forest of fungoid vegetation. It is admitted that the spores of such common moulds as *Aspergillus* and *Penicillium* are so widely diffused, that it is almost impossible to exclude them from closed vessels, or the most carefully guarded preparations. Special contrivances for the dispersion of the spores in the different groups follow a few general types, and it is only rarely that we meet with any method that is confined only to a species or genus. Some of the more significant forms of spores may be illustrated, with their modes of dissemination.

Basidiospores is a term which we may employ here to designate all spores borne at the tips of such supports as are found in the *Hymenomycetes* and *Gasteromycetes*, to which the name of basidia has been given. In fact, under this section we may include all the spores of those two orders, although we may be ignorant of the precise mode in which the fruit of most of the *Myxogastres* is developed. Guarding ourselves at the outset against any misinterpretation as to the use of this term, which, in fact, we employ simply to designate the fruit of *Hymenomycetes*, we may have excuse in our desire to limit special terms as much as possible. In the *Agaricini* the spores are plentiful, and are distributed over the hymenium or gill plates, the surface of which is studded with basidia, each of which normally terminates with four short, erect, delicate, thread-like processes, each of which is surmounted by a spore. These spores are colourless or coloured, and it is upon this fact that primary divisions in the genus *Agaricus* are based, inasmuch as colour in the

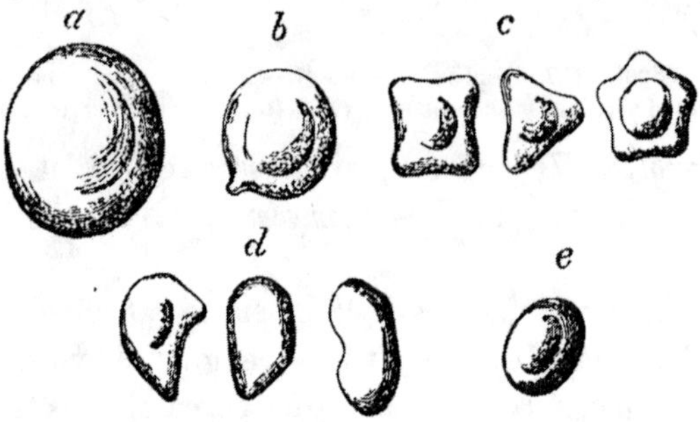

FIG. 45.—Spores of (*a*) *Agaricus mucidus*; (*b*) *Agaricus vaginatus*; (*c*) *Agaricus pascuus*; (*d*) *Agaricus nidorosus*; (*e*) *Agaricus campestris*. (Smith.)

spores appears to be a permanent feature. In white-spored species the spores are white in all the individuals, not mutable as the colour of the pileus, or the corolla in phanerogamic plants. So also with the pink spored, rusty spored, black spored, and others. This may serve to explain why colour, which is so little relied upon in classification amongst the higher plants, should be introduced as an element of classification in one of the largest genera of fungi.

There are considerable differences in size and form amongst the spores of the *Agaricini*, although at first globose; when mature they are globose, oval, oblong, elliptic, fusiform, and either smooth or tuberculated, often maintaining in the different

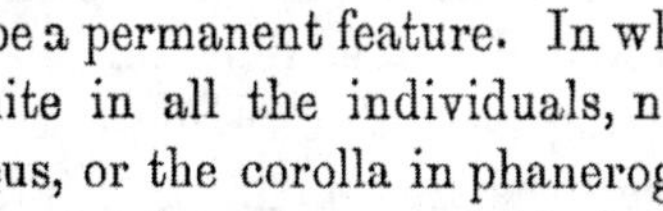

FIG. 46.—Spores of (*a*) *Lactarius blennius*; (*b*) *Lactarius fuliginosus*; (*c*) *Lactarius quietus*. (Smith.)

genera or subgenera one particular characteristic, or typical form. It is unnecessary here to particularize all the modifications which the form and colour of the spores undergo in different species, as this has already been alluded to. The spores

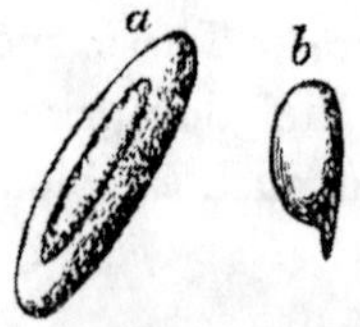

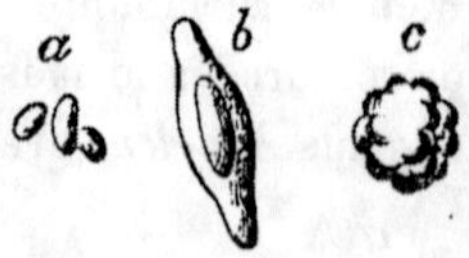

FIG. 46*.—(a) Spore of *Gomphidius viscidus;* (b) spore of *Coprinus micaceus.*

FIG. 47.—Spores of (a) *Polyporus cæsius;* (b) *Boletus parasiticus;* (c) *Hydnum.*

in the *Polyporei*, *Hydnei*, &c., are less variable, of a similar character, as in all the *Hymenomycetes*, except perhaps the *Tremellini*.

When an Agaric is mature, if the stem is cut off close to the gills, and the pileus inverted, with the gills downwards on a sheet of black paper (one of the pale-spored species is best for this purpose), and left for a few hours, or all night, in that position, the paper will be found imprinted in the morning with a likeness of the under side of the pileus with its radiating gills, the spores having been thrown down upon the paper in such profusion, from the hymenium, and in greater numbers from the opposed surfaces of the gills. This little experiment will be instructive in two or three points. It will illustrate the facility with which the spores are disseminated, the immense number in which they are produced, and the adaptability of the gill structure to the economy of space, and the development of the largest number of basidiospores from a given surface. The tubes or pores in *Polyporei*, the spines in *Hydnei*, are modifications of the same principles, producing a like result.

In the *Gasteromycetes* the spores are produced in many cases, probably in most, if not all, at the tips of sporophores; but the hymenium, instead of being exposed, as in the *Hymenomycetes*, is enclosed within an outer peridium or sac, which is sometimes double. The majority of these spores are globose in form, some of them extremely minute, variously coloured, often dark, nearly black, and either externally smooth or echinulate. In some genera, as *Enerthenema*, *Badhamia*, &c., a definite number of spores are at first enclosed in delicate cysts, but these are exceptions to the general rule: this also is the case in at least one species of *Hymenogaster*. As the spores approach maturity, it may be observed in such genera as *Stemonitis*, *Arcyria*, *Diachea*, *Dictydium*, *Cribraria*, *Trichia*, &c., that they are accompanied by a sort of reticulated skeleton of threads, which remain permanent, and served in earlier stages, doubtless, as supports for the spores; being, in fact, the skeleton of the hymenium. It has been suggested that the spiral character of the threads in *Trichia* calls to mind the elaters in the *Hepaticæ*, and like them may, by elasticity, aid in the dispersion of the spores. There is nothing known, however, which will warrant this view. When the spores are mature, the peridium ruptures either by an external orifice, as in *Geaster*, *Lycoperdon*, &c., or by an irregular opening, and the light, minute, delicate spores are disseminated by the slightest breath of air. Specimens of *Geaster* and *Bovista* are easily separated from the spot on which they grew; when rolling from place to place, the spores are deposited over a large surface. In the *Phalloidei* the spores are involved in a slimy mucus which would prevent their diffusion in such a manner. This gelatinous substance has nevertheless a peculiar attraction for insects, and it is not altogether romantic to believe that in sucking up the fetid slime, they also imbibe the spores and transfer them from place to place, so that even amongst fungi insects aid in the dissemination of species. Whether or not the *Myxogastres* should be included here is matter of opinion, since the mode in which the spores are developed is but little known; analogy with the *Trichogastres* in other points alone leading to the conclusion that they may produce basidiospores. The slender, elastic stems which support the peridia in many species are undoubted aids to the dissemination of the spores.*

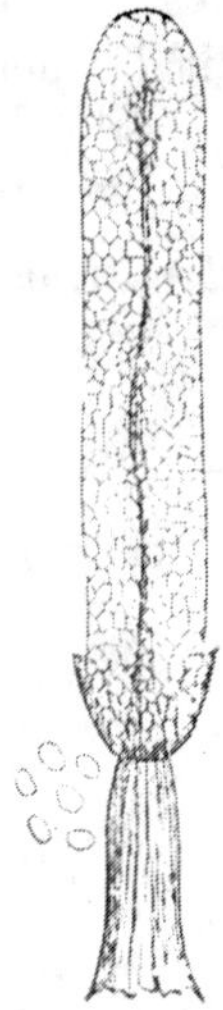

FIG. 48.—*Diachea elegans.*

Under the name of STYLOSPORES may be classed those spores which in some orders of *Coniomycetes* are produced at the apex

* See "Corda Icones," tab. 2.

of short threads, either enclosed in a perithecium, or seated upon a kind of stroma. These are exceedingly variable, sometimes large, and multiseptate, at other times minute, resembling spermatia. In such genera as are chiefly epiphytal, in *Septoria*, *Phyllosticta*, and their allies, the minute spores are enclosed within membranaceous perithecia, and when mature these are ejected from the orifice at the apex, or are exposed by the breaking off of the upper portion of the perithecia. In *Diplodia* and *Hendersonia* the spores are larger, mostly coloured, often very fine in the latter genus, and multiseptate, escaping from the perithecia by a terminal pore. Probably the species are only pycnidia of *Sphæriacei*, but that is of no consequence in relation to our present inquiry. Of stylospores which deserve mention on account of their singularity of form, we may note those of *Dilophospora graminis*, which are straight, and have two or three hair-like appendages at each extremity. In *Discosia* there is a single oblique bristle at each end, or at the side of the septate spores, whilst in *Neottiospora* a tuft of

FIG. 49.—Spore of *Hendersonia polycystis*.

FIG. 50.—Spores of *Dilophospora graminis*.

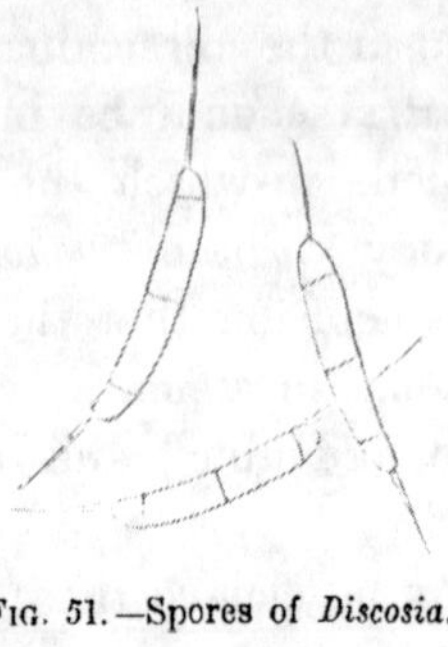

FIG. 51.—Spores of *Discosia*.

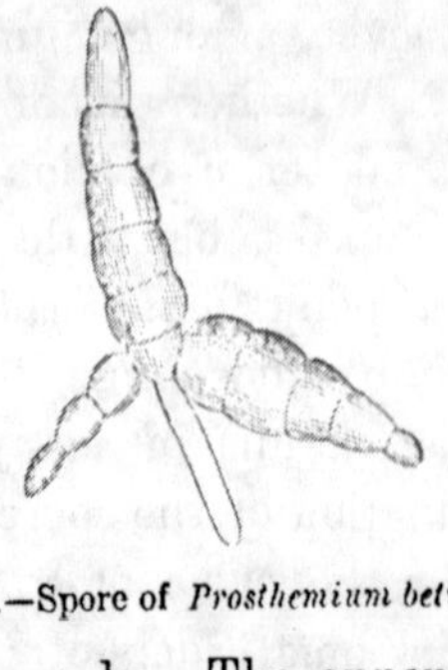

FIG. 52.—Spore of *Prosthemium betulinum*.

delicate hairs is found at one extremity only. The appendages in *Dinemasporium* are similar to those of *Discosia*. The spores in *Prosthemium* may be said in some sort to resemble compound *Hendersonia*, being fusiform and multiseptate, often united at the base in a stellate manner. In this genus, as in *Darluca*, *Cytispora*, and the most of those belonging to the *Melanconiei*, the spores when mature are expelled from the orifice of the perithecium or spurious perithecium, either in the form of tendrils, or in a pasty mass. In these instances the spores are more or less involved in gelatine, and when expelled lie spread over the matrix, around the orifice; their ultimate diffusion being due to moisture washing them over other parts of the same tree, since it is probable that their natural area of dissemination is not large, the higher plants, of which they are mostly conditions, being developed on the same branches. More must be known of the relations between *Melanconium* and Tulasne's sphæriáceous genus *Melanconis* before we can appreciate entirely the advantage to *Melanconium* and some other genera, that the wide diffusion of their spores should be checked by involving them in mucus, or their being agglutinated to the surface of the matrix, only to be softened and diffused by rain. The spores in many species amongst the *Melanconiei* are

FIG. 53.—Spore of *Stegonosporium cellulosum*.

FIG. 54.—Stylospores of *Coryneum disciforme*.

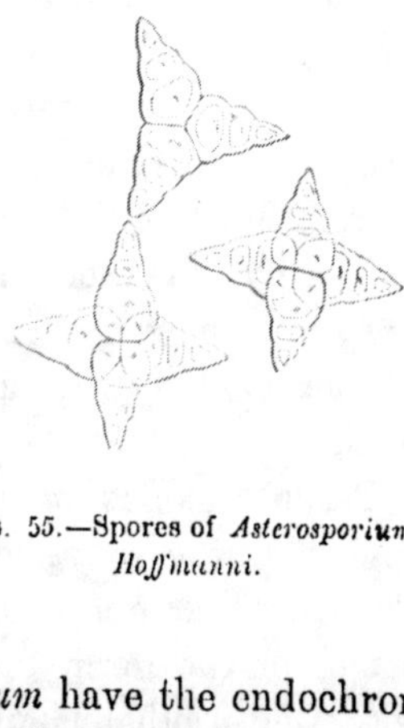

FIG. 55.—Spores of *Asterosporium Hoffmanni*.

remarkably fine; those of *Stegonosporium* have the endochrome partite and cellular. In *Stilbospora* and *Coryneum* the spores are multiseptate, large, and mostly coloured. In *Asterosporium* the spores are stellate, whilst in *Pestalozzia* they are septate, with a permanent peduncle, and crested above with two or three hyaline appendages.

The *Torulacei* externally, and to the naked eye, are very similar to the black moulds, and the mode of dissemination will be alike in both. The spores are chiefly compound, at first resembling septate threads, and at length breaking up into

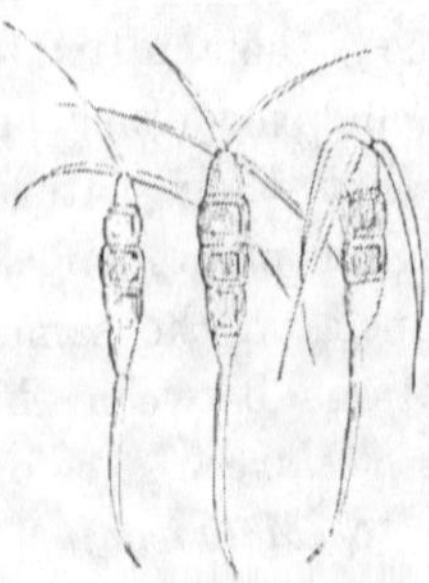

FIG. 56.—Spores of *Pestalozzia*.

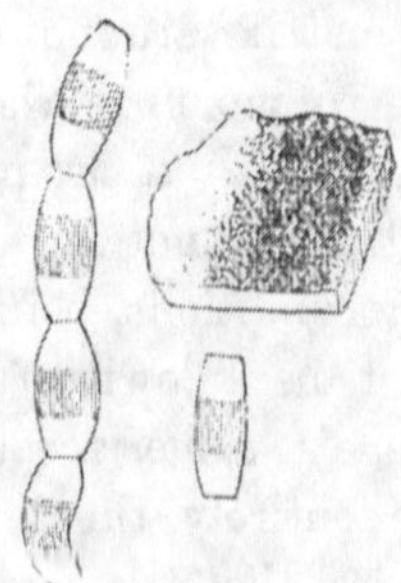

FIG. 57.—*Bispora monilioides*.

joints, each joint of which possesses the function of a spore. In some instances the threads are connate, side by side, as in *Torula hysterioides*, and in *Speira*, being concentrically arranged in laminæ in the latter genus. The structure in *Sporochisma* is very peculiar, the joints breaking up within an external tube or membrane. The spores in *Sporidesmium* appear to consist of irregular masses of cells, agglomerated into a kind of compound spore. Most of the species become pulverulent, and the spores are easily diffused through the air like an impalpable dust. They form a sort of link between the stylospores of one section of the *Coniomycetes*, and the pseudospores of the parasitical section.

PSEUDOSPORE is, perhaps, the most fitting name which can be applied to the so-called spores of the parasitical *Coniomycetes*. Their peculiar germination, and the production of reproductive bodies on the germ tubes, prove their analogy to some extent with the prothallus of other cryptogams, and necessitate the use of some term to distinguish them from such spores as are reproductive without the intervention of a promycelium. The differences between these pseudospores in the several genera are confined in some instances to their septation, in others to their mode of development. In the *Æcidiacei* the pseudospores are more or less globose, produced in chains within an external cellular peridium. In the *Cæomacei* they are simple, sometimes produced in chains, and sometimes free, with or without a caduceous peduncle. In the *Ustilaginei* they are simple, dark coloured, and occasionally attached in subglobose masses, as in *Urocystis* and *Thecaphora*, which are more or less compact.

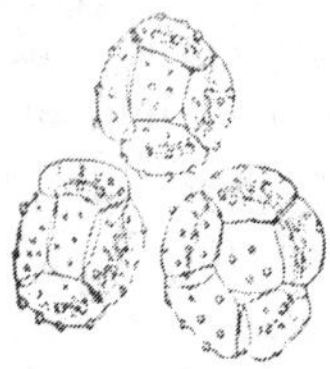

FIG. 58.—Pseudospores of *Thecaphora hyalina*.

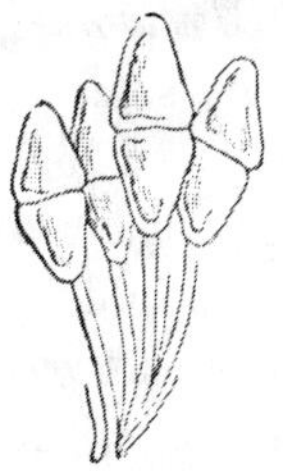

FIG. 59.—Pseudospores of *Puccinia*.

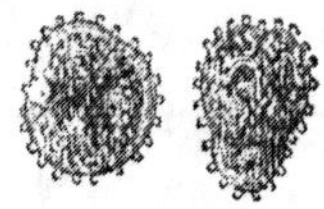

FIG. 60.—Pseudospores of *Triphragmium*.

In the *Pucciniæi* the distinctive features of the genera are based upon the more or less complex nature of the pseudospores, which

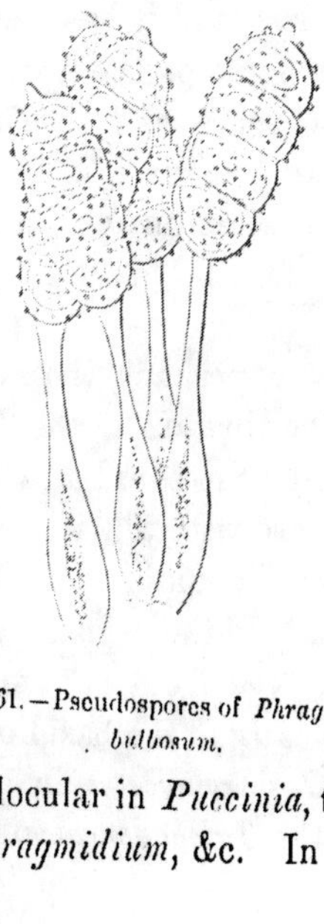

FIG. 61.—Pseudospores of *Phragmidium bulbosum*.

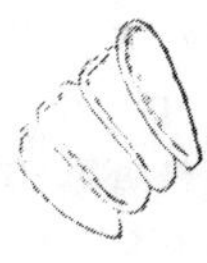

FIG. 62.—*Melampsora salicina*. (Winter fruit.)

are bilocular in *Puccinia*, trilocular in *Triphragmium*, multilocular in *Phragmidium*, &c. In the curious genus *Podisoma* the septate pseudospores are involved in a gelatinous element. The diffusion of these fruits is more or less complete according to their compact or pulverulent nature. In some species of *Puccinia* the sori are so compact that they remain attached to the leaves long after they are dead and fallen. In the genus *Melampsora*, the wedge-shaped winter-pseudospores are not perfected until after the dead leaves have for a long time remained and almost rotted on the ground. It is probable that their ultimate diffusion is only accomplished by the rotting and disintegration of the matrix. In the *Cæomacei*, *Ustilaginei*, and *Æcidiacei* the pseudospores are pulverulent, as in some species of *Puccinia*, and are easily diffused by the motion of the leaves in the wind, or the contact of passing bodies. Their diffusion in the atmosphere seems to be much less than in the case of the *Hyphomycetes*. By what means such a species as *Puccinia malvacearum*, which has very compact sori, has become within so short a period diffused over such a wide area, is a problem which in the present state of our knowledge must remain unsolved. It may be through minute and plentiful secondary spores.

Spermatia are very minute delicate bodies found associated with many of the epiphyllous *Coniomycetes*, and it has been supposed are produced in conjunction with some of the *Sphæriacei*, but their real function is at present obscure, and the name is applied rather upon conjecture than knowledge. It is by no means improbable that spermatia do exist extensively amongst fungi, but we must wait in patience for the history of their relationship.

Trichospores might be applied better, perhaps, than *conidia* to the spores which are produced on the threads of the *Hyphomycetes*. Some of them are known to be the conidia of higher plants; but as this is by no means the case with all, it would be assuming too much to give the name of conidia to the whole. By whatever name they may be called, the spores of the *Hyphomycetes* are of quite a different type from any yet mentioned, approximating, perhaps, most closely to the basidiospores of the *Hymenomycetes* in some, and *Gasteromycetes* in others; as, for instance, in the *Sepedoniei* and the *Trichodermacei*. The form of the spores and their size differ materially, as well as the manner in which they are produced on the threads. In many they are very minute and profuse, but larger and less plentiful in the *Dematiei* than in the *Mucedines*. The spores of some species of *Helminthosporium* are large and multiseptate, calling to mind the spores of the *Melanconiei*. Others are very curious, being stellate in *Triposporium*, circinate in *Helicoma* and *Helicoryne*, angular in *Gonatosporium*, and ciliate in *Menispora ciliata*. Some are produced singly and some in chains, and in some the threads are nearly obsolete. In *Peronospora*, it has been demonstrated that certain species produce minute zoospores from the so-called spores. The dissemination of the minute spores of the *Mucedines* through the air is undoubted; rain also certainly assists not only in the dispersion of the spores in this as in other groups, but also in the production of zoospores which require moisture for that purpose. The form of the threads, and the mode of attachment of the spores, is far more variable amongst the *Mucedines* than the form of the spores, but the latter are in all instances so slightly attached to their supports as to be dissevered by the least motion. This aids also in the diffusion of the spores through the atmosphere.

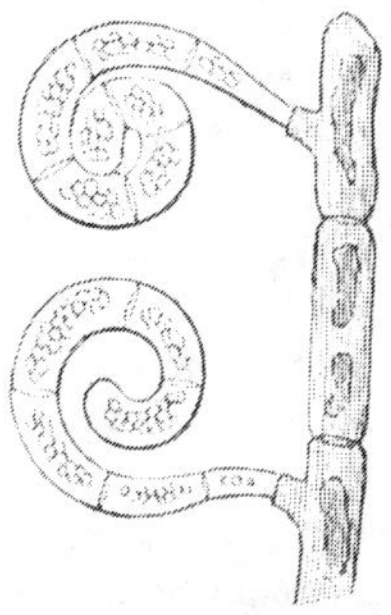

FIG. 63.—Spores of *Helicocoryne*.

SPORANGIA are produced in the *Physomycetes* usually on the tips or branches of delicate threads, and these when mature dehisce and set free the minute sporidia. These are so small and uniform in their character that they require but a passing mention. The method of diffusion agrees much with that of the *Mucedines*, the walls of the sporangia being usually so thin and delicate as to be easily ruptured. Other modes of fructification prevail in some species by the production of cysts, which are the result of conjugation of the threads. These bodies are for the most part furnished with thicker and more resistant walls, and the diffusion of their contents will be regulated by other circumstances than those which influence the dispersion of the minute sporidia from the terminal cysts. Probably they are more perennial in their character, and are assimilated more to the oogonia of *Cystopus* and *Peronospora*, being rather of the nature of resting spores, inasmuch as the same threads usually bear the terminal fruits.

THECASPORES is a term which may be applied generally to all sporidia produced in asci, but these are in turn so innumerable and variable that it will be necessary to treat of some of the groups individually. The *Thecaspores*, for instance, of the *Tuberacei* offer several features whereby they may be distinguished from other thecaspores. The asci in which these sporidia are generated mostly partake of a broadly saccate, ovate form. The number of sporidia contained in an individual ascus is usually less than in the majority of the *Ascomycetes*, and the sporidia approximate more nearly to the globose form. Usually, also, they are comparatively large. Many have been figured by Corda* and Tulasne.† Three types of spores may be said to prevail in the *Tuberacei:* the smooth spored, the warted or spinulose, and the areolate. The first of these may be represented by the *Stephensia bombycina*, in which the globose sporidia are quite smooth and colourless. The warted sporidia may be observed in *Genea verrucosa*, the spinulose in *Tuber nitidum*, and the areolate are present in *Tuber æstivum* and *Tuber excavatum*, in which the epispore is divided into polygonal alveoli, bounded by thin, membranaceous, prominent partitions. This form of sporidium is very beautiful. In all no special provision is made for the dissemination of the sporidia, as, from their subterranean habit, none would be available save the ultimate dissolution of the external integuments. As they are greedily devoured by several animals, it is possible that they may be dispersed through the excrements.

FIG. 64.—Sporidium of *Genea verrucosa*.

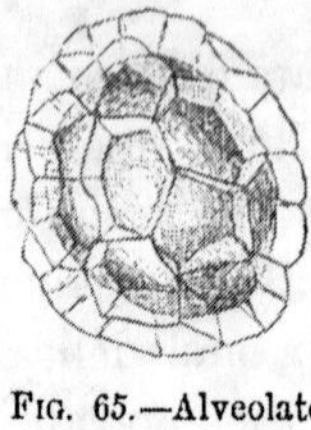

FIG. 65.—Alveolate sporidium of *Tuber*.

* Corda, "Icones Fungorum," vol. vi. Prague.
† Tulasne, "Fungi Hypogæi." Paris.

In the *Perisporiacei* the perithecium has no proper orifice, or ostiolum, for the discharge of the mature sporidia, which are usually small, and are disseminated by the irregular rupture of the somewhat fragile conceptacles. The asci are usually more or less saccate, and the sporidia approximate to a globose form. The asci are often very diffluent. In *Perisporium vulgare* the ovate brown sporidia are at first, and for some time, attached together in fours in a concatenate or beaded manner. In some species of *Erysiphei* the conceptacle encloses but a single sporangium, in others several, which are attached together at the base. In some species the sporangia contain two, in others four, in others eight, and in others numerous sporidia. In *Chætomium* the asci are cylindrical, and in most cases the coloured sporidia are lemon-shaped. When the conceptacles are fully matured, it is commonly the case that the asci are absorbed and the sporidia are free in the interior of the conceptacles.

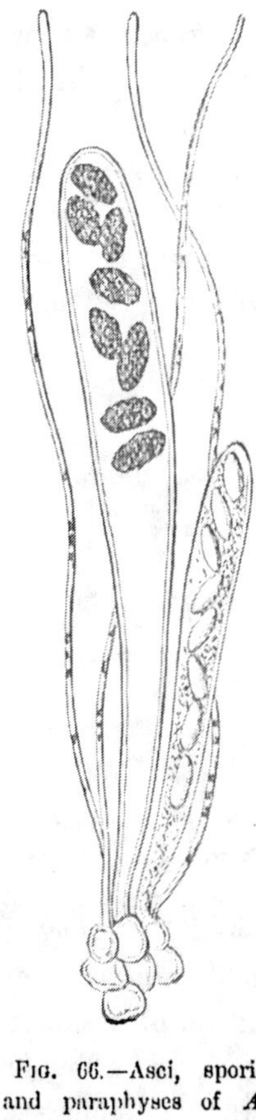

FIG. 66.—Asci, sporidia, and paraphyses of *Ascobolus* (Boudier).

Of the fleshy *Discomycetes* the genus *Peziza* may be taken as the type. If the structure which prevails in this genus be brought to mind, it will be remembered that the hymenium lines an expanded cup, and that the asci are packed together, side by side, with their apices outwards, and their bases attached to a substratum of cells which form the inner layer of the receptacle. The sporidia are usually eight in each ascus, either arranged in single or double rows, or irregularly grouped together. The asci are produced in succession; the later, pressing themselves upwards between those previously developed, cause the rupture of the mature asci at the apex and the ejection of the sporidia with considerable force. When a large *Peziza* is observed for a time a whitish cloud will be seen to rise suddenly from the surface of the disc, which is repeated again and again whenever the specimen is moved. This cloud consists of sporidia ejected simultaneously from several asci. Sometimes the ejected sporidia lie like frost on the surface of the disc. Theories have been devised to account for this sudden extrusion of the sporidia, in *Ascobolus*, and a few species of *Peziza*, of the asci also, the most feasible one being the successive growth of the asci; contraction of the cup may also assist, as well as some other less potent causes. It may be remarked here that the sporidia in *Peziza* and *Helotium* are mostly colourless, whilst in *Ascobolus* they pass through pink to violet, or dark brown, and the epispore, which is of a waxy nature, becomes fissured in a more or less reticulated manner.

The sporidia in *Hysterium* proper are usually coloured, often multiseptate, sometimes fenestrate, and occasionally of considerable size. There is no evidence that the sporidia are ever excluded in the same manner as in *Peziza*, the lips closing over the disc so much as to prevent this. The diffusion of the sporidia probably depends on the dissolution of the asci, and hence they will not be widely dispersed, unless, perhaps, by the action of rain.

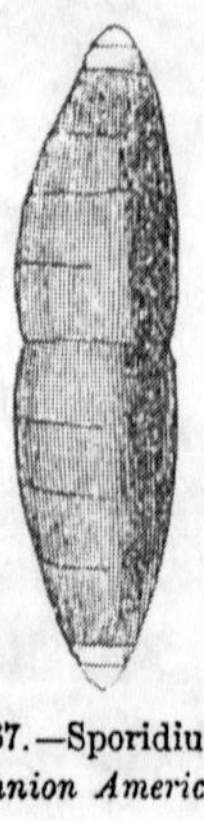

FIG. 67.—Sporidium of *Ostreichnion Americanum*.

In *Tympanis*, asci of two kinds have been observed in some species; one kind containing an indefinite number of very minute bodies resembling spermatia, and the other octosporous, containing sporidia of the usual type.

The *Sphæriacei* include an almost infinite variety in the form and character of the sporidia. Some of these are indefinite in the number contained in an ascus, although the majority are eight, and a few less. In the genera *Torrubia* and *Hypocrea* the structure differs somewhat from other groups, inasmuch as in the former the long thread-like sporidia break up into short joints, and in the latter the ascus contains sixteen subglobose or subquadrate sporidia. Other species contain linear sporidia, which are often the length of the ascus, and may either be simple or septate. In *Sphæria ulnaspora* the sporidia are abruptly bent at the second joint. Shorter fusiform sporidia are by no means uncommon, varying in the number of septa, and in constriction at the joints in different species. Elliptic or ovate sporidia are common, as are those of the peculiar form which may be termed sausage-shaped. These are either hyaline or coloured of some shade of brown. Coloured sporidia of this kind are common in

FIG. 68.—Ascus and sporidia of *Hypocrea.*

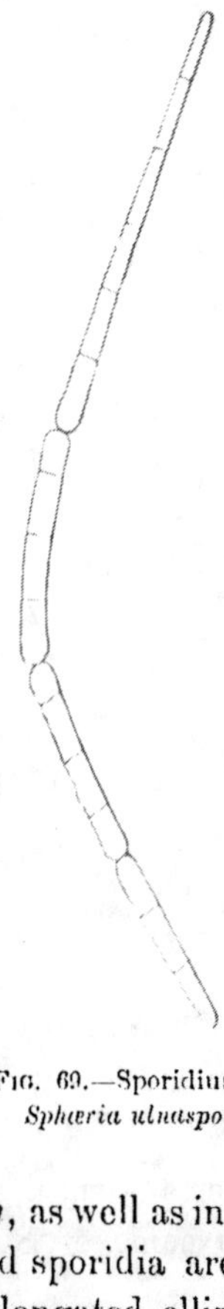

FIG. 69.—Sporidium of *Sphæria ulnaspora.*

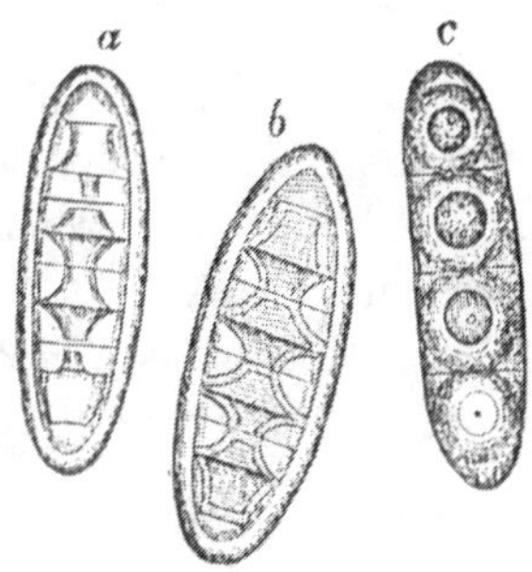

FIG. 70.—Sporidia of *Valsa profusa* (Currey).

Xylaria and *Hypoxylon*, as well as in certain species of the section *Superficiales.* Coloured sporidia are often large and beautiful: they are mostly of an elongated, elliptical form, or fusiform. As noteworthy may be mentioned the sporidia of *Melanconis lanci-*

formis, those of *Valsa profusa*, and some species of *Massaria*, the latter being at first invested with a hyaline coat. Some coloured sporidia have hyaline appendages at each extremity, as

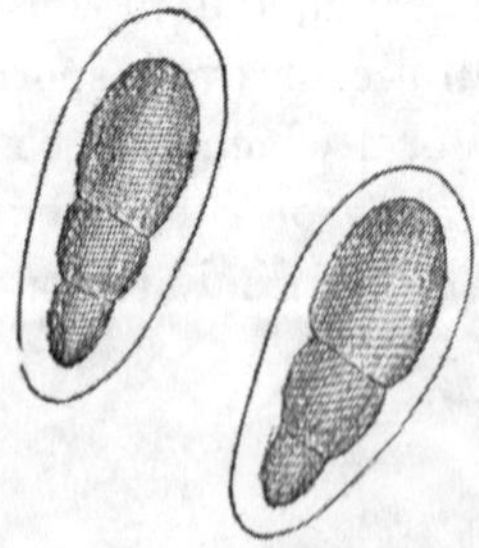

Fig. 71.—Sporidia of *Massaria fœdans*. × 400.

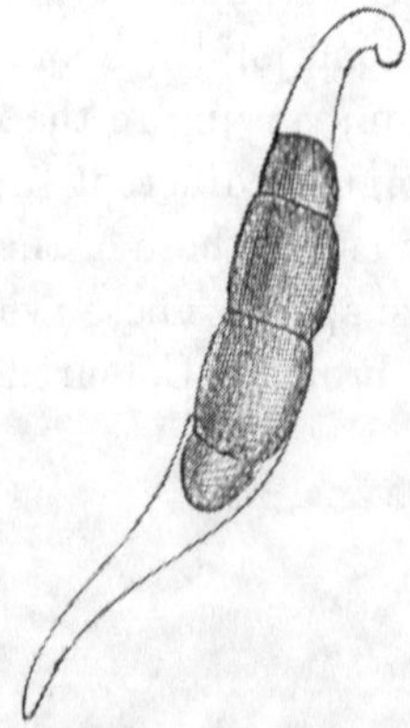

Fig. 72.—Sporidium of *Melanconis bicornis*, Cooke.

in *Melanconis Berkeleii*, and an allied species, *Melanconis bicornis*, from the United States, also some dung *Sphæriæ*, as *S. fimiseda*, included under the proposed genus *Sordaria*.* Hyaline sporidia occasionally exhibit a delicate bristle-like appendage at each extremity, as in the *Valsa thelebola*, or with two additional cilia at the central constriction, as in *Valsa taleola*. A peculiar form

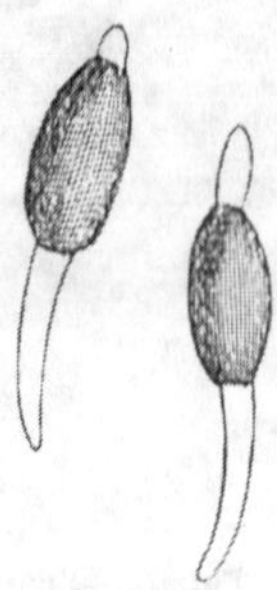

Fig. 73.—Caudate sporidia of *Sphæria fimiseda*.

Fig. 74.—Sporidia of *Valsa thelebola*.

of sporidium is present in certain species of *Sphæria* found on dung, for which the generic name of *Sporormia* has been pro-

* Winter, "Die Deutschen Sordarien" (1873).

posed, in which the sporidium (as in *Perisporium vulgare*) consists of four coloured ovate joints, which ultimately separate. Multiseptate fenestrate sporidia are not uncommon in *Cucurbi-*

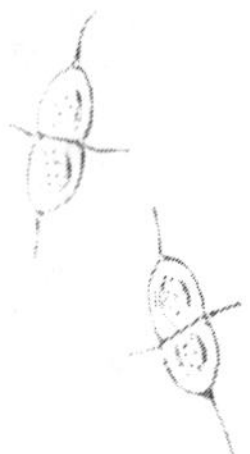

FIG. 75.—Sporidia of *Valsa taleola*. × 400.

FIG. 76.—Sporidium of *Sporormia intermedia*.

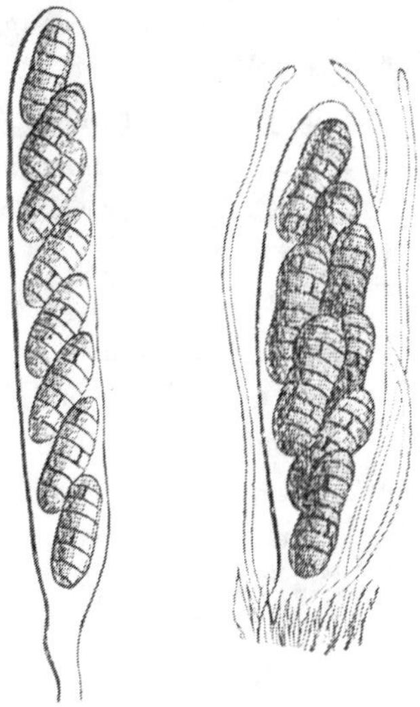

FIG. 77.

taria and *Pleospora*, as well as in *Valsa fenestrata* and some other species. In the North American *Sphæria putaminum* the sporidia are extraordinarily large.

The dissemination of the sporidia may, from identity of structure in the perithecium, be deemed to follow a like method in all. When mature, they are in a great measure expelled from the mouth of the perithecia, as is evident in species with large dark sporidia, such as exist in the genera *Hypoxylon*, *Melanconis*, and *Massaria*. In these genera the sporidia, on maturity, may be observed blackening the matrix round the mouths of the perithecia.

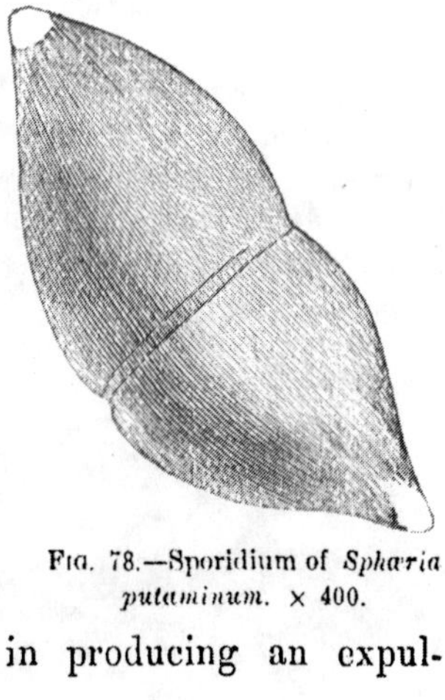

FIG. 78.—Sporidium of *Sphæria putaminum*. × 400.

As moisture has an evident effect in producing an expulsion of sporidia by swelling the gelatinous nucleus, it may be assumed that this is one of the causes of expulsion, and therefore of aids to dissemination. When *Sphæriæ* are submitted to extra moisture, either by placing the twig which bears them on damp sand, or dipping one end in a vessel of water, the sporidia will exude and form a gelatinous bead at the orifice. There may be other methods, and possibly the successive production of new asci may also be one, and the increase in bulk by growth of the sporidia another; but of this the evidence is scanty.

Finally, OOGONIA may be mentioned as occurring in such genera as *Peronospora* amongst moulds, *Cystopus* amongst Uredines, and the *Saprolegniaceæ* amongst the *Physomycetes*. The zoospores being furnished with vibratile cilia, are for some time active, and need only water in which to disseminate themselves, and this is furnished by rain.

We have briefly indicated the characteristics of some of the more important types of spores to be found in fungi, and some of the modes by which it is known, or presumed, that their dissemination takes place. In this summary we have been compelled to rest content with suggestions, since an exhaustive essay would have occupied considerable space. The variability in the fruit of fungi, in so far as we have failed to demonstrate, will be found exhibited in the illustrated works devoted more especially to the minute species.*

* Corda, "Icones Fungorum," 6 vols. (1837–1842); Sturm, "Deutschlands Flora," Pilze (1841); Tulasne, "Selecta Fungorum Carpologia;" Bischoff, "Kryptogamenkunde" (1860); Corda, "Anleitung zum Studium der Mykologie" (1842); Fresenius, "Beiträge zur Mykologie" (1850); Nees von Esenbeck, "Das System der Pilze" (1816); Bonorden, "Handbuch der Allgemeinen Mykologie" (1851).

VII.

GERMINATION AND GROWTH.

In describing the structure of these organisms in a previous chapter, the modes of germination and growth from the spores have been purposely excluded and reserved for the present. It may be assumed that the reader, having followed us to this point, is prepared for our observations by some knowledge of the chief features of structure in the principal groups, and of the main distinctions in the classification, or at least sufficient to obviate any repetition here. In very many species it is by no means difficult to induce germination of the spores, whilst in others success is by no means certain.

M. de Seynes made the *Hymenomycetes* an especial object of study,* but he can give us no information on the germination and growth of the spore. Hitherto almost nothing is positively known. As to the form of the spore, it is always at first spherical, which it retains for a long time, while attached to the basidia, and in some species, but rarely, this form is final, as in *Ag. terreus*, &c. The most usual form is either ovoid or regularly elliptic. All the *Coprini* have the spores oval, ovoid, more or less elongated or attenuated from the hilum, which is more translucent than the rest of the spore. This last form is rather general amongst the Leucospores, in *Amanita*, *Lepiota*, &c. At other times the spores are fusiform, with regularly attenuated extremities, as in *Ag. ermineus*, Fr., or with obtuse extremities, as

* Seynes, J. de, "Essai d'une Flore Mycologique de la Montpellier," &c. (1863), p. 30.

in *Ag. rutilans*, Sch. In *Hygrophorus* they are rather irregular, reniform, or compressed in the centre all round. Hoffmann* has given a figure taken from *Ag. chlorophanus*, and Seynes verified it upon *Ag. ceraceus*, Sow. (See figures on page 121.)

The exospore is sometimes roughened, with more or less projecting warts, as may be seen in *Russula*, which much resembles *Lactarius* in this as in some other particulars. The spores of the *Dermini* and the *Hyporhodii* often differ much from the sphærical form. In *Ag. pluteus*, Fr., and *Ag. phaiocephalus*, Bull, there is already a commencement of the polygonal form, but the angles are much rounded. It is in *Ag. sericeus*, *Ag. rubellus*, &c., that the polygonal form becomes most distinct. In *Dermini* the angles are more or less pronounced, and become rather acute in *Ag. murinus*, Sow., and *Ag. ramosus*, Bull. The passage from one to the other may be seen in the stellate form of the conidia of *Nyctalis*.

It is almost always the external membrane that is coloured, which is subject to as much variation as the form. The more fine and more delicate shades are of rose, yellow-dun or yellow, violet, ashy-grey, clear fawn colour, yellow-orange, olive-green, brick-red, cinnamon-brown, reddish-brown, up to sepia-black and other combinations. It is only by the microscope and transparency that one can make sure of these tints; upon a sufficient quantity of agglomerated spores the colour may be distinguished by the naked eye. Colour, which has only a slight importance when considered in connection with other organs, acquires much in the spores, as a basis of classification.

With the growth of Agarics from the mycelium, or spawn, we are not deficient in information, but what are the conditions necessary to cause the spores themselves to germinate before our eyes and produce this mycelium is but too obscure. In the cultivated species we proceed on the assumption that the spores have passed a period of probation in the intestines of the horse, and by this process have acquired a germinating power, so that when expelled we have only to collect them, and the excrement in which

* Hoffman, "Icones Analyticæ Fungorum."

they are concealed, and we shall secure a crop.* As to other species, we know that hitherto all attempts to solve the mystery of germination and cultivation has failed. There are several species which it would be most desirable to cultivate if the conditions could be discovered which are essential to germination.† In the same manner the *Boleti* and *Hydnei*—in fact, all other hymenomycetal fungi, with the exception of the *Tremellini*—still require to be interrogated by persevering experiment and close inquiry as to their mode of germination, but more especially as to the essential conditions under which alone a fruitful mycelium is produced.

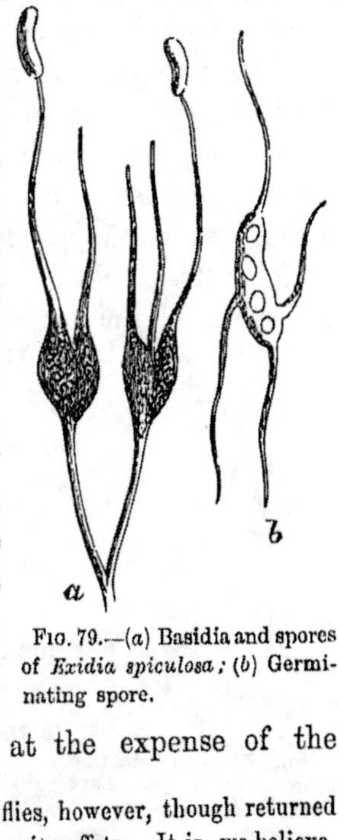

FIG. 79.—(*a*) Basidia and spores of *Exidia spiculosa*; (*b*) Germinating spore.

The germination of the spore has been observed in some of the *Tremellini*. Tulasne described it in *Tremella violacea*.‡ These spores are white, unilocular, and filled with a plastic matter of homogeneous appearance. From some portion of their surface an elongated germ filament is produced, into which the contents of the reproductive cell pass until quite exhausted. Other spores, perhaps more abundant, have a very different kind of vegetation. From their convex side, more rarely from the outer edge, these particular spores emit a conical process, generally shorter than themselves, and directed perpendicularly to the axis of their figure. This appendage becomes filled with protoplasm at the expense of the

* The spores of Agarics which are devoured by flies, however, though returned in their dung in an apparently perfect state, are quite effete. It is, we believe, principally by the *Syrphidæ*, which devour pollen, that fungus spores are consumed.

† All attempts at Chiswick failed with some of the more esculent species, and Mr. Ingram at Belvoir, and the late Mr. Henderson at Milton, were unsuccessful with native and imported spawn.

‡ Tulasne, "On the Organization of the Tremellini," "Ann. des. Sci. Nat." 3me sér. xix. (1853), p. 193.

spore, and its free and pointed extremity finally dilated into a sac, at first globose and empty. This afterwards admits into its cavity the plastic matter contained in its support, and, increasing, takes exactly the form of a new spore, without, however, quite equalling in size the primary or mother spore. The spore of the new formation long retains its pedicel, and the mother spore which produced it, but these latter organs are then entirely empty and extremely transparent. Sometimes two secondary spores are thus engendered from the same spore, and their pedicels may be implanted on the same or on different sides, so as to be parallel in the former case, and growing in opposite directions in the latter. The fate of these secondary spores was not determined.

In *Dacrymyces deliquescens* are found mingled amongst the spores immense numbers of small round or ovoid unilocular bodies, without appendages of any kind, which long puzzled mycologists. Tulasne ascertained that they are derived from the spores of this fungus when they have become free, and rest on the surface of the hymenium. Each of the cells of the spore emits exteriorly one or several of these corpuscles, supported on very short slender pedicels, which remain after the corpuscles are detached from them. This latter circumstance evidences that new corpuscles succeed the firstborn one on each pedicel as long as there remains any plastic matter within the spore. The latter, in fact, in consequence of this labour of production, becomes gradually emptied, and yet preserves the generative pedicels of the corpuscles, even when it no longer contains any solid or coloured matter. These pedicels are not all in the same plane, as may be ascertained by turning the spore on its longitudinal axis; but it often seems to be so when they are looked at in profile, on account of the very slight distance which then separates them one from another. It will also be remarked that they are in this case often implanted all on the same side of the

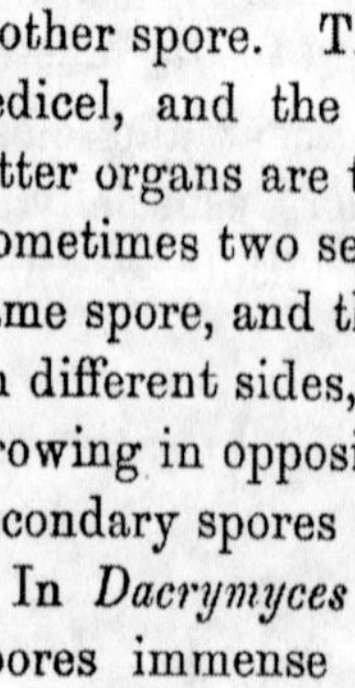

FIG. 80. — Germinating spore and (*a*) corpuscles of *Dacrymyces deliquescens*.

reproductive body, and most often on its convex side. Their fecundity is exhausted with the plastic contents of the spore. The corpuscles, when placed in the most favourable conditions, have never given the least sign of vegetation; they have also remained for a long time in water without experiencing any appreciable alteration.

All the individuals of *Dacrymyces deliquescens* do not produce these corpuscles in the same abundance; those which bear the most are recognizable by the pale tint of the reproductive dust with which they are covered; in others, where this dust preserves its golden appearance, only a few corpuscles are found. The spores which produce corpuscles do not appear at all apt to germinate. On the other hand, multitudes of spores will germinate which had not produced any corpuscles. Tulasne remarks on this, that these observations would authorize us to think that all spores, though perfectly identical to our eyes, have not, without distinction, the same fate, nor doubtless the same nature; and, in the second place, that these two kinds of bodies, if they are not always isolated, yet are most frequently met with on distinct individuals. This author claims for the corpuscles in question that they are spermatia, and thinks that their origin is only so far unusual in that they proceed from veritable spores.

The whole of the *Gasteromycetes* have as yet to be challenged as to the mode and conditions of germination and development. It is probable that these will not materially differ from those which prevail in *Hymenomycetes.*

The germination in *Æcidium* has been followed out by Tulasne,* either by placing the pseudospores in a drop of water, or confining them in a moist atmosphere, or by placing the leaves on which the *Æcidium* flourishes upon water. The pseudospores plunged in water germinated more readily than the others. If the conditions were favourable, germination would take place in a few hours. *Æcidium Ranunculacearum*, D. C., on leaves of figwort, gives rarely more than one germinating filament, which soon attains three times the length of the diameter of the pseudospore. This filament generally remains simple, sometimes torulose, and

* Tulasne, "Mémoire sur les Urédinées."

distorted in a long spire. Sometimes it has been seen divided into two branches, nearly equal to each other. The spore in germinating empties itself of its plastic contents, contracts, and diminishes in size. The pseudospores of *Æcidium crassum*, P., emit three long filaments, which describe spirals, imitating the twistings of the stem of a bean or bindweed. In *Æcidium Violæ*, Schum, one filament is produced, which frequently rolls up its anterior extremity into a spire, but more often this same extremity rises in a large ovoid, irregular vesicle, which continues the axis of the filament, or makes with it a more or less decided angle. In whatever manner placed, this vesicle attracts to it all the orange protoplasm, and hardly does this become settled and complete before the vesicle becomes the starting point of a new development, for it begins to produce at its apex a filament, more slender than the previous one, stiff, and unbranched.

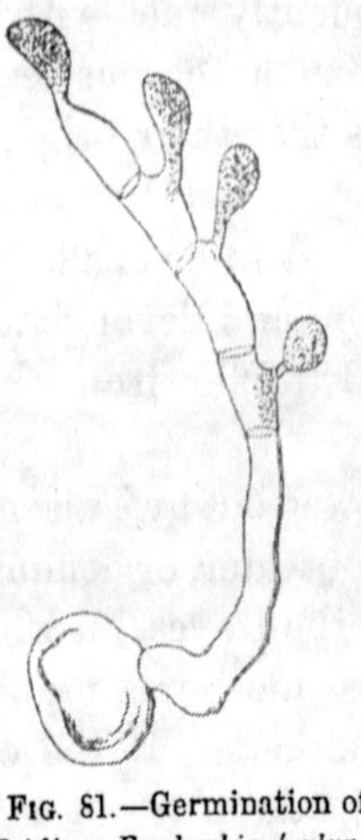

FIG. 81.—Germination of *Æcidium Euphorbia* (*sylvaticæ*), Tulasne.

According to M. Tulasne, the germination of the pseudospores of *Æcidium Euphorbiæ* on *Euphorbia sylvatica* differ in some respects from the preceding. When dropped upon water these spores very soon emit a short tube, which ordinarily curves in an arch or circle, almost from its origin, attaining a length of from three to six times the diameter of the spore; then this tube gives rise to four spicules, each of which produces a small obovate or reniform sporule; the generation of these sporules absorbs all the plastic matter contained in the germ-tube, which permits of the observation that it was divided into four cells corresponding with the number of spicules. These sporules germinate very rapidly from an indefinite point of their surface, emitting a filiform process, which is flexuous and very delicate, not extending more in length than three times that of the long axis of the sporule, often less, reproducing at its summit a new sporule, differing in form and size from that which preceded it. This sporule of the second formation becomes at its apex a vital centre, and sprouts one or more linear buds, of which the elongation is occasionally interrupted by the formation of vesicular swellings. As Tulasne observes, the pseudospores of the *Æcidium* and the greater number of Uredines are easily wetted with water before arriving at maturity; but when they are ripe, on the contrary, they appear to be clothed with a greasy matter which protects them from the liquid, forcing them almost all to rest on the surface.

The pseudospores of *Ræstelia* are produced in strings or chaplets, as in *Æcidium*, with this difference, that instead of being contiguous they are separated by narrow isthmuses. The ripe pseudospores are enveloped in a thick tegument, of a dark brown colour. They germinate readily on water, producing a filament fifteen times as long as the diameter of the spore. This filament is sometimes rolled or curved. Towards its extremity it exhibits protuberances which resemble the rudiments of ramuli, or they terminate in a vesicle which gives rise to a slender filament. The tegument of these pseudospores, above all in those which have germinated, and have consequently become more transparent, it is easy to see has many pores, or round ostioles.

In *Peridermium* the pseudospores, when dropped upon water, germinate at any point of their surface. Sometimes two unequal filaments issue from the same spore. After forty-eight hours of vegetation in the air, the greater part had already emitted a multitude of thick little branches, themselves either simple or branched, giving to the filaments a peculiar aspect. Tulasne did not on any occasion observe the formation of secondary spores.

In the Uredines proper the germination seems to be somewhat similar, or at least not offering sufficient differences to warrant special reference in *Uredo*, *Trichobasis*, *Lecythea*, &c. In *Coleosporium* there are two kinds of spores, one kind consisting of pulverulent single cells, and the other of elongated septate cells, which break up into obovate joints. Soon after the maturity of the pulverulent spores, each begins to emit a long tube, which is habitually simple, and produces at its summit a reproductive cellule, or reniform sporule. The orange protoplasm passes along the colourless tubes to the terminal sporule at the end of its vegetation. The two forms of spores in this genus are constantly found on the same leaf, and in the same pulvinule, but generally the pulverulent spores abound at the commencement of the summer. The reniform sporules begin to germinate in a great number as soon as they are free; some few extend a

FIG. 82.—Germinating pseudospores of (*b*) *Coleosporium Sonchi;* (*s s*) secondary spores, or sporules (Tulasne).

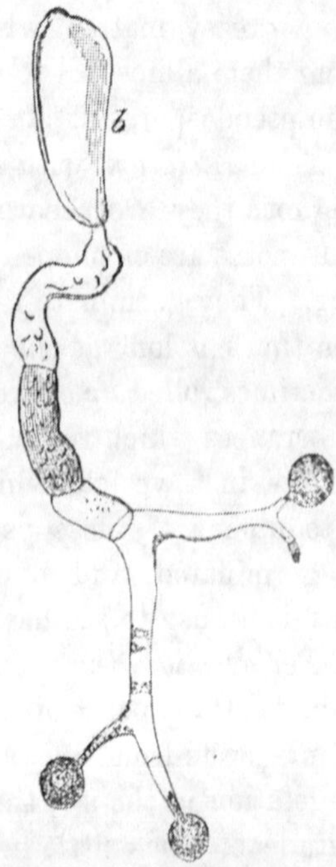

FIG. 83.—Germinating pseudospore (*b*) of *Melampsora betulina* (Tulasne).

filament which remains simple and uniform, but more commonly it forms at its extremity a second sporule. If this does not become isolated, to play an independent life, the filament is continued, and new vesicles are repeated many times.

In *Melampsora* the summer spores are of the *Lecythea* type, and were included in that genus till their relation with *Melampsora* was clearly made out. The winter spores are in solid pulvinules, and their fructification takes place towards the end of winter or in the spring. This phenomenon consists in the production of cylindrical tubes, which start from the upper extremity of the wedge-shaped spores, or more rarely from the base. These tubes are straight or twisted, simple or bifurcated, and each of them very soon emits four monosporous spicules, at the same time that they become septate. The sporules are in this instance globose.

In *Uromyces* germination follows precisely the same type as that of the upper cell of *Puccinia;* in fact, Tulasne states that it is very difficult to say in what they differ from the *Pucciniæ* which are accidentally unilocular.

FIG. 84. — Germinating pseudospore of *Uromyce appendiculatus.* (Tulasne.)

In *Cystopus* a more complex method prevails, which will be examined more closely hereafter.

In *Puccinia*, as already observed when describing their structure, the pseudospores are two-celled. From the pores of each cell, which are near the central septum, springs a clavate tube, which attains two or three times the total length of the fruit, and of which the very obtuse extremity curves more or less in the manner of a crozier.* This tube, making a perfectly uncoloured transparent membrane, is filled with a granular and very pale plastic matter at the expense of the generative cell, which is soon rendered vacant; then it gives rise to four spicules, usually on the same side, and at the summit of these produces a reniform cellule. The four sporules so engendered exhaust all the protoplasm at first contained in the generative cell, so that their united capacity proves to be evidently much insufficient to contain it, the more so as it leads to the belief that this matter undergoes as it condenses an elaboration which diminishes its size. In all cases the spicule originates before the sporule which it carries, and also attains its full length when the sporule ap-

* Tulasne, in his "Memoirs on the Uredines."

pears. The form of the latter is at first globular, then ellipsoid, and more or less curved. All these phases of vegetation are accomplished in less than twelve hours, and if the spore is mature and ready for germination, it is sufficient to provoke it by keeping the pseudospores in a humid atmosphere. During this process the two cells do not separate, nor does one commence germination before the other, but both simultaneously. When the sporules are produced, the protospore, somewhat analogous to a prothallus, has performed its functions and decays. Towards the time of the falling of the sporules they are nearly all divided into four unequal cells by transverse and parallel septa. These sporules in time produce, from any point on their surface, a filament, which reproduces a new sporule, resembling the first, but generally smaller. This sporule of the second generation ordinarily detaches itself from its support before germinating.

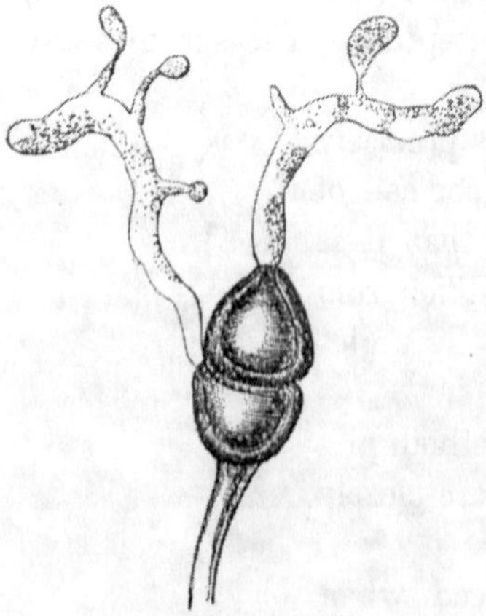

Fig. 85.—Germinating pseudospore of *Puccinia Moliniæ*. (Tulasne.)

The pseudospores of *Triphragmium ulmariæ* have been seen in April germinating on old leaves of the meadowsweet which survived the winter, whilst at the same time new tufts of the spores were being developed on the leaves of the year. These fruits of the spring vegetation would not germinate the same year. Each cell in germination emits a long cylindrical filament, con-

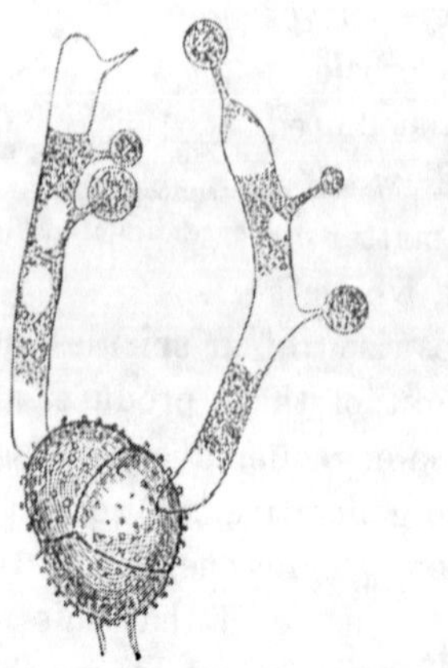

Fig. 86.—Germinating pseudospore of *Triphragmium ulmariæ*. (Tulasne.)

taining a brownish protoplasm, on which four spicules, bearing as many sporules, are generated.

The germination of the black fruits of *Phragmidium* only appears to take place in the spring. It greatly resembles that in *Puccinia*, except that the filament is shorter, and the sporules are spherical and orange-coloured, instead of being kidney-shaped and pale. In the species found on the leaves of the common bramble, the filament emitted by each cell attains three or four times the length of the fruit. The granular orange protoplasm which fills it passes ere long into the sporules, which are engendered at the extremity of pointed spicules. After the long warty fruits are emptied of their contents they still seem as dark as before, but the pores which are pierced in the sides, through which the germinating filaments have proceeded, are more distinctly visible.

FIG. 87. — Germinating pseudospore of *Phragmidium bulbosum*. (Tulasne.)

It will be observed that throughout all these allied genera of *Uromyces*, *Puccinia*, *Triphragmium*, and *Phragmidium* the same type of germination prevails, which confirms the accuracy of their classification together, and renders still less probable the supposed affinity of *Phragmidium* with *Sporidesmium*, which was at one time held by very astute mycologists, but which is now abandoned. This study of germination leads also to a very definite conclusion with regard to the genus *Uromyces*—that it is much more closely related to *Puccinia* and its immediate allies than to other unicellular Uredines.

The germination of the pseudospores of the gelatinous Uredines of the genus *Podisoma* was studied by Tulasne.* These

* Mr. Berkeley has lately published a species under the name of *P. Ellisii*, in which the gelatinous element is scarcely discernible till the plant is moistened. There are two septa in this species, and another species or form has lately been received from Mr. Ellis which has much shorter pedicels, and resembles more

pretended spores, he writes, are formed of two large conical cells, opposed by their base and easily separating. They vary in length. The membrane of which they are formed is thin and completely colourless in most of them, though much thicker and coloured brown in others. It is principally the spores with thin membranes that emit from near the middle very obtuse tubes, into which by degrees, as they elongate, the contents of the parent utricles pass. Each of the two cells of the supposed spore may originate near its base four of these tubes, opposed to each other at their point of origin, and their subsequent direction; but it is rather rare for eight tubes, two by two, to decussate from the same spore or basidium. Usually there are only two or three

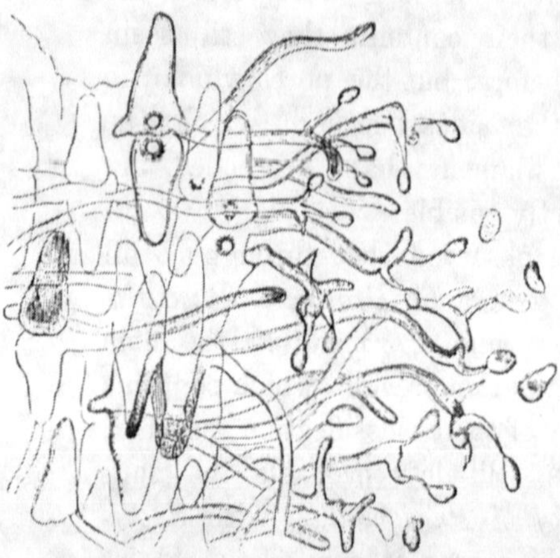

FIG. 88.—Germinating pseudospores of *Podisoma Juniperi.* (Tulasne.)

which are completely developed, and these tend together towards the surface of the fungus, which they pass, and expand at liberty in the air. The tubes generally become thicker by degrees as they elongate, some only slightly exceeding the length of the protospores. Others attain three or four times that length, according to the greater or less distance between the protospore and the surface of the plant. In the longest tubes it is easy to observe how the colouring matter passes to their outer extremity,

closely *Puccinia*, from which it is chiefly distinguished by its revivescent character.

leaving the portion nearest to the parent cell colourless and lifeless. When nearly attaining their ultimate dimensions, all the tubes are divided towards their outer extremity by transverse septa into unequal cells; then simple and solitary processes, of variable length and form, but attenuated upwards, proceed from each segment of the initial tube, and produce at their extremity an oval spore (teleutospore, Tul.), which is slightly curved and unilocular. These spores absorb all the orange endochrome from the original tubes. They appear in immense numbers on the surface of the fungus, and when detached from their spicules fall upon the ground or on any object which may be beneath them. So freely are they deposited that they may be collected on paper, or a slip of glass, like a fine gold-coloured powder. Again, these secondary spores (teleutospores) are capable of germination, and many of them will be found to have germinated on the surface of the *Podisoma* whence they originated. The germ filament which they produce springs habitually from the side, at a short distance from the hilum, which indicates the point of attachment to the original spicule. These filaments will attain to from fifteen to twenty times the diameter of the spore in length before branching, and are in themselves exceedingly delicate. The tubes which issue from the primary spores (protospores, Tul.) are not always simple, but sometimes forked; and the cells which are ultimately formed at their extremities, though producing filiform processes, do not always generate secondary spores (teleutospores) at their apices. This mode of germination, it will be seen, resembles greatly that which takes place in *Puccinia.*

The germination of the Ustilagines was in part examined by Tulasne, but since has received accessions through the labours of Dr. A. Fischer von Waldheim.* Nothing, however, of any importance is added to our knowledge of the germination of *Tilletia*, which was made known as early as 1847.† After some

* Von Waldheim, on the "Development of the Ustilagineæ," in "Pringsheim's Jahrbucher," vol. vii. (1869); translated in "Transactions of N. Y. State Agricultural Society for 1870."

† Berkeley, on the "Propagation of Bunt," in "Trans. Hort. Soc. London,"

days a little obtuse tube is protruded through the epispore, bearing at its apex long fusiform bodies, which are the sporules of the first generation. These conjugate by means of short transverse tubes, after the manner of the threads of *Zygnema*. Afterwards long elliptical sporules of the second generation are produced on short pedicels by the conjugated fusiform bodies of the first generation. (Fig. 89, *ss.*) Ultimately these sporules of the second generation germinate, and generate, on short spicules, similar sporules of a third generation. (Fig. 89, *st.*)

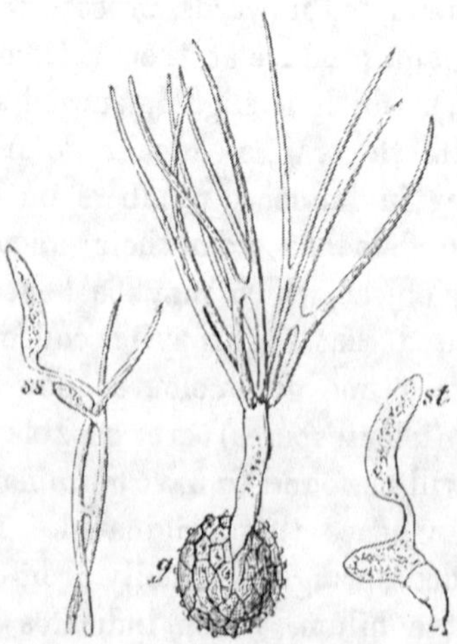

FIG. 89.—Germinating pseudospore (*g*) of *Tilletia caries* with secondary spores in conjugation. (Tul.)

In *Ustilago* (*flosculorum*) germination takes place readily in warm weather. The germ tube is rather smaller at its base than further on. In from fifteen to eighteen hours the contents become coarsely granular; at the same time little projections appear on the tube which are narrowed at the base, into which some of the protoplasm passes. These ultimately mature into sporules. At the same time a terminal sporule generally appears on the threads. Secondary sporules frequently grow from the primary, which are rather smaller, and these occasionally give rise to a third generation.

In *Urocystis* (*pompholygodes*) the germinating tubes spring exclusively from the darker central cells of the clusters. From these are developed at their extremity three or four linear bodies, as in *Tilletia*, but after this no further development has as yet been traced. It may be remarked here that Waldheim observed similar conjugation of the sporules in some species of

ii. (1847), p. 113; Tulasne, second memoir, in "Ann. des. Sci. Nat." ii. (4me sér.), p. 77; Cooke, in "Journ. Quekett Micro. Club," i. p. 170.

Ustilago as have been remarked in the sporules of the first generation in *Tilletia.*

Returning to *Cystopus*, as the last of the Uredines, we must briefly recapitulate the observations made by Professor de Bary,* who, by the bye, claims for them an affinity with *Peronospora* (Mucedines but too well known in connection with the potato disease), and *not* with the Uredines and their allies. In this genus there are two kinds of reproductive organs, those produced on the surface of the plant bursting through the cuticle in white pustules, and which De Bary terms *conidia*, which are generated in chains, and certain globose bodies termed *oogonia*, which are developed on the mycelium in the internal tissues of the foster plant. When the conidia are sown on water they rapidly absorb the moisture, and swell; the centre of one of the extremities soon becomes a large obtuse papilla resembling the neck of a bottle. This is filled with a granular protoplasm, in which vacuoles are formed. Soon, however, these vacuoles disappear, and very fine lines of demarcation separate the protoplasm into from five to eight polyhedric portions, each presenting a little faintly-coloured vacuole in the centre (*a*). Soon after this division the papilla at the extremity swells, opens itself, and at the same time the five to eight bodies which had formed in the interior are expelled one by one (*b*). These are zoospores,

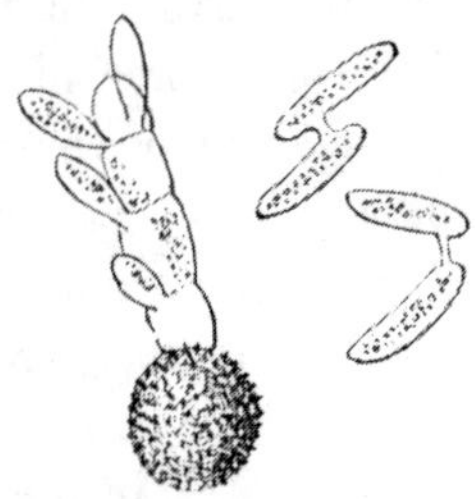

FIG. 90.—Pseudospore of *Ustilago receptaculorum* in germination, and secondary spores in conjugation. (Tul.)

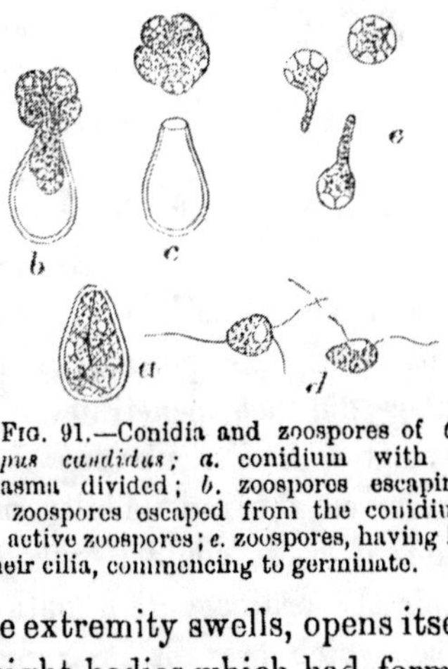

FIG. 91.—Conidia and zoospores of *Cystopus candidus*; *a.* conidium with the plasma divided; *b.* zoospores escaping; *c.* zoospores escaped from the conidium; *d.* active zoospores; *e.* zoospores, having lost their cilia, commencing to germinate.

* De Bary, "Recherches," &c. in "Annales des Sciences Naturelles" (4me sér.), xx. p. 5; Cooke in "Pop. Sci. Rev." iii. (1864), p. 459.

which at first take a lenticular form, and group themselves before the mouth of the parent cell in a globose mass (*c.*) Very soon, however, they begin to move, and then vibratile cilia show themselves (*d*), and by means of these appendages the entire globule moves in an oscillating manner as one by one the zoospores disengage themselves, each becoming isolated and swimming freely in the surrounding fluid. The movement is precisely that of the zoospores of Algæ.

The generation of the zoospores commences within from an hour and a half to three hours after the sowing of the conidia on water. From the oogonia, or resting spores, similar zoospores, but in greater number, are generated in the same manner, and their conduct after becoming free is identical. Their movements in the water usually last from two to three hours, then they abate, the cilia disappear, and the spore becomes immovable, takes a globose form, and covers itself with a membrane of cellulose. Afterwards the spore emits, from any point whatever of its surface, a thin, straight or flexuous tube, which attains a length of from two to ten times the diameter of the spore. The extremity becomes clavate or swollen, after the manner of a vesicle, which receives by degrees the whole of the protoplasm.

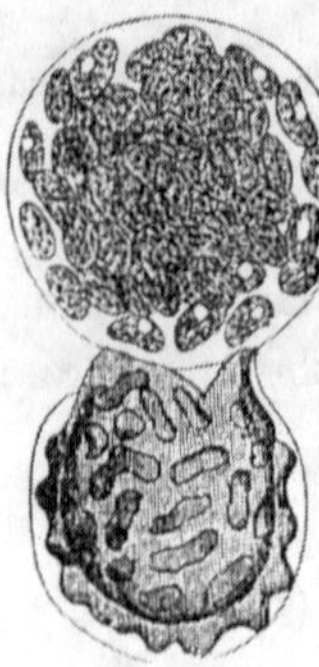

FIG. 92.—Resting spore of *Cystopus candidus* with zoospores escaped.

De Bary then proceeds to describe experiments which he had performed by watering growing plants with these zoospores, the result being that the germinating tubes did not penetrate the epidermis, but entered by the stomates, and there put forth an abundant mycelium which traversed the intercellular passages. Altogether the germination of these conidia or zoospores offers so many differences from the ordinary germination of the Uredines, and is so like that which prevails in *Peronospora*, in addition to the fact of both genera producing winter spores or oogonia, that we cannot feel surprised that the learned mycologist who made these observations should claim for *Cystopus* an affinity with *Perono-*

spora rather than with the plants so long associated with it amongst the *Coniomycetes.*

In passing from these to the *Mucedines*, therefore, we cannot do so more naturally than by means of that genus of white moulds to which we have just alluded. The erect branched threads bear at the tip of their branchlets spores, or conidia, which conduct themselves in a like manner to the organs so named in *Cystopus*, and oogonia or resting spores developed on the mycelium within the tissues of the foster plant also give origin to similar zoospores.

The conidia are borne upon erect, elongated filaments, originating from the creeping mycelium. These threads are hollow, and rarely septate; the upper portion divided into numerous branches, and these again are subdivided, the ultimate ramuli each terminated by a single conidium. This body when mature is oval or elliptical, filled with protoplasm, but there is a diversity in their mode of germination. In the greater part, of which *P. effusa* may be taken as an example, the conidia have the function of simple spores. Placed in favourable conditions, each of them puts forth a germ-tube, the formation of which does not differ in any essential point from what is known of the spores of the greater part of fungi.

The short oval conidia of *P. gangliformis* have little obtuse papillæ at their apex, and it is at this point that germination commences.

The conidia of *P. densa* are similar, but the germination is different. When placed in a drop of water, under favourable circumstances, the following changes may be observed in from four to six hours. The protoplasm, at first uniformly distributed in all the conidia, appears strewn with semi-lenticular, and nearly equidistant vacuoles, of which the plane face is immediately in contact with the periphery of the protoplasm. These vacuoles number from sixteen to eighteen in *P. macrocarpa*, but are less numerous in *P. densa.* A short time after the appearance of the vacuoles the entire conidium extends itself so that the papilla disappears. Suddenly it reappears, elongates itself, its attenuated membrane vanishes, and the protoplasm is expelled by the narrow opening that remains in place of the papilla. In normal cases the protoplasm remains united in a single mass that shows a clear but very delicate outline. When it has reached the front of the opening in the conidium, which is thus emptied, the mass remains immovable. In *P. densa* it is at first of a very irregular form, but assumes by degrees a regular globose shape. This is deprived of a distinct membrane, the vacuoles that disappeared in the expulsion again become visible, but soon disappear for a second time. The globule becomes surrounded with a membrane of cellulose, and soon puts out from the point opposite to the opening of the conidium a thick tube which grows in the same manner as the germ-tube of the conidia in other species. Sometimes the expulsion of the protoplasm is not completely accomplished; a portion of it remaining in the membrane of the conidium detaches itself from the expelled portion, and while this is undergoing changes takes the form of a vesicle, which is destroyed with the membrane. It is very rare that the protoplasm is not evacuated, and that the conidia give out terminal or lateral tubes in the manner that is normal to other species without papillæ. The germination just described does not take place unless the conidia are entirely surrounded by water; it is not sufficient that they repose upon its surface. Besides, there is another condition which, without being indispensable, has a sensible influence on the germination of *P. macrocarpa*, and that is the exclusion of light. To ascertain if the light or the darkness had any influence, two equal sowings were placed side by side, the one under a clear glass bell, the other under a blackened glass bell. Repeated many times, these experiments always gave the same result—germination in from four to six hours in the conidia under the blackened glass; no change in those under the clear glass up to the evening. In the morning germination was completed.

The conidia of *P. umbelliferarum* and *P. infestans* * show an analogous structure. These bodies, if their development be normal, become zoosporangia. When they are sown upon water, one sees at the end of some hours the protoplasm divided by

* This is the mould which produces the potato murrain.

very fine lines, and each of the parts furnished with a small central vacuole. Then the papilla of the conidium disappears. In its place appears a rounded opening, by which the parts of the protoplasm are expelled rapidly, one after the other. Each of these, when free, immediately takes the form of a perfect zoospore, and commences to agitate itself. In a few moments the sporangium is empty and the spores disappear from the field of the microscope.

The zoospores are oval or semi-oval, and in *P. infestans* the two cilia spring from the same point on the inferior border of the vacuole. Their number in a sporangium are from six to sixteen in *P. infestans*, and from six to fourteen in *P. umbelliferarum*. The movement of the zoospores ceases at the end of from fifteen to thirty minutes. They become motionless, cover themselves with a membrane of cellulose, and push out slender bent germ-tubes which are rarely branched. It is but seldom that two tubes proceed from the same spore. The same development of the zoospores in *P. infestans* is favoured by the exclusion of the light. Placed in a position moderately lighted or protected by a blackened bell, the conidia very readily produced zoospores.

A second form of germination of the conidia in *P. infestans*, when sown upon a humid body or on the surface of a drop of water, consists in the conidium emitting from its summit a simple tube, the extremity of which swells itself into the form of an oval vesicle, drawing to itself, little by little, all the protoplasm contained in the conidium. Then it isolates itself from the germ-tube by a septum, and takes all the essential characteristics of the parent conidium. This secondary conidium can sometimes engender a third cellule by a similar process. These secondary and tertiary productions have equally the character of sporangia. When they are plunged into water, the ordinary production of zoospores takes place.

Lastly, there is a third mode of germination which the conidia of *P. infestans* manifest, and which consists in the conidium emitting from its summit a simple or branched germ-tube. This grows in a similar manner to the conidia first named as of such species as *P. effusa.* The conditions which control this orm of germination cannot be indicated, since some conidia which germinate after this manner will sometimes be found mixed with others, the majority of which furnish zoospores. It may be that the conidia themselves are in some sort of abnormal condition.

In all the species examined the conidia possess the power of germination from the moment of their maturity. The younger they are the more freely they germinate. They can retain this power for some days or weeks, provided they are not entirely dried. Dessication in an ordinary temperature seemed sufficient to destroy the faculty of germinating in twenty-four hours, when the conidia had been removed from the leaves on which they were produced. They none of them retained the faculty during a few months, hence they cannot preserve it during the winter.

The germs of *Peronospora* enter the foster plant if the spores are sown upon a part suitable for the development of the parasite. It is easy to convince one's self that the mycelium, springing from the penetrating germs, soon takes all the characters that are found in the adult state. Besides, when cultivated for some time, conidiiphorous branches can be seen growing, identical with those to which it owes its origin. Such cultivation is so readily accomplished that it can be made upon cut leaves preserved fresh in a moist atmosphere.

In the species of *Peronospora* that inhabit perennial plants, or annual plants that last through the winter, the mycelium hidden in the tissues of the foster-plant lasts with it. In the spring it recommences vegetation, and emits its branches into the newly-formed organs of its host, there to fructify. The *Peronospora* of the potato is thus perennial by means of its mycelium contained in the browned tissue of the diseased tubers. When in the spring a diseased potato begins to grow, the mycelium rises in the stalk, and soon betrays itself by blackish spots. The parasites can fructify abundantly on these little stalks, and in consequence propagate themselves in the new season by the conidia coming from the vivacious mycelium.

The diseased tubers of the potato always contain the mycelium of *P. infestans*, which never fructifies there as long as the skin of the tuber is intact. But when, in cutting the tuber, the parenchyma occupied by the mycelium is exposed to the contact of the air, it covers itself with conidia-bearing branches at the end of from twenty-four to forty-eight hours. Analogous results are obtained with the stalks of the potato. It is evident that in these experiments nothing is changed except the contact of the air; the specific conditions particularly remain the same. It appears, therefore, that it is this contact alone which determines generally the production of the conidiiferous branches.*

The mode of germination and development in the Mucors has been studied by several observers, but most recently by Van Tieghem and Le Monnier.† In one of the common forms, the *Mucor phycomyces* of some authors, and the *Phycomyces nitens* of others, the process is given in detail. In this species germination will not take place in ordinary water, but it readily takes place in orange juice and other media. The spore loses colour, swells, and absorbs fluid around it until double its original size and ovoid. Then a thick thread is emitted from one or both extremities, which elongates and becomes branched in a pinnate manner. Sometimes the exospore is ruptured and detached loosely from the germinating spore. After about forty-eight hours from the first sowing, the mycelium will send branches into the air, which again become abundantly branched; other short submerged branches will also remain simple, or have tuft-like ramifications, each terminating in a point, so as to bristle with spiny hairs. In two or three days abruptly swollen branches, of a club shape, will make their appearance on the threads both in the air and in the fluid. Sometimes these branches are prolonged into an equal number of sporangia-bearing threads, but most frequently they divide first at their swollen summits into numerous branches, of which usually one,

* De Bary, "Champignons parasitiques," in "Annales des Sci. Nat." (4me sér.), xx. p. 5; Cooke, "Microscopic Fungi," cap. xi. p. 138; "Popular Science Review," iii. 193 (1864).

† Van Tieghem and Le Monnier, "Researches on Mucorini," in "Ann. des Sci. Nat." (1873), xvii. p. 261; Summary in "Quart. Journ. Micro. Science" (2nd ser.), xiv. p. 49.

sometimes two or three, develop into sporangia-bearing threads, while the rest are short, pointed, and form a tuft of rootlets. Sometimes these rootlets reduce themselves to one or more rounded protuberances towards the base of the sporangia-bearing threads.

There are often also a certain number of the branches which had acquired a clavate shape, and do not erect themselves above the surface, instead of producing a fertile thread, which would seem to have been their first intention, become abruptly attenuated, and are merely prolonged into a mycelial filament. Although in other species chlamydospores are formed in such places on the mycelium, nothing of the kind has been traced in this species, more than here indicated. Occasionally, when germination is arrested prematurely, certain portions of the hyphæ, in which the protoplasm maintains its vitality, become partitioned off. This may be interpreted as a tendency towards the formation of chlamydospores, but there is no condensation of protoplasm, or investiture with a special membrane. Later on this isolated protoplasm is gradually altered, separating into somewhat regular ovoid or fusiform

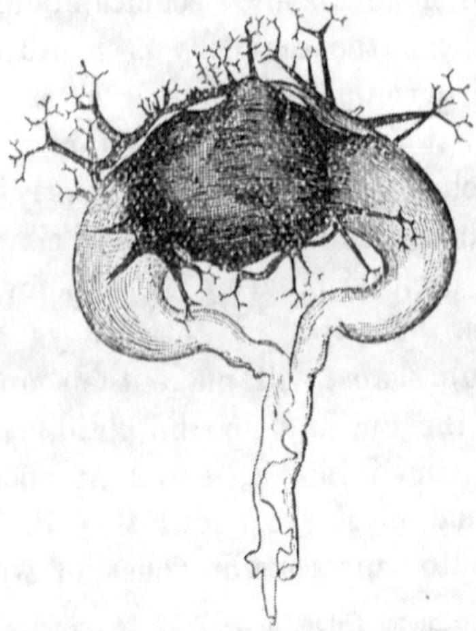

FIG. 93.—Zygospores of *Mucor phycomyces*. (Van Tieghem.)

granules, which have, to a certain extent, the appearance of spores in an ascus, but they seem to be incapable of germination.

Another method of reproduction, not uncommon in *Mucorini*, is described by Van Tieghem in this species. Conjugating threads on the substratum by degrees elaborate zygospores, but these, contrary to the mode in other species, are surrounded by curious branched processes which emanate from the arcuate cells on either side of the newly-developed zygospore. This system of reproduction is again noticed more in detail in the chapter on polymorphism.

M. de Seynes has given the details of his examination of the sporidia of *Morchella esculenta* during germination.* A number of these sporidia, placed in water in the morning, presented, at nine o'clock of the same evening, a sprout from one of the extremities, measuring half the length of the spore. In the morning of the next day this sprout had augmented, and become a filament three or four times as long. The next day these elongated filaments exhibited some transverse divisions and some ramifications. On the third day, the germination being more advanced, many more of the sporidia were as completely changed, and presented, in consequence of the elongation, the appearance of a cylindrical ruffle, the cellular prolongations arising from the germination having a tendency towards one of the extremities of the longer axis of the sporidium, and more often to the two opposed extremities, either simultaneously or successively. Out of many hundreds of sporidia examined during germination, he had only seen a very few exceptions to this rule, among which he had encountered the centrifugal tendency to vegetate by two opposed filaments, proving that if it bears a second by the side of the primal filament situated at one of the poles, a second would also be seen from the side of the filament coming from the opposite pole.

Before being submitted to the action of water, the contents of the sporidia seemed formed of two distinct parts, one big drop of yellow oil of the same form as the sporidium, with the space between it and the cell wall occupied by a clear liquid, more fluid and less refractive, nearly colourless, or at times, slightly roseate. As the membrane absorbed the water by

* Seynes, "Essai d'une Flore Mycologique."

which it was surrounded, the quantity of this clear liquid was augmented, and the rosy tint could be more easily distinguished. All the contents of the spore, which up to this time remained divided into two parts, presented altogether one aspect, only containing numerous granulations, nearly of equal size, completely filling it, and reaching the inner face of the sporic membrane.

After this time the sporidium augments in size very rapidly, becoming at times irregular, and sometimes even as much as from two to three times its original dimensions, then there appears at the surface, usually at one of the poles of the ellipse, a small prominence, with an extremely fine membrane, which does not appear to separate itself from that which surrounds the sporidium, and it is difficult to say whether it is a prolongation of the internal membrane going across the outside, or simply a prolongation caused by a continuation of tissue of an unique membrane. Sometimes there may be seen at the point where the primal filament issues from the sporidium a circular mark, which appears to indicate the rupture of the external membrane. From this time another change comes over the contents. We again find the yellow oily liquid, now occupying the external position, with some drops of colourless or roseate liquid in the centre, so that the oily liquid and the more limpid fluid interchange the positions which they occupied previous to the commencement of germination. Whether these two fluids have undergone any change in their constitution is difficult to determine, at all events the oily liquid appears to be less refractive and more granular, and it may be that it is a product of new formation, containing some of the elements of the primitive oily drop. Having regard to the delicate character of the membrane of the germinating filaments, De Seynes supposed that it might offer greater facility for the entrance of water by endosmose, and account for the rapid enlargement of the sporidia. By a series of experiments he became satisfied that this was the case to a considerable extent, but he adds:—"I cannot help supposing that a greater absorption of greasy matter in the cell which is the first product of germination raises an objection to an aqueous endosmose. One can also see in this experience a proof of the existence of two special membranes, and so suppose that the germinative cell is the continuation of the internal membrane, the external membrane alone being susceptible of absorbing the liquids, at least with a certain rapidity."

In other *Discomycetes* germination takes place in a similar manner. Boudier * narrates that in *Ascobolus*, when once the spore reaches a favourable place, if the circumstances are good, *i.e.*, if the temperature is sufficiently high and the moisture sufficient, it will germinate. The time necessary for this purpose is variable, some hours sufficing for some species; those of *A. viridis*, for example, germinate in eight or ten hours, doubtless because, being terrestrial, it has in consequence less heat. The spore slightly augments in size, then opens, generally at one or other extremity, sometimes at two, or at any point on its surface, in order to pass the mycelium tubes. At first simple, without septa, and granular in the interior, above all at the extremity, these tubes, the rudiment of the mycelium, are not long in elongating, in branching, and later in having partitions. These filaments are always colourless, only the spore may be coloured, or not. Coemans has described them as giving rise to two kinds of conidia,† the one having the form of *Torula*, when they give rise to continuous filaments, the other in the form of *Penicillium*, when they give birth to partitioned filaments. De Seynes could never obtain this result. Many times he had seen the *Penicillium glaucum* invade his sowings, but he feels confident that it had nothing to do with the *Ascobolus*. M. Worouin‡ has detailed some observations on the sexual phenomena which he has observed in *Ascobolus* and *Peziza*, and so far as the scolecite is concerned these have been confirmed by M. Boudier.

FIG. 94. — Sporidium of *Ascobolus* germinating.

* Boudier, "Mémoire sur l'Ascoboles," pt. i. iv. f. 13–15.

† Coemans, "Spicilége Mycologique," i. p. 6.

‡ Woronin, "Abhandlungen der Senchenbergischen Naturfor. Gesellschaft" (1865), p. 333.

There is no reason for doubt that in other of the *Discomycetes* the germination of the sporidia is very similar to that already seen and described, whilst in the *Pyrenomycetes*, as far as we are aware, although the production of germinating tubes is by no means difficult, development has not been traced beyond this stage.*

* In the very important observations made by Dr. Cunningham at Calcutta, on substances floating in the atmosphere, it appeared that the sporidia of many *Sphæriæ* actually germinated after being taken up by the air. The multitude of fungus spores which were observed in every case was quite extraordinary.

VIII.

SEXUAL REPRODUCTION.

The existence of some sort of sexual reproduction in Fungi has long been suspected, although in earlier instances upon insufficient grounds; but of late years observations have multiplied and facts accumulated which leave no doubt of its existence. If the *Saprolegniæ* are left out of the question as disputed Fungi, there still remain a number of well authenticated instances of the phenomena of copulation, and many other facts which indicate some sort of sexual relationship. The precise manner in which those minute bodies, so common amongst the *Sphæronemei*, which we prefer to call stylospores, perform their functions is still to a great extent a mystery; yet it is no longer doubted that certain species of *Aposphæria*, *Phoma*, *Septoria*, &c., are only conditions of some species of *Sphæria*, often developed and matured in close proximity to them on the same host. In *Æcidium*, *Ræstelia*, &c., spermogonia are produced plentifully on or near the same spots on which the fructification appears, either simultaneously or at a later period.* The relation of *Cytispora* to *Valsa* was suspected by Fries very many years ago, and, as since demonstrated, with very good reason. All attempts, however, to establish anything like sexual reproduction in the higher forms of *Hymenomycetes* have at present been unsuccessful; and the same may be said of the *Gasteromycetes;* but in *Ascomycetes* and *Physomycetes* instances abound.

We know not whether any importance is to be attached to the

* M. Tulasne has devoted a chapter to the spermogonia of the Uredines in his memoir, to which we have already alluded.

views of M. A. S. Œrsted,* which have not since been confirmed, but which have been cited with some approval by Professor de Bary, as to a trace of sexual organs in *Hymenomycetes*. He is supposed to have seen in *Agaricus variabilis*, P., oocysts or elongated reniform cells, which spring up like rudimentary branches of the filaments of the mycelium, and enclose an abundant protoplasm, if not even a nucleus. At the base of these oocysts appear the presumed antheridia, that is to say, one or two slender filaments, which generally turn their extremities towards the oocysts, and which more rarely are applied to them. Then, without ulteriorily undergoing any appreciable modifications, the fertile cell or oocyst becomes enveloped in a network of filaments of mycelium which proceed from the one which bears it, and this tissue forms the rudiments of the cap. The reality of some kind of fecundation in this circumstance, and the mode of the phenomena, if there is one, are for the present equally uncertain. If M. Œrsted's opinion is confirmed, naturally the whole of the cap will be the product of fecundation. Probably Karsten (Bonplandia, 1862, p. 62) saw something similar in *Agaricus campestris*, but his account is obscure.

In *Phycomyces* the organs of reproduction have been subjected to close examination by Van Tieghem,† and although he failed to discover chlamydospores in this, he describes them in other Mucors. In this species, besides the regular sexual development, by means of sporangia, there is a so-called sexual reproduction by means of zygospores, which takes place in this wise. The threads which conjugate to form the zygospores are slender and erect on the surface of the substratum. Two of these threads come into close contact through a considerable length, and clasp each other by alternate protuberances and depressions. Some of the protuberances are prolonged into slender tubes. At the same time the free extremities of the threads dilate, and arch

* Œersted, in "Verhandl der König. Dän. Gesell. Der Wissensch," 1st January, 1865; De Bary, "Handbuch der Physiol. Botanik" (1866), p. 172; "Annales des Sci. Nat." (5me sér.), vol. v. (1866), p. 366.

† Van Tieghem and Le Monnier, in "Annales des Sci. Nat." (1873), vol. xvii. p. 261.

over one towards the other until their tops touch like a vice, each limb of which rapidly increases in size. Each of these arcuate, clavate cells has now a portion of its extremity isolated by a partition, by means of which a new hemispherical cell is formed at the end of each thread at its point of junction with the opposed thread. These cells become afterwards cylindrical by pressure, the protoplasm is aggregated into a mass, the double membrane at the point of first contact is absorbed, and the two confluent masses of protoplasm form a zygospore invested with a tubercular coat and enveloped by the primary wall of the two

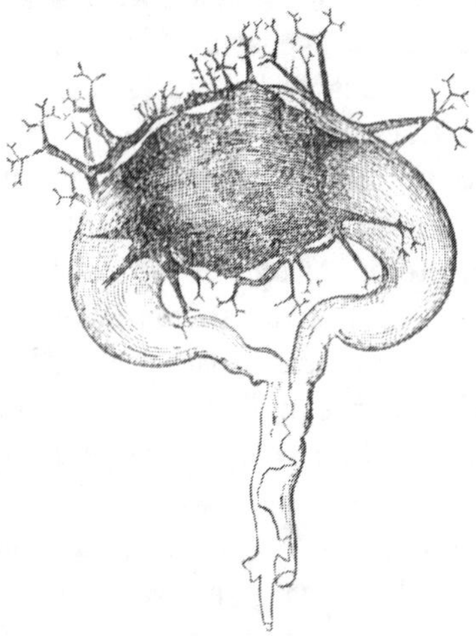

FIG. 95.—Zygospore of *Mucor phycomyces*.

conjugating cells. During this formation of the zygospore, the two arched cells whence the zygospore originated develop a series of dichotomous processes in close proximity to the walls which separate them from the zygospore. These processes appear at first on one of the arcuate cells in successive order. The first makes its appearance above upon the convex side; the succeeding ones to the right and left in descending order; the last is in the concavity beneath. It is only after the development of this that the first process appears on the opposite cell, which is followed by others in the same order. These dichotomous processes are nothing more than branches developed from the arcuate, or mother cells. During all these changes, while the zygospore enlarges, the wall of the arcuate cells becomes coloured brown. This colouring is more marked on the convex side, and it shows itself first in the cell on which the dichotomous branches are first produced, and which retains the darker tint longer than the other. The zone from whence the processes issue, and also the processes themselves, have their walls blackened deeply, while the walls of the conjugated cells, which continue to clothe the zygospore during the whole of its development, are bluish-black. By pressure, the thin brittle coat which envelopes the zygospore is ruptured, and the coat of the zygospore exposed, formed of a thick cartilaginous membrane, studded with large irregular warts.

The germination of the zygospores in this species has not as yet been observed, but it is probably the same or very similar to that observed in other species of *Mucor*. In these the rough tuberculate epispore splits on one side, and its internal coat elongates itself and protrudes as a tube filled with protoplasm and oil globules, terminating in an ordinary sporangium. Usually the amount of nutriment contained in the zygospore is exhausted by the formation of the terminal sporangium, according to Brefeld ;* but Van Tieghem and Le Monnier remark that in their examinations they have often seen a partition formed at about a third of the length of the principal filament from the base, below which a strong branch is given off, and this is also terminated by a large sporangium.

De Bary has given a precise account of the formation of the zygospore in another of the Mucors, *Rhizopus nigricans*, in which he says that the filaments which conjugate are solid rampant tubes, which are branched without order and confusedly intermingled. Where two of these filaments meet each of them pushes towards the other an appendage which is at first cylindrical and of the same diameter. From the first these two processes are applied firmly one to the other by their extremities; they increase in size, become clavate, and constitute together a fusiform body placed across the two conjugated filaments. Between the two halves of this body there exists no constant difference of size ; often they are both perfectly equal. In each

* Brefeld, "Bot. Unt. uber Schimmelpilze," p. 31.

there is collected an abundance of protoplasm, and when they have attained a certain development the largest extremity of each is isolated by a septum from the clavule, which thus becomes the support or suspender of the copulative cell. The two conju-

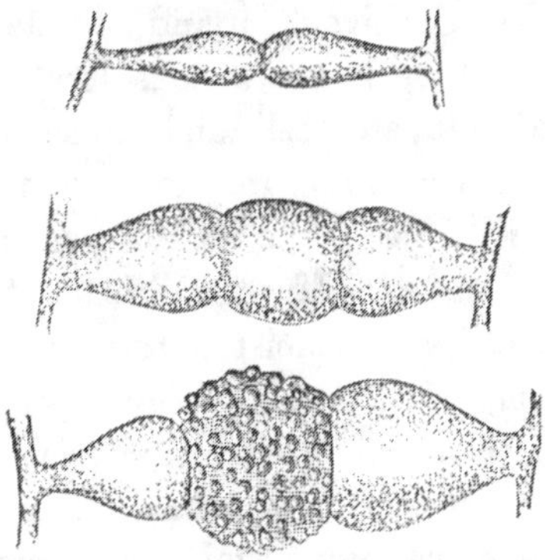

FIG. 95.--Zygospore of *Rhizopus* in different stages. (De Bary.)

gated cells of the fusiform body are generally unequal; the one is a cylinder as long as it is broad, the other is disciform, and its length is only equal to half its breadth. The primitive membrane of the clavule forms between the copulative cells a solid partition of two membranes, but soon after the cells have become defined the medial partition becomes pierced in the centre, and then soon entirely disappears, so that the two twin cells are confounded in one single zygospore, which is due to the union of two more or less similar utricles. After its formation the zygospore still increases considerably in size, and acquires a diameter of more than one-fifth of a millimetre. Its form is generally spherical, and flattened on the faces which are united to the suspenders, or it resembles a slightly elongated cask. The membrane thickens considerably, and consists at the time of maturity of two superposed integuments; the exterior or epispore is solid, of a dark blackish-blue colour, smooth on the plane faces in contact with the suspenders, but covered everywhere else with thick warts, which are hollow beneath. The endospore is thick and composed of several layers, colourless, and covered with warts, which correspond and fit into those of the epispore. The contents of the zygospore are a coarsely granular protoplasm, in which float large oleaginous drops. While the zygospore is increasing in size, the suspender of the smaller copulative cell becomes a rounded and stipitate utricle, often divided at the base by a septum, and which attains almost to the size of the zygospore. The suspender of the larger copulative cell preserves its primitive form and becomes scarcely any larger. It is rare that there is not a considerable difference of size between the two conjugated cells and the suspenders.*

Similar conjugation with like results also takes place in *Syzygites megalocarpus.* In this species the germination of the zygospores has been observed. If, after a certain time of repose, these bodies are placed on a moist substratum, they emit a germ-like tube, which, without originating a proper mycelium, develops at the expense of the nutritive material stored in the zygospore into a carpophore or fruit bearer, which is many times dichotomously branched, bearing terminal sporangia characteristic of the species.

It has already been remarked by us that the *Saprolegnei* are claimed by some authors as Algæ, whilst we are more disposed to regard them as closely allied to the Mucors, and as they exhibit in themselves strong evidence in support of the existence of sexual reproduction, we cannot forbear giving a summary of what has been observed by De Bary and others in this very interesting and singular group of plants, to which M. Cornu has recently dedicated an exhaustive monograph.†

In *Saprolegnia monoica*, and others, the female organs consist of oogonia—that is to say, of cells which are at first globose and rich in plastic matter, which most generally terminate short branches of the mycelium, and which are rarely seen in an interstitial position. The constitutive membrane of the adult oogonia is reabsorbed in a great many points, and is there pierced with rounded holes. At the same time the plasma is divided into a larger or smaller number of distinct portions, which are rounded into little spheres, and separate from the

* De Bary, "Morphologie und Physiologie der Pilze," cap. 5, p. 160; "Ann. des. Sci. Nat." (1866), p. 343.

† Cornu, in "Ann. des Sci. Nat." (5me sér.), vol. xv. p. 1 (1872).

walls of the conceptacle in order to group themselves at the centre, where they float in a watery fluid. These gonospheres are then smooth and bare, with no membrane on their surface of the nature of cellulose.

During the formation of the oogonia there arise from its pedicel or from neighbouring filaments slight cylindrical curved branches, sometimes turned round the support of the oogonia, and which all tend towards this organ. Their superior extremity is intimately applied to its wall, then ceases to be elongated, becomes slightly inflated, and is limited below by a partition; it is then an oblong cell, slightly curved, filled with protoplasm, and intimately applied to the oogonia—in fact, an antheridium or organ of the male sex. Each oogonium possesses one or several antheridia. Towards the time when the gonospheres are formed it may be observed that each antheridium sends to the interior of the oogonia one or several tubular processes, which have crossed its side wall, and which open at their extremity in order to discharge their contents. These, while they are flowing out, present some very agile corpuscles, and which, considering their resemblance to those in *Vaucheria*, to which the name of spermatozoids are applied, ought to be considered as the fecundating corpuscles. After the evacuation of the antheridia the gonospheres are found to be covered with cellulose; they then constitute so many oospores, with solid walls. De Bary considers that, bearing in mind analogous phenomena observed in *Vaucheria*, and the direct observations of Pringsheim,* the cellulose membrane on the surface of the gonospheres is only the consequence of a sexual fecundation.

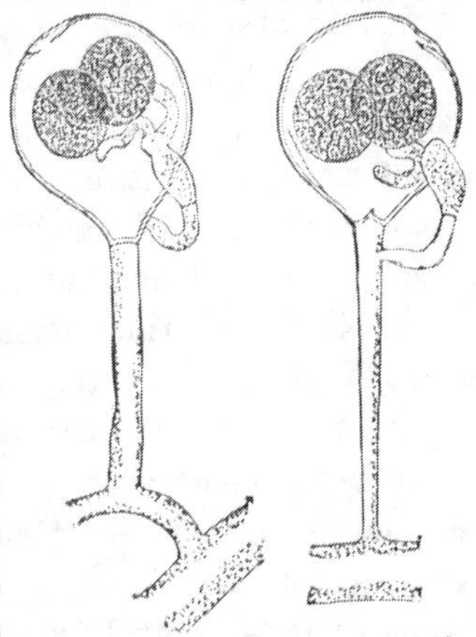

FIG. 97.—Conjugation in *Achlya racemosa*. (Cornu.)

In *Achlya dioica* the antheridium is cylindrical, the plasma which it encloses is divided into particles, which attain nearly

* Pringsheim's "Jahrbucher," vol. ii. p. 169.

the size of the zoospores of the same plant. These particles become globose cells, grouped in the centre of the antheridium. Afterwards the contents of these latter cells become divided into numerous bacillary spermatozoids, which first break the wall of their mother cell, and then issue from the antheridium. These rod-like corpuscles, which resemble the spermatozoids in *Vaucheria*, have their movements assisted by a long cilium. It is presumable that here, as in the Algæ, the spermatozoids introduce themselves into the cavity of the oogonium, and unite with the gonospheres.

Amongst obscure and doubtful bodies are those described by Pringsheim, which have their origin in thick filaments or tubes, similar to those which form the zoosporangia, and represent so many distinct little masses of plasma within an homogeneous parietal ganglion. The contour of these plastic masses is soon delineated in a more precise manner. We see in their interior some homogeneous granules, which are at first globose, then oval, and finally travel to the enlarged and ampullæform extremity of the generating tube. There they become rounded or oval cells covered with cellulose, and emit from their surface one or several cylindrical processes, which elongate towards the wall of the conceptacle, and pierce it, without, however, ever projecting very far beyond it. At the same time the lacunose protoplasm of each cell becomes divided into a number of corpuscles, which escape by the open extremity of the cylindrical neck. They resemble in their organization and agility the spermatozoids of *Achlya dioica*. They soon become motionless in water, and do not germinate. During the development of these organs, the protoplasm of the utricle which contains them offers at first completely normal characteristics, and disappears entirely by degrees as they increase. De Bary and Pringsheim believe that these organs constitute the antheridia of the species of *Saprolegnia* to which they belong.

The oospores of the *Saprolegniæ*, when arrived at maturity, possess a tolerably thick double integument, consisting of an epispore and an endospore. After a considerable time of repose they give rise to tubular or vesicular germs, which, without being much elongated, produce zoospores.*

De Bary has claimed for the oogonia in *Cystopus* and *Peronospora* a kind of fecundation which deserves mention here.† These same fruits, he says, which owe their origin to sexual organs, should bear the names of *oogonia* and *antheridia*, according to the terminology proposed by Pringsheim for analogous organs in the Algæ. The formation of the oogonia, or female organs, commences by the terminal or interstitial swelling of the tubes of the mycelium, which increase and take the form of large spherical or oboval cells, and which separate themselves by septa from the tube which carries them. Their membrane encloses granules of opaque protoplasm, mingled with numerous bulky granules of colourless fatty matter.

The branches of the mycelium which do not bear oogonia apply their obtuse extremities against the growing oogonia; this extremity swells, and, by a transverse partition, separates itself from the supporting tube. It is the antheridium, or male organ, which is formed by this process; it takes the form of an obliquely clavate or obovate cellule, which is always considerably smaller than the oogonium, and adheres to its walls by a plane or convex area. The slightly thickened membrane of the antheridia encloses protoplasm which is finely granular. It is seldom that more than one antheridium applies itself to an oogonium.

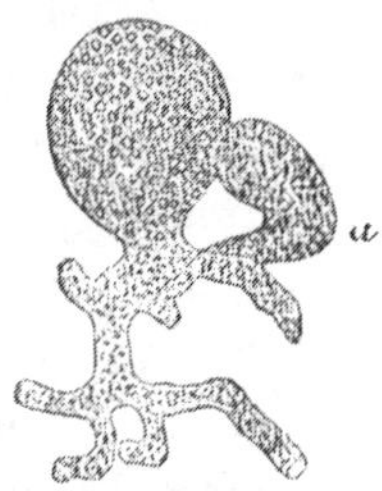

FIG. 98.—Conjugation in *Peronospora*; *a.* *antheridium.* (De Bary.)

The two organs having together achieved their development, the large granules contained in the oogonium accumulate at its centre to group themselves under the form of an irregular globule deprived of a proper membrane, and surrounded by a bed of almost homogeneous protoplasm. This globule is the *gonosphere*, or reproductive sphere, which, through the means of

* De Bary, in "Annales des Sciences Naturelles" (5me sér.), vol. v. (1866), p. 343; Hoffmeister's "Handbook" (Fungi), cap. v. p. 155.

† De Bary, in "Annales des Sci. Nat." (4me sér.), vol. xx. p. 129.

fecundation, should become the reproductive body, vegetable egg, or oospore. The gonosphere having been formed, the antheridium shoots out from the centre of its face, close against the oogonium, a straight tube, which perforates the walls of the female cell, and traversing the protoplasm of its periphery, directs itself to the gonosphere. It ceases to elongate itself as soon as it touches it, and the gonosphere becomes clothed with a membrane of cellulose, and takes a regular spheroidal form.

Considering the great resemblance of these organs with the sexual organs of the Saprolegniæ, which are closely allied to the Algæ, and of which the sexuality has been proved, De Bary adds, we have no doubt whatever that the phenomena just described represent an act of fecundation, and that the tube pushed out by the antheridium should be regarded as a fecundating tube. It is remarkable that amongst these fungi the tube projected by the antheridium effects fecundation only by contact. Its extremity never opens, and we never find antherozoids; on the contrary, the antheridium presents, up to the maturity of the oospore, the appearance which it presented at the moment of fecundation.

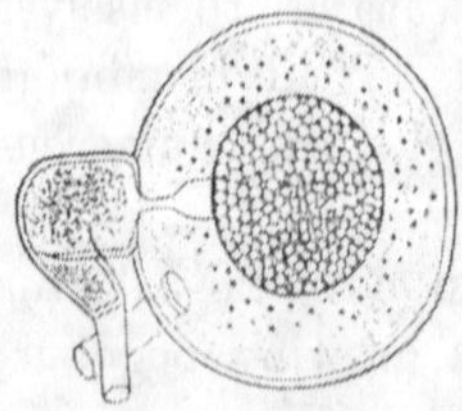

FIG. 99. — Antheridia and oogonium of *Peronospora*. (De Bary.)

The primitive membrane of the oospore, at first very thin, soon acquires a more sensible thickness, and becomes surrounded by an external layer (epospore), which is formed at the expense of the protoplasm of the periphery. This disappears in proportion as the epispore attains maturity, and finally there only remains a quantity of granules, suspended in a transparent watery fluid. At the period of maturity, the epispore is a slightly thickened, resistant membrane, of a yellowish-brown colour, and finely punctate. The surface is almost always provided with brownish warts, which are large and obtuse, sometimes isolated, and sometimes confluent, forming irregular crests. These warts are composed of cellulose, which reagents colour of a deep blue, whilst the membrane which bears them preserves its primitive colour.

One of the warts, larger than the rest, and recognizable by its cylindrical form, always forms a kind of thick sheath around the fecundating tube. The ripe endospore is a thick, smooth, colourless membrane, composed of cellulose containing a bed of finely granulated protoplasm, which surrounds a great central vacuole. This oospore, or resting spore, may remain dormant in this state within the tissues of the foster plant for some months. Its ultimate development by production of zoospores is similar to the production of zoospores from conidia, which it is unnecessary to repeat here. The oospore becomes an oosporangium, and from it at least a hundred germinating bodies are at length expelled.

Amongst the principal observers of certain phenomena of copulation in cells formed in the earliest stages of the *Discomycetes* are Professor de Bary,* Dr. Woronin,† and Messrs. Tulasne.‡ In the *Ascobolus pulcherrimus* of Crouan, Woronin ascertained that the cup derives its origin from a short and flexible tube, thicker than the other branches of the mycelium, and which is soon divided by transverse septa into a series of cells, the successive increase of which finally gives to the whole a torulose and unequal appearance. The body thus formed he calls a "vermiform body." The same observer also seems to have convinced himself that there exists always in proximity to this body certain filaments, the short arched or inflected branches of which, like so many antheridia, rest their anterior extremities on the utriform cells. This contact seems to communicate to the vermiform body a special vital energy, which is immediately directed towards the production of a somewhat filamentous tissue, on which the hymenium is at a later period developed. This "vermiform body" of M. Woronin has since come to be recognized under the name of "scolecite."

Tulasne observes that this "scolecite" or ringed body can be readily isolated in *Ascobolus furfuraceus*. When the young re-

* De Bary, in "Annales des Sciences Naturelles" (5me sér.), p. 343.

† Woronin, in De Bary's "Beitr. zur. Morph. und Physiol. der Pilze," ii. (1866), pp. 1–11.

‡ Tulasne, "Ann. des Sci. Nat." (5me sér.), October, 1866, p. 211.

ceptacles are still spherical and white, and have not attained a diameter exceeding the one-twentieth of a millimetre, it is sufficient to compress them slightly in order to rupture them at the summit and expel the "scolecite." This occupies the centre of the little sphere, and is formed of from six to eight cells, curved in the shape of a comma.

In *Peziza melanoloma*, A. and S., the same observer succeeded still better in his searches after the scolecite, which he remarks is in this species most certainly a lateral branch of the filaments of the mycelium. This branch is isolated, simple, or forked at a short distance from its base, and in diameter generally exceeding that of the filament which bears it. This branch is soon arcuate or bent, and often elongated in describing a spiral, the irregular turns of which are lax or compressed. At the same time its interior, at first continuous, becomes divided by transverse septa into eight or ten or more cells. Sometimes this special branch terminates in a crozier shape; which is involved in the bent part of another crozier which terminates a neighbouring filament. In other cases the growing branch is connected, by its extremity, with that of a hooked branch. These contacts, however, did not appear to Tulasne to be so much normal as accidental. But of the importance of the ringed body, or "scolecite," there was no room for doubt, as being the certain and habitual rudiment of the fertile cup. In fact, inferior cells are produced from the flexuous filaments which creep about its surface, cover and surround it on all sides, while joining themselves to each other. At first continuous, then septate, these cells by their union constitute a cellular tissue, which increases little by little until the scolecite is so closely enveloped that only its superior extremity can be seen. These cellular masses attain a considerable volume before the hymenium begins to show itself in a depression of their summit. So long as their smallness permits of their being seen in the field of the microscope, it can be determined that they adhere to a single filament of the mycelium by the base of the scolecite which remains naked.

Although Tulasne could not satisfy himself of the presence of any act of copulation in *Ascobolus furfuraceus*, or *Peziza melanoloma*, he was more successful with *Peziza omphalodes*. As early as 1860 he recognized the large globose, sessile, and grouped vesicles which originate the fertile tissue, but did not comprehend the part which these macrocysts were to perform. Each of these emits from its summit a cylindrical tube, generally flexuous, but always more or less bent in a crozier shape, sometimes attenuated at the extremity. Thus provided, these utricles resemble so many tun-shaped, narrow-necked retorts, filled with a granular thick roseate protoplasm. In the middle of these, and from the same filaments, are generated elongated clavate cells, with paler contents, more vacuoles, which Tulasne names *paracysts*. These, though produced after the *macrocysts*, finally exceed them in height, and seem to carry their summit so as to meet the crozier-like prolongations. It would be difficult to determine to which of these two orders of cells belongs the initiative of conjugation. Sometimes the advance seems to be on one side, and sometimes on the other. However this may be, the meeting of the extremity of the connecting tube with the summit of the neighbouring paracyst is a constant fact, observed over and over again a hundred times. There is no real junction between the dissimilar cells above described, except at the very limited point where they meet, and there a circular perforation may be discerned at the end, defined by a round swelling, which is either barely visible or sometimes very decided. Everywhere else the two organs may be contiguous, or more or less near together, but they are free from any adherence whatever. If the plastic matters contained in the conjugated cells influence one another reciprocally, no notable modification in their appearance results at first. The large appendiculate cell seems, however, to yield to its consort a portion of the plasma it contains. One thing only can be affirmed from these phenomena, that the con-

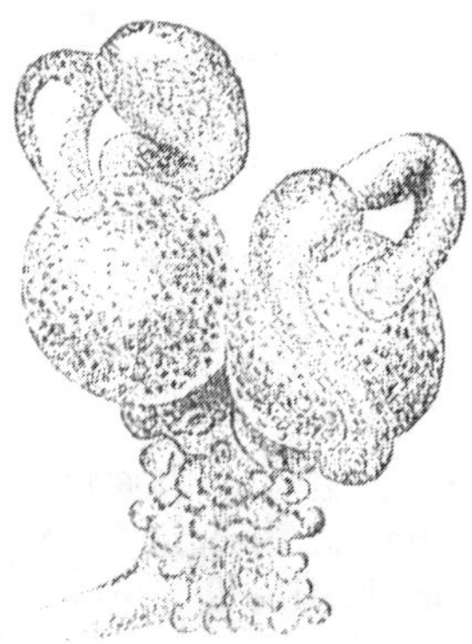

FIG. 100.—Conjugation in *Peziza omphalodes*. (Tulasne.)

jugated cells, especially the larger, wither and empty themselves, while the upright compressed filaments, which will ultimately constitute the asci, increase and multiply.*

Certain phenomena concerned in the development of the *Erysiphei* belong also to this connection. The mycelium of *Erysiphe cichoracearum*, like that of other species, consists of branched filaments, crossed in all directions, which adhere as they climb to the epidermis of the plant on which the fungus lives as a parasite. The perithecia are engendered where two filaments cross each other. These swell slightly at this point,

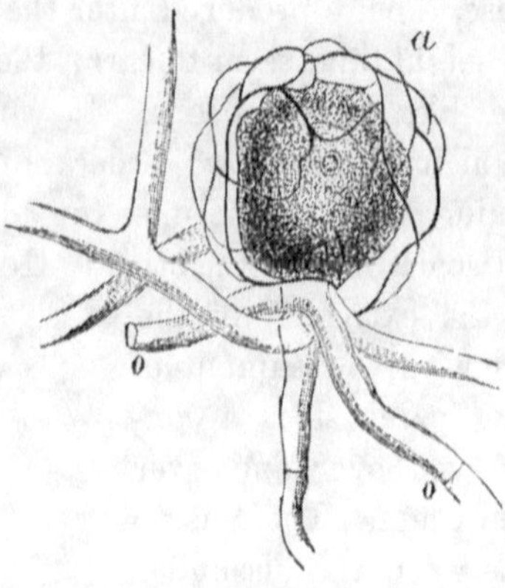

Fig. 100*.

and each emits a process which imitates a nascent branch, and remains upright on the surface of the epidermis. The process originating from the inferior filament soon acquires an oval form and a diameter double that of the filament; then it becomes isolated from it by a septum, and constitutes a distinct cell, which De Bary † terms an oocyst. The appendage which proceeds from the inferior filament always adheres intimately to this cell, and elongates into a slender cylindrical tube, which

* Tulasne, "On the Phenomena of Copulation in certain Fungi," in "Ann. des Sci. Nat." (1866), p. 211.

† De Bary, "Morphologie und Phys. der Pilze," cap. v. p. 162.

terminates in an obtuse manner at the summit of the same cell. At its base it is also limited by a septum, and soon after another appears a little below its extremity at a point indicated beforehand by a constriction. This new septum defines a terminal short obtuse cell, the antheridium, which is thus borne on a narrow tube like a sort of pedicel. Immediately after the formation of the antheridia new productions show themselves, both around the oocyst and within it. Underneath this cell eight or ten tubes are seen to spring from the filament which bears it; these join themselves by the sides to each other and to the pedicel of the antheridium, while they apply their inner face to the oocyst, above which their extremities soon meet. Each of the tubes is then divided by transverse septa into two or three distinct cells, and in this manner the cellular walls of the perithecia come into existence.

During this time the oocyst enlarges and divides, without its being possible precisely to determine the way in which it happens, into a central cell and an outer layer, ordinarily simple, of smaller cells, contiguous to the general enveloping wall. The central cell becomes the single ascus, which is characteristic of the species, and the layer which surrounds it constitutes the inner wall of its perithecium. The only changes afterwards observed are the increase in size of the perithecium, the production of the root-like filaments which proceed from its outer wall, the brown tint which it assumes, and finally the formation of the sporidia in the ascus. The antheridium remains for a long time recognizable without undergoing any essential modification, but the dark colour of the perithecium soon hides it from the observer's eye. De Bary thinks that he is authorized in assuming the probability that the conceptacles and organs of fructification of others of the *Ascomycetes*, including the *Discomycetes* and the *Tuberacei*, are the results of sexual generation.

Certain phenomena which have been observed amongst the *Coniomycetes* are cited as examples of sexual association. Amongst these may be named the conjugation of the slender spores of the first generation, produced on the germinating threads of *Tilletia*,* and similar acts of conjugation, as observed in some species of *Ustilago.* Whether this interpretation should be placed on those phenomena in the present condition of our knowledge is perhaps an open question.

Finally, the spermogonia must be regarded as in some occult manner, which as yet has baffled detection, influencing the perfection of sporidia.† In *Rhytisma*, found on the leaves of maple and willow, black pitchy spots at first appear, which contain within them a golden pulp, in which very slender corpuscles are mixed with an abundant mucilage. These corpuscles are the spermatia, which in *Rhytisma acerinum* are linear and short, in *Rhytisma salicinum* globose. When the spermatia are expelled, the stroma thickens for the production of asci and sporidia, which are afterwards developed during the autumn and winter.

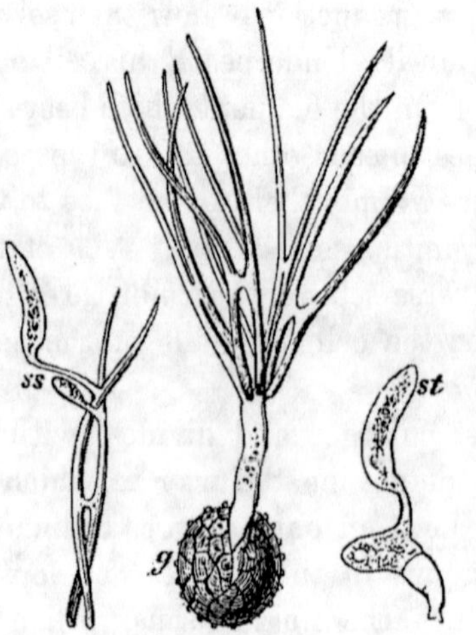

FIG. 101.—*Tilletia caries* with conjugating cells.

Several of the species of *Hysterium* also possess spermogonia, notably *H. Fraxini*, which may be distinguished from the ascigerous perithecia with which they are associated by their smaller size and flask-like shape. From these the spermatia are expelled long before the maturity of the spores. In *Hypoderma virgultorum*, *H. commune*, and *H. scirpinum*, the spermogonia are small depressed black capsules, which contain an abundance of minute spermatia. These were formerly regarded as distinct species, under the name of *Leptostroma*. In *Stictis ocellata* a great number of the tubercles do not pass into the perfect state

* Berkeley, in "Journ. Hort. Soc." vol. ii. p. 107; Tulasne, "Ann. d. Sc. Nat." (4me sér.), vol. ii. tab. 12.

† Tulasne, "New Researches on the Reproductive Apparatus of Fungi;" "Comptes Rendus," vol. xxxv. (1852), p. 841.

until after they have produced either linear, very short spermatia, or stylospores, the latter being reproductive bodies of an oblong shape, equal in size to the perfect sporidia. Some of the tubercles never pass beyond this stage.

Again, there is a very common fungus which forms black discoid spots on dead holly leaves, called *Ceuthospora phacidioides*, figured by Greville in his "Scottish Cryptogamic Flora," which expels a profusion of minute stylospores; but later in the season, instead of these, we find the asci and sporidia of *Phacidium ilicis*, so that the two are forms and conditions the one of the other.

In *Tympanis conspersa* the spermogonia are much more commonly met with than the complete fruit. There is a great external resemblance in them to the ascigerous cups, but there is no evidence that they are ever transformed into such. The perfect sporidia are also very minute and numerous, being contained in asci borne in cups, which usually surround the spermogonia.

In several species of *Dermatea* the stylospores and spermatia co-exist, but they are disseminated before the appearance of the ascigerous receptacles, yet they are produced upon a common stroma not unlike that of *Tubercularia*.

In its early stage the common and well-known *Bulgaria inquinans*, which when mature looks like a black *Peziza*, is a little tubercle, the whole mass of which is divided into ramified lobes, the extremities of which become, towards the surface of the tubercle, receptacles from whence escape waves of spermatia which are colourless, or stylospores mixed with them which are larger and nearly black.

Amongst the *Sphæriacei* numerous instances might be cited of minute stylosporous bodies in consort with, or preceding, the ascigerous receptacles. A very familiar example may be found at the base of old nettle stems in what has been named *Aposphæria acuta*, but which truly are only the stylospores of the *Sphæria coniformis*, the perithecia of which flourish in company or in close proximity to them. Most of these bodies are so minute, delicate, and hyaline that the difficulties in the way of tracing them in their relations to the bodies with which they are associated are very great. Nevertheless there is strong presumption in favour of regarding some of them as performing the functions which the name applied to them indicates.

Professor de Bary cautiously refrains from accepting spermatia other than as doubtful or at least uncertain sexual bodies.* He says that the Messrs. Tulasne have supposed that the spermogonia represented the male sex, and that the spermatia were analogous to spermatozoids. Their opinion depends on two plausible reasons,—the spermatia, in fact, do not germinate, and the development of the spermogonia generally precedes the appearance of the sporophorous organs, a double circumstance which reminds us of what is known of the spermatozoids and antheridia of other vegetables. It remained to discover which were the female organs which underwent fecundation from the spermatia.

Many organs placed at first amongst spermatia have been recognized by M. Tulasne as being themselves susceptible of germination, and consequently ought to take their place among legitimate spores. Then it must be considered that very many spores can only germinate under certain conditions. It is, therefore, for the present a doubtful question whether there exist really any spermatia incapable of germination, or if the default of germination of these corpuscles does not rather depend on the experiments hitherto attempted not having included the conditions required by the phenomena. Moreover, as yet no trace has been discovered of the female organs which are specially fecundated by the spermatia.

Finally, there exist in the *Ascomycetes* certain organs of reproduction, diverse spore-bearing apparatus, pycnidia, and others, which, like the spermogonia, usually precede ascophorous fruits. The real nature of the spermogonia and spermatia should therefore be regarded as, at present, very uncertain; as regards, however, the spermatia which have never been seen to germinate, perhaps it is as well not to absolutely reject the first opinion formed concerning them, or

* De Bary, "Morphologie und Physiologie der Pilze," cap. v. p. 168.

perhaps they might be thought to perform the part of androspores, attributing to that expression the meaning which Pringsheim gives it in the *Conferoæ.* The experiments performed with the spermatia which do not germinate, and with the spermogonia of the Uredines, do not, at any rate, appear to justify the reputed masculine or fecundative nature of these organs. The spermogonia constantly accompany or precede fruits of *Æcidium*, whence naturally follows the presumption that the first are in a sexual relation to the second. Still, when Tulasne cultivated *Endophyllum sempervivum*, he obtained on some perfectly isolated rosettes of *Sempervivum* some *Æcidium* richly provided with normal and fertile spores, without any trace of spermogonia or of spermatia.

IX.

POLYMORPHISM.

A GREAT number of very interesting facts have during late years been brought to light of the different forms which fungi assume in the course of their development. At the same time, we fear that a great many assumptions have been accepted for fact, and supposed connections and relations between two or three or more so-called species, belonging to different genera, have upon insufficient data been regarded as so many states or conditions of one and the same plant. Had the very pertinent suggestions of Professor de Bary been more generally acted upon, these suspicions would have been baseless. His observations are so valuable as a caution, that we cannot forbear prefacing our own remarks on this subject by quoting them.* In order to determine, he says, whether an organic form, an organ, or an organism, belongs to the same series of development as another, or that which is the same is developed from it, or *vice versâ*, there is only one way, viz., to observe how the second grows out of the first. We see the commencement of the second begin as a part of the first, perfect itself in connection with it, and at last it often becomes independent; but be it through spontaneous dismembering from the first, or that the latter be destroyed and the second remains, both their disunited bodies are always connected together in organic continuity, as parts of a whole (single one) that can cease earlier or later.

By observing the organic continuity, we know that the apple is the product of development of an apple-tree, and not hung on

* De Bary, in "Quarterly German Magazine" (1872), p. 197.

it by chance, that the pip of an apple is a product of the development of the apple, and that from the pip an apple-tree can at last be developed, that therewith all these bodies are members of a sphere of development or form. It is the same with every similar experience of our daily life, that where an apple-tree stands, many apples lie on the ground, or that in the place where apple-pips are sown seedlings, little apple-trees, grow out of the ground, is not impôrtant to our view of the course of development. Every one recognizes that in his daily life, because he laughs at a person who thinks a plum which lies under an apple-tree has grown on it, or that the weeds which appear among the apple seedlings come from apple-pips. If the apple-tree with its fruit and seed were microscopically small, it would not make the difference of a hair's breadth in the form of the question or the method of answering it, as the size of the object can be of no importance to the latter, and the questions which apply to microscopical fungi are to be treated in the same manner.

If it then be asserted that two or several forms belong to a series of development of one kind, it can only be based on the fact of their organic continuity. The proof is more difficult than in large plants, partly because of the delicacy, minuteness, and fragility of the single parts, particularly the greater part of the mycelia, partly because of the resemblance of the latter in different species, and therefore follows the danger of confusing them with different kinds, and finally, partly in consequence of the presence of different kinds in the same substratum, and therefore the mixture not only of different sorts of mycelia, but also that different kinds of spores are sown. With some care and patience, these difficulties are in no way insurmountable, and they must at any rate be overcome; the organic continuity or non-continuity must be cleared up, unless the question respecting the course of development, and the series of forms of special kinds, be laid on one side as insolvable.

Simple and intelligible as these principles are, they have not always been acted upon, but partly neglected, partly expressly rejected, not because they were considered false, but because the difficulties of their application were looked upon as insurmountable. Therefore another method of examination was adopted; the spores of a certain form were sown, and sooner or later they were looked after to see what the seed had produced—not every single spore—but the seed *en masse*, that is, in other words, what had grown on that place where the seed had been sown. As far as it relates to those forms which are so widely spread, and above all grow in conjunction with one another—and that is always the case in the specimens of which we speak—we can never be sure that the spores of the form which we mean to test are not mingled with those of another species. He who has made an attentive and minute examination of this kind knows that we may be sure to find such a mixture, and that such an one was there can be afterwards decidedly proved. From the seed which is sown, these spores, for which the substratum was most suitable, will more easily germinate, and their development will follow the more quickly. The favoured germs will suppress the less favoured, and grow up at their expense. The same relation exists between them as between the seeds, germs, and seedlings of a sown summer plant, and the seeds which have been undesignedly sown with it, only in a still more striking manner, in consequence of the relatively quick development of the mildew fungus.

Therefore, that from the latter a decided form, or a mixture of several forms, is to be found sown on one spot, is no proof of their generic connection with one which has been sown for the purpose of experiments; and the matter will only be more confused if we call imagination to our aid, and place the forms which are found near one another, according to a real or fancied resemblance, in a certain series of development. All those statements on the sphere of form and connection, which have for their basis such a superficial work, and are not based on the clear exposition of the continuity of development, as by the origin of the connection of the *Mucor* with *Penicillium*, *Oidium lactis* and *Mucor*, *Oidium* and *Penicillium*, are rejected as unfounded.

A source of error, which can also interfere in the last-named superficial method of cultivation for experiments, is, viz., that heterogeneous unwished-for spores intrude themselves from without, among the seed which is sown, but that has been until now quite disregarded. It is of great importance in practice, but in truth, for our present purpose, synonymous with what we have already written. Those learned in the science of this kind of culture lay great stress on its importance, and many apparatuses have been constructed, called "purely cultivating machines," for the purpose of destroying the spores which are contained in the substratum, and preventing the intrusion of those from without. The mixture in the seed which is sown has of course not been obviated. These machines may, perhaps, in every other respect, fulfil their purpose, but they cannot change the form of the question, and the most ingeniously constructed apparatus cannot replace the attention and intellect of the observer.*

Two distinct kinds of phenomena have been grouped under the term "polymorphy." In one series two or more forms of fruit occur consecutively or simultaneously on the same individual, and in the other two or more forms appear on a different mycelium, on a different part of the same plant, or on a matrix wholly distinct and different; in the latter case the connection being attested or suspected circumstantially, in the former proved by the method suggested by De Bary. It will at once be conceded that in cases where actual growth and development substantiate the facts the polymorphy is undoubted, whilst in the other series it can at best be little more than suspected. We will endeavour to illustrate both these series by examples.

One of the first and earliest suspected cases of dualism, which long puzzled the older mycologists, was observed amongst the Uredines, and many years ago it was held that there must be some mysterious association between the "red rust" (*Trichobasis rubigo vera*) of wheat and grasses and the "corn mildew" (*Puccinia*

* The method pursued by Messrs. Berkeley and Hoffmann of surrounding the drop of fluid, in which a definite number of spores or yeast globules had been placed, with a pellicle of air, into which the germinating threads might pass and fructify, is perhaps the most satisfactory that has been adopted, though it requires nice manipulation. If carefully managed, the result is irrefragable, though doubts have been cast, without any reason, on their observations.

graminis) which succeeded it. The simple spored rust first makes its appearance, and later the bilocular "mildew." It is by no means uncommon to find the two forms in the same pustule. Some have held, without good reason, that the simple cells became afterwards divided and converted into *Puccinia*, but this is not the case; the uredo-spores are always simple, and remain so except in *Uredo linearis*, where every intermediate stage has been observed. Both are also perfect in their kind, and capable of germination.

What the precise relations between the two forms may be has as yet never been revealed to observers, but that the two forms belong to one species is not now doubted. Very many species of *Puccinia* have already been found associated with a corresponding *Trichobasis*, and of *Phragmidium* with a relative *Lecythea*, but it may be open to grave doubt whether some of the very many species associated by authors are not so classed upon suspicion rather than observation. We are ready to admit that the evidence is strong in favour of the dimorphism of a large number of species—it *may* be in all, but this awaits proof, or substantial presumption on good grounds. Up to the present we know that there are species of *Trichobasis* which have never been traced to association with a *Puccinia*, and doubtless there will be species of *Puccinia* for which no corresponding *Uredo* or *Trichobasis* can be found.

Tulasne remarks, in reference to *Puccinia sonchi*, in one of his memoirs, that this curious species exhibits, in effect, that a *Puccinia* may unite three sorts of reproductive bodies, which, taking part, constitute for the mycologists of the day three entirely different plants—a *Trichobasis*, a *Uromyces*, and a *Puccinia*. The Uredines are not less rich, he adds, in reproductive bodies of divers sorts than the *Pyrenomycetes* and the *Discomycetes;* and we should not be surprised at this, since it seems to be a law, almost constant in the general harmony of nature, that the smaller the organized beings are, the more their races are prolific.

In *Puccinia variabilis*, Grev., it is common to find a unicellular form, species of *Trichobasis*, in the same pustules. A like circumstance occurs with *Puccinia violarum*, Link., and *Trichobasis violarum*, B.; with *Puccinia fallens*, C., and *Trichobasis fallens*, Desm.; also with *Puccinia menthæ*, P., and *Trichobasis Labiatarum*, D. C. In *Melampsora*, again, the prismatic pseudospores of *Melampsora salicina*, Lev., are the winter fruits of *Lecythea caprearum*, Lev., as those of *Melampsora populina*, Lev., are of *Lecythea populina*, Lev. In the species of *Lecythea* themselves will be found, as De Bary * has shown, hyaline cysts of a larger size, which surround the pseudospores in the pustules in which they are developed.

A good illustration of dimorphism in one of the commonest of moulds is given by De Bary in a paper from which we have already quoted.† He writes thus:—In every household there is a frequent unbidden guest, which appears particularly on preserved fruits, viz., the *mould* which is called *Aspergillus glaucus*. It shows itself to the naked eye as a woolly floccy crust over the substance, first purely white, then gradually covered with little fine glaucous, or dark green dusty heads. More minute microscopical examination shows that the fungus consists of richly ramified fine filaments, which are partly disseminated in the substratum, and partly raised obliquely over it. They have a cylindrical form with rounded ends, and are divided into long outstretched members, each of which possesses the property which legitimatizes it as a vesicle in the ordinary sense of the word; it contains, enclosed within a delicate structureless wall, those bodies which bear the appearance of a finely granulated mucous substance, which is designated by the name of protoplasm, and which either equally fills the cells, or the older the cell the more it is filled with watery cavities called vacuoles.

All parts are at first colourless. The increase in the length of the filaments takes place through the preponderating growth near their points; these continually push forward, and, at a short distance from them, successive new partitions rise up, but at a greater distance, the growth in the length ceases. This kind of growth is called point growth. The twigs and

* De Bary, "Uber die Brandpilze" (Berlin, 1853), pl. iv. figs. 3, 4, 5.

† A. de Bary, on Mildew and Fermentation, in "Quarterly German Magazine," vol. ii. 1872.

branches spring up as lateral dilatations of the principal filament, which, once designed, enlarges according to the point growth. This point growth of every branch is, to a certain extent, unlimited. The filaments in and on the substratum are the first existing members of the fungus; they continue so long as it vegetates. As the parts which absorb nourishment from and consume the substance, they are called the *mycelium*. Nearly every fungus possesses a mycelium, which, without regard to the specific difference of form and size, especially shows the described nature in its construction and growth.

The superficial threads of the mycelium produce other filaments beside those numerous branches which have been described, and which are the fruit thread (carpophore) or conidia thread. These are on an average thicker than the mycelium threads, and only exceptionally ramified or furnished with partitions; they rise almost perpendicularly into the air, and attain a length of, on an average, half a millimetre, or one-fiftieth of an inch, but they seldom become longer, and then their growth is at an end. Their free upper end swells in a rounded manner, and from this is produced, on the whole of its upper part, rayed divergent protuberances, which attain an oval form, and a length almost equal to their radius, or, in weaker specimens, the diameter of the rounded head. The rayed divergent protuberances are the direct producers and bearers of the propagating cells, spores, or conidia, and are called sterigmata. Every sterigma at first produces at its point a little round protuberance, which, with a strong narrow basis, rests upon the sterigma. These are filled with protoplasm, swell more and more, and, after some time, separate themselves by a partion from the sterigma into independent cells, spores, or conidia.

The formation of the first spore takes place at the same end of the sterigma, and in the same manner a second follows, then a third, and so on; every one which springs up later pushes its predecessor in the direction of the axis of the sterigma in the same degree in which it grows itself; every successive spore formed from a sterigma remains for a time in a row with one another. Consequently every sterigma bears on its apex a chain of spores, which are so much the older, the farther they stand from the sterigma. The number of the links in a chain of spores reaches in normal specimens to ten or more. All sterigmata spring up at the same time, and keep pace with one another in the formation of the spores. Every spore grows for a time, according to its construction, and at last separates itself from

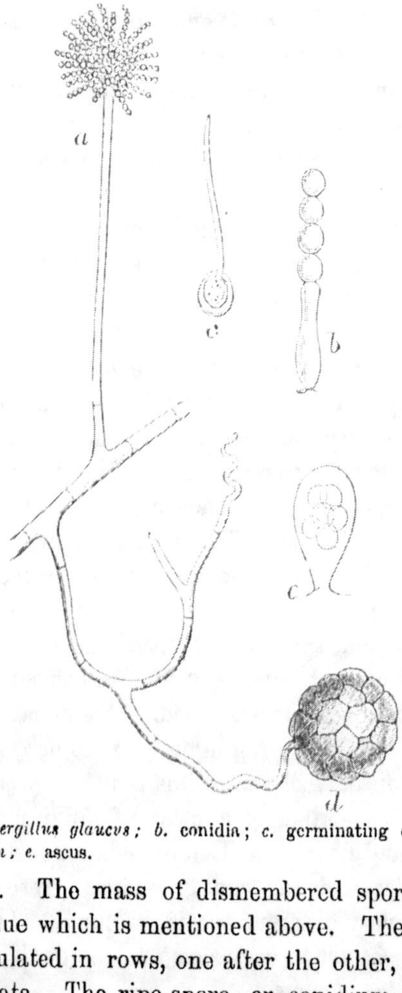

FIG. 102.—*a. Aspergillus glaucus*; *b.* conidia; *c.* germinating conidium; *d.* conceptacle of *Eurotium*; *e.* ascus.

its neighbours. The mass of dismembered spores forms that fine glaucous hue which is mentioned above. The spores, therefore, are articulated in rows, one after the other, from the ends of the sterigmata. The ripe spore, or conidium, is a cell of a round or broadly oval form, filled with a colourless protoplasm, and, if observed separately, is found to be provided with a brownish, finely verruculose, dotted wall.

The same mycelium which forms the pedicel for the conidia when it is near the end of its development, forms by normal vegetation a second kind of fructification. It begins as delicate thin little branches, which are not to be distinguished by the naked eye, and which mostly in four or six turns, after a quickly terminated growth, wind their ends like a corkscrew. (Fig. 102.) The sinuations decrease in width more and more, till they at last reach close to one another, and the whole end changes from the form of a corkscrew into that of a hollow screw. In and on that screw-like body, a change of a complicated kind takes place, which is a productive process. In consequence of this, from the screw body a globose receptacle is formed, consisting of a thin wall of delicate cells, and a closely entwined row of cells surrounded by this dense mass (*d*). By the enlargement of all these parts the round body grows so much, that by the time it is ripe it is visible to the naked eye. The outer surface of the wall assumes a compactness and a bright yellow colour; the greater part of the cells of the inner mass become asci for the formation of sporidia, while they free themselves from the reciprocal union, take a broad oval form, and each one produces within its inner space eight sporidia (*e*). These soon entirely fill the ascus. When they are quite ripe, the wall of the conceptacle becomes brittle, and from irregular fissures, arising easily from contact, the colourless round sporidia are liberated.

The pedicels of both kinds of fruit are formed from the same mycelium in the order just described. If we examine attentively, we can often see both springing up close to one another from the same filament of a mycelium. This is not very easy in the close interlacing of the stalks of a mass of fungi in consequence of their delicacy and fragility. Before their connection was known, the conceptacles and the conidia pedicels were considered as organs of two very different species of fungi. The conceptacles were called *Eurotium herbariorum*, and the conidia bearers were called *Aspergillus glaucus*.

Allied to *Eurotium* is the group of *Erysiphei*, in which well-authenticated polymorphy prevails. These fungi are developed on the green parts of growing plants, and at first consist of a white mouldy stratum, composed of delicate mycelium, on which erect threads are produced, which break up into subglobose joints or conidia. The species on grass was named *Oidium monilioides* before its relationship was known, but undoubtedly this is only the conidia of *Erysiphe graminis*. In like manner the vine disease (*Oidium Tuckeri*) is most probably only the conidia of a species of *Erysiphe*, of which the perfect condition has not yet been discovered. On roses the old *Oidium leuco-conium* is but the conidia of *Sphærotheca pannosa*, and so of other species. The *Erysiphe* which ultimately appears on the same mycelium consists of globose perithecia, externally

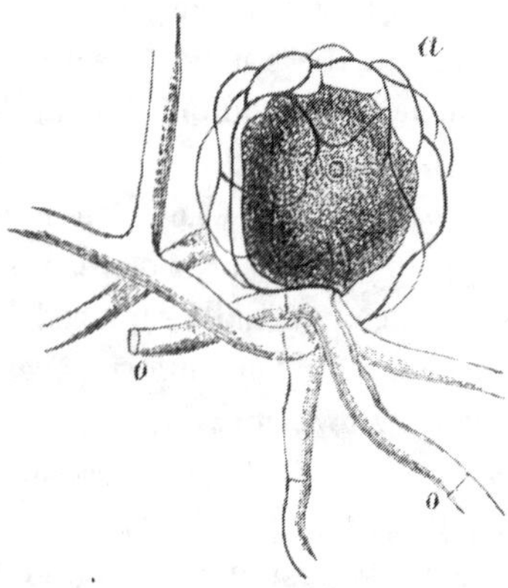

FIG. 103.—*Erysiphe cichoracearum*. *a*. Receptacle; *o*. mycelium. (De Bary.)

furnished with thread-like appendages, and internally with asci containing sporidia. In this genus there are no less than five different forms of fruit,* the multiform threads on the mycelium, already alluded to as forms of *Oidium*, the asci contained in the sporangia, which is the proper fruit of the *Erysiphe*, larger stylospores which are produced in other sporangia, the smaller stylospores which are generated in the pycnidia, and separate sporules which are sometimes formed in the joints of the necklaces of the conidia. These forms are figured in the "Introduction

* Berkeley, "Introd. Crypt. Bot." p. 78, fig. 20.

to Cryptogamic Botany" from *Sphærotheca Castagnei*, which is the hop mildew.* The vine disease, hop mildew, and rose mildew, are the most destructive species of this group, and the constant annoyance of cultivators.

When first describing an allied fungus found on old paper, and named *Ascotricha chartarum*, the Rev. M. J. Berkeley called attention to the presence of globose conidia attached to the threads which surround the conceptacles,† and this occurred as long since as 1838. In a recent species of *Chætomium* found on old sacking, *Chætomium griseum*, Cooke,‡ we have found tufts in all respects similar externally to the *Chætomium*, but no perithecium was formed, naked conidia being developed apparently at the base of the coloured threads. In *Chætomium funicolum*, Cooke, a black mould was also found which may possibly prove to be its conidia, but at present there is no direct evidence.

The brothers Tulasne have made us acquainted with a greater number of instances amongst the *Sphæriacei* in which multiple organs of reproduction prevail. Very often old and decaying individuals belonging to species of *Boletus* will be found filled, and their entire substance internally replaced, by the threads and multitudinous spores of a golden yellow parasite, to which the name of *Sepedonium chrysospermum* has been given. According to Tulasne, this is merely a condition of a sphæriaceous fungus belonging to his genus *Hypomyces*.§

The same observers also first demonstrated that *Trichoderma viride*, P., was but the conidia-bearing stage of *Hypocrea rufa*, P., another sphæriaceous fungus. The ascigerous stroma of the latter is indeed frequently associated in a very close manner with the cushions of the pretended *Trichoderma*, or in other cases the same stroma will give rise to a different apparatus of conidia, of which the principal elements are acicular filaments, which are short, upright, and almost simple, and which give rise to small

* See also Berkeley, in "Trans. Hort. Soc. London," vol. ix. p. 68.

† Berkeley, in "Ann. Nat. Hist." (June, 1838), No. 116.

‡ "Grevillea," vol. i. p. 176.

§ Tulasne, "On Certain Fungicolous Sphæriæ," in "Ann. des Sci. Nat." 4me sér. xiii. (1860), p. 5.

oval conidia which are solitary on the tips of the threads. Therefore this *Hypocrea* will possess two different kinds of conidia, as is the case in many species of *Hypomyces.*

A most familiar instance of dualism will be found in *Nectria cinnabarina*, of which the conidia form is one of the most common of fungi, forming little reddish nodules on all kinds of dead twigs.*

Almost any small currant twig which has been lying on the ground in a damp situation will afford an opportunity of studying this phenomenon. The whole surface of the twig will be covered from end to end with little bright pink prominences, bursting through the bark at regular distances, scarcely a quarter of an inch apart. Towards one end of the twig probably the prominences will be of a deeper, richer colour, like powdered cinnabar. The naked eye is sufficient to detect some difference between the two kinds of pustules, and where the two merge into each other specks of cinnabar will be visible on the pink projections. By removing the bark it will be seen that the pink bodies have a sort of paler stem, which spreads above into a somewhat globose head, covered with a delicate mealy bloom. At the base it penetrates to the inner bark, and from it the threads of mycelium branch in all directions, confined, however, to the bark, and not entering the woody tissues beneath. The head, placed under examination, will be found to consist of delicate parallel threads compacted together to form the stem and head. Some of these threads are simple, others are branched, bearing here and there upon them delicate little bodies, which are readily detached, and which form the mealy bloom which covers the surface. These are the conidia, little slender cylindrical bodies, rounded at the ends.

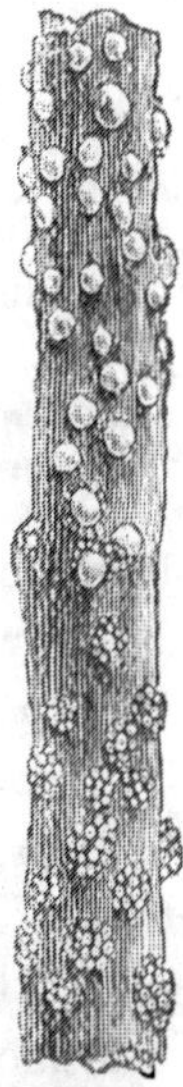

FIG. 104. — Twig with *Tubercularia* on the upper portion, *Nectria* on the lower.

Passing to the other bodies, which are of a deeper colour, it

* "A Currant Twig, and Something on it," in "Gardener's Chronicle," January 28, 1871.

will soon be discovered that, instead of being simple rounded heads, each tubercle is composed of numerous smaller, nearly globose bodies, closely packed together, often compressed, all

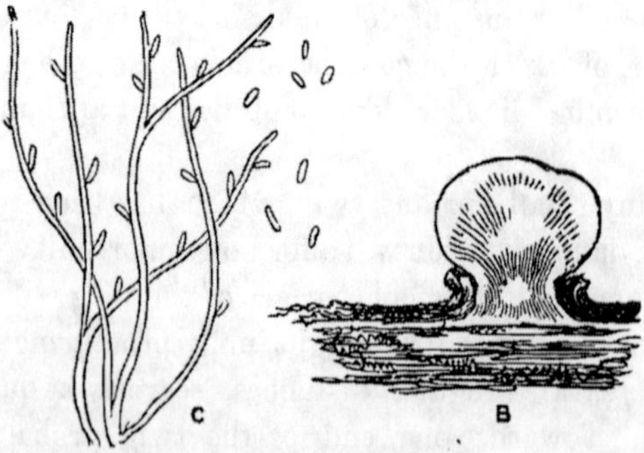

FIG. 105.—Section of *Tubercularia*. *c.* Threads with conidia.*

united to a base closely resembling the base of the other tubercles. If for a moment we look at one of the tubercles near the spot where the crimson tubercles seem to merge into the pink, we shall not only find them particoloured, but that the red points are the identical globose little heads just observed in clusters. This will lead to the suspicion, which can afterwards be verified, that the red heads are really produced on the stem or stroma of the pink tubercles.

A section of one of the red tubercles will show us how much the internal structure differs. The little subglobose bodies which spring from a common stroma or stem are hollow shells or capsules, externally granular, internally filled with a gelatinous nucleus. They are, indeed, the perithecia of a sphæriaceous fungus of the genus *Nectria*, and the gelatinous nucleus contains the fructification. Still further examination will show that this fructification consists of cylindrical asci, each enclosing eight elliptical sporidia, closely packed together, and mixed with slender threads called paraphyses.

Here, then, we have undoubted evidence of *Nectria cinnabarina*, with its fruit, produced in asci growing from the stroma or stem, and in intimate relationship with what was formerly named *Tubercularia vulgaris*. A fungus with two forms of fruit,

* Figs. 104 to 106 by permission from the "Gardener's Chronicle."

one proper to the pink, or *Tubercularia* form, with naked slender conidia, the other proper to the mature fungus, enclosed in asci, and generated within the walls of a perithecium. Instances of this kind are now known to be far from uncommon, although

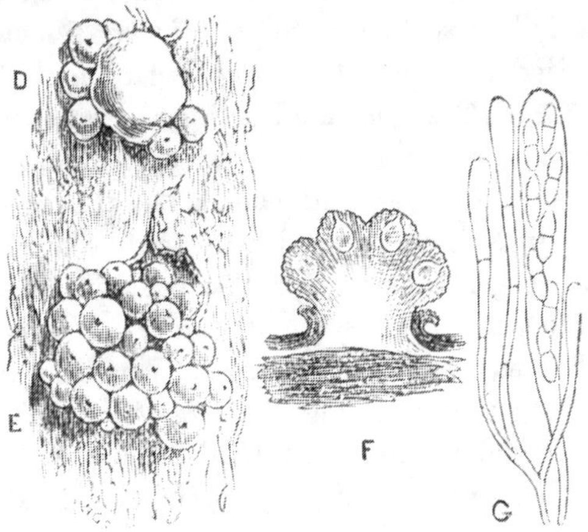

FIG. 106.—D. *Nectria* surrounding *Tubercularia*; E. tuft of *Nectria cinnabarina*; F. section of stroma; G. ascus and paraphyses.

they cannot always, or often, be so clearly and distinctly traced as in the illustration which we have selected.

It is not uncommon for the conidia of the *Sphæria* to partake of the characteristics of a mould, and then the perithecia are developed amongst the conidial threads. A recently recorded instance of this relates to *Sphæria Epochnii*, B. and Br.,* the conidia form of which was long known before the *Sphæria* related to it was discovered, under the name of *Epochnium, fungorum.* The *Epochnium* forms a thin stratum, which overruns various species of *Corticium.* The conidia are at first uniseptate. The perithecia of the *Sphæria* are at first pale bottle-green, crowded in the centre of the *Epochnium*, then black green granulated, sometimes depressed at the summit, with a minute pore. The sporidia are strongly constricted in the centre, at first uniseptate, with two nuclei in each division.

Another *Sphæria* in which the association is undoubted is the

* Berkeley and Broome, in "Annals of Natural History" (1866), No. 1177, pl. v. fig. 36; Cooke, "Handbook," ii. p. 866.

Sphæria aquila, Fr.,* which is almost always found nestling in a woolly brown subiculum, for the most part composed of barren brown jointed threads. These threads, however, produce, under favourable conditions, mostly before the perfection of the perithecia, minute subglobose conidia, and in this state constitute what formerly bore the name of *Sporotrichum fuscum*, Link., but now recognized as the conidia of *Sphæria aquila.*

In *Sphæria nidulans*, Schw., a North American species, we have more than once found the dark brown subiculum bearing large triseptate conidia, having all the characters of the genus *Helminthosporium.* In *Sphæria pilosa*, P., Messrs. Berkeley and Broome have observed oblong conidia, rather irregular in outline, terminating the hairs of the perithecium.† The same authors have also figured the curious pentagonal conidia springing from flexuous threads accompanying *Sphæria felina*, Fckl.,‡ and also the threads resembling those of a *Cladotrichum* with the angular conidia of *Sphæria cupulifera*, B. and Br.§ A most remarkable example is also given by the Brothers Tulasne in *Pleospora polytricha*, in which the conidia-bearing threads not only surround, but grow upon the perithecia, and are crowned by fascicles of septate conidia.‖

Instances of this kind have now become so numerous that only a few can be cited as examples of the rest. It is not at all improbable that the majority of what are now classed together as species under the genus of black moulds, *Helminthosporium*, will at some not very distant period be traced as the conidia of different species of ascomycetous fungi. The same fate may also await other allied genera, but until this association is established, they must keep the rank and position which has been assigned to them.

Another form of dualism, differing somewhat in character

* Cooke, "Handbook," ii. p. 853, No. 2549 ; specimens in Cooke's "Fungi Britannici Exsiccati," No. 270.

† Berk. and Br. "Ann. Nat. Hist." (1865), No. 1096.

‡ "Ann. Nat. Hist." (1871), No. 1332, pl. xx. fig. 23.

§ Ibid. No. 1333, pl. xxi. fig. 24.

‖ Tulasne, "Selecta Fungorum Carpologia," ii. p. 269, pl. 29.

from the foregoing, finds illustration in the sphæriaceous genus *Melanconis*, of Tulasne, in which the free spores are still called conidia, though in most instances produced in a sort of spurious conceptaculum, or borne on short threads from a kind of cushion-shaped stroma. In the *Melanconis stilbostoma*,* there are three forms, one of slender minute bodies, oozing out in the form of yellow tendrils, which may be spermatia, formerly called *Nemaspora crocea*. Then there are the oval brown or olive brown conidia, which are at first covered, then oozing out in a black pasty mass, formerly *Melanconium bicolor*, and finally the sporidia in asci of *Sphæria stilbostoma*, Fries. In *Melanconis Berkeleii*, Tul., the conidia are quadrilocular, previously known as *Stilbospora macrosperma*, B. and Br. In a closely-allied species from North America, *Melanconis bicornis*, Cooke, the appendiculate sporidia are similar, and the conidia would also appear to partake of the character of *Stilbospora*. We may remark here that we have seen a brown mould, probably an undescribed species of *Dematiei*, growing in definite patches around the openings in birch bark caused by the erumpent ostiola of the perithecia of *Melanconis stilbostoma*, from the United States.

In *Melanconis lanciformis*,† Tul., there are, it would appear, four forms of fruit. One of these consists of conidia, characterized by Corda as *Coryneum disciforme*.‡ Stylospores, which are also figured by Corda under the name of *Coniothecium betulinum*; pycnidia,§ first discovered by Berkeley and Broome, and named by them *Hendersonia polycystis*; || and the ascophorous fruits which constituted the *Sphæria lanciformis* of Fries. Mr. Currey indicated *Hendersonia polycystis*, B. and Br., as a form of fruit of this species in a communication to the Royal Society in 1857.¶ He says this plant grows upon birch, and is in perfection in very moist weather, when it may be recognized by the

* Cooke, "Handbook," ii. p. 878; Tulasne, "Carpologia," ii. p. 120, plate 14.

† Tulasne, "Selecta Fung. Carp.," ii. plate 16.

‡ Corda, "Icones Fungorum," vol. iii. fig. 91.

§ Corda, "Icones," vol. i. fig. 25.

|| Berk. and Br. "Ann. Nat. Hist." No. 415.

¶ Currey, in "Philosoph. Trans. Roy. Soc." (1857), pl. 25.

large black soft gelatinous protuberances on the bark, formed by spores escaping and depositing themselves upon and about the apex of the perithecium. This I suspect to be an abnormal state of a well-known Sphæria (*S. lanciformis*), which grows upon birch, and upon birch only.

We might multiply, almost indefinitely, instances amongst the *Sphæriacei*, but have already given sufficient for illustration, and will therefore proceed briefly to notice some instances amongst the *Discomycetes*, which also bear their complete or perfect fruit in asci.

The beautiful purple stipitate cups of *Bulgaria sarcoides*, which may be seen flourishing in the autumn on old rotten wood, are often accompanied by club-shaped bodies of the same colour; or earlier in the season these clavate bodies may be found alone, and at one time bore the name of *Tremella sarcoides*. The upper part of these clubs disseminate a great abundance of straight and very slender spermatia. Earlier than this they are covered with globose conidia. The fully-matured *Bulgaria* develops on its hymenium clavate delicate asci, each enclosing eight elongated hyaline sporidia, so that we have three forms of fruit belonging to the same fungus, viz. conidia and spermatia in the *Tremella* stage, and sporidia contained in asci in the mature condition.* The same phenomena occur with *Bulgaria purpurea*, a larger species with different fruit, long confounded with *Bulgaria sarcoides*.

On the dead stems of nettles it is very common to meet with small orange tubercles, not much larger than a pin's head, which yield at this stage a profusion of slender linear bodies, produced on delicate branched threads, and at one time bore the name of *Dacrymyces Urticæ*, but which are now acknowledged to be only a condition of a little tremelloid *Peziza* of the same size and colour, which might be mistaken for it, if not examined with the microscope, but in which there are distinct asci and sporidia. Both forms together are now regarded as the same fungus, under the name of *Peziza fusarioides*, B.

* Tulasne, "On the Reproductive Apparatus of Fungi," in "Comptes Rendus" (1852), p. 841; and Tulasne, "Selecta Fungorum Carpologia," vol. iii.

The other series of phenomena grouped together under the name of polymorphism relate to forms which are removed from each other, so that the mycelium is not identical, or, more usually, produced on different plants. The first instance of this kind to which we shall make reference is one of particular interest, as illustrative of the old popular creed, that berberry bushes near corn-fields produced mildewed corn. There is a village in Norfolk, not far from Great Yarmouth, called "Mildew Rollesby," because of its unenviable notoriety in days past for mildewed corn, produced, it was said, by the berberry bushes, which were cut down, and then mildew disappeared from the corn-fields, so that Rollesby no longer merited its *sobriquet*. It has already been shown that the corn-mildew (*Puccinia graminis*) is dimorphous, having a one-celled fruit (*Trichobasis*), as well as a two-celled fruit (*Puccinia*). The fungus which attacks the berberry is a species of cluster-cup (*Æcidium berberidis*), in which little cup-like peridia, containing bright orange pseudospores, are produced in tufts or clusters on the green leaves, together with their spermogonia.

De Bary's observations on this association of forms were published in 1865.* In view of the popular belief, he determined to sow the spores of *Puccinia graminis* on the leaves of the berberry. For this purpose he selected the septate resting spores from *Poa pratensis* and *Triticum repens*. Having caused the spores to germinate in a moist atmosphere, he placed fragments of the leaves on which they had developed their secondary spores on young but full-grown berberry leaves, under the same atmospheric conditions. In from twenty-four to forty-eight hours a quantity of the germinating threads had bored through the walls and penetrated amongst the subjacent cells. This took place both on the upper and under surface of the leaves. Since, in former experiments, it appeared that the spores would penetrate only in those cases where the plant was adapted to develop the parasite, the connection between *P. graminis* and

* "Monatsbericht der Koniglichen Preuss, Acad. der Wissenschaften au Berlin," Jan. 1865; Summary, in "Journ. Roy. Hort. Soc., London," vol. i. n.s. p. 107.

Æcid. berberidis seemed more than ever probable. In about ten days the spermogonia appeared. After a time the cut leaves began to decay, so that the fungus never got beyond the spermogonoid stage. Some three-year-old seedlings were then taken, and the germinating resting spores applied as before. The plants were kept under a bell-glass from twenty-four to forty-eight hours, and then exposed to the air like other plants. From the sixth to the tenth day, yellow spots appeared, with single spermogonia; from the ninth to the twelfth, spermógonia appeared in numbers on either surface; and, a few days later, on the under surface of the leaves, the cylindrical sporangia of the *Æcidium* made their appearance, exactly as in the normally developed parasite, except that they were longer, from being protected from external agents. The younger the leaves, the more rapid was the development of the parasite, and sometimes, in the younger leaves, the luxuriance was far greater than in free nature. Similar plants, to the number of two hundred, were observed in the nursery, and though some of them had *Æcidium* pustules, not one fresh pustule was produced; while two placed under similar circumstances, but without the application of any resting spores, remained all the summer free from *Æcidium.* It seems, then, indubitable so far that *Æcidium berberidis* does spring from the spores of *Puccinia graminis.*

It has, however, to be remarked that De Bary was not equally successful in producing the *Puccinia* from the spores of the *Æcidium.* In many cases the spores do not germinate when placed on glass, and they do not preserve their power of germinating very long. He reverts then to the evidence of experiments instituted by agriculturists. Bönninghausen remarked, in 1818, that wheat, rye, and barley which were sown in the neighbourhood of a berberry bush covered with *Æcidium* contracted rust immediately after the maturation of the spores of the *Æcidia.* The rust was most abundant where the wind carried the spores. The following year the same observations were repeated; the spores of the *Æcidium* were collected, and applied to some healthy plants of rye. After five or six days these plants were affected with rust, while the remainder of the crop was sound. In 1863 some winter rye was sown round a berberry bush, which in the following year was infested with *Æcidium*, which was mature in the middle of May, when the rye was completely covered with rust. Of the wild grasses near the bush, *Triticum repens* was most affected. The distant plants of rye were free from rust.

The spores of the *Æcidium* would not germinate on berberry leaves; the berberry *Æcidium* could not therefore spring from the previous *Æcidium.* The uredospores of *Puccinia graminis* on germinating penetrate into the parenchym of the grass on which they are sown; but on berberry leaves, if the tips of the threads enter for a short distance into the stomates their growth at once ceases, and the leaves remain free from parasites.

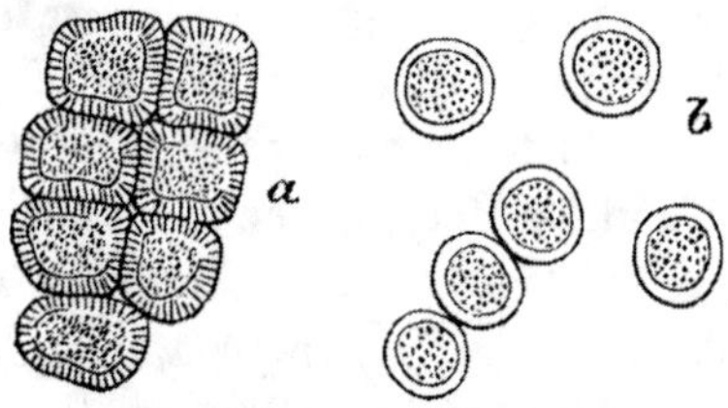

FIG. 107.—Cells and pseudospores of *Æcidium berberidis.*

Montagne has, however, described a *Puccinia berberidis* on leaves of *Berberis glauca* from Chili, which grows in company

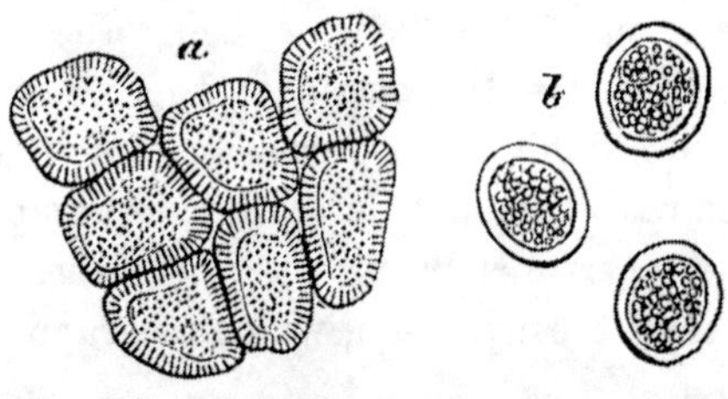

FIG. 108.—Cells and pseudospores of *Æcidium graveolens.*

with *Æcidium berberidis.* This at first sight seems to contradict the above conclusions; but the *Æcidium* which from the same disc produces the puccinoid resting spores, appears to be different from the European species, inasmuch as the cells of the wall of the sporangium are twice as large, and the spores decidedly of greater diameter.* The resting spores, moreover,

* We have before us an *Æcidium* on leaves of *Berberis vulgaris,* collected at

differ not only from those of *Puccinia graminis*, but from those of all other European species.

From this account, then, it is extremely probable that the *Æcidium* of the berberry enters into the cycle of existence of *Puccinia graminis*, and, if this be true, wherefore should not other species of *Puccinia* be related in like manner to other *Æcidia?* This is the conclusion to which many have arrived, and, taking advantage of certain presumptions, have, we fear, rashly associated many such forms together without substantial evidence. On the leaves of the primrose we have commonly a species of *Æcidium*, *Puccinia*, and *Uromyces* nearly at the same time; we may imagine that all these belong to one cycle, but it has not yet been proved. Again, *Uromyces cacaliæ*, Unger, *Uredo cacaliæ*, Unger, and *Æcidium cacaliæ*, Thumen, are considered by Heufler * to form one cycle. Numerous others are given by Fuckel,† and De Bary, in the same memoir from which we have already cited, notes *Uromyces appendiculatus*, Link., *U. phaseolorum*, Tul., and *Puccinia tragopogonis*, Ca., as possessing five kinds of reproductive organs. Towards the end of the year, shortly stipitate spores appear on their stroma, which do not fall off. These spores, which do not germinate till after a shorter or longer winter rest, may conveniently be called resting spores, or, as De Bary calls them, *teleutospores*, being the last which are produced. These at length germinate, become articulated, and produce ovate or kidney-shaped spores, which in their turn germinate, penetrating the cuticle of the mother plant, avoiding the stomates or apertures by which it breathes. After about two or three weeks, the mycelium, which has ramified among the

Berne by Shuttleworth in 1833. It is named by him *Æcidium graveolens*, and differs in the following particulars from *Æcidium berberidis*. The peridia are scattered as in *Æ. Epilobii*, and not collected in clusters. They are not so much elongated. The cells are larger, and the orange spores nearly twice the diameter. There is a decided, strong, but unpleasant odour in the fresh plant; hence the name. The above figures (figs. 107, 108). of the cells and spores of both species are drawn by camera lucida to the same scale—380 diameters.

* Freiherrn von Hohenbühel-Heufler, in "Œsterr. Botan. Zeitschrift," No. 3, 1870.

† "Fuckel Symbolæ Mycologicæ" (1869), p. 49.

tissues, produces an *Æcidium*, with its constant companion, spermogonia—distinct cysts, that is, from which a quantity of minute bodies ooze out, often in the form of a tendril, the function of which is imperfectly known at present, but which from analogy we regard as a form of fruit, though it is just possible that they may be rather of the nature of spermatozoids. The *Æcidia* contain, within a cellular membranous sac, a fructifying disc, which produces necklaces of spores, which ultimately separate from each other in the form of a granular powder. The grains of which it is composed germinate in their turn, no longer avoiding the stomates as before, but penetrating through their aperture into the parenchym. The new resultant mycelium reproduces the *Uredo*, or fifth form of fructification, and the *Uredo* spores fall off like those of the *Æcidium*, and in respect of germination, and mode of penetration, present precisely the same phenomena. The disc which has produced the *Uredo* spores now gives rise to the resting spores, and so the cycle is complete.*

The late Professor Œrsted, of Copenhagen, was of opinion that he had demonstrated the polymorphy of the Tremelloid Uredines, and satisfied himself that the one condition known as *Podisoma* was but another stage of *Rœstelia*.† Some freshly gathered specimens of *Gymnosporangium* were damped with water, and during the night following the spores germinated profusely, so that the teleutospores formed an orange-coloured powder. A little of this powder was placed on the leaves of five small sorbs, which were damped and placed under bell-glasses. In five days yellow spots were seen on the leaves, and in two days more indications of spermogonia. The spermatia were discharged, and in two months from the first sowing,

* Almost simultaneously with De Bary, the late Professor Œrsted instituted experiments, from which the same results ensued, as to *Æcidium berberidis* and *Puccinia graminis*. See "Journ. Hort. Soc. Lond." new ser. i. p. 85.

† "Oversigt over det Kon. Danske Videns. Selskabs" (1866), p. 185, t. 3, 4; (1867,) p. 208, t. 3, 4; "Résumé du Bulletin de la Soc. Roy. Danoise des Sciences" (1866), p. 15; (1867), p. 38; "Botanische Zeitung" (1867), p. 104; "Quekett Microscopical Club Journal," vol. ii. p. 260.

the peridia of *Rœstelia* appeared, and were developed. "This trial of spores," says Œrsted, "has conduced to the result expected, and proves that the teleutospores of *Gymnosporangium*, when transported upon the sorb, give rise to a totally different fungus, the *Rœstelia cornuta*, that is to say, that an alternate generation comes between these fungi. They appertain in consequence to a single species, and the *Gymnosporangium* ceased to be an independent species, and must be considered as synonymous with the first generation of *Rœstelia*. The spores have been transported upon young shoots of the juniper-tree, and have now commenced to produce some mycelium in the bark. There is no doubt that in next spring it will result in *Gymnosporangium*."

Subsequently the same learned professor instituted similar experiments upon other hosts, with the spores of *Podisoma*, and from thence he concluded that *Rœstelia* and *Podisoma*, in all their known species, were but forms the one of the other. Hitherto we are not aware that these results have been confirmed, or that the sowing of the spores of *Rœstelia* on juniper resulted in *Podisoma*. Such experiments should be received always with care, and not too hastily accepted in their apparent results as proven facts. Who shall say that *Rœstelia* would not have appeared on *Sorbus* within two months without the sowing of *Podisoma* spores?—because it is not by any means uncommon for that fungus to appear upon that plant. It is true many mycologists write and speak of *Rœstelia* and *Podisoma* (or *Gymnosporangium*) as identical; but, as we think, without the evidence being so complete as to be beyond suspicion. It is, nevertheless, a curious fact that in Europe the number of species of *Rœstelia* and *Podisoma* are equal, if one species be excluded, which is certainly not a good *Podisoma*, for the reception of which a new genus has been proposed.*

Amongst the ascigerous fungi will be found a curious but interesting genus formerly called *Cordyceps*, but for which Tulasne, in consequence of the discovery of secondary forms of fruit,

* This is *Podisoma foliicola*, B. and Br., or, as proposed in "Journ. Quekett Club," ii. p. 267, *Sarcostroma Berkeleyi*, C.

has substituted that of *Torrubia.** These curious fungi partake more or less of a clavate form, and are parasitic on insects. The pupæ of moths are sometimes seen bearing upon them the white branched mould, something like a *Clavaria* in appearance, to which the name of *Isaria farinosa* has been given. According to Tulasne, this is the conidia form of the bright scarlet, club-shaped body which is also found on dead pupæ, called *Torrubia militaris*. An American mould of the same genus, *Isaria sphingum*, found on mature moths,† is in like manner declared to be the conidia of *Torrubia sphingum;* whereas a similar mould, found on dead spiders, called *Isaria arachnophila*,‡ is probably of a similar nature. An allied kind of compact mould, which is parasitic on *Cocci*, on the bark of trees, recently found in England by Mr. C. E. Broome, and named *Microcera coccophila*,§ is said by Tulasne to be a condition of *Sphærostilbe*, and it is intimated that other productions of a similar character bear like relations to other sphœriaceous fungi. For many species of *Torrubia* no corresponding conidia are yet known.

Some instances might be noted, not without interest, in which the facts of dimorphism or polymorphism have not been satisfactorily proved, but final judgment is held in suspense until suspicion is replaced by conviction. Some years since, a quantity of dead box leaves were collected, on which flourished at the time a mould named *Penicillium roseum*. This mould has a roseate tint, and occurs in patches on the dead leaves lying upon the ground; the threads are erect and branched above, bearing chains of oblong, somewhat spindle-shaped spores, or, perhaps more accurately, conidia. When collected, these leaves were examined, and nothing was observed or noted upon them except this *Penicillium*. After some time, certainly between two and three years, during which period the box remained undisturbed, circumstances led to the examination again of one or two of the leaves, and afterwards of the greater number of them, when the

* Tulasne, "Selecta Fungorum Carpologia," iii. p. 6, pl. i. figs. 19-31.

† Cramer's "Papilio Exotic" (1782), fig. 267.

‡ Cooke, "Handbook," p. 548, No. 1639.

§ Ibid. p. 556, No. 1666.

patches of *Penicillium* were found to be intermixed with another mould of a higher development, and far different character. This mould, or rather *Mucor*, consists of erect branching threads, many of the branches terminating in a delicate globose, glassy head, or sporangium, containing numerous very minute subglobose sporidia. This species was named *Mucor hyalinus*.* The habit is very much like that of the *Penicillium*, but without any roseate tint. It is almost certain that the *Mucor* could not have been present when the *Penicillium* was examined, and the leaves on which it had grown were enclosed in the tin box, but that the *Mucor* afterwards appeared on the same leaves, sometimes from the same patches, and, as it would appear, from the same mycelium. The great difference in the two species lies in the fructification. In the *Penicillium*, the spores are naked, and in moniliform threads; whilst in *Mucor* the spores are enclosed within globose membraneous heads or sporangia. Scarcely can we doubt that the *Mucor* alluded to above, found thus intermixed, under peculiar circumstances, with *Penicillium roseum*, is no other than the higher and more complete form of that species, and that the *Penicillium* is only its conidiiferous state. The presumption in this case is strong, and not so open to suspicion as it would be did not analogy render it so extremely probable that such is the case, apart from the fact of both forms springing from the same mass of mycelium. In such minute and delicate structures it is very difficult to manipulate the specimens so as to arrive at positive evidence. If a filament of mycelium could be isolated successfully, and a fertile thread, bearing the fruit of each form, could be traced from the same individual mycelium thread, the evidence would be conclusive. In default of such conclusive evidence, we are compelled to rest with assumption until further researches enable us to record the assumption as fact.†

Apropos of this very connection of *Penicillium* with *Mucor*, a similar suspicion attaches to an instance noted by a wholly dis-

* Specimens were published under this name in Cooke's "Fungi Britannici Exsiccati," No. 359.

† Cooke, "On Polymorphism in Fungi," in "Popular Science Review."

interested observer to this effect. "On a preparation preserved in a moist chamber, on the third day a white speck was seen on the surface, consisting of innumerable 'yeast' cells, with some filaments, branching in all directions. On the fourth day tufts of *Penicillium* had developed two varieties—*P. glaucum* and *P. viride.* This continued until the ninth day, when a few of the filaments springing up in the midst of the *Penicillium* were tipped with a dewdrop-like dilatation, excessively delicate—a mere distended pellicle. In some cases they seemed to be derived from the same filament as others bearing the ordinary branching spores of *Penicillium*, but of this I could not be positive. This kind of fructification increased rapidly, and on the fourteenth day spores had undoubtedly developed within the pellicle, just as had been observed in a previous cultivation, precisely similar revolving movements being also manifested."* Although we have here another instance of *Mucor* and *Penicillium* growing in contact, the evidence is insufficient to warrant more than a suspicion of their identity, inasmuch as the equally minute spores of *Mucor* and *Penicillium* might have mingled, and each producing its kind, no relationship whatever have existed between them, except their development from the same matrix.

Another case of association—for the evidence does not proceed further—was recorded by us, in which a dark-coloured species of *Penicillium* was closely associated with what we now believe to be a species of *Macrosporium*—but then designated a *Sporidesmium*—and a minute *Sphæria* growing in succession on damp wall-paper. Association is all that the *facts* warrant us in calling it.

We cannot forbear alluding to one of the species of *Sphæria* to which Tulasne † attributes a variety of forms of fruit, and we do so here because we think that a circumstance so extraordinary should be confirmed before it is accepted as absolutely true. This refers to the common *Sphæria* found on herbaceous plants,

* Lewis's "Report on Microscopic Objects found in Cholera Evacuations," Calcutta, 1870.

† Tulasne, "Selecta Fungorum Carpologia," ii. p. 261.

known as *Sphæria* (*Pleospora*) *herbarum*. First of all the very common mould called *Cladosporium herbarum* is constituted as conidia, and of this again *Macrosporium sarcinula*, Berk., is considered to be another condition. In the next place, *Cytispora orbicularis*, Berk., and *Phoma herbarum*, West, are regarded as pycnidia, enclosing stylospores. Then *Alternaria tenuis*, Pr.,* which is said to be parasitic on *Cladosporium herbarum*, is held to be only a form of that species, so that here we have (including the *perithecia*) no less than six forms or phases for the same fungus. As *Macrosporium Cheiranthi*, Pr., often is found in company with *Cladosporium herbarum*, that is also open to suspicion.

We have adduced in the foregoing pages a few instances which will serve to illustrate the polymorphism of fungi. Some of these it will be observed are accepted as beyond doubt, occurring as they do in intimate relationship with each other. Others are considered as scarcely so well established, but probable, although developed sometimes on different species of plants. Finally, some are regarded as hitherto not satisfactorily proved, or, it may be, only suspicious. In this latter group, however much probability may be in their favour, it can hardly be deemed philosophical to accept them on such slender evidence as in some cases alone is afforded. It would not have been difficult to have extended the latter group considerably by the addition of instances enumerated by various mycologists in their works without any explanation of the data upon which their conclusions have been founded. In fact, altogether this chapter must be accepted as illustrative and suggestive, but by no means as exhaustive.

* Corda, "Prachtflora," plate vii.

X.

INFLUENCES AND EFFECTS.

It is no longer doubted that fungi exercise a large and very important influence in the economy of nature. It may be that in some directions these influences are exaggerated; but it is certain that on the whole their influence is far more important for evil and for good than that of any other of the Cryptogamia. In our endeavour to estimate the character and extent of these influences it will prove advantageous to examine them under three sections. 1. Their influence on man. 2. Their influence on lower animals. 3. Their influence on vegetation. Under these sections the chief facts may be grouped, and some approximate idea obtained of the very great importance of this family of inferior plants, and consequently the advisability of pursuing their study more thoroughly and nationally than has hitherto been done.

I. In estimating the influence of fungi upon man, we naturally enough seek in the first instance to know what baneful effects they are capable of producing on food. Although in the case of "poisonous fungi," popularly understood, fungi may be the passive agents, yet they cannot be ignored in an inquiry of this nature. Writing of the Uses of Fungi, we have already shown that a large number are available for food, and some of these real delicacies; so, on the other hand, it becomes imperative, even with stronger emphasis, to declare that many are poisonous, and some of them virulently so. It is not sufficient to say that they are perfectly harmless until voluntarily introduced into the human system, whilst it is well known that accidents are always possible, and probably would be if every baneful fungus had the word POISON inscribed in capitals on its pileus.

The inquiry is constantly being made as to what plain rules can be given for distinguishing poisonous from edible fungi, and we can answer only that there are none other than those which apply to flowering plants. How can aconite, henbane, œnanthe, stramonium, and such plants, be distinguished from parsley, sorrel, watercress, or spinach? Manifestly not by any general characters, but by specific differences. And so it is with the fungi. We must learn to discriminate *Agaricus muscarius* from *Agaricus rubescens*, in the same manner as we would discriminate parsley from *Æthusa cynapium.* Indeed, fungi have an advantage in this respect, since one or two general cautions can be given, when none such are applicable for higher plants. For instance, it may be said truly that all fungi that exhibit a rapid change to blue when bruised or broken should be avoided; that all Agarics are open to suspicion which possess an acrid taste; that fungi found growing on wood should not be eaten unless the species is well known; that no species of edible fungus has a strong, unpleasant odour, and similar cautions, which, after all, are insufficient. The only safe guide lies in mastering, one by one, the specific distinctions, and increasing the number of one's own esculents gradually, by dint of knowledge and experience, even as a child learns to distinguish a filbert from an acorn, or with wider experience will thrust in his mouth a leaf of *Oxalis* and reject that of the white clover.

One of the most deleterious of fungi that we possess is at the same time one of the most beautiful. This is the *Agaricus muscarius*, or Fly Agaric, which is sometimes used as a fly poison.* It has a bright crimson pileus studded with pale whitish (sometimes yellowish) warts, and a stem and gills of ivory whiteness. Many instances have been recorded of poisoning by this fungus, and amongst them some British soldiers abroad, and yet it cannot be doubted that this fungus is eaten in

* A detailed account of the peculiar properties of this fungus and its employment as a narcotic will be found in Cooke's "Seven Sisters of Sleep," p. 337. It is figured in Greville's "Scottish Cryptogamic Flora," plate 54.

Russia. Two instances have come under our notice of persons with some botanical knowledge, and one a gardener, who had resided in Russia and eaten of this fungus. In one case the Fly Agaric was collected and shown to us, and in the other the figure was indicated, so that we might be under no doubt as to the species. Only one hypothesis can be advanced in explanation. It is known that a large number of fungi are eaten in Russia, and that they enter much into the domestic cookery of the peasantry, but it is also known that they pay considerable attention to the mode of cooking, and add a large amount of salt and vinegar, both of which, with long boiling, must be powerful agents in counteracting the poison (probably somewhat volatile) of such fungi as the Fly Agaric. In this place we may give a recipe published by a French author of a process for rendering poisonous fungi edible. It must be taken on his authority, and not our own, as we have never made the experiment, notwithstanding it seems somewhat feasible:—For each pound of mushrooms, cut into moderately small pieces, take a quart of water acidulated with two or three spoonfuls of vinegar, or two spoonfuls of bay salt. Leave the mushrooms to macerate in the liquid for two hours, then wash them with plenty of water; this done, put them in cold water and make them boil. After a quarter or half hour's boiling take them off and wash them, then drain, and prepare them either as a special dish, or use them for seasoning in the same manner as other species.*

This method is said to have been tried successfully with some of the most dangerous kinds. Of these may be mentioned the emetic mushroom, *Russula emetica*, with a bright red pileus and

* Pour chaque 500 grammes de champignons coupes en morceaux d'assez mediocre grandeur, il faut un litre d'eau acidulée par deux ou trois cuillerées de vinaigre, ou deux cuillerées de sel gris. Dans le cas ou l'on n'aurait que de l'eau à sa disposition, il faut la renouveler une ou deux fois. On laisse les champignons macérer dans le liquide pendant deux heures entières, puis on les lave à grande eau. Ils sont alors mis dans de l'eau froide qu'on porte à l'ébullition, et après un quart d'heure ou une demi-heure, on les retire, on les lave, on les essuie, et on les apprête soit comme un mets spécial, et ils comportent les mêmes assaisonnements que les autres, soit comme condiment.—*Morel Traité des Champignons*, p. lix. Paris, 1865.

white gills, which has a clear, waxy, tempting appearance, but which is so virulent that a small portion is sufficient to produce disagreeable consequences. It would be safer to eschew all fungi with a red or crimson pileus than to run the risk of indulging in this. A white species, which, however, is not very common, with a bulbous base enclosed in a volva, called *Agaricus vernus*, should also be avoided. The pink spored species should also be regarded with suspicion. Of the *Boleti* several turn blue when cut or broken, and these again require to be discarded. This is especially the case with *Boletus luridus** and *Boletus Satanas*,† two species which have the under surface or orifice of the pores of a vermilion or blood-red colour.

Not only are species which are known to be poisonous to be avoided, but discretion should be used in eating recognized good species. Fungi undergo chemical changes so rapidly that even the cultivated mushroom may cause inconvenience if kept so long after being gathered as to undergo chemical change. It is not enough that they should be of a good kind, but also fresh. The employment of plenty of salt in their preparation is calculated very much to neutralize any deleterious property. Salt, pepper, and vinegar are much more freely employed abroad in preparing fungi than with us, and with manifest advantage.

It is undoubtedly true that fungi exert an important influence in skin diseases. This seems to be admitted on all hands by medical men,‡ however much they may differ on the question of the extent to which they are the cause or consequence of disease. Facts generally seem to bear out the opinion that a great number of skin diseases are aggravated, and even produced, by fungi. Robin § insists that a peculiar soil is necessary, and Dr. Fox says it is usually taught that tuberculous, scrofulous, and dirty people furnish the best nidus. It is scarcely necessary to enu-

* Smith's "Chart of Poisonous Fungi," fig. 10.

† Ibid. fig. 27. It would be well to become acquainted with all these figures.

‡ "Skin Diseases of Parasitic Origin," by Dr. Tilbury Fox. London, 1863.

§ Robin, "Hist. Nat. des Végétaux Parasites." Paris, 1853. Kuchenmeister, "Animal and Vegetable Parasites of the Human Body." London, Sydenham Society, 1857.

merate all these diseases, with which medical men are familiar, but simply to indicate a few. There is favus or scall-head, called also "porrigo," which has its primary seat in the hair follicles. Plica polonica, which is endemic in Russia, is almost cosmopolitan. Then there is Tinea tonsurans, Alopecia, Sycosis, &c., and in India a more deeply-seated disease, the Madura Foot, has been traced to the ravages of a fungus described under the name of *Chionyphe Carteri.** It is probable that the application of different names to the very often imperfect forms of fungi which are associated with different diseases is not scientifically tenable. Perhaps one or two common moulds, such as *Aspergillus* or *Penicillium*, lie at the base of the majority, but this is of little importance here, and does not affect the general principle that some skin diseases are due to fungi.

Whilst admitting that there are such diseases, it must be understood that diseases have been attributed to fungi as a primary cause, when the evidence does not warrant such a conclusion. Diphtheria and thrush have been referred to the devastations of fungi, whereas diphtheria certainly may and does occur without any trace of fungi. Fevers may sometimes be accompanied by fungoid bodies in the evacuations, but it is very difficult to determine them. The whole question of epidemic diseases being caused by the presence of fungi seems based on most incomplete evidence. Dr. Salisbury was of opinion that camp measles was produced by *Puccinia graminis*, the pseudospores of which germinated in the damp straw, disseminated the resultant secondary bodies in the air, and caused the disease. This has never been verified. Measles, too, has been attributed freely, as well as scarlatina,† to fungal influences, and the endeavours to implicate fungi in being the cause of cholera have been pertinaciously persevered in with no conviction. The presence of certain cysts, said to be those of *Urocystis*, derived from rice, was announced by Dr.

* Berkeley, in "Intellectual Observer," Nov., 1862. "Mycetoma," H. Vandyke Carter, 1874.

† Hallier and Zurn, "Zeitschrift für Parasitenkunde." Jena, 1869-71.

Hallier, but when it was shown that no such fungus was found on rice, this phase of the theory collapsed. Special and competent experts were sent from this country to examine the preparations and hear the explanations of Dr. Hallier on his theory of cholera contagion, but they were neither convinced nor satisfied.

As long ago as 1853, Dr. Lauder Lindsay examined and reported on cholera evacuations, and in 1856 he declared—"It will be evident that I can see no satisfactory groundwork for the fungus theory of cholera, which I am not a little surprised to find still possesses powerful advocates." * And of the examinations undertaken by him he writes:—"The mycelium and sporules of various species of fungi, constituting various forms of vegetable mould, were found in the scum of the vomit, as well as of the stools, but only at some stage of decomposition. They are found, however, under similar circumstances, in the vomit and stools of other diseases, and, indeed, in all decomposing animal fluids, and they are therefore far from peculiar to cholera."

Some writers have held that the atmosphere is often highly charged with fungi spores, others have denied the presence of organic bodies to any extent in the air. The experiments conducted in India by Dr. Cunningham † have been convincing enough on this point. This report states that spores and similar cells were of constant occurrence, and were generally present in considerable numbers. That the majority of the cells were living and ready to undergo development on meeting with suitable conditions was very manifest, as in those cases in which preparations were retained under observation for any length of time, germination rapidly took place in many of the cells; indeed, many spores already germinating were deposited on the slides. In few instances did any development take place beyond the

* Dr. Lauder Lindsay, "On Microscopical and Clinical Characters of Cholera Evacuations," reprinted from "Edinburgh Medical Journal," February and March, 1856; also "Clinical Notes on Cholera," by W. Lauder Lindsay, M.D., F.L.S., in "Association Medical Journal" for April 14, 1854.

† "Microscopic Examinations of Air," from the "Ninth Annual Report of the Sanitary Commissioner," Calcutta, 1872.

formation of mycelium or masses of toruloid cells, but in one or two distinct sporules were developed on the filaments arising from some of the larger septate spores, and in a few others *Penicillium* and *Aspergillus* produced their characteristic heads of fructification.

With regard to the precise nature of the spores and other cells present in various instances little can be said, as, unless their development were to be carefully followed out through all its stages, it is impossible to refer them to their correct species or even genera. The greater number of them are apparently referable to the old orders of fungi—*Sphæronemei*, *Melanconei*, *Torulacei*, *Dematiei*, and *Mucedines*, while some probably belonged to the *Pucciniei* and *Coæmacei*. Amongst those belonging to the *Torulacei*, the most interesting was a representative of the rare genus *Tetraploa*. Distinct green algoid cells occurred in some specimens. Then follow in the report details of observations made on the rise and fall of diseases, of which diarrhœa, dysentery, cholera, ague, and dengue were selected and compared with the increase or diminution of atmospheric cells. The conclusions arrived at are :—

"Spores and other vegetable cells are constantly present in atmospheric dust, and usually occur in considerable numbers; the majority of them are living, and capable of growth and development. The amount of them present in the air appears to be independent of conditions of velocity and direction of the wind, and their number is not diminished by moisture.

"No connection can be traced between the numbers of bacteria, spores, &c., present in the air, and the occurrence of diarrhœa, dysentery, cholera, ague, or dengue, nor between the presence or abundance of any special form or forms of cells, and the prevalence of any of these diseases.

"The amount of inorganic and amorphous particles and other débris suspended in the atmosphere is directly dependent on conditions of moisture and velocity of wind."

This report is accompanied by fourteen large and well-executed plates, each containing hundreds of figures of organic bodies collected from the air between February and September. It is valuable both for its evidence as to the number and character of the spores in the air, and also for the tables showing the relation between five forms of disease, and their fluctuations, as compared with the amount of spores floating in the atmosphere.

We are fain to believe that we have represented the influence of fungi on man as far as evidence seems to warrant. The presence of forms of mould in some of their incipient conditions in different diseased parts of the human body, externally and internally, may be admitted without the assumption that they are in any manner the cause of the diseased tissues, except in such cases as we have indicated. Hospital gangrene may be alluded to in this connection, and it is possible that it may be due to some fungus allied to the crimson spots (blood rain) which occur on decayed vegetation and meat in an incipient stage of decomposition. This fungus was at one time regarded as an algal, at another as animal; but it is much more probable that it is a low condition of some common mould. The readiness with which the spores of fungi floating in the atmosphere adhere to and establish themselves on all putrid or corrupt substances is manifest in the experience of all who have had to do with the dressing of wounds, and in this case it is a matter of the greatest importance that, as much as possible, atmospherical contact should be avoided.

Recently a case occurred at the Botanic Gardens at Edinburgh which was somewhat novel. The assistant to the botanical professor was preparing for demonstration some dried specimens of a large puff-ball, filled with the dust-like spores, which he accidentally inhaled, and was for some time confined to his room under medical attendance from the irritation they caused. This would seem to prove that the spores of some fungi are liable, when inhaled in large quantities, to derange the system and become dangerous; but under usual and natural conditions such spores are not likely to be present in the atmosphere in sufficient quantity to cause inconvenience. In the autumn a very large number of basidiospores must be present in the atmosphere of woods, and yet there is no reason to believe that it is more unhealthy to breathe the atmosphere of a wood in September or October than in January or May. Dreadful effects are said to be produced by a species of black rust which attacks the large South of Europe reed, *Arundo donax*. This is in all probability the same species with that which attacks *Arundo phragmitis* in this country, the spores of which produce violent headaches and other disorders amongst the labourers who cut the reeds for thatching. M. Michel states that the spores from the parasite on *Arundo donax*, either inhaled or injected, produce violent papular eruption on the face, attended with great swelling, and a variety of alarming symptoms which it is unnecessary to particularize, in various parts of the body.* Perhaps if *Sarcina* should ultimately prove to be a fungus, it may be added to the list of those which aggravate, if they are not the primary cause of, disease in the human subject.

II. What influences can be attributed to fungi upon animals other than man? Clearly instinct preserves animals from many dangers. It may be presumed that under ordinary circumstances there is not much fear of a cow or a sheep poisoning itself in a pasture or a wood. But under extraordinary circumstances it is not only possible, but very probable, that injuries may occur. For instance, it is well known that not only rye and wheat, but also many of the grasses, are liable to infection from a peculiar form of fungus called "ergot." In certain seasons this ergot is much more common than others, and the belief is strong in those who ought to know something of the subject from experience, viz., farmers and graziers, that in such seasons it is not uncommon for cattle to slip their young through feeding on ergotized grass. Then, again, it is fairly open to inquiry whether, in years when "red rust" and "mildew" are more than usually plentiful on grasses, these may not be to a certain extent injurious. Without attempting to associate the cattle plague in any way with fungi on grass, it is nevertheless a most remarkable coincidence that the year in which the cattle disease was most prevalent in this country was one in which there was—at least in some districts—more "red rust" on grasses than we ever remem-

* "Gardener's Chronicle," March 26, 1864.

ber to have seen before or since; the clothes of a person walking through the rusty field soon became orange-coloured from the abundance of spores. Graziers on this point again seem to be generally agreed, that they do not think "red rust" has been proved to be injurious to cattle. The direct influence of fungi on quadrupeds, birds, reptilia, &c., seems to be infinitesimally small.

Insects of various orders have been observed from time to time to become the prey of fungi.* That known at Guadaloupe under the name of *La Guêpe Végétale*, or vegetable wasp, has been often cited as evidence that, in some instances at least, the fungus attacks the insect whilst still living. Dr. Madianna states that he has noticed the wasp still living with its incumbrance attached to it, though apparently in the last stage of existence, and seeming about to perish from the influence of its destructive parasite.† This fungus is called by Tulasne *Torrubia sphecocephala.*‡ About twenty-five species of this genus of sphæriaceous fungi have been described as parasitic on insects. Five species are recorded in South Carolina, one in Pennsylvania, found on the larvæ of the May-bug, and one other North American species on Nocturnal Lepidoptera, one in Cayenne, one in Brazil, on the larva of a *Cicada*, and one on a species of ant, two in the West Indies, one in New Guinea on a species of *Coccus*, and one on a species of *Vespa* in Senegal. In Australia two species have been recorded, and two are natives of New Zealand. Dr. Hooker found two in the Khassya mountains of India, and one American species has also been found at Darjeeling. It has long been known that one species, which has a medicinal repute there, is found in China, whilst three have been recorded in Great Britain. Opinions are divided as to whether in these instances the fungus causes or is subsequent to the death of the insect. It is generally the belief of entomologists that the death of the insect is caused by the fungus.

* Gray, G., "Notices of Insects that are Known to Form the Bases of Fungoid Parasites." London, 1858.

† Halsey, "Ann. Lyceum," New York, 1824, p. 125.

‡ Tulasne, "Selecta Fung. Carp." vol. iii. p. 17.

In the case of *Isaria sphingum*, which is the conidia form of a species of *Torrubia*, the moth has been found standing on a leaf, as during life, with the fungus sprouting from its body.

Other and less perfect forms of fungi also attack insects. During the summer of 1826, Professor Sebert collected a great many caterpillars of *Arctia villica*, for the purpose of watching their growth. These insects on arriving at their full size became quite soft, and then suddenly died. Soon after they became hard, and, if bent, would easily break into two pieces. Their bodies were covered with a beautiful shining white mould. If some of the caterpillars affected with the parasitic mould were placed on the same tree with those apparently free from its attack, the latter soon exhibited signs that they also were attacked in the same manner, in consequence of coming into contact with each other.*

During the spring of 1851, some twelve or twenty specimens were found from amongst myriads of *Cicada septemdecim*, which, though living, had the posterior third of the abdominal contents converted into a dry, powdery, ochreous-yellow compact mass of sporuloid bodies. The outer coverings of that portion of the insect were loose and easily detached, leaving the fungoid matter in the form of a cone affixed by its base to the unaffected part of the abdomen of the insect. The fungus may commence, says Dr. Leidy, its attacks upon the larva, develop its mycelium, and produce a sporular mass within the active pupa, when many are probably destroyed; but should some be only affected so far as not to destroy the organs immediately essential to life, they might undergo their metamorphosis into the imago, in which case they would be affected in the manner previously described.†

The common house-fly in autumn is very usually subject to the attacks of a mouldy fungus called *Sporendonema muscæ*, or *Empusa muscæ* in former times, which is now regarded as the terrestrial condition of one of the *Saprolegniei*.‡ The flies become sluggish, and at last fix themselves to some object on

* "Berlin Entom. Zeitung," 1858, p. 178.

† "Smithsonian Contributions to Knowledge," v. p. 53.

‡ "Wiegmann Archiv." 1835, ii. p. 354; "Ann. Nat. Hist." 1841, p. 405.

which they die, with their legs extended and head depressed, the body and wings soon becoming covered with a minute white mould, the joints of which fall on the surrounding object. Examples are readily distinguished when they settle on windows and thus succumb to their foe. Mr. Gray says that a similar mould has been observed on individuals of the wasp family.

A *Gryllotalpa* was found in a wood near Newark, Delaware, U.S., upon turning over a log. The insect was seen standing very quietly at the mouth of its oval cell, which is formed in the earth, having a short curved tube to the surface. Upon taking it up it exhibited no signs of movement, though perfectly fresh and lifelike in appearance. On examining it next morning it still presented no signs of life. Every part of the insect was perfect, not even the antennæ being broken. Upon feeling it, it was very hard and resistant, and on making an incision through the thorax it exhaled a fungoid odour. The insect had been invaded by a parasitic fungus which everywhere filled the animal, occupying the position of all the soft tissue, and extending even into the tarsal joints. It formed a yellowish or cream-coloured compact mass.*

The destructive silk-worm disease, *Botrytis Bassiana*, is also a fungus which attacks and destroys the living insect, concerning which an immense deal has been written, but which has not yet been eradicated. It has also been supposed that a low form or imperfect condition of a mould has much to do with the disease of bees known as "foul brood."†

Penicillium Fieberi, figured by Corda on a beetle, was doubtless developed entirely after death, with which event it had probably nothing whatever to do.‡ Sufficient, however, has been written to show that fungi have an influence on insect life, and this might be extended to other animal forms, as to spiders, on which one or two species of *Isaria* are developed, whilst Dr. Leidy has recorded observations on *Julus*§ which may be

* Leidy, "Proc. Acad. Nat. Sci. Phil." 1851, p. 204.

† "Gardener's Chronicle," November 21, 1868.

‡ Corda, "Prachtflora," pl. ix.

§ Leidy, "Fauna and Flora within Living Animals," in "Smithsonian Contributions to Knowledge."

perused with advantage. Fish are subject to a mouldy-looking parasite belonging to the *Saprolegniei*, and a similar form attacks the ova of toads and frogs. Gold fish in globes and aquaria are very subject to attack from this mouldy enemy, and although we have seen them recover under a constant change of water, this is by no means always the case, for in a few weeks the parasite will usually prevail.

The influence of fungi upon animals in countries other than European is very little known, except in the case of the species of *Torrubia* found on insects, and the diseases to which silk-worms are subject. Instances have been recorded of the occurrence of fungoid mycelium—for in most it is nothing more—in the tissues of animals, in the hard structure of bone and shell, in the intestines, lungs, and other fleshy parts, and in various organs of birds.* In some of the latter cases it has been described as a Mucor, in most it is merely cells without sufficient character for determination. It is by no means improbable that fungi may be found in such situations; the only question with regard to them is whether they are not accidental, and not the producers of unhealthy or diseased tissues, even when found in proximity thereto.

There is one phase of the influences of fungi on the lower animals which must not be wholly passed over, and that is the relation which they bear to some of the insect tribes in furnishing them with food. It is especially the case with the *Coleoptera* that many species seem to be entirely dependent on fungi for existence, since they are found in no other situations. Beetle-hunters tell us that old *Polyporei*, and similar fungi of a corky or woody nature, are always sought after for certain species which they seek in vain elsewhere,† and those who possess herbaria know how destructive certain minute members of the animal kingdom are to their choicest specimens, against whose depredations even poison is sometimes unavailing.

Some of the Uredines, as *Trichobasis suaveolens* and *Coleosporium sonchi*, are generally accompanied by a little orange larva

* Murie, in "Monthly Microscopical Journal" (1872), vii. p. 149.

† See genus *Mycetophagus*, "Stephen's Manual Brit. Coleopt." p. 132.

which preys upon the fungus; and in the United States Dr. Bolles informs us that some species of *Æcidium* are so constantly infested with this red larva that it is scarcely possible to get a good specimen, or to keep it from its sworn enemy. Minute *Anguillidæ* revel in tufts of mould, and fleshy Agarics, as they pass into decay, become colonies of insect life. Small *Lepidoptera*, belonging to the *Tineina*, appear to have a liking for such *Polyporei* as *P. sulfureus* when it becomes dry and hard, or *P. squamosus* when it has attained a similar condition. *Acari* and *Psocidæ* attack dried fungi of all kinds, and speedily reduce them to an unrecognizable powder.

III. What are the influences exerted by fungi on other plants? This is a broad subject, but withal an important one, since these influences act indirectly on man as well as on the lower animals. On man, inasmuch as it interferes with the vegetable portion of his food, either by checking its production or depreciating its quality. On the lower animals, since by this means not only is their natural food deteriorated or diminished, but through it injurious effects are liable to be produced by the introduction of minute fungi into the system. These remarks apply mainly to fungi which are parasitic on living plants. On the other hand, the influence of fungi must not be lost sight of as the scavengers of nature when dealing with dead and decaying vegetable matter. Therefore, as in other instances, we have here also good and bad influences intermingled, so that it cannot be said that they are wholly evil, or unmixed good.

Wherever we encounter decaying vegetable matter we meet with fungi, living upon and at the expense of decay, appropriating the changed elements of previous vegetable life to the support of a new generation, and hastening disintegration and assimilation with the soil. No one can have observed the mycelium of fungi at work on old stumps, twigs, and decayed wood, without being struck with the rapidity and certainty with which disintegration is being carried on. The gardener casts on one side, in a pile as rubbish, twigs and cuttings from his trees, which are useless to him, but which have all derived much from the soil on which they flourished. Shortly fungi make their appearance in species almost innumerable, sending their subtle threads of mycelium deep into the tissues of the woody substance, and the whole mass teems with new life. In this metamorphosis as the fungi flourish so the twigs decay, for the new life is supported at the expense of the old, and together the destroyers and their victims return as useful constituents to the soil from whence they were derived, and form fresh pabulum for a succeeding season of green leaves and sweet flowers. In woods and forests we can even more readily appreciate the good offices of fungi in accelerating the decay of fallen leaves and twigs which surround the base of the parent trees. In such places Nature is left absolutely to her own resources, and what man would accomplish in his carefully attended gardens and shrubberies must here be done without his aid. What we call decay is merely change; change of form, change of relationship, change of composition; and all these changes are effected by various combined agencies—water, air, light, heat, these furnishing new and suitable conditions for the development of a new race of vegetables. These, by their vigorous growth, continue what water and oxygen, stimulated by light and heat, had begun, and as they flourish for a brief season on the fallen glories of the past summer, make preparation for the coming spring.

Unfortunately this destructive power of fungi over vegetable tissues is too often exemplified in a manner which man does not approve. The dry rot is a name which has been given to the ravages of more than one species of fungus which flourishes at the expense of the timber it destroys. One of these forms of dry rot fungus is *Merulius lacrymans*, which is sometimes spoken of as if it were the only one, though perhaps the most destructive in houses. Another is *Polyporus hybridus*, which attacks oak-built vessels; * and these are not the only ones which are capable of mischief. It appears that the dry rot fungus acts indirectly on the wood, whose cells are saturated with its juice, and in consequence lose their lignine and cellulose, though their walls suffer no corrosion. The different forms of decay in wood

* Sowerby's "Fungi," plates 289 and 387, fig. 6.

are accompanied by fungi, which either completely destroy the tissue, or alter its nature so much by the abstraction of the cellulose and lignine, that it becomes loose and friable. Thus fungi induce the rapid destruction of decaying wood. These are the conclusions determined by Schacht, in his memoir on the subject.*

We may allude, in passing, to another phase of destructiveness in the mycelium of fungi, which traverse the soil and interfere most injuriously with the growth of shrubs and trees. The reader of journals devoted to horticulture will not fail to notice the constant appeals for advice to stop the work of fungi in the soil, which sometimes threatens vines, at others conifers, and at others rhododendrons. Dead leaves, and other vegetable substances, not thoroughly and completely decayed, are almost sure to introduce this unwelcome element.

Living plants suffer considerably from the predations of parasitic species, and foremost amongst these in importance are those which attack the cereals. The corn mildew and its accompanying rust are cosmopolitan, as far as we know, wherever corn is cultivated, whether in Australia or on the slopes of the Himalayas. The same may also be said of smut, for *Ustilago* is as common in Asia and America as in Europe. We have seen it on numerous grasses as well as on barley from the Punjab, and a species different from *Ustilago maydis* on the male florets of maize from the same locality. In addition to this, we learn that in 1870 one form made its appearance on rice. It was described as constituting in some of the infested grains a whitish, gummy, interlaced, ill-defined, thread-like mycelium, growing at the expense of the tissues of the affected organs, and at last becoming converted into a more or less coherent mass of spores, of a dirty green colour, on the exterior of the deformed grains. Beneath the outer coating the aggregated spores are of a bright orange red; the central portion has a vesicular appearance, and is white in colour.† It is difficult to

* Schacht, "Fungous Threads in the Cells of Plants," in Pringsheim's "Jahrbuch." Berlin, 1863.

† "Proceedings of the Agri. Hort. Soc. of Indi " (1871), p. 85.

determine from the description what this so-called *Ustilago* may be, which was said to have affected a considerable portion of the standing rice crop in the vicinity of Diamond Harbour.

Bunt is another pest (*Tilletia caries*) which occupies the whole farinaceous portion of the grains of wheat. Since dressing the seed wheat has been so widely adopted in this country, this pest has been of comparatively little trouble. Sorghum and the small millets, in countries where these are cultivated for food, are liable to attacks from allied parasites. Ergot attacks wheat and rice as well as rye, but not to such an extent as to have any important influence upon the crop. Two or three other species of fungi are sometimes locally troublesome, as *Dilophospora graminis*, and *Septoria nodorum* on wheat, but not to any considerable extent. In countries where maize is extensively grown it has not only its own species of mildew (*Puccinia*), but also one of the most enormous and destructive species of *Ustilago*.

A singular parasite on grasses was found by Cesati in Italy, in 1850, infesting the glumes of *Andropogon*.* It received the name of *Cerebella Andropogonis*, but it never appears to have increased and spread to such an extent as was at first feared.

Even more destructive than any of these is the potato disease † (*Peronospora infestans*), which is, unfortunately, too well known to need description. This disease was at one time attributed to various causes, but long since its ascertained source has been acknowledged to be a species of white mould, which also attacks tomatoes, but less vigorously. De Bary has given considerable attention to this disease, and his opinions are clearly detailed in his memoir on *Peronospora*, as well as in his special pamphlet on the potato disease.‡ One sees the cause of the epidemic, he says, in the diseased state of the potato itself, produced either accidentally by unfavourable conditions of soil and atmosphere, or by a depravation that the plant has experi-

* "Gardener's Chronicle" (1852), p. 643, with fig.

† Berkeley, "On the Potato Murrain," in "Jour. Hort. Soc." vol. i. (1846), p. 9.

‡ De Bary, "Die gegenwartig herrschende Kartoffelkrankheit."

enced in its culture. According to these opinions, the vegetation of the parasite would be purely accidental, the disease would be independent of it, the parasite would be able frequently even to spare the diseased organs. Others see in the vegetation of the *Peronospora* the immediate or indirect cause of the various symptoms of the disease; either that the parasite invades the stalks of the potato, and in destroying them, or, so to speak, in poisoning them, determines a diseased state of the tubercles, or that it introduces itself into all the organs of the plant, and that its vegetation is the immediate cause of all the symptoms of the disease that one meets with in any organ whatever. His observations rigorously proved that the opinions of the latter were those only which were well founded. All the alterations seen on examining spontaneous individuals are found when the *Peronospora* is sown in a nourishing plant. The most scrupulous examination demonstrates the most perfect identity between the cultivated and spontaneous individuals as much in the organization of the parasite as in the alteration of the plant that nourishes it. In the experiments that he had made he affirms that he never observed an individual or unhealthy predisposition of the nourishing plant. It appeared to him, on the contrary, that the more the plant was healthy, the more the mould prospered.

We cannot follow him through all the details of the growth and development of the disease, or of his experiments on this and allied species, which resulted in the affirmation that the mould immediately determines the disease of the tubercles as well as that of the leaves, and that the vegetation of the *Peronospora* alone determines the redoubtable epidemic to which the potato is exposed.* We believe that this same observer is still engaged in a series of observations, with the view, if possible, of suggesting some remedy or mitigation of the disease.

Dr. Hassall pointed out, many years since, the action of fungous mycelium, when coming in contact with cellular tissue,

* De Bary, "Memoir on Peronospora," in "Annales des Sci. Nat."

of inducing decomposition, a fact which has been fully confirmed by Berkeley.

Unfortunately there are other species of the same genus of moulds which are very destructive to garden produce. *Peronospora gangliformis*, B., attacks lettuces, and is but too common and injurious. *Peronospora effusa*, Grev., is found on spinach and allied plants. *Peronospora Schleideniana*, D. By., is in some years very common and destructive to young onions, and field crops of lucerne are very liable to attack from *Peronospora trifoliorum*, D. By.

The vine crops are liable to be seriously affected by a species of mould, which is but the conidia form of a species of *Erysiphe*. This mould, known under the name of *Oidium Tuckeri*, B., attacks the vines in hothouses in this country, but on the Continent the vineyards often suffer severely * from its depredations; unfortunately, not the only pest to which the vine is subject, for an insect threatens to be even more destructive.

Hop gardens suffer severely, in some years, from a similar disease; in this instance the mature or ultimate form is perfected. The hop mildew is *Sphærotheca Castagnei*, Lév., which first appears as whitish mouldy blotches on the leaves, soon becoming discoloured, and developing the black receptacles on either surface of the leaf. These may be regarded as the cardinal diseases of fungoid origin to which useful plants are subject in this country.

Amongst those of less importance, but still troublesome enough to secure the anathemas of cultivators, may be mentioned *Puccinia Apii*, Ca., often successful in spoiling beds of celery by attacking the leaves; *Cystopus candidus*, Lév., and *Glæosporium concentricum*, Grev., destructive to cabbages and other cruciferous plants; *Trichobasis Fabæ*, Lév., unsparing when once established on beans; *Erysiphe Martii*, Lév., in some seasons a great nuisance to the crop of peas.

* "Reports of H. M. Secretaries of Embassy and Legation on the Effects of the Vine Disease on Commerce, 1859;" "Reports of H. M. Secretaries of Embassy, &c., on Manufactures and Commerce, Vine Disease in Bavaria and Switzerland, 1859," pp. 54 and 62.

Fruit trees do not wholly escape, for *Rœstelia cancellata*, Tul., attacks the leaves of the pear. *Puccinia prunorum* affects the leaves of almost all the varieties of plum. Blisters caused by *Ascomyces deformans*, B., contort the leaves of peaches, as *Ascomyces bullatus*, B., does those of the pear, and *Ascomyces juglandis*, B., those of the walnut. Happily we do not at present suffer from *Ascomyces pruni*, Fchl., which, on the Continent, attacks young plum-fruits, causing them to shrivel and fall. During the past year pear-blossoms have suffered from what seems to be a form of *Helminthosporium pyrorum*, and the branches are sometimes infected with *Capnodium elongatum ;* but orchards in the United States have a worse foe in the " black knot,"* which causes gouty swellings in the branches, and is caused by the *Sphæria morbosa* of Schweinitz.

Cotton plants in India † were described by Dr. Shortt as subject to the attacks of a kind of mildew, which from the description appeared to be a species of *Erysiphe*, but on receiving specimens from India for examination, we found it to be one of those diseased conditions of tissue formerly classed with fungi under the name of *Erineum ;* and a species of Torula attacks cotton pods after they are ripe. Tea leaves in plantations in Cachar have been said to suffer from some sort of blight, but in all that we have seen insects appear to be the depredators, although on the decaying leaves *Hendersonia theicola*, Cooke, establishes itself.‡ The coffee plantations of Ceylon suffer from the depredations of *Hemiliea vastatrix*, as well as from insects.§ Other useful plants have also their enemies in parasitic fungi.

Olive-trees in the south of Europe suffer from the attacks of a species of *Antennaria*, as do also orange and lemon trees from a *Capnodium*, which covers the foliage as if with a coating of soot. In fact most useful plants appear to have some enemy to contend with, and it is fortunate, not only for the plant, but its cultiva-

* C. H. Peck, "On the Black Knot," in "Quekett Microscopical Journal," vol. iii. p. 82.

† Cooke, "Microscopic Fungi," p. 177.

‡ "Grevillea," i. p. 90.

§ "Gardener's Chronicle," 1873.

tors, if this enemy is less exacting than is the case with the potato, the vine, and the hop.

Forestry in Britain is an insignificant interest compared to what it is in some parts of Europe, in the United States, and in our Indian possessions. In these latter places it becomes a matter of importance to inquire what influence fungi exert on forest trees. It may, however, be predicated that the injury caused by fungi is far outstripped by insects, and that there are not many fungi which become pests in such situations. Coniferous trees may be infested with the species of *Peridermium*, which are undoubtedly injurious, *Peridermium elatinum*, Lk., distorting and disfiguring the silver fir, as *Peridermium Thomsoni*, B,* does those of *Abies Smithiana* in the Himalayas. This species occurred at an elevation of 8,000 feet. The leaves become reduced in length one-half, curved, and sprinkled, sometimes in double rows, with the large sori of this species, which gives the tree a strange appearance, and at length proves fatal, from the immense diversion of nutriment requisite to support a parasite so large and multitudinous. The dried specimens have a sweet scent resembling violets. In Northern Europe *Cœoma pinitorquum*, D. By., seems to be plentiful and destructive. All species of juniper, both in Europe and the United States, are liable to be attacked and distorted by species of *Podisoma* † and *Gymnosporangium*. *Antennaria pinophila*, Fr., is undoubtedly injurious, as also are other species of *Antennaria*, which probably attain their more complete development in *Capnodium*, of which *Capnodium Citri* is troublesome to orange-trees in the south of Europe, and other species to other trees. How far birch-trees are injured by *Dothidea betulina*, Fr., or *Melampsora betulina*, Lév., or poplars and aspens by *Melampsora populina*, Lév., and *Melampsora tremulæ*, Lév., we cannot say. The species of *Lecythea* found on willow leaves have decidedly a prejudicial effect on the growth of the affected plant.

Floriculture has to contend with many fungoid enemies, which sometimes commit great ravages amongst the choicest flowers.

* "Gardener's Chronicle," 1852, p. 627, with fig.

† "Podisoma Macropus," Hook, "Journ. Bot." vol. iv. plate xii. fig. 6.

Roses have to contend against the two forms of *Phragmidium mucronatum* as well as *Asteroma Rosæ*. Still more disastrous is a species of *Erysiphei*, which at first appears like a dense white mould. This is named *Sphærotheca pannosa*. Nor is this all, for *Peronospora sparsa*, when it attacks roses in conservatories, is merciless in its exactions.* Sometimes violets will be distorted and spoiled by *Urocystis Violæ*. The garden anemone is freely attacked by *Æcidium quadrifidum*. Orchids are liable to spot from fungi on the leaves, and recently the whole of the choicest hollyhocks have been threatened with destruction by a merciless foe in *Puccinia malvacearum*. This fungus was first made known to the world as an inhabitant of South America many years ago. It seems next to have come into notoriety in the Australian colonies. Then two or three years ago we hear of it for the first time on the continent of Europe, and last year for the first time in any threatening form in our own islands. During the present year its ravages are spreading, until all admirers of hollyhocks begin to feel alarm lest it should entirely exterminate the hollyhock from cultivation. It is common on wild mallows, and cotton cultivators must be on the alert, for there is a probability that other malvaceous plants may suffer.

A writer in the "Gardener's Chronicle" has proposed a remedy for the hollyhock disease, which he hopes will prove effectual. He says, "This terrible disease has now, for twelve months, threatened the complete annihilation of the glorious family of hollyhock, and to baffle all the antidotes that the ingenuity of man could suggest, so rapidly does it spread and accomplish its deadly work. Of this I have had very sad evidence, as last year at this time I had charge of, if not the largest, one of the largest and finest collections of hollyhocks anywhere in cultivation, which had been under my special care for eleven years, and up to within a month of my resigning that position I had observed nothing uncommon amongst them; but before taking my final leave of them I had to witness the melancholy spectacle of bed after bed being smitten down, and amongst them many splendid seedlings, which had cost me years of patience and

* Berkeley, in "Gardener's Chronicle," 1862, p. 308.

anxiety to produce. And again, upon taking a share and the management of this business, another infected collection fell to my lot, so that I have been doing earnest battle with this disease since its first appearance amongst us, and I must confess that, up to a very short time back, I had come in for a great deal the worst of the fight, although I had made use of every agent I could imagine as being likely to aid me, and all that many competent friends could suggest. But lately I was reminded of Condy's patent fluid, diluted with water, and at once procured a bottle of the green quality, and applied it in the proportion of a large tablespoonful to one quart of water, and upon examining the plants dressed, twelve hours afterwards, was delighted to find it had effectually destroyed the disease (which is easily discernible, as when it is living and thriving it is of a light grey colour, but when killed it becomes of a rusty black). Further to test the power at which the plant was capable of bearing the antidote without injury, I used it double the strength. This dose was instant death to the pest, leaving no trace of any injury to the foliage. As to its application, I advocate sponging in all dressings of this description. Syringing is a very ready means, but very wasteful. No doubt sponging consumes more time, but taking into consideration the more effectual manner in which the dressing can be executed alone, it is in the end most economical, especially in regard to this little parasite. I have found it difficult by syringing, as it has great power of resisting and throwing off moisture, and if but a very few are left living, it is astonishing how quickly it redistributes itself. I feel confident, that by the application of this remedy in time another season, I shall keep this collection clean. I believe planting the hollyhock in large crowded beds should be avoided, as I have observed the closer they are growing the more virulently does the disease attack them, whereas isolated rows and plants are but little injured." *

The "Gardener's Chronicle" has also sounded a note of warning that a species of Uredine has been very destructive to pelargoniums at the Cape of Good Hope. Hitherto these plants

* "Gardener's Chronicle," August 22, 1874, p. 243.

have not suffered much in this country from parasites. Besides these, there are many other less troublesome parasites, such as *Uredo filicum,* on ferns; *Puccinia Lychnidearum*, on leaves of sweet-william; *Uredo Orchidis*, on leaves of orchids, &c.

If we would sum up the influences of fungi in a few words, it could be done somewhat in the following form.

Fungi exert a deleterious influence—

On *Man*,

When eaten inadvertently.
By the destruction of his legitimate food.
In producing or aggravating skin diseases.

On *Animals*,

By deteriorating or diminishing their food supplies.
By establishing themselves as parasites on some species.

On *Plants*,

By hastening the decay of timber.
By establishing themselves as parasites.
By impregnating the soil.

But it is not proved that they produce epidemic diseases in man or animals, or that the dissemination of their multitudinous spores in the atmosphere has any appreciable influence on the health of the human race. Hence their association with cholera, diarrhœa, measles, scarlatina, and the manifold ills that flesh is heir to, as producing or aggravating causes, must, in the present state of our knowledge and experience, be deemed apocryphal.

XI.

HABITATS.

It commonly happens that one of the first inquiries which the student seeks to have answered, after an interest is excited in fungi, is—Where, and under what circumstances, are they to be found? The inexperienced, indeed, require some guide, or much labour will be expended and patience lost in seeking microscopic forms in just such places as they are least likely to inhabit. Nor is it wholly unprofitable or uninteresting for others, who do not claim to be students, to summarize the habitats of these organisms, and learn how much the circumstances of their immediate surrounding elements influence production. For reasons which will at once be recognized by the mycologist, the most satisfactory method of study will be somewhat that of the natural groups into which fungi are divided.

Agaricini.—There is such a close affinity between all the genera of this group that it will be a manifest advantage to take together all those fleshy pileate fungi, the fruit of which is borne on folded plates or gills. It must be premised of this group that, for the majority, shade, a moderate amount of moisture, and steady warmth, but not too great heat, are required. A stroll through a wood in autumn will afford good evidence of the predilection of *Agaricini*, as well as some smaller groups, for such spots. A larger proportion will be found in woods, where shade is afforded, than on open heaths or pastures. These wood-loving forms will consist, again, of those which appear on the soil, and those which are found on rotten stumps and decaying trees. Many of those which grow on trees have a lateral stem, or scarcely any stem at all. It may be remarked, that some species which spring from the soil delight most in the shelter of particular trees. The Agarics of a beech wood will materially differ largely from those in an oak wood, and both will differ from those which spring up beneath coniferous trees.

It may be accepted as true of the largest proportion of terrestrial species, that if they do not spring directly from rotten leaves, and vegetable débris in the last stage of decay, the soil will be rich in vegetable humus. A few only occur on sandy spots. The genus *Marasmius* is much addicted to dead leaves; *Russula*, to open places in woods, springing immediately from the soil. *Lactarius* prefers trees, and when found in exposed situations, occurs mostly under the shadow of trees.* *Cantharellus*, again, is a woodland genus, many of the species loving to grow amongst grass or moss, and some as parasites on the latter. *Coprinus* is not a genus much addicted to woods, but is rather peculiar in its attachment to man—if such expression, or one even implying domesticity, might be employed—farm-yards, gardens, dunghills, the base of old gateposts and railings, in cellars, on plaster walls, and even on old damp carpets. *Hygrophorus* loves "the open," whether pastures, lawns, heaths, commons, or up the slopes of mountains, nearly to the top of the highest found in Great Britain. *Cortinarius* seems to have a preference for woods, whilst *Bolbitius* affects dung, or a rich soil. *Lentinus*, *Panus*, *Lenzites*, and *Schizophyllum* all grow on wood. Coming to the subgenera of *Agaricus*, we find *Pleurotus*, *Crepidotus*, *Pluteus*, *Collybia*, *Pholiota*, *Flammula*, *Hypholoma*, and some species of *Psathyra* growing on wood, old stumps, or charcoal; *Amanita*, *Tricholoma*, and *Hebeloma* most attached to woods; *Clitocybe* and *Mycena* chiefly amongst leaves; *Nolanea* amongst grass; *Omphalia* and *Galera* chiefly in swampy places; *Lepiota*, *Leptonia*, *Psalliota*, *Stropharia*, *Psilocybe*, and *Psathyrella* mostly in open places and pastures; *Deconica* and *Panæolus* mostly on dung; *Entoloma* and *Clitopilus* chiefly terrestrial, and the rest variable.

* These predilections must be accepted as general, to which there will be exceptions.

Of special habitats, we may allude to *Nyctalis*, of which the species are parasitic on dead fungi belonging to the genus *Russula*. One or two species of *Agaricus*, such as *Agaricus tuberosus* and *Agaricus racemosus*, P., grow on decaying Agarics, whilst *Agaricus Loveianus* flourishes on *Agaricus nebularis* even before it is thoroughly decayed. A few species grow on dead fir cones, others on old ferns, &c. *Agaricus cepæstipes*, Sow., probably of exotic origin, grows on old tan in hothouses. *Agaricus caulicinalis*, Bull, flourishes on old thatch, as well as twigs, &c. *Agaricus juncicola*, Fr., affects dead rushes in boggy places, whilst *Agaricus affricatus*, Fr., and *Agaricus sphagnicola*, B., are attached to bog moss in similar localities. Some few species are almost confined to the stems of herbaceous plants. *Agaricus petasatus*, Fr., *Agaricus cucumis*, P., and *Paxillus panuoides*, F., have a preference for sawdust. *Agaricus carpophilus*, Fr., and *Agaricus balaninus*, P., have a predilection for beech mast. *Agaricus urticæcola*, B. and Br., seems to confine itself to nettle roots. *Coprinus radians*, Fr., makes its appearance on plaster walls, *Coprinus domesticus*, Fr., on damp carpets. The only epizoic species, according to M. Fries, is *Agaricus cerussatus v. nauseosus*, which has been met with in Russia on the carcase of a wolf; this, however, might have been accidental. Persoon described *Agaricus Neapolitanus*, which was found growing on coffee-grounds at Naples; and more recently Viviani has described another species, *Agaricus Coffeæ*, with rose-coloured spores, found on old fermenting coffee-grounds at Genoa.* Tratinnick figures a species named *Agaricus Markii*, which was found in wine casks in Austria. A *Coprinus* has, both in this country and on the Continent, been found, after a very short time, on the dressing of wounds, where there has been no neglect. A curious case of this kind, which at the time excited great interest, occurred some fifty years since at St. George's Hospital. Some species appear to confine themselves to particular trees, some to come up by preference on soil in garden pots. Certain species have a solitary, others a gregarious habit, and, of the latter, *Agaricus grammopodius*, Bull,

* Viviani, "I Funghi d'Italia."

Agaricus gambosus, Fr., *Marasmius oreades*, Fr., and some others grow in rings. Hence it will be seen that, within certain limits, there is considerable variation in the habitats of the *Agaricini.*

Boleti do not differ much from *Agaricini* in their localization. They seem to prefer woods or borders of woods to pastures, seldom being found in the latter. One species, *B. parasiticus*, Bull, grows on old specimens of *Scleroderma*, otherwise they are for the most part terrestrial.

Polypori also have no wide range of habitat, except in choice of trees on which to grow, for the majority of them are corticolous. The section *Mesopus*, which has a distinct central stem, has some species which prefer the ground. *Polyporus tuberaster*, P., in Italy springs from the *Pietra funghaia*,* and is cultivated for food as well as *Polyporus avellanus*, which is reared from charred blocks of cob-nut trees.

In other genera of the *Polyporei* similar habitats prevail. *Merulius lacrymans*, Fr., one form of dry rot, occurs in cellars, and too often on worked timber; whilst *Merulius himantoides*, Fr., is much more delicate, sometimes running over plants in conservatories.

HYDNEI.—There is nothing calling for special note on the habitats of these fungi. The stipitate species of *Hydnum* are some of them found in woods, others on heaths, one on fir-cones, while the rest have similar habitats to the species of *Polyporus.*

AURICULARINI.—The genera *Hymenochæte*, *Stereum*, and *Corticium*, with some species of *Thelephora*, run over corticated or decorticated wood; other species of *Thelephora* grow on the ground. The Pezizoid forms of *Cyphella* and *Solenia*, like species of *Peziza*, sometimes occur on bark, and of the former genus some on grasses and others on moss.

CLAVARIEI.—The interesting, often brightly-coloured, tufts of *Clavaria* are usually found amongst grass, growing directly from the ground. Only in rare instances do they occur on dead leaves or herbaceous stems. *Calocera* probably should be classed with the *Tremellini*, to which its structure seems more closely allied. The species are developed on wood. The species of *Typhula*

* Badham's "Esculent Funguses," Ed. i. pp. 42, 116.

and *Pistillaria* are small, growing chiefly on dead herbaceous plants. One or two are developed from a kind of *Sclerotium*, which is in fact a compact perennial mycelium.

TREMELLINI.—These curious gelatinous fungi are, with rare exceptions, developed on branches or naked wood; *Tremella versicolor*, B. and Br., one of the exceptions, being parasitic on a species of *Corticium*, and *Tremella epigæa*, B. and Br., spreading over the naked soil. This completes our rapid survey of the habitats of the *Hymenomycetes*. Very few of them are really destructive to vegetation, for the Agarics and Polypori found on growing trees are seldom to be seen on vigorous, but rather on dead branches or partly-decayed trunks.

The GASTEROMYCETES are far less numerous in species, and also in individuals, but their habitats are probably more variable. The *Hypogæi*, or subterranean species, are found either near the surface or buried in the soil, usually in the neighbourhood of trees.

PHALLOIDEI.—In most cases the species prefer woody places. They are mostly terrestrial, and have the faculty of making their presence known, even when not seen, by the fetid odour which many of them exhale. Some of them occur in sandy spots.

PODAXINEI.—These resemble in their localities the *Trichogastres*. Species of *Podaxon* affect the nests of Termites in tropical countries.* Others are found growing amongst grass.

TRICHOGASTRES.—These are chiefly terrestrial. The rare but curious *Batarrea phalloides*, P., has been found on sand-hills, and in hollow trees. *Tulostoma mammosum*, Fr., occurs on old stone walls, growing amongst moss. *Geaster striatus*, D. C., was at one time usually found on the sand of the Denes at Great Yarmouth. Although *Lycoperdon giganteum*, Batsch, occurs most frequently in pastures, or on hedge banks in fields, we have known it to occur annually for some consecutive years in a garden near London. The species of *Scleroderma* seem to prefer a sandy soil. *Aglæocystis* is rather an anomalous genus, occurring on the fruit heads of *Cyperus*, in India. *Broomeia* occurs at the Cape on rotten wood.

* An excellent white Agaric occurs on ant nests in the Neilgherries, and a curious species is found in a similar position in Ceylon.

Myxogastres.—Rotten wood is one of the most favoured of matrices on which these fungi develop themselves; some of them, however, are terrestrial. *Æthalium* will grow on spent tan and other substances. Species of *Diderma* flourish on mosses, jungermanniæ, grass, dead leaves, ferns, &c. *Angioridium sinuosum*, Grev., will run over growing plants of different kinds, and *Spumaria*, in like manner, encrusts living grasses. *Badhamia* not only flourishes on dead wood, but one species is found on the fading leaves of coltsfoot which are still green. *Craterium* runs over almost any substance which lies in its way. *Licea perreptans* was found in a cucumber frame heated with spent hops. One or two *Myxogastres* have been found on lead, or even on iron which had been recently heated. Sowerby found one on cinders, in one of the galleries of St. Paul's Cathedral.

Nidulariacei grow on the ground, or on sticks, twigs, chips, and other vegetable substances, such as sawdust, dung, and rotten wood.

The Coniomycetes consist of two sections, which are based on their habitats. In one section the species are developed on dead or dying plants, in the other they are parasitic on living plants. The former includes the *Sphæronemei*, which are variable in their proclivities, although mostly preferring dead herbaceous plants and the twigs of trees. The exceptions are in favour of *Sphæronema*, some of which are developed upon decaying fungi. In the large genera, *Septoria*, *Ascochyta*, *Phyllosticta*, *Asteroma*, &c., the favourite habitat is fading and dying leaves of plants of all kinds. In the majority of cases these fungi are not autonomous, but are merely the stylosporous conditions of *Sphæria*. They are mostly minute, and the stylospores are of the simplest kind. The *Melanconiei* have a preference for the twigs of trees, bursting through the bark, and expelling the spores in a gelatinous mass. A few of them are foliicolous, but the exceptions are comparatively rare, and are represented chiefly in *Glœosporium*, species of which are found also on apples, peaches, nectarines, and other fruits. The *Torulacei* are superficial, having much of the external appearance of the black moulds, and like them are found on decaying vegetable substances, old stems of herbaceous plants, dead twigs, wood, stumps of trees, &c. The exceptions are in favour of such species as *Torula sporendonema*, which is the red mould of cheese, and also occurs on rats' dung, old glue, &c., and *Sporendonema Muscæ*, which is only the conidia of a species of *Achlya*. One species of *Bactridium* is parasitic on the hymenium of *Peziza*, and *Echinobotryum atrum*, on the flocci of black moulds.

In the other section of *Coniomycetes* the species are parasitic upon, and destructive to, living plants, very seldom being found on really dead substances, and even in such rare cases undoubtedly developed during the life of the tissues. Mostly the ultimate stage of these parasites is exhibited in the ruptured cuticle, and the dispersion of the dust-like spores; but in *Tilletia caries*, *Thecaphora hyalina*, and *Puccinia incarcerata*, they remain enclosed within the fruit of the foster-plant. The different genera exhibit in some instances a liking for plants of certain orders on which to develop themselves. *Peridermium* attacks the *Coniferæ; Gymnosporangium* and *Podisoma* the different species of Juniper; *Melampsora* chiefly the leaves of deciduous trees; *Ræstelia* attaches itself to pomaceous trees, whilst *Graphiola* affects the *Palmaceæ*, and *Endophyllum* the succulent leaves of houseleek. In *Æcidium* a few orders seem to be more liable to attack than others, as the *Compositæ*, *Ranunculaceæ*, *Leguminosæ*, *Labiatæ*, &c., whilst others, as the *Graminaceæ*, *Ericaceæ*, *Malvaceæ*, *Cruciferæ*, are exempt. There are, nevertheless, very few natural orders of phanerogamous plants in which some one or more species, belonging to this section of the *Coniomycetes*, may not be found; and the same foster-plant will occasionally nurture several forms. Recent investigations tend to confirm the distinct specific characters of the species found on different plants, and to prove that the parasite of one host will not vegetate upon another, however closely allied. This admission must not, however, be accepted as universally applicable, and therefore it should not be assumed, because a certain parasite is found developed on a special host, that it is distinct, unless distinctive characters, apart from habitat, can be detected. *Æcidium compositarum* and *Æcidium ranunculacearum*, for instance, are found on various composite and ranunculaceous plants, and as yet no sufficient evidence has been adduced to prove that the different forms are other than varieties of one of the two species. On the other hand, it is not improbable that two species of *Æcidium* are developed on the common berberry, as De Bary has indicated that two species of mildew, *Puccinia graminis*, and *Puccinia straminis*, are found on wheat.

HYPHOMYCETES.—The moulds are much more universal in their habitats, especially the *Mucedines*. The *Isariacei* have a predilection for animal substances, though not exclusively. Some species occur on dead insects, others on decaying fungi, and the rest on sticks, stems, and rotten wood. The *Stilbacei* have also similar habitats, except that the species of *Illosporium* seem to be confined to parasitism on lichens. The black moulds, *Dematiei*, are widely diffused, appearing on herbaceous stems, twigs, bark, and wood in most cases, but also on old linen, paper, millboard, dung, rotting fruit, &c., whilst forms of *Cladosporium* and *Macrosporium* are met with on almost every kind of vegetable substance in which the process of decay has commenced.

Mucedines, in some instances, have not been known to appear on more than one kind of matrix, but in the far greater number of cases they flourish on different substances. *Aspergillus glaucus* and *Penicillium crustaceum* are examples of these universal *Mucedines*. It would be far more difficult to mention substances on which these moulds are never developed than to indicate where they have been found. With the species of *Peronospora* it is different, for these are truly parasitic on living plants, and, as far as already known, the species are confined to certain special plants, and cannot be made to vegetate on any other. The species which causes the potato murrain, although liable to attack the tomato, and other species of *Solanaceæ*, does not extend its ravages beyond that natural order, whilst *Peronospora parasitica* confines itself to cruciferous plants. One species is restricted to the *Umbelliferæ*, another, or perhaps two, to the *Leguminosæ*, another to *Rubiaceæ*, two or three to *Ranunculaceæ*, and two or three to *Caryophyllaceæ*. All the experiments made by De Bary seem to prove that the species of *Peronospora* will only flourish on certain favoured plants, to the exclusion of all others. The non-parasitic moulds are scarcely exclusive. In *Oidium* some species are parasitic, but probably all the parasitic forms are states of *Erysiphe*, the non-parasitic alone being autonomous; of these one occurs on *Porrigo lupinosa*, others on putrefying oranges, pears, apples, plums, &c., and one on honeycomb. *Acrospeira* grows in the interior of sweet chestnuts, and we have seen a species growing within the hard testa of the seeds of *Guilandina Bonduc*, from India, to which there was no external opening visible, and which was broken with considerable difficulty. Several *Mucedines* are developed on the dung of various animals, and seldom on anything else.

The *Physomycetes* consist of two orders, *Antennariei* and *Mucorini*, which differ from each other almost as much in habitat as in external appearance. The former, if represented by *Antennaria*, runs over the green and fading leaves of plants, forming a dense black stratum, like a congested layer of soot; or in *Zasmidium*, the common cellar fungus, runs over the walls, bottles, corks, and other substances, like a thick sooty felt. In the *Mucorini*, as in the *Mucedines*, there is usually less restriction to any special substance. *Mucor mucedo* occurs on bread, paste, preserves, and various substances; other species of *Mucor* seem to have a preference for dung, and some for decaying fungi, but rotting fruits are nearly sure to support one or other of the species. The two known species of the curious genus *Pilobolus*, as well as *Hydrophora*, are confined to dung. *Sporodinia*, *Syzygites*, &c., flourish on rotten Agarics, where they pass through their somewhat complicated existence.

The *Ascomycetes* contain an immense number of species, and in general terms we might say that they are found everywhere. The *Tuberacei* are subterraneous, with a preference for calcareous districts. The *Perisporiacei* are partly parasitical and partly not. The *Erysiphei* include those of the former which flourish at the expense of the green parts of roses, hops, maples, poplars, peas, and many other plants, both in Europe and in North America, whilst in warmer latitudes the genus *Meliola* appears to take their place.

The *Elvellacei* are fleshy fungi, of which the larger forms are terrestrial; *Morchella*, *Gyromitra*, and *Helvella* mostly growing in woods, *Mitrula*, *Spathularia*, and *Leotia* in swampy places, and *Geoglossum* amongst grass. The very large genus *Peziza* is divided into groups, of which *Aleuriæ* are mostly terrestrial. This group includes nearly all the large-sized species, although a few belong to the next. *Lachneæ* are partly terrestrial and partly epiphytal, the most minute species being found on twigs and leaves of dead plants. In *Phialea* the species are nearly entirely epiphytal, as is also the case in *Helotium* and allied genera. Some species of *Peziza* are developed from the curious masses of compact mycelium called *Sclerotia*. A few are rather eccentric in their habitats. *P. viridaria*, *P. domestica*, and *P. hæmastigma*, grow on damp walls; *P. granulata* and some others on dung. *Peziza Bullii* was found growing on a cistern. *P. theleboloides* appears in profusion on spent hops. *P. episphæria*, *P. clavariarum*, *P. vulgaris*, *Helotium pruinosum*, and others are parasitic on old fungi. One or two species of *Helotium* grow on submerged sticks, so as to be almost aquatic, a circumstance of rare occurrence in fungi. Other *Discomycetes* are similar in their habitats to the *Elvellacei*. The group to which the old genus *Ascobolus* belongs is in a great measure confined to the dung of various animals, although there are two or three lignicolous species; and *Ascophanus saccharinus* was first found on old leather, *Ascophanus testaceus* on old sacking, &c. *Ascomyces* is, perhaps, the lowest form which ascomycetous fungi assume, and the species are parasitic on growing plants, distorting the leaves and fruit, constituting themselves pests to the cultivators of peach, pear, and plum trees.

The *Sphæriacei* include a very large number of species which grow on rotten wood, bark, sticks, and twigs; another group is developed on dead herbaceous stems; yet another is confined to dead or dying leaves. One genus, *Torrubia*, grows chiefly on insects; *Hypomyces* is parasitic on dead fungi; *Claviceps* is developed from ergot, *Poronia* on dung, *Polystigma* on living leaves, as well as some species of *Stigmatea* and *Dothidea*. Of the genus *Sphæria*, a considerable number are found on dung, now included by some authors under *Sordaria* and *Sporormia*, genera founded, as we think, on insufficient characters. A limited number of species are parasitic on lichens, and one species only is known to be aquatic.

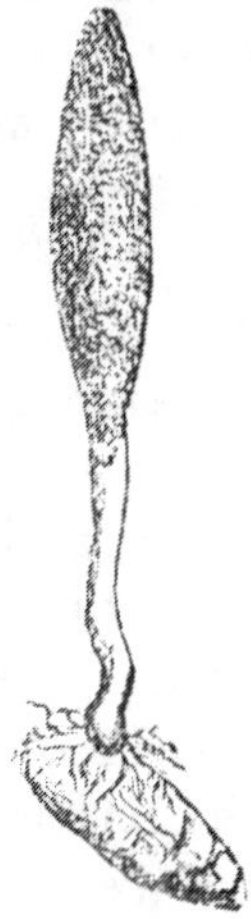

FIG. 109. — *Torrubia militaris* on pupa of a moth.

We have thus rapidly, briefly, and casually indicated the habitats to which the majority of the larger groups of fungi are attached, regarding them from a systematic point of view. There is, however, another aspect from which we might approach the subject, taking the host or matrix, or in fact the habitat, as the basis, and endeavouring to ascertain what species of fungi are to be found in such positions. This has partly been done by M. Westendorp; * but every year adds considerably to the number of species, and what might have been moderately accurate twelve years since can scarcely be so now. To carry this out fully a special work would be necessary, so that we shall be content to indicate or suggest, by means of a few illustrations, the forms of fungi, often widely distinct in structure and character, to be found in the same locality.

The stems of herbaceous plants are favourite habitats for minute fungi. The old stems of the common nettle, for example, perform the office of host to about thirty species.† Of these about nine are *Pezizæ*, and there are as many sphæriaceous fungi, whilst three species of *Dendryphium*, besides other moulds, select this plant. Some of these have not hitherto been detected growing on any other stems, such as *Sphæria urticæ* and *Lophiostoma sex-nucleatum*, to which we might add *Peziza fusarioides* and *Dendryphium griseum*. These do not, however, include the whole of the fungi found on the nettle, since others are parasitic upon

* Westendorp, "Les Cryptogams après leurs stations naturelles."

† Cooke, "On Nettle Stems and their Micro-Fungi," in "Journ. Quekett Micro. Club," iii. p. 69.

its living green parts. Of these may be named *Æcidium urticæ* and *Peronospora urticæ*, as well as two species described by Desmazières as *Fusisporium urticæ* and *Septoria urticæ*. Hence it will be seen how large a number of fungi may attach themselves to one herbaceous plant, sometimes whilst living, but most extensively when dead. This is by no means a solitary instance, but a type of what takes place in many others. If, on the other hand, we select such a tree as the common lime, we shall find that the leaves, twigs, branches, and wood bear, according to M. Westendorp,* no less than seventy-four species of fungi, and of these eleven occur on the leaves. The spruce fir, according to the same authority, nourishes one hundred and fourteen species, and the oak not less than two hundred.

It is curious to note how fungi are parasitic upon each other in some instances, as in that of *Hypomyces*, characteristic of the genus, in which sphæriaceous fungi make hosts of dead *Lactarii*, &c. We have already alluded to *Nyctalis*, growing on decayed *Russulæ*, to *Boletus parasiticus*, flourishing on old *Scleroderma*, and to *Agaricus Loveianus*, on the pileus of *Agaricus nebularis*. To these we may add *Torrubia ophioglossoides* and *T. capitata*, which flourish on decaying *Elaphomyces*, *Stilbum tomentosum* on old *Trichia*, *Peziza Clavariarum* on dead *Clavaria*, and many others, the mere enumeration of which would scarcely prove interesting. A very curious little parasite was found by Messrs. Berkeley and Broome, and named by them *Hypocrea inclusa*, which makes itself a home in the interior of truffles. Mucors and moulds flourish on dead and decaying Agarics, and other fleshy forms, in great luxuriance and profusion. *Mucor ramosus* is common on *Boletus luridus*, and *Syzygites megalocarpus* on Agarics, as well as *Acrostalagmus cinnabarinus*. A very curious little parasite, *Echinobotryum atrum*, occurs like minute nodules on the flocci of black moulds. *Bactridium Helvellæ* usurps the fructifying disc of species of *Peziza*. A small *Sphinctrina* is found both in Britain and the United States on old *Polypori*. In *Sphæria nigerrima*, *Nectria episphæria*, and two or three

* Westendorp, "Les Cryptogams après leurs stations naturelles," 1865.

others, we have examples of one sphæriaceous fungus growing upon another.

Mr. Phillips has recently indicated the species of fungi found by him on charcoal beds in Shropshire,* but, useful as it is, that only refers to one locality. A complete list of all the fungi which have been found growing on charcoal beds, burnt soil, or charred wood, would be rather extensive. The fungi found in hothouses and stoves are also numerous, and often of considerable interest from the fact that they have many of them never been found elsewhere. Those found in Britain,† for instance, are excluded from the British Flora as doubtful, because, growing upon or with exotic plants, they are deemed to be of exotic origin, yet in very few cases are they known to be inhabitants of any foreign country. Some species found in such localities are not confined to them, as *Agaricus cœpestipes*, *Agaricus cristatus*, *Æthalium vaporarium*, &c. It is somewhat singular that certain species have a predilection for growing in proximity with other plants with which they do not appear to have any more intimate relation. Truffles, for instance, in association with oaks, *Peziza lanuginosa* under cedar-trees, *Hydnangium carneum* about the roots of *Eucalypti*, and numerous species of *Agaricini*, which are only found under trees of a particular kind. As might be anticipated, there is no more fertile habitat for fungi than the dung of animals, and yet the kinds found in such locations belong to but a few groups. Amongst the *Discomycetes*, a limited number of the genus *Peziza* are fimicolous, but the allied genus *Ascobolus*, and its own immediate allies, include amongst its species a large majority that are found on dung. If we take the number of species at sixty-four, there are only seven or eight which do not occur on dung, whilst fifty-six are fimicolous. The species of *Sphæria* which are found on the same substances are also closely allied, and some Continental authors have grouped them under the two proposed

* "Gardener's Chronicle," 1874.

† W. G. Smith, in "Journ. Botany," March, 1873; Berkeley, in "Grevillea," vol. i. p. 88.

genera *Sporormia* and *Sordaria*, whilst Fuckel * proposes a distinct group of *Sphæriacei*, under the name of *Fimicoli*, in which he includes as genera *Coprolepa*, *Hypocopra*, *Delitschia*, *Sporormia*, *Pleophragmia*, *Malinvernia*, *Sordaria*, and *Cercophora*. The two species of *Pilobolus*, and some of *Mucor*, are also found on dung, *Isaria felina* on that of cats, *Stilbum fimetarium* and a few other moulds, and amongst Agarics some species of *Coprinus*. Animal substances are not, as a rule, prolific in the production of fungi. *Ascobolus saccharinus* and one or two others have been found upon old leather. *Onygena* of two or three species occurs on old horn, hoofs, &c. Cheese, milk, &c., afford a few forms, but the largest number infest dead insects, either under the mouldy form of *Isaria* or the more perfect condition of *Torrubia*, and occasionally under other forms.

Robin † has recorded that three species of *Brachinus*, of the order Coleoptera, have been found infected, whilst living, with a minute yellow fungus which he calls *Laboulbenia Rougeti*, and the same species has been noted on other beetles. *Torrubia Melolonthæ* ‡ has been described by Tulasne as occurring on the maybug or cockchafer, which is allied to, if not identical with, *Cordyceps Ravenelii*, B. and C., and also that described and figured by M. Fougeroux de Bondaroy.§ *Torrubia curculionum*, Tul., occurs on several species of beetles, and seems to be by no means uncommon in Brazil and Central America. *Torrubia cæspitosa*, Tul., which may be the same as *Cordyceps Sinclairi*, B.,‖ is found on the larvæ of *Orthoptera* in New Zealand, *Torrubia Miquelii* on the larvæ of *Cicada* in Brazil, and *Torrubia sobolifera* on the pupæ of *Cicada* in the West Indies. A romantic account is given of this in an extract cited by Dr. Watson in his communication to the Royal Society.¶ "The vegetable fly is found in the island Dominica, and (excepting that it has no wings) re-

* Fuckel, "Symbolæ Mycologicæ," p. 240.

† Robin, "Végét. Parasites," p. 622, t. viii. f. 1, 2.

‡ Tulasne, "Selecta Fung. Carp." iii. p. 12.

§ "Hist. de l'Acad. des Sciences," 1769. Paris, 1772.

‖ Berkeley, "Crypt. Bot." p. 73; Hooker, "New Zealand Flora," ii. 338.

¶ "Philosophical Transactions," liii. (1763), p. 271.

sembles the drone, both in size and colour, more than any other English insect. In the month of May it buries itself in the earth and begins to vegetate. By the latter end of July, the tree is arrived at its full growth, and resembles a coral branch, and is about three inches high, and bears several little pods, which, dropping off, become worms, and from thence flies, like the English caterpillar." *Torrubia Taylori*, which grows from the caterpillar of a large moth in Australia, is one of the finest examples of the genus. *Torrubia Robertsii*, from New Zealand, has long been known as attacking the larva of *Hepialus virescens*. There are several other species on larvæ of different insects, on spiders, ants, wasps, &c., and one or two on mature Lepidoptera, but the latter seem to be rare.

That fungi should make their appearance and flourish in localities and conditions generally considered inimical to vegetable life is no less strange than true. We have already alluded to the occurrence of some species on spent tan, and some others have been found in locations as strange. We have seen a yellow mould resembling *Sporotrichum* in the heart of a ball of opium, also a white mould appears on the same substance, and more than one species is troublesome in the opium factories of India. A mould made its appearance some years since in a copper solution employed for electrotyping in the Survey Department of the United States,* decomposing the salt, and precipitating the copper. Other organisms have appeared from time to time in various inorganic solutions, some of which were considered destructive to vegetable life, and it is not improbable that some of these organisms were low conditions of mould. It may well occasion some surprise that fungi should be found growing within cavities wholly excluded from the external air, as in the hollow of filberts, and the harder shelled nuts of *Guilandina*, in the cavities of the fruit of tomato, or in the interior of an egg. It is scarcely less extraordinary that *Hypocrea inclusa* should flourish in the interior of a kind of truffle.

From the above it will be concluded that the habitats of fungi are exceedingly variable, that they may be regarded as almost

* Berkeley's "Outlines," p. 30.

universal wherever decaying vegetable matter is found, and that under some conditions animal substances, especially of vegetable feeders, such as insects, furnish a pabulum for their development.

A very curious and interesting inquiry presents itself to our minds, which is intimately related to this subject of the habitats of fungi. It shapes itself into a sort of "puzzle for the curious," but at the same time one not unprofitable to think about. How is the occurrence of new and before unknown forms to be accounted for in a case like the following?*

It was our fortune—good fortune as far as this investigation was concerned—to have a portion of wall in our dwelling persistently damp for some months. It was close to a cistern which had become leaky. The wall was papered with "marbled" paper, and varnished. At first there was for some time nothing worthy of observation, except a damp wall—decidedly damp, discoloured, but not by any means mouldy. At length, and rather suddenly, patches of mould, sometimes two or three inches in diameter, made their appearance. These were at first of a snowy whiteness, cottony and dense, just like large tufts of cotton wool, of considerable expansion, but of miniature elevation. They projected from the paper scarcely a quarter of an inch. In the course of a few weeks the colour of the tufts became less pure, tinged with an ochraceous hue, and resembling wool rather than cotton, less beautiful to the naked eye, or under a lens, and more entangled. Soon after this darker patches made their appearance, smaller, dark olive, and mixed with, or close to, the woolly tufts; and ultimately similar spots of a dendritic character either succeeded the olive patches, or were independently formed. Finally, little black balls, like small pin heads, or grains of gunpowder, were found scattered about the damp spots. All this mouldy forest was more than six months under constant observation, and during that period was held sacred from the disturbing influences of the housemaid's broom and duster.

Curiosity prompted us from the first to submit the mouldy

* "Popular Science Review," vol. x. (1871), p. 25.

denizens of the wall to the microscope, and this curiosity was increased week by week, on finding that none of the forms found vegetating on nearly two square yards of damp wall could be recognized as agreeing specifically with any described moulds with which we were acquainted. Here was a problem to be solved under the most favourable conditions, a forest of mould indoors, within a few yards of the fireside, growing quite naturally, and all strangers. Whence could these new forms proceed ?

The cottony tufts of white mould, which were the first to appear, had an abundant mycelium, but the erect threads which sprang from this were for a long time sterile, and closely interlaced. At length fertile threads were developed in tufts, mixed with the sterile threads. These fruit-bearers were shorter and stouter, more sparingly branched, but beset throughout nearly their whole length with short patent, alternate branchlets. These latter were broadest towards the apex, so as to be almost clavate, and the extremity was beset with two or three short spicules. Each spicule was normally surmounted by an obovate spore. The presence of fertile threads imparted the ochraceous tint above alluded to. This tint was slight, and perhaps would not have been noticed, but from the close proximity of the snow-white tufts of barren threads. The fertile flocci were decumbent, probably from the weight of the spores, and the tufts were a little elevated above the surface of the matrix. This mould belonged clearly to the *Mucedines*, but it hardly accorded well with any known genus, although most intimately related to *Rhinotrichum*, in which it was placed as *Rhinotrichum lanosum*.*

The white mould having become established for a week or two, small blackish spots made their appearance on the paper, sometimes amongst thin patches of the mould, and sometimes outside them. These spots, at first cloudy and indefinite, varied in size, but were usually less than a quarter of an inch in diameter. The varnish of the paper was afterwards pushed off

* Specimens of this mould were distributed in Cooke's "Fungi Britannici Exsiccati," No. 356, under the name of *Clinotrichum lanosum*.

in little translucent flakes or scales, an erect olivaceous mould appeared, and the patches extended to nearly an inch in diameter, maintaining an almost universal circular form. This new mould sometimes possessed a dirty reddish tint, but was commonly dark olive. There could be no mistake about the genus to which this mould belonged; it had all the essential characters of *Penicillium*. Erect jointed threads, branched in the upper portion in a fasciculate manner, and bearing long beaded threads of spores, which formed a tassel-like head, at the apex of each fertile thread. Although at first reminded of *Penicillium olivaceum*, of Corda, by the colour of this species, it was found to differ in the spores being oblong instead of globose, and the ramifications of the flocci were different. Unable again to find a described species of *Penicillium* with which this new mould would agree, it was described under the name of *Penicillium chartarum.**

Almost simultaneously, or but shortly after the perfection of the spores of *Penicillium*, other and very similar patches appeared, distinguished by the naked eye more particularly by their dendritic form. This peculiarity seemed to result from the dwarfed habit of the third fungus, since the varnish, though cracked and raised, was not cast off, but remained in small angular fragments, giving to the spots their dendritic appearance, the dark spores of the fungus protruding through the fissures. This same mould was also found in many cases growing in the same spots amongst *Penicillium chartarum*, but whether from the same mycelium could not be determined.

The distinguishing features of this fungus consist in an extensive mycelium of delicate threads, from which arise numerous erect branches, bearing at the apex dark brown opaque spores. Sometimes the branches were again shortly branched, but in the majority of instances were single. The septate spores had from two to four divisions, many of them divided again by cross septa in the longitudinal direction of the spore, so as to impart a muriform appearance. As far as the structure and appearance of the spores are concerned, they re-

* Cooke's "Handbook of British Fungi," p. 602.

sembled those of *Sporidesmium polymorphum*, under which name specimens were at first published,* but this determination was not satisfactory. The mycelium and erect threads are much too highly developed for a good species of *Sporidesmium*, although the name of *Sporidesmium alternaria* was afterwards adopted. In fresh specimens of this fungus, when seen *in situ* by a half-inch objective, the spores appear to be moniliform, but if so, all attempts to see them so connected, when separated from the matrix, failed. On one occasion, a very immature condition was examined, containing simple beaded, hyaline bodies, attached to each other by a short neck. The same appearance of beaded spores, when seen *in situ*, was recognized by a mycological friend, to whom specimens were submitted for confirmation.†

The last production which made its appearance on our wall-paper burst through the varnish as little black spheres, like grains of gunpowder. At first the varnish was elevated by pressure from beneath, then the film was broken, and the little blackish spheres appeared. These were, in the majority of cases, gregarious, but occasionally a few of the spheres appeared singly, or only two or three together. As the whole surface of the damp paper was covered by these different fungi, it was scarcely possible to regard any of them as isolated, or to declare that one was not connected with the mycelium of the others. The little spheres, when the paper was torn from the wall, were also growing from the under surface, flattened considerably by the pressure. The spherical bodies, or perithecia, were seated on a plentiful hyaline mycelium. The walls of the perithecia, rather more carbonaceous than membranaceous, are reticulated, reminding one of the conceptacles of *Erysiphe*, to which the perithecia bear considerable resemblance. The ostiolum is so

* Cooke's "Fungi Britannici Exsiccati," No. 329, under the name of *Sporidesmium polymorphum* var. *chartarum*.

† This reminds one of Preuss's *Alternaria*, figured in Sturm's "Flora;" it has been suggested that the mould, as seen when examined under a power of 320 diam., is very much like a *Macrosporium*. Again arises the question of the strings of spores attached end to end.

obscure that we doubt its existence, and hence the closer affinity of the plant to the *Perisporiacei* than to the *Sphæriacei.* The interior of the perithecium is occupied by a gelatinous nucleus, consisting of elongated cylindrical asci, each enclosing eight globose hyaline sporidia, with slender branched paraphyses. A new genus has been proposed for this and another similar form, and the present species bears the name of *Orbicula cyclospora.**

The most singular circumstance connected with this narrative is the presence together of four distinctly different species oi fungi, all of them previously unknown and undescribed, and no trace amongst them of the presence of any one of the very common species, which would be supposed to develop themselves under such circumstances. It is not at all unusual for *Sporocybe alternata*, B., to appear in broad black patches on damp papered walls, but in this instance not a trace was to be found. What were the peculiar conditions present in this instance which led to the manifestation of four new forms, and none of the old ones? We confess that we are unable to account satisfactorily for the mystery, but, at the same time, feel equally unwilling to invent hypotheses in order to conceal our own ignorance.

* "Handbook of British Fungi," vol. ii. p. 926, No. 2,788.

XII.

CULTIVATION.

THE cultivation of fungi in this country for esculent purposes is confined to a single species, and yet there is no reason why, by a series of well-conducted experiments, means should not be devised for the cultivation of others, for instance, *Marasmius oreades*, and the morel. Efforts have been made on the Continent for the cultivation of truffles, but the success has hitherto been somewhat doubtful. For the growth of the common mushroom, very little trouble and care is required, and moderate success is certain. A friend of ours some years since was fortunate enough to have one or two specimens of the large puff-ball, *Lycoperdon giganteum*, growing in his garden. Knowing its value, and being particularly fond of it when fried for breakfast, he was anxious to secure its permanence. The spot on which the specimens appeared was marked off and guarded, so that it was never desecrated by the spade, and the soil remained consequently undisturbed. Year after year, so long as he resided on the premises, he counted upon and gathered several specimens of the puff-ball, the mycelium continuing to produce them year after year. All parings, fragments, &c., not utilized of the specimens eaten were cast on this spot to rot, so that some of the elements might be returned to the soil. This was not true cultivation perhaps, as the fungus had first established itself, but it was preservation, and had its reward. It must be admitted, however, that the size and number of specimens diminished gradually, probably from exhaustion of the soil. This fungus, though strong, is much approved by many palates, and its cultivation might be attempted. Burying a ripe specimen in similar soil, and watering ground with the spores, has been tried without success.*

As to the methods adopted for cultivation of the common mushroom, it is unnecessary to detail them here, as there are several special treatises devoted to the subject, in which the particulars are more fully given than the limits of this chapter will permit.† Recently, M. Chevreul exhibited at the French Academy some splendid mushrooms, said to have been produced by the following method: he first develops the mushrooms by sowing spores on a pane of glass, covered with wet sand; then he selects the most vigorous individuals from among them, and sows, or plants their mycelium in a cellar in a damp soil, consisting of gardener's mould, covered with a layer of sand and gravel two inches thick, and another layer of rubbish from demolitions, about an inch deep. The bed is watered with a diluted solution of nitrate of potash, and in about six days the mushrooms grow to an enormous size.‡ The cultivation of mushrooms for the market, even in this country, is so profitable, that curious revelations sometimes crop up, as at a recent trial at the Sheriffs' Court for compensa-

* Experiments were made at Belvoir, by Mr. Ingram, in the cultivation of several species of *Agaricini*, but without success, and a similar fate attended some spawn of a very superior kind from the Swan River, which was submitted to the late Mr. J. Henderson. No result was obtained at Chiswick, either from the cultivation of truffles or from the inoculation of grass-plots with excellent spawn. Mr. Disney's experiments at the Hyde, near Ingatestone, were made with dried truffles, and were not likely to succeed. The Viscomte Nôe succeeded in obtaining abundant truffles, in an enclosed portion of a wood fenced from wild boars, by watering the ground with an infusion of fresh specimens; but it is possible that as this took place in a truffle country, there might have been a crop without any manipulation. Similar trials, and it is said successfully, have been made with *Boletus edulis*. Specimens of prepared truffle-spawn were sent many years since to the "Gardener's Chronicle," but they proved useless, if indeed they really contained any reliable spawn.

† Robinson, "On Mushroom Culture," London, 1870. Cuthill, "On the Cultivation of the Mushroom," 1861. Abercrombie, "The Garden Mushroom; its Culture, &c." 1802.

‡ This has, however, not been confirmed, and is considered (how justly we cannot say) a "canard."

tion by the Metropolitan Railway Company for premises and business of a nurseryman at Kensington. The Railway had taken possession of a mushroom-ground, and the claim for compensation was £716. It was stated in evidence that the profits on mushrooms amounted to 100 or 150 per cent. One witness said if £50 were expended, in twelve months, or perhaps in six months, the sum realized would be £200.

Immense quantities of mushrooms are produced in Paris, as is well known, in caves, and interesting accounts have been written of visits to these subterranean mushroom-vaults of the gay city. In one of these caves, at Montrouge, the proprietor gathers largely every day, occasionally sending more than 400 pounds weight per day to market, the average being about 300 pounds. There are six or seven miles' run of mushroom-beds in this cave, and the owner is only one of a large class who devote themselves to the culture of mushrooms. Large quantities of preserved mushrooms are exported, one house sending to England not less than 14,000 boxes in a year. Another cave near Frépillon was in full force in 1867, sending as many as 3,000 pounds of mushrooms to the Parisian markets daily. In 1867, M. Renaudot had over twenty-one miles of mushroom-beds in one great cave at Méry, and in 1869 there were sixteen miles of beds in a cave at Frépillon. The temperature of these caves is so equal that the cultivation of the mushroom is possible at all seasons of the year, but the best crops are gathered in the winter.

Mr. Robinson gives an excellent account, not only of the subterranean, but also of the open-air culture of mushrooms about Paris. The open-air culture is never pursued in Paris during the summer, and rarely so in this country.* What might be termed the domestic cultivation of mushrooms is easy, that is, the growth by inexperienced persons, for family consumption, of a bed of mushrooms in cellars, wood-houses, old tubs, boxes, or other unconsidered places. Even in towns and cities it is not impracticable, as horse-dung can always be obtained from mews

* This method is pursued with great success by Mr. Ingram, at Belvoir, and by Mr. Gilbert, at Burleigh.

and stables. Certainly fungi are never so harmless, or seldom so delicious, as when collected from the bed, and cooked at once, before the slightest chemical change or deterioration could possibly take place.

Mr. Cuthill's advice may be repeated here. He says:—"I must not forget to remind the cottager that it would be a shilling or two a week saved to him during the winter, if he had a good little bed of mushrooms, even for his own family, to say nothing about a shilling or two that he might gain by selling to his neighbours. I can assure him mushrooms grow faster than pigs, and the mushrooms do not eat anything; they only want a little attention. Addressing myself to the working classes, I advise them, in the first place, to employ their children or others collecting horse-droppings along the highway, and if mixed with a little road-sand, so much the better. They must be deposited in a heap during summer, and trodden firmly. They will heat a little, but the harder they are pressed the less they will heat. Over-heating must be guarded against; if the watch or trial stick which is inserted into them gets too hot for the hand to bear, the heat is too great, and will destroy the spawn. In that case artificial spawn must be used when the bed is made up, but this expedient is to be avoided on account of the expense. The easiest way for a cottager to save his own spawn would be to do so when he destroys his old bed; he will find all round the edges or driest parts of the dung one mass of superior spawn; let him keep this carefully in a very dry place, and when he makes up his next bed it can then be mixed with his summer droppings, and will insure a continuance and excellent crop. These little collections of horse-droppings and road-sand, if kept dry in shed, hole, or corner, under cover, will in a short time generate plenty of spawn, and will be ready to be spread on the surface of the bed in early autumn, say by the middle of September or sooner. The droppings during the winter must be put into a heap, and allowed to heat gently, say up to eighty or ninety degrees; then they must be turned over twice daily to let off the heat and steam; if this is neglected the natural spawn of the droppings is destroyed. The cottager should provide himself with a few barrowfuls of strawy dung to form the foundation of his bed, so that the depth, when all is finished, be not less than a foot. Let the temperature be up to milk heat. He will then, when quite sure that the bed will not overheat, put on his summer droppings. By this time these will be one mass of natural spawn, having a grey mouldy and thready appearance, and a smell like that of mushrooms. Let all be pressed very hard; then let mould, unsifted, be put on, to the thickness of four inches, and trodden down hard with the feet and watered all over; and the back of a spade may now be used to make it still harder, as well as to plaster the surface all over." * Mushrooms are cultivated very extensively by Mr. Ingram, at Belvoir, without artificial spawn. There is a great riding-house there, in which the litter is ground down by the horses' feet into very small shreds. These are placed in a heap and turned over once or twice during the season, when a large quantity of excellent spawn is developed which, placed in asparagus beds or laid under thin turf, produces admirable mushrooms, in the latter case as clean as in our best pastures.†

Other species will sometimes be seen growing on mushroom-beds besides the genuine mushroom, the spawn in such cases being probably introduced with the materials employed. We have seen a pretty crisped variety of *Agaricus dealbatus* growing in profusion in such a place, and devoured it accordingly. Sometimes the mushrooms will, when in an unhealthy condition, be subject to the ravages of parasitic species of mould, or perhaps of *Hypomyces*. *Xylaria vaporaria* has, in more than one instance, usurped the place of mushrooms. Mr. Berkeley has received abundant specimens in the Sclerotioid state, which he succeeded in developing in sand under a bell glass. Of course under such conditions there is much loss. The little fairy-ring champignon is an excellent and useful species, and it is a great pity that some effort should not be made to procure it by cultivation. In

* Cuthill, "Treatise on the Cultivation of the Mushroom," p. 9.

† Mr. Berkeley lately recommended, at one of the meetings of the Horticultural Society at South Kensington, that the railway arches should be utilized for the cultivation of mushrooms.

Italy a kind of *Polyporus*, unknown in this country, is obtained by watering the *Pietra funghaia*, or fungus stone, a sort of tufa impregnated with mycelium. The *Polypori*, it is said, take seven days to come to perfection, and may be obtained from the foster mass, if properly moistened, six times a year. There are specimens which were fully developed in Mr. Lee's nursery at Kensington many years since. Another fungus is obtained from the pollard head of the black poplar. Dr. Badham says that it is usual to remove these heads at the latter end of autumn, as soon as the vintage is over, and their marriage with the vine is annulled; hundreds of such heads are then cut and transported to different parts; they are abundantly watered during the first month, and in a short time produce that truly delicious fungus *Agaricus caudicinus*, which, during the autumn of the year, makes the greatest show in the Italian market-places. These pollard blocks continue to bear for from twelve to fourteen years.

Another fungus, which Dr. Badham himself reared (*Polyporus avellanus*), is procured by singeing, over a handful of straw, a block of the cob-nut tree, which is then watered and put by. In about a month the fungi make their appearance, and are quite white, of from two to three inches in diameter, and excellent to eat, while their profusion is sometimes so great as entirely to hide the wood from whence they spring.* It has been said that *Boletus edulis* may be propagated by watering the ground with a watery infusion of the plants, but we have no knowledge of this method having been pursued with success.

The culture of truffles has been partially attempted, on the principle that, in some occult manner, certain trees produced truffles beneath their shade. It is true that truffles are found under trees of special kinds, for Mr. Broome remarks that some trees appear more favourable to the production of truffles than others. Oak and hornbeam are specially mentioned; but, besides these, chestnut, birch, box, and hazel are alluded to. He generally found *Tuber œstivum* under beech-trees, but also under hazel, *Tuber macrosporum* under oaks, and *Tuber brumale* under

* Badham, "Esculent Funguses," 1st ed. p. 43.

oaks and abele. The men who collect truffles for Covent Garden Market obtain them chiefly under beech, and in mixed plantations of fir and beech.*

Some notion may be obtained of the extent to which the trade of truffles is carried in France, when we learn that in the market of Apt alone about 3,500 pounds of truffles are exposed for sale every week during the height of the season, and the quantity sold during the winter reaches upwards of 60,000 pounds, whilst the Department of Vaucluse yields annually upwards of 60,000 pounds. It may be interesting here to state that the value of truffles is so great in Italy that precautions are taken against truffle poachers, much in the same way as against game poachers in England. They train their dogs so skilfully that, while they stand on the outside of the truffle grounds, the dogs go in and dig for the fungi. Though there are multitudes of species, they bring out those only which are of market value. Some dogs, however, are employed by botanists, which will hunt for any especial species that may be shown to them. The great difficulty is to prevent them devouring the truffles, of which they are very fond. The best dogs, indeed, are true retrievers.

The Count de Borch and M. de Bornholz give the chief accounts of the efforts that have been made towards the cultivation of these fungi. They state that a compost is prepared of pure mould and vegetable soil mixed with dry leaves and sawdust, in which, when properly moistened, mature truffles are placed in winter, either whole or in fragments, and that after the lapse of some time small truffles are found in the compost.† The most successful plan consists in sowing acorns over a considerable extent of land of a calcareous nature; and when the young oaks have attained the age of ten or twelve years, truffles are found in the intervals between the trees. This process was carried on in the neighbourhood of Loudun, where truffle-beds had formerly existed, but where they had long ceased to be productive—a fact indicating the aptitude of the soil for the purpose. In this case

* Broome, "On Truffle Culture," in "Journ. Hort. Soc." i. p. 15 (1866).

† No faith, however, is, in general, placed on these realises, as they were merely conjectural.

no attempt was made to produce truffles by placing ripe specimens in the earth, but they sprang up themselves from spores probably contained in the soil. The young trees were left rather wide apart, and were cut, for the first time, about the twelfth year after sowing, and afterwards at intervals of from seven to nine years. Truffles were thus obtained for a period of from twenty-five to thirty years, after which the plantations ceased to be productive, owing, it was said, to the ground being too much shaded by the branches of the young trees. It is the opinion of the Messrs. Tulasne that the regular cultivation of the truffle in gardens can never be so successful as this so-called indirect culture at Loudun, but they think that a satisfactory result might be obtained in suitable soils by planting fragments of mature truffles in wooded localities, taking care that the other conditions of the spots selected should be analogous to those of the regular truffle-grounds, and they recommend a judicious thinning of the trees and clearing the surface from brushwood, etc., which prevents at once the beneficial effects of rain and of the direct sun's rays. A truffle collector stated to Mr. Broome that whenever a plantation of beech, or beech and fir, is made on the chalk districts of Salisbury Plain, after the lapse of a few years truffles are produced, and that these plantations continue productive for a period of from ten to fifteen years, after which they cease to be so.

M. Gasparin reported to the jurors of the Paris Exhibition of 1855, concerning the operations of M. Rousseau, of Carpentras, on the production of oak truffles in France. The acorns of evergreen and of common oaks were sown about five yards apart. In the fourth year of the plantation three truffles were found; at the date of the report the trees were nine years old, and over a yard in height. Sows were employed to search for the truffles. Although these plantations consist both of the evergreen and common oak, truffles cannot be gathered at the base of the latter species, it so happening that it arrives later at a state of production. The common oak, however, produces truffles like the evergreen oak, this report states, for a great number of the natural truffle-grounds at Vaucluse are planted with common oaks. It is remarked that the truffles produced from these are larger but less regular than those of the evergreen oak, which are smaller, but nearly always spherical. The truffles are gathered at two periods of the year; in May only white truffles are to be found, which never blacken and have no odour; they are dried and sold for seasoning. The black truffles (*Tuber melanosporum*) commence forming in June, enlarging towards the frosty season; then they become hard, and acquire all their perfume. They are dug a month before and a month after Christmas. It is also asserted that truffles are produced about the vine, or at any rate that the association of the vine is favourable to the production of truffles, because truffle-plots near vines are very productive. The observation of this decided M. Rousseau to plant a row of vines between the oaks. The result of this experiment altogether does not appear to have been by any means flattering, for at the end of eight years only little more than fifteen pounds were obtained from a hectare of land, which, if valued at 45 francs, would leave very little profit. M. Rousseau also called attention to a meadow manured (*sic*) with parings of truffles, which was said to have given prodigious results.

The cultivation of minute fungi for scientific purposes has been incidentally alluded to and illustrated in foregoing chapters, and consequently will not require such full and particular details here. Somewhat intermediately, we might allude to the species of *Sclerotium*, which are usually compact, externally blackish, rounded or amorphous bodies, consisting of a cellular mass of the nature of a concentrated mycelium. Placed in favourable conditions, these forms of *Sclerotium* will develop the peculiar species of fungus belonging to them, but in certain cases the production is more rapid and easy than in others. In this country, Mr. F. Currey has been the most successful in the cultivation of *Sclerotia*. The method adopted is to keep them in a moist, somewhat warm, but equable atmosphere, and with patience await the results. The well-known ergot of rye, wheat, and other grasses may be so cultivated, and Mr. Currey has developed the ergot of the common reed by keeping the stem immersed in water. The final conditions are small clavate bodies of the order *Sphæriacei*, belonging to the genus *Claviceps*. The *Sclerotium* of the *Eleocharis* has been found in this country, but we are not aware that the *Claviceps* developed from it has been met with or induced by cultivation. One method recommended for this sort of experiment is to fill a garden-pot half full of crocks, over which to place sphagnum broken up until the pot is nearly full, on this to place the *Sclerotia*, and cover with silver sand; if the pot is kept standing in a pan of water in a warm room, it is stated that production will ensue. Ergot of the grasses will not always develop under these conditions, but perseverance may ultimately ensure success.

A species of *Sclerotium* on the gills of dead Agarics originates *Agaricus tuberosus*, another *Agaricus cirrhatus*,* but this should be kept *in situ* when cultivated artificially, and induced to develop whilst still attached to the rotten Agarics. *Peziza tuberosa*, in like manner, is developed from *Sclerotia*, usually found buried in the ground in company with the roots of *Anemone nemorosa*. At one time it was supposed that some relationship existed between the roots of the anemone and the *Sclerotia*. From another *Sclerotium*, found in the stems of bulrushes, Mr. Currey has developed a species of *Peziza*, which has been named *P. Curreyana*.† This *Peziza* has been found growing naturally from the *Sclerotia* imbedded in the tissue of common rushes. De Bary has recorded the development of *Peziza Fuckeliana* from a *Sclerotium* of which the conidia take the form of a species of *Polyactis*. *Peziza ciborioides* is developed from a *Sclerotium* found amongst dead leaves; and recently we have received from the United States an allied *Peziza* which originated from the *Sclerotia* found on the petals of *Magnolia*, and which has been named *Peziza gracilipes*, Cooke, from its very slender, thread-like stem. Other species of *Peziza* are also known to be developed from similar bases, and these Fuckel has associated

* Dr. Bull has been very successful in developing the *Sclerotium* of *Agaricus cirrhatus*.

† Currey, "On Development of *Sclerotium roseum*," in "Journ. Linn. Soc." vol. i. p. 148.

together under a proposed new genus with the name of *Sclerotinia*. Two or three species of *Typhula*, in like manner, spring from forms of *Sclerotium*, long known as *Sclerotium complanatum* and *Sclerotium scutellatum*. Other forms of *Sclerotium* are known, from one of which, found in a mushroom-bed, Mr. Currey developed *Xylaria vaporaria*, B., by placing it on damp sand covered with a bell glass.* Others, again, are only known in the sclerotioid state, such as the *Sclerotium stipitatum* found in the nests of white ants in South India.† From what is already known, however, we feel justified in the conclusion that the so-called species of *Sclerotium* are a sort of compact mycelium, from which, under favourable conditions, perfect fungi may be developed. Mr. Berkeley succeeded in raising from the minute *Sclerotium* of onions, which looks like grains of coarse gunpowder, a species of *Mucor*. This was accomplished by placing a thin slice of the *Sclerotium* in a drop of water under a glass slide, surrounded by a pellicle of air, and luted to prevent evaporation and external influences.‡

As to the cultivation of moulds and *Mucors*, one great difficulty has to be encountered in the presence or introduction of foreign spores to the matrix employed for their development. Bearing this in mind, extensive cultivations may be made, but the conditions must influence the decision upon the results. Rice paste has been used with advantage for sowing the spores of moulds, afterwards keeping them covered from external influences. In cultivation on rice paste of rare species, the experimenter is often perplexed by the more rapid growth of the common species of *Mucor* and *Penicillium*. Mr. Berkeley succeeded in developing up to a certain point the fungus of the Madura Foot, but though perfect sporangia were produced, the further development was masked by the outgrowth of other species. In like manner, orange juice, cut surfaces of fruits,

* Currey, in "Linn. Trans." xxiv. pl. 25, figs. 17, 26.

† Berkeley, "On Two Tuberiform Veg. Productions from Travancore," in "Trans. Linn. Soc." vol. xxiii. p. 91.

‡ Berkeley, "On a Peculiar Form of Mildew in Onions," "Journ. Hort. Soc." vol. iii. p. 91.

slices of potato tubers, etc., have been employed. Fresh horse-dung, placed under a bell glass and kept in a humid atmosphere, will soon be covered with *Mucor*, and in like manner the growth of common moulds upon decayed fruit may be watched; but this can hardly be termed cultivation unless the spores of some individual species are sown. Different solutions have been proposed for the growth of such conditions as the cells which induce fermentation, to which yeast plants belong. A fly attacked by *Empusa muscæ*, if immersed in water, will develop one of the *Saprolegniæ*.

The *Uredines* and other epiphyllous *Coniomycetes* will readily germinate by placing the leaf which bears them on damp sand, or keeping them in a humid atmosphere. Messrs. Tulasne and De Bary have, in their numerous memoirs, detailed the methods adopted by them for different species, both for germination of the pseudospores and for impregnating healthy foster plants. The germination of the pseudospores of the species of *Podisoma* may easily be induced, and secondary fruits obtained. The germination of the spores of *Tilletia* is more difficult to accomplish, but this may be achieved. Mr. Berkeley found no difficulty, and had the stem impregnated as well as the germen. On the other hand, the pseudospores of *Cystopus*, when sown in water on a slip of glass, will soon produce the curious little zoospores in the manner already described.

The sporidia of the *Discomycetes*, and some of the *Sphæriacei*, germinate readily in a drop of water on a slip of glass, although not proceeding further than the protrusion of germ-tubes. A form of slide has been devised for growing purposes, in which the large covering glass is held in position, and one end of the slip being kept immersed in a vessel of water, capillary attraction keeps up the supply for an indefinite period, so that there is no fear of a check from the evaporation of the fluid. Even when saccharine solutions are employed this method may be adopted.

The special cultivation of the *Peronosporei* occupied the attention of Professor De Bary for a long time, and his experiences are detailed in his memoir on that group,* but which are too

* De Bary, "Ann. des Sci. Nat." 4th series, vol. xx.

long for quotation here, except his observations on the development of the threads of *Peronospora infestans* on the cut surface of the tubers of diseased potatoes. When a diseased potato is cut and sheltered from dessication, the surface of the slice covers itself with the mycelium and conidiiferous branches of *Peronospora*, and it can easily be proved that these organs originate from the intercellulary tubes of the brown tissue. The mycelium that is developed upon these slices is ordinarily very vigorous; it often constitutes a cottony mass of a thickness of many millimetres, and it gives out conidiiferous branches, often partitioned, and larger and more branched than those observed on the leaves. The appearance of these fertile branches ordinarily takes place at the end of from twenty-four to forty-eight hours; sometimes, nevertheless, one must wait for many days. These phenomena are observed in all the diseased tubercles without exception, so long as they have not succumbed to putrefaction, which arrests the development of the parasite and kills it.

Young plants of the species liable to attack may be inoculated with the conidia of the species of *Peronospora* usually developed on that particular host, in the same manner that young cruciferous plants, watered with an infusion of the spores of *Cystopus candidus*, will soon exhibit evidence of attack from the white rust.

It is to the cultivation and close investigation of the growth and metamorphoses of the minute fungi that we must look for the most important additions which have yet to be made to our knowledge of the life-history of these most complex and interesting organisms.

XIII.

GEOGRAPHICAL DISTRIBUTION.

UNFORTUNATELY no complete or satisfactory account can be given of the geographical distribution of fungi. The younger Fries,* with all the facilities at his disposal which the lengthened experience and large collections of his father afforded, could only give a very imperfect outline, and now we can add very little to what he has given. The cause of this difficulty lies in the fact that the Mycologic Flora of so large a portion of the world remains unexplored, not only in remote regions, but even in civilized countries where the Phanerogamic Flora is well known. Europe, England, Scotland, and Wales are as well explored as any other country, but Ireland is comparatively unknown, no complete collection having ever been made, or any at least published. Scandinavia has also been well examined, and the northern portions of France, with Belgium, some parts of Germany and Austria, in Russia the neighbourhood of St. Petersburg, and parts of Italy and Switzerland. Turkey in Europe, nearly all Russia, Spain, and Portugal are almost unknown. As to North America, considerable advances have been made since Schweinitz by Messrs. Curtis and Ravenel, but their collections in Carolina cannot be supposed to represent the whole of the United States; the small collections made in Texas, Mexico, etc., only serve to show the richness of the country, not yet half exhausted. It is to be hoped that the young race of botanists in the United States will apply themselves to the task of investi-

* Mr. E. P. Fries, in "Ann. des Sci. Nat." 1861, xv. p. 10.

gating the Mycologic Flora of this rich and fertile region. In Central America very small and incomplete collections have as yet been made, and the same may be said of South America and Canada. Of the whole extent of the New World, only the Carolina States of North America can really be said to be satisfactorily known. Asia is still less known, the whole of our vast Indian Empire being represented by the collections made by Dr. Hooker in the Sikkim Himalayas, and a few isolated specimens from other parts. Ceylon has recently been removed from the category of the unknown by the publication of its Mycologic Flora.* All that is known of Java is supplied by the researches of Junghuhn; whilst all the rest is completely unknown, including China, Japan, Siam, the Malayan Peninsula, Burmah, and the whole of the countries in the north and west of India. A little is known of the Philippines, and the Indian Archipelago, but this knowledge is too fragmentary to be of much service. In Africa no part has been properly explored, with the exception of Algeria, although something is known of the Cape of Good Hope and Natal. The Australasian Islands are better represented in the Floras published of those regions. Cuba and the West Indies generally are moderately well known from the collections of Mr. C. Wright, which have been recorded in the journal of the Linnæan Society, and in the same journal Mr. Berkeley has described many Australian species.

It will be seen from the above summary how unsatisfactory it must be to give anything like a general view of the geographical distribution of fungi, or to estimate at all approximately the number of species on the globe. Any attempt, therefore, must be made and accepted subject to the limitations we have expressed.

The conditions which determine the distribution of fungi are not precisely those which determine the distribution of the higher plants. In the case of the parasitic species they may be said to follow the distribution of their foster-plants, as in the case of the rust, smut, and mildew of the cultivated cereals,

* Berkeley and Broome, "Enumeration of the Fungi of Ceylon," in "Journ. Linn. Soc." xiv. Nos. 73, 74, 1873.

which have followed those grains wherever they have been distributed, and the potato disease, which is said to have been known in the native region of the potato plant before it made its appearance in Europe. We might also allude to *Puccinia malvacearum*, Ca., which was first made known as a South American species; it then travelled to Australia, and at length to Europe, reaching England the next year after it was recorded on the Continent. In the same manner, so far as we have the means of knowing, *Puccinia Apii*, Ca., was known on the Continent of Europe for some time before it was detected on the celery plants in this country. Experience seems to warrant the conclusion that if a parasite affects a certain plant within a definite area, it will extend in time beyond that area to other countries where the foster-plant is found. This view accounts in some part for the discovery of species in this country, year after year, which had not been recorded before; some allowance being made for the fact that an increased number of observers and collectors may cause the search to be more complete, yet it must be conceded that the migration of Continental species must to some extent be going on, or how can it be accounted for that such large and attractive fungi as *Sparassis crispa, Helvellas gigas*, and *Morchella crassipes* had never been recorded till recently, or amongst parasitic species such as the two species of *Puccinia* above named? In the same manner it is undoubtedly true that species which at one time were common gradually become somewhat rare, and at length nearly extinct. We have observed this to apply to the larger species as well as to the microscopic in definite localities. For instance, *Craterellus cornucopioides* some ten years ago appeared in one wood, at a certain spot, by hundreds, whereas during the past three or four years we have failed to find a single specimen. As many years since, and in two places, where the goat's-beard was abundant, as it is now, we found nearly half the flowering heads infested with *Ustilago receptaculorum*, but for the past two or three years, although we have sought it industriously, not a single specimen could be found. It is certain that plants found by Dickson, Bolton, and Sowerby, have not been detected since, whilst it is not improbable that species common with us may be very rare fifty years hence. In this manner it would really appear that fungi are much more liable than flowering plants to shift their localities, or increase and diminish in number.

The fleshy fungi, *Agaricini* and *Boleti* especially, are largely dependent upon the character of woods and forests. When the undergrowth of a wood is cleared away, as it often is every few years, it is easy to observe a considerable difference in the fungi. Species seem to change places, common ones amongst a dense undergrowth are rare or disappear with the copsewood, and others not observed before take their place. Some species, too, are peculiar to certain woods, such as beech woods and fir woods, and their distribution will consequently depend very much on the presence or absence of such woods. Epiphytal species, such as *Agaricus ulmarius*, *Agaricus mucidus*, and a host of others, depend on circumstances which do not influence the distribution of flowering plants. It may be assumed that such species as flourish in pastures and open places are subject to fewer adverse conditions than those which affect woods and forests.

Any one who has observed any locality with reference to its Mycologic Flora over a period of years will have been struck with the difference in number and variety caused by what may be termed a "favourable season," that is, plenty of moisture in August with warm weather afterwards. Although we know but little of the conditions of germination in Agarics, it is but reasonable to suppose that a succession of dry seasons will considerably influence the flora of any locality. Heat and humidity, therefore, are intimately concerned in the mycologic vegetation of a country. Fries has noted in his essay the features to which we have alluded. "The fact," he says, "must not be lost sight of that some species of fungi which have formerly been common in certain localities may become, within our lifetime, more and more scarce, and even altogether cease to grow there. The cause of this, doubtless, is the occurrence of some change in the physical constitution of a locality, such as that resulting from the destruction of a forest, or from the drainage, by ditches and cuttings, of more or less extensive swamps, or from the cultivation of the soil—all of them circumstances which cause the destruction of the primitive fungaceous vegetation and the production of a new one. If we compare the fungal flora of America with that of European countries, we observe that the former equals, in its richness and the variety of its forms, that of the phanerogamous flora; it is probable, however, that, in the lapse of more or fewer years, this richness will decrease, in consequence of the extension of cultivation—as is illustrated, indeed, in what has already taken place in the more thickly peopled districts, as, for example, in the vicinity of New York."

Although heat and humidity influence all kinds of vegetation, yet heat seems to exert a less, and humidity a greater, influence on fungi than on other plants. It is chiefly during the cool moist autumnal weather that the fleshy fungi flourish most vigorously in our own country, and we observe their number to increase with the humidity of the season. Rain falls copiously in the United States, and this is one of the most fruitful countries known for the fleshy fungi. Hence it is a reasonable deduction that moisture is a condition favourable to the development of these plants. The *Myxogastres*, according to Dr. Henry Carter, are exceedingly abundant—in individuals, at least, if not in species—in Bombay, and this would lead to the conclusion that the members of this group are influenced as much by heat as humidity in their development, borne out by the more plentiful appearance of the species in this country in the warmer weather of summer.

In the essay to which we have alluded, Fries only attempts the recognition of two zones in his estimate of the distribution of fungi, and these are the temperate and tropical. The frigid zone produces no peculiar types, and is poor in the number of species, whilst no essential distinction can be drawn between the tropical and sub-tropical with our present limited information. Even these two zones must not be accepted too rigidly, since tropical forms will in some instances, and under favourable conditions, extend far upwards into the temperate zone.

"In any region whatever," writes Fries, "it is necessary, in the first instance, to draw a distinction between its open naked plains and its wooded tracts. In the level open country there is a more rapid evaporation of the moisture by the conjoined action of the sun and wind; whence it happens that such a region is more bare of fungi than one that is mountainous or covered by woods. On the other hand, plains possess several species peculiar to themselves; as, for example, *Agaricus pediades*, certain *Tricholomata*, and, above all, the family *Coprini*, of which they may be regarded as the special habitat. The species of this family augment in number, in any given country, in proportion to the extent and degree of its cultivation; for instance, they grow more luxuriantly in the province of Scania, in Sweden—a district further distinguished above all others by its cultivation and fertility. In well-wooded countries moisture is retained a much longer time, and, as a result, the production of fungi is incomparably greater; and it is here desirable to make a distinction between the fungi growing in forests of resinous-wooded trees (*Coniferæ*) and those which inhabit woods of other trees, for these two descriptions of forests may be rightly regarded, as to their fungaceous growths, as two different regions. Beneath the shade of *Coniferæ*, fungi are earlier in their appearance; so much so, that it often happens they have attained their full development when their congeners in forests of non-resinous trees have scarcely commenced their growth. In woods of the latter sort, the fallen leaves, collected in thick layers, act as an obstacle to the soaking of moisture into the earth, and thereby retard the vegetation of fungi; on the other hand, such woods retain moisture longer. These conditions afford to several large and remarkable species the necessary time for development. The beech is characteristic of our own region, but further north this tree gives place to the birch. Coniferous woods are, moreover, divisible into two regions—that of the pines and that of the firs. The latter is richer in species than the former, because, as is well known, fir-trees flourish in more fertile and moister soils. Whether, with respect to the South of Europe, other subdivisions into regions are required, we know not; still less are we able to decide on the like question in reference to the countries beyond Europe." *

In very cold countries the higher fungi are rare, whilst in tropical countries they are most common at elevations which secure a temperate climate. In Java, Junghuhn found them most prolific at an elevation of 3,000 to 5,000 feet; and in India, Dr. Hooker remarked that they were most abundant at an elevation of 7,000 to 8,000 feet above the sea level.

For the higher fungi we must be indebted to the summary made by Fries, to which we have little to add.

The genus *Agaricus* occupies the first place, and surpasses, in the number of species, all the other generic groups known. It appears, from our present knowledge, that the *Agarici* have their geographic centre in the temperate zone, and especially in the colder portion of that zone. It is a curious circumstance that all the extra-European species of this genus *Agaricus* may be referred to various European subgenera.

In tropical countries it appears that the *Agarici* occupy only a secondary position in relation to other genera of fungi, such as *Polyporus*, *Lenzites*, etc. North America, on the other hand, is richer in species of *Agaricus* than Europe; for whilst the majority of typical forms are common to both continents, America further possesses many species peculiar to itself. In the temperate zone, so close is the analogy prevailing between the various countries in respect to the *Agaricini*, that from Sweden to Italy, and as well in England as North America, the same species are to be found. Of 500 *Agaricini* met with in St. Petersburg, there are only two or three which have not been discovered in Sweden; and again, of fifty species known in Greenland, there is not one that is not common in Sweden. The same remarks hold good in reference to the *Agaricini* of Siberia, Kamtschatka, the Ukraine, etc. The countries bordering upon the Mediterranean possess, however, several peculiar types; and Eastern and Western Europe present certain dissimilarities in their Agaric inhabitants. Several species, for example, of *Armil-*

* Fries, "On the Geographical Distribution of Fungi," in "Ann. and Mag. Nat. Hist." ser. iii. vol. ix. p. 279.

laria and *Tricholoma*, which have been found in Russia, have been met with in Sweden only in Upland, that is, in the most eastern province; all the species which belong to the so-called *abiegno-rupestres* and *pineto-montanæ* regions of Sweden are wanting in England; and it is only in Scotland that the species of northern mountainous and pine-bearing regions are met with—a circumstance explicable from the similarity in physical features between Sweden and the northern portions of Great Britain.

The species of *Coprinus* appear to find suitable habitats in every quarter of the globe.

The *Cortinariæ* predominate in the north; they abound in Northern latitudes, especially on wooded hills; but the plains offer also some peculiar species which flourish during the rainy days of August and September. In less cold countries they are more scarce or entirely absent. The species of the genus *Hygrophorus* would at first seem to have a similar geographical distribution to those of the last group; but this is really not the case, for the same *Hygrophori* are to be found in nearly every country of Europe, and even the hottest countries (and those under the equator) are not destitute of representatives of this wide-spread genus.

The *Lactarii*, which are so abundant in the forests of Europe and North America, appear to grow more and more scarce towards both the south and north. The same may be stated in regard to *Russula*.

The genus *Marasmius* is dispersed throughout the globe, and everywhere presents numerous species. In inter-tropical countries they are still more abundant, and exhibit peculiarities in growth which probably might justify their collection into a distinct group.

The genera *Lentinus* and *Lenzites* are found in every region of the world; their principal centre, however, is in hot countries, where they attain a splendid development. On the contrary, towards the north they rapidly decrease in number.

The *Polypori* constitute a group which, unlike that of the Agarics, especially belongs to hot countries. The *Boleti* constitute the only exception to this rule, since they select the temperate and frigid zones for their special abode, and some of them at times find their way to the higher regions of the Alps. No one can describe the luxuriance of the torrid zone in *Polypori* and *Trametes*, genera of *Hymenomycetes*, which flourish beneath the shade of the virgin forests, where perpetual moisture and heat promote their vegetation and give rise to an infinite variety of forms. But though the genus *Polyporus*, which rivals *Agaricus* in the number of its species, inhabits, in preference, warm climates at large, it nevertheless exhibits species peculiar to each country. This arises from the circumstance that the *Polypori*, for the most part, live upon trees, and are dependent on this or that particular tree for a suitable habitat; and the tropical flora being prolific in trees of all kinds, a multitude of the most varied forms of these fungi is a necessary consequence. *Hexagona*, *Favolus*, and *Laschia* are common in inter-tropical countries, but they are either entirely absent or extremely rare in temperate climes.

When the majority of the species of a genus are of a fleshy consistence, it may generally be concluded that that genus belongs to a Northern region, even if it should have some representatives in lands which enjoy more sunshine. Thus the *Hydna* are the principal ornaments of Northern forests, where they attain so luxuriant a growth and beauty that every other country must yield the palm to Sweden in respect to them. In an allied genus, that of *Irpex*, the texture assumes a coriaceous consistence, and we find its species to be more especially inhabitants of warm climates.

Most of the genera of *Auricularini* are cosmopolitan, and the same is true of some species of *Stereum*, of *Corticium*, etc., which are met with in countries of the most different geographical position. In tropical countries, these genera of fungi assume the most curious and luxuriant forms. The single and not considerable genus *Cyphella* appears to be pretty uniformly distributed over the globe. The *Clavariæi* are equally universal in their diffusion, although more plentiful in the north; however, the genus *Pterula* possesses several exotic forms, though in Europe it has but two representative species. That beautiful genus of

Hymenomycetes, *Sparassis*, occupies a similar place next the *Clavariæi*, and is peculiarly a production of the temperate zone and of the coniferous region.

The fungi which constitute the family of *Tremellini* prevail in Europe, Asia, and North America, and exhibit no marked differences amongst themselves, notwithstanding the distances of the several countries apart. It must, however, be stated that the *Hirneolæ* for the most part inhabit the tropics.

We come now to the *Gasteromycetes*—an interesting family, which exhibits several ramifications or particular series of developments. The most perfect *Gasteromycetes* almost exclusively belong to the warmer division of the temperate, and to the tropical zone, where their vegetation is the most luxuriant. Of late the catalogue of these fungi has been greatly enriched by the addition of numerous genera and species, proper to hot countries, previously unknown. Not uncommonly, the exotic floras differ from ours, not merely in respect of the species, but also of the genera of *Gasteromycetes*. It must, besides, be observed that this family is rich in well-defined genera, though very poor in distinct specific forms. Among the genera found in Europe, many are cosmopolitan.

The *Phalloidei* present themselves in the torrid zone under the most varied form and colouring, and comprise many genera rich in species. In Europe their number is very restricted. As we advance northward they decrease rapidly, so that the central districts of Sweden possess only a single species, the *Phallus impudicus*, and even this solitary representative of the family is very scarce. In Scania, the most southern province of Sweden, there is likewise but one genus and one species belonging to it, viz., the *Mutinus caninus*. Among other members of the *Phalloidei*, may be further mentioned the *Lysurus* of China, the *Aseröe* of Van Diemen's Land, and the *Clathrus*, one species of which, *C. cancellatus*, has a very wide geographical range; for instance, it is found in the south of Europe, in Germany, and in America; it occurs also in the south of England and the Isle of Wight; whereas the other species of this genus have a very limited distribution.

The *Tuberacei** are remarkable amongst the fungi in being all of them more or less hypogeous. They are natives of warm countries, and are distributed into numerous genera and species. The *Tuberacei* constitute in Northern latitudes a group of fungi very poor in specific forms. The few species of the *Hymenogastres* belonging to Sweden, with the exception of *Hyperrhiza variegata* and one example of the genus *Octaviana*, are confined to the southern provinces. The greater part of this group, like the *Lycoperdacei*, are met with in the temperate zone. Most examples of the genus *Lycoperdon* are cosmopolitan.

The *Nidulariacei* and the *Trichodermacei* appear to be scattered over the globe in a uniform manner, although their species are not everywhere similar. The same statement applies to the *Myxogastres*, which are common in Lapland, and appear to have their central point of distribution in the countries within the temperate zone. At the same time, they are not wanting in tropical regions, notwithstanding that the intensity of heat, by drying up the mucilage which serves as the medium for the development of their spores, is opposed to their development.†

Of the *Coniomycetes*, the parasitic species, as the *Cæomacei*, the *Pucciniei*, and the *Ustilagines*, accompany their foster-plants into almost all regions where they are found; so that smut, rust, and mildew are as common on wheat and barley in the Himalayas and in New Zealand as in Europe and America. *Ravenelia* and *Cronartium* only occur in the warmer parts of the temperate zone, whilst *Sartvellia* is confined to Surinam. Species of *Podisoma* and *Ræstelia* are as common in the United States as in Europe, and the latter appears also at the Cape and Ceylon. Wherever species of *Sphæria* occur there the *Sphæronemei* are found, but they do not appear, according to our present knowledge, to be so plentiful in tropical as in temperate countries. The *Torulacei* and its allies are widely diffused, and probably occur to a considerable extent in tropical countries.

Hyphomycetes are widely diffused; some species are peculiarly

* The *Hypogæi* are evidently intended here by Fries.

† Fries, "On the Geographical Distribution of Fungi," in "Ann. and Mag. Nat. Hist." ser. 3, vol. ix. p. 285.

cosmopolitan, and all seem to be less influenced by climatic conditions than the more fleshy fungi. The *Sepedoniei* are represented by at least one species wherever *Boletus* is found. The *Mucedines* occur everywhere in temperate and tropical regions, *Penicillium* and *Aspergillus* flourishing as much in the latter as in the former. *Botrytis* and *Peronospora* are almost as widely diffused and as destructive in warmer as in temperate countries, and although from difficulty in preservation the moulds are seldom represented to any extent in collections, yet indications of their presence constantly occur in connection with other forms, to such an extent as to warrant the conclusion that they are far from uncommon. The *Dematiei* are probably equally as widely diffused. Species of *Helminthosporium*, *Cladosporium*, and *Macrosporium* seem to be as common in tropical as temperate climes. The distribution of these fungi is imperfectly known, except in Europe and North America, but their occurrence in Ceylon, Cuba, India, and Australasia indicated a cosmopolitan range. *Cladosporium herbarum* would seem to occur everywhere. The *Stilbacei* and *Isariacei* are not less widely diffused, although as yet apparently limited in species. *Isaria* occurs on insects in Brazil as in North America, and species of *Stilbum* and *Isaria* are by no means rare in Ceylon.

The *Physomycetes* have representatives in the tropics, species of *Mucor* occurring in Cuba, Brazil, and the southern states of North America, with the same and allied genera in Ceylon. *Antennaria* and *Pisomyxa* seem to reach their highest development in hot countries.

The *Ascomycetes* are represented everywhere, and although certain groups are more tropical than others, they are represented in all collections. The fleshy forms are most prolific in temperate countries, and only a few species of *Peziza* affect the tropics, yet in elevated districts of hot countries, such as the Himalayas of India, *Peziza*, *Morchella*, and *Geoglossum* are found. Two or three species of *Morchella* are found in Kashmir, and at least one or two in Java, where they are used as food. The genus *Cyttaria* is confined to the southern parts of South America and Tasmania. The United States equal if they do not exceed

European states in the number of species of the *Discomycetes.* The *Phacidiacei* are not confined to temperate regions, but are more rare elsewhere. *Cordierites* and *Acroscyphus* (?) are tropical genera, the former extending upwards far into the temperate zone, as *Hysterium* and *Rhytisma* descend into the tropics. Amongst the *Sphæriacei*, *Xylaria* and *Hypoxylon* are well represented in the tropics, such species as *Xylaria hypoxylon* and *Xylaria corniformis* being widely diffused. In West Africa an American species of *Hypoxylon* is amongst the very few specimens that have ever reached us from the Congo, whilst *H. concentricum* and *Ustulina vulgaris* seem to be almost cosmopolitan. *Torrubia* and *Nectria* extend into the tropics, but are more plentiful in temperate and sub-tropical countries. *Dothidea* is well represented in the tropics, whilst of the species of *Sphæria* proper, only the more prominent have probably been secured by collectors; hence the *Superficiales* section is better represented than the *Obtectæ*, and the tropical representatives of foliicolous species are but few. *Asterina*, *Micropeltis*, and *Pemphidium* are more sub-tropical than temperate forms. The *Perisporiacei* are represented almost everywhere; although species of *Erysiphe* are confined to temperate regions, the genus *Meliola* occupies its place in warmer climes. Finally, the *Tuberacei*, which are subterranean in their habits, are limited in distribution, being confined to the temperate zone, never extending far into the cold, and but poorly represented out of Europe. One species of *Mylitta* occurs in Australia, another in China, and another in the Neilgherries of India; the genus *Paurocotylis* is found in New Zealand and Ceylon. It is said that a species of *Tuber* is found in Himalayan regions, but in the United States, as well as in Northern Europe, the *Tuberacei* are rare.

The imperfect condition of our information concerning very many countries, even of those partially explored, must render any estimate or comparison of the floras of those countries most fragmentary and imperfect. Recently, the mycology of our own islands has been more closely investigated, and the result of many years' application on the part of a few individuals has appeared in a record of some 2,809 species,* to which subsequent additions have been made, to an extent of probably not much less than 200 species,† which would bring the total to about 3,000 species. The result is that no material difference exists between our flora and that of Northern France, Belgium, and Scandinavia, except that in the latter there are a larger number of Hymenomycetal forms. The latest estimates of the flora of Scandinavia are contained in the works of the illustrious Fries,‡ but these are not sufficiently recent, except so far as regards the *Hymenomycetes*, for comparison of numbers with British species.

The flora of Belgium has its most recent exponent in the posthumous work of Jean Kickx; but the 1,370 species enumerated by him can hardly be supposed to represent the whole of the fungi of Belgium, for in such case it would be less than half the number found in the British Islands, although the majority of genera and species are the same.§

For the North of France no one could have furnished a more complete list, especially of the microscopic forms, than M. Desmazières, but we are left to rely solely upon his papers in "Annales des Sc. Nat." and his published specimens, which, though by no means representative of the fleshy fungi, are doubtless tolerably exhaustive of the minute species. From what we know of French *Hymenomycetes*, their number and variety appear to be much below those of Great Britain.‖

The mycologic flora of Switzerland has been very well investi-

* Cooke's "Handbook of British Fungi," 2 vols. 1871.

† "Grevillea," vols. i. and ii. London, 1872–1874.

‡ Fries, "Summa Vegetabilium Scandinaviæ" (1846), and "Monographia Hymenomycetum Sueciæ" (1863); "Epicrisis Hymenomycetum Europ." (1874).

§ "Flore cryptogamique des Flanders" (1867).

‖ "Ainé Plantes Cryptogames-cellulaires du Départment de Saone et Loire" (1863); Bulliard, "Hist. des Champignons de la France" (1791); De Candolle, "Flore Française" (1815); Duby, "Botanicon Gallicum" (1828–1830); Paulet, "Iconographie des Champignons" (1855); Godron, "Catalogue des Plantes Cellulaires du Départment de la Meurthe" (1845); Crouan, "Florule du Finistère" (1867); De Seynes, "Essai d'une Flore Mycologique de la Région de Montpellier et du Gard" (1863).

gated, although requiring revision. Less attention having been given to the minute forms, and more to the *Hymenomycetes* than in France and Belgium, may in part account for the larger proportion of the latter in the Swiss flora.*

In Spain and Portugal scarce anything has been done; the small collection made by Welwitsch can in no way be supposed to represent the Peninsula.

The fungi of Italy† include some species peculiar to the Peninsula. The *Tuberacei* are well represented, and although the *Hymenomycetes* do not equal in number those of Britain or Scandinavia, a good proportion is maintained.

Bavaria and Austria (including Hungary and the Tyrol) are being more thoroughly investigated than hitherto, but the works of Schæffer, Tratinnick, Corda, and Krombholz have made us acquainted with the general features of their mycology,‡ to which more recent lists and catalogues have contributed. § The publication of dried specimens has of late years greatly facilitated acquaintance with the fungi of different countries in Europe, and those issued by Baron Thümen from Austria do not differ materially from those of Northern Germany, although Dr. Rehm has made us acquainted with some new and interesting forms from Bavaria.||

Russia is to a large extent unknown, except in its northern borders.¶ Karsten has investigated the fungi of Finland,** and

* Secretan, "Mycographie Suisse" (1833); Trog. "Verzeichniss Schweizerischer Schwämme" (1844).

† Passerini, "Funghi Parmensi," in "Giorn. Bot. Italiano" (1872–73); Venturi, "Miceti dell' Agro Bresciano" (1845); Viviani, "Funghi d'Italia" (1834); Vittadini, "Funghi Mangerecci d'Italia" (1835).

‡ Schæffer, "Fungorum qui in Bavaria," &c. (1762-1774); Tratinnick, "Fungi Austriaci" (1804-1806 and 1809-30); Corda, "Icones Fungorum" (Prague, 1837-1842); Krombholz, "Abbildungen der Schwämme" 1831-1849).

§ Reichardt, "Flora von Iglau;" Niessl, "Cryptogamenflora Nieder-Œsterreichs" (1857, 1859); Schulzer, "Schwämme Ungarns, Slavoniens," &c.

|| Rehm, "Ascomyceten," fasc. i.-iv.

¶ Weinmann, "Hymeno- et Gasteromycetes," in "Imp. Ross" (1836); Weinmann, "Enumeratio Stirpium, in Agro Petropolitano" (1837).

** Karsten, "Fungi in insulis Spetsbergen collectio" (1872); Karsten, "Mono added considerably to the number of *Discomycetes*, for which the climate seems to be favourable; but, as a whole, it may be concluded that Western and Northern Europe are much better explored than the Eastern and South-Eastern, to which we might add the South, if Italy be excepted.

We have only to add, for Europe, that different portions of the German empire have been well worked, from the period of Wallroth to the present.* Recently, the valley of the Rhine has been exhaustively examined by Fuckel;† but both Germany and France suffered checks during the late war which made their mark on the records of science not so speedily to be effaced. Denmark, with its splendid Flora Danica still in progress, more than a century after its commencement,‡ has a mycologic flora very like to that of Scandinavia, which is as well known.

If we pass from Europe to North America, we find there a mycologic flora greatly resembling that of Europe, and although Canada and the extreme North is little known, some parts of the United States have been investigated. Schweinitz § first made known to any extent the riches of this country, especially Carolina, and in this state the late Dr. Curtis and H. W. Ravenel continued their labours. With the exception of Lea's collections in Cincinnati, Wright's in Texas, and some contributions from Ohio, Alabama, Massachusetts, and New York, a great portion of this vast country is mycologically unknown. It is remarkably rich in fleshy fungi, not only in *Agaricini*, but also in *Discomycetes*, containing a large number of European forms, mostly

graphia Pezizarum fennicarum" (1869); Karsten, "Symbolæ ad Mycologiam fennicam" (1870).

* Rabenhorst, "Deutschlands Kryptogamen Flora" (1844); Wallroth, "Flora Germanica" (1833); Sturm, "Deutschlands Flora, iii. die Pilze" (1837, &c.).

† Fuckel, "Symbolæ mycologicæ" (1869).

‡ "Flora Danica" (1766-1873); Holmskjold, "Beata ruris otia Fungis Danicis impensa" (1799); Schumacher, "Enumeratio plantarum Sellandiæ" (1801).

§ Schweinitz, "Synopsis Fungorum," in "America Boreali," &c. (1834). Lea, "Catalogue of Plants of Cincinnati" (1849); Curtis, "Catalogue of the Plants of North Carolina" (1867); Berkeley, "North American Fungi," in "Grevillea," vols. i.-iii.; Peck, in "Reports of New York Museum Nat. Hist."

European genera, with many species at present peculiar to itself. Tropical forms extend upwards into the Southern States.

The islands of the West Indies have been more or less examined, but none so thoroughly as Cuba, at first by Ramon de la Sagra, and afterwards by Wright.* The three principal genera of *Hymenomycetes* represented are *Agaricus*, *Marasmius*, and *Polyporus*, represented severally by 82, 51, and 120 species, amounting to more than half the entire number. Of the 490 species, about 57 per cent. are peculiar to the island; 13 per cent. are widely dispersed species; 12 per cent. are common to the island and Central America, together with the warmer parts of South America and Mexico; 3 per cent. are common to it with the United States, especially the Southern; while 13 per cent. are European species, including, however, 13 which may be considered as cosmopolitan. Some common tropical species do not occur, and, on the whole, the general character seems sub-tropical rather than tropical. Many of the species are decidedly those of temperate regions, or at least nearly allied. Perhaps the most interesting species are those which occur in the genera *Craterellus* and *Laschia*, the latter genus, especially, yielding several new forms. The fact that the climate is, on the whole, more temperate than that of some other islands in the same latitudes, would lead us to expect the presence of a comparatively large number of European species, or those which are found in the more northern United States, or British North America, and may account for the fact that so small a proportion of species should be identical with those from neighbouring islands.

In Central America only a few small collections have been made, which indicate a sub-tropical region.

From the northern parts of South America, M. Leprieur collected in French Guiana.† Southwards of this, Spruce collected in the countries bordering on the River Amazon, and

* Berkeley and Curtis, "Fungi Cubensis," in "Journ. Linn. Soc." (1868); Ramon de la Sagra, "Hist. Phys. de l'Isle de Cuba, Cryptogames, par Montagne" (1841); Montagne, in "Ann. des Sci. Nat." February, 1842.

† Montagne, "Cryptogamia Guyanensis," "Ann. Sci. Nat." 4me sér. iii.

Gardner in Brazil,* Gaudichaud in Chili and Peru,† Gay in Chili,‡ Blanchet in Bahia,§ Weddell in Brazil,|| and Auguste de Saint Hiliare ¶ in the same country. Small collections have also been made in the extreme south. All these collections contain coriaceous species of *Polyporus*, *Favolus*, and allied genera, with *Auricularini*, together with such *Ascomycetes* as *Xylaria*, and such forms of *Peziza* as *P. tricholoma*, *P. Hindsii*, and *P. macrotis*. As yet we cannot form an estimate of the extent or variety of the South American flora, which has furnished the interesting genus *Cyttaria*, and may yet supply forms unrecognized elsewhere.

The island of Juan Fernandez furnished to M. Bertero a good representative collection,** which is remarkable as containing more than one-half its number of European species, and the rest possessing rather the character of those of a temperate than a sub-tropical region.

Australasia has been partly explored, and the results embodied in the Floras of Dr. Hooker and subsequent communications. In a note to an enumeration of 235 species in 1872, the writer observes that "many of them are either identical with European species, or so nearly allied that with dried specimens only, unaccompanied by notes or drawings, it is impossible to separate them; others are species which are almost universally found in tropical or sub-tropical countries, while a few only are peculiar to Australia, or are undescribed species, mostly of a tropical type. The collections on the whole can scarcely be said to be of any great interest, except so far as geographical distribution is concerned, as the aberrant forms are few." ††

* Berkeley, in "Hooker's Journal of Botany" for 1843, &c.

† Montagne, in "Ann. des Sci. Nat." 2me sér. vol. ii. p. 73 (1834).

‡ Gay, "Hist. fisica y politica de Chile" (1845).

§ Berkeley and Montagne, "Ann. des Sci. Nat." xi. (April, 1849).

|| Montagne, in "Ann. des Sci. Nat." 4me sér. v. No. 6.

¶ Montagne, in "Ann. des Sci. Nat." (July, 1839).

** Montagne, "Prodromus Floræ Fernandesianæ," in "Ann. des Sci. Nat." (June, 1835).

†† Berkeley, "On Australian Fungi," in "Journ. Linn. Society," vol. xiii. (May, 1872).

The fungi collected by the Antarctic Expedition in Auckland and Campbell's Islands, and in Fuegia and the Falklands,* were few and of but little interest, including such cosmopolitan forms as *Sphæria hebarum* and *Cladosporium herbarum*, *Hirneola auricula-judaæ*, *Polyporus versicolor*, *Eurotium herbariorum*, etc.

In New Zealand a large proportion have been found, and these may be taken to represent the general character of the fungi of the islands, which is of the type usually found in temperate regions.†

The fungi of Asia are so little known that no satisfactory conclusions can be drawn from our present incomplete knowledge. In India, the collections made by Dr. Hooker in his progress to the Sikkim Himalayas,‡ a few species obtained by M. Perottet in Pondicherry, and small collections from the Neilgherries,§ are almost all that have been recorded. From these it may be concluded that elevations such as approximate a temperate climate are the most productive, and here European and North American genera, with closely allied species, have the preponderance. The number of *Agaricini*, for instance, is large, and amongst the twenty-eight subgenera into which the genus *Agaricus* is divided, eight only are unrepresented. Casual specimens received from other parts of India afford evidence that here is a vast field unexplored, the forests and mountain slopes of which would doubtless afford an immense number of new and interesting forms.

Of the Indian Archipelago, Java has been most explored, both by Junghuhn|| and Zollinger.¶ The former records 117 species in 40 genera, Nees von Esenbeck and Blume 11 species in 3 genera, and Zollinger and Moritzi 31 species in 20 genera, making a total of 159 species, of which 47 belong to *Polyporus*.

* Hooker's "Cryptogamia Antarctica," pp. 57 and 141.

† Hooker's "New Zealand Flora."

‡ Berkeley, "Sikkim Himalayan Fungi," in Hooker's "Journal of Botany" (1850), p. 42, &c.

§ Montagne, "Cryptogamæ Neilgherrensis," in "Ann. des Sci. Nat." 2me sér. xviii. p. 21 (1842).

|| Junghuhn, "Premissa in Floram Crypt. Javæ."

¶ Zollinger, "Fungi Archipalegi Malaijo Neerlandici novi."

Léveillé added 87 species, making a total of 246 species. The fungi of Sumatra, Borneo, and other islands are partly the same and partly allied, but of a similar tropical character.

The fungi of the island of Ceylon, collected by Gardner, Thwaites, and König, were numerous. The Agarics comprise 302 species, closely resembling those of our own country.* It is singular that every one of the subgenera of Fries is represented, though the number of species in one or two is greatly predominant. *Lepiota* and *Psalliota* alone comprise one-third of the species, while *Pholiota* offers only a single obscure species. The enumeration recently published of the succeeding families contains many species of interest.

In Africa, the best explored country is Algeria, although unfortunately the flora was never completed.† The correspondence between the fungi of Algeria and European countries is very striking, and the impression is not removed by the presence of a few sub-tropical forms. It is probable that were the fungi of Spain known the resemblance would be more complete.

From the Cape of Good Hope and Natal collections have been made by Zeyher,‡ Drége, and others, and from these we are enabled to form a tolerable estimate of the mycologic flora. Of the *Hymenomycetes*, the greater part belong to *Agaricus;* there are but four or five *Polypori* in Zeyher's collection, one of which is protean. The *Gasteromycetes* are interesting, belonging to many genera, and presenting two, *Scoleciocarpus* and *Phellorinia*, which were founded upon specimens in this collection. *Batarrea*, *Tulostoma*, and *Mycenastrum* are represented by European species. There are also two species of *Lycoperdon*, and one of *Podaxon*. Besides these, there is the curious *Secotium Gueinzii*. The genus *Geaster* does not appear in the collection, nor *Scleroderma*. Altogether the Cape flora is a peculiar one, and can scarcely be compared with any other.

At the most, only scattered and isolated specimens have been

* Berkeley and Broome, "Fungi of Ceylon," in "Journ. Linn. Soc." for May, 1871.

† "Flore d'Algerie, Cryptogames" (1846, &c.).

‡ Berkeley, in Hooker's "Journal of Botany," vol. ii. (1843), p. 408.

recorded from Senegal, from Egypt, or from other parts of Africa, so that, with the above exceptions, the continent may be regarded as unknown.

From this imperfect summary it will be seen that no general scheme of geographical distribution of fungi can as yet be attempted, and the most we can hope to do is to compare collection with collection, and what we know of one country with what we know of another, and note differences and agreements, so as to estimate the probable character of the fungi of other countries of which we are still in ignorance. It is well sometimes that we should attempt a task like the present, since we then learn how much there is to be known, and how much good work lies waiting to be done by the capable and willing hands that may hereafter undertake it.

XIV.

COLLECTION AND PRESERVATION.

THE multitudinous forms which fungi assume, the differences of substance, and variability in size, render a somewhat detailed account of the modes adopted for their collection and preservation necessary. The habitats of the various groups have already been indicated, so that there need be no difficulty in selecting the most suitable spots, and as to the period of the year, this will be determined by the class of objects sought. Although it may be said that no time, except when the ground is covered with snow, is entirely barren of fungi, yet there are periods more prolific than others.* Fleshy fungi, such as the *Hymenomycetes*, are most common from September until the frosts set in, whereas many microscopic species may be found in early spring, and increase in number until the autumn.

The collector may be provided with an ordinary collecting box, but for the Agarics an open shallow basket is preferable. A great number of the woody kinds may be carried in the coat-pocket, and foliicolous species placed between the leaves of a pocket-book. It is a good plan to be provided with a quantity of soft bibulous paper, in which specimens can be wrapped when collected, and this will materially assist in their preservation when transferred to box or basket. A large clasp-knife, a small pocket-saw, and a pocket-lens will complete the outfit for ordinary occasions. In order to preserve the fleshy fungi for the herbarium, there is but one method, which has often been described.

* The genus *Chionyphe* occurs on granaries under snow, as well as in that formidable disease, the Madura fungus-foot. (*See* Carter's "Mycetoma."

The Agaric, or other similar fungus, is cut perpendicularly from the pileus downwards through the stem. A second cut in the same direction removes a thin slice, which represents a section of the fungus; this may be laid on blotting paper, or plant-drying paper, and put under slight pressure to dry. From one-half of the fungus the pileus is removed, and with a sharp knife the gills and fleshy portion of the pileus are cut away. In the same manner the inner flesh of the half stem is also cleared. When dried, the half of the pileus is placed in its natural position on the top of the half stem, and thus a portrait of the growing fungus is secured, whilst the section shows the arrangement of the hymenium and the character of the stem. The other half of the pileus may be placed, gills downward, on a piece of black paper, and allowed to rest there during the night. In the morning the spores will have been thrown down upon the paper, which may be placed with the other portions. When dry, the section, profile, and spore paper may be mounted together on a piece of stiff paper, and the name, locality, and date inscribed below, with any additional particulars. It is advisable here to caution the collector never to omit writing down these particulars at once when the preparations are made, and to place them together, between the folds of the drying paper, in order to prevent the possibility of a mistake. Some small species may be dried whole or only cut down the centre, but the spores should never be forgotten. When dried, either before or after mounting, the specimens should be poisoned, in order to preserve them from the attacks of insects. The best medium for this purpose is carbolic acid, laid on with a small hog-hair brush. Whatever substance is used, it must not be forgotten by the manipulator that he is dealing with poison, and must exercise caution. If the specimens are afterwards found to be insufficiently poisoned, or that minute insects are present in the herbarium, fresh poisoning will be necessary. Some think that benzine or spirits of camphor is sufficient, but as either is volatile, it is not to be trusted as a permanent preservative. Mr. English, of Epping, by an ingenious method of his own, preserves a great number of the fleshy species in their natural position, and although valueless for an herbarium, they are not only very ornamental, but useful, if space can be devoted to them.

Leaf parasites, whether on living or dead leaves, may be dried in the usual way for drying plants, between folds of bibulous paper under pressure. It may be sometimes necessary with dead leaves to throw them in water, in order that they may be flattened without breaking, and then dry them in the same manner as green leaves. All species produced on a hard matrix, as wood, bark, etc., should have as much as possible of the matrix pared away, so that the specimens may lie flat in the herbarium. This is often facilitated in corticolous species by removing the bark and drying it under pressure.

The dusty *Gasteromycetes* are troublesome, especially the minute species, and if mounted openly on paper are soon spoiled. A good plan is to provide small square or round cardboard boxes, of not more than a quarter of an inch in depth, and to glue the specimen to the bottom at once, allowing it to dry in that position before replacing the cover. The same method should be adopted for many of the moulds, such as *Polyactis*, etc., which, under any circumstances, are difficult to preserve.

In collecting moulds, we have found it an excellent plan to go out provided with small wooden boxes, corked at top and bottom, such as entomologists use, and some common pins. When a delicate mould is collected on a decayed Agaric, or any other matrix, after clearing away with a penknife all unnecessary portions of the matrix, the specimen may be pinned down to the cork in one of these boxes. Another method, and one advisable also for the *Myxogastres*, is to carry two or three pill-boxes, in which, after being wrapped in tissue paper, the specimen may be placed.

A great difficulty is often experienced with microscopic fungi, such, for instance, as the *Sphæriacei*, in the necessity, whenever a new examination is required, to soak the specimen for some hours, and then transfer the fruit to a slide, before it can be compared with any newly-found specimen that has to be identified. To avoid this, mounted specimens ready for the microscope are an acquisition, and may be secured in the following manner. After the fungus has been soaked in water, where that is necessary, and the hymenium extracted on the point of a penknife, let it be transferred to the centre of a clean glass slide. A drop of glycerine is let fall upon this nucleus, then the covering glass placed over it. A slight pressure will flatten the object and expel all the superfluous glycerine around the edges of the covering glass. A spring clip holds the cover in position, whilst a camel-hair pencil is used to remove the glycerine which may have been expelled. This done, the edges of the cover may be fixed to the slide by painting round with gum-dammar dissolved in benzole. In from twelve to twenty-four hours the spring clip may be removed, and the mount placed in the cabinet. Glycerine is, perhaps, the best medium for mounting the majority of these objects, and when dammar and benzole are used for fixing, there is no difficulty experienced, as is the case with Canada balsam, if the superfluous glycerine is not wholly washed away. Specimens of *Puccinia* mounted in this way when fresh gathered, and before any shrivelling had taken place, are as plump and natural in our cabinet as they were when collected six or seven years ago.

Moulds are always troublesome to preserve in a herbarium in a state sufficiently perfect for reference after a few years. We have found it an excellent method to provide some thin plates of mica, the thinner the better, of a uniform size, say two inches square, or even less. Between two of these plates of mica enclose a fragment of the mould, taking care not to move one plate over the other after the mould is placed. Fix the plates by a clip, whilst strips of paper are gummed or pasted over the edges of the mica plates so as to hold them together. When dry, the clip may be removed, and the name written on the paper. These mounts may be put each in a small envelope, and fastened down in the herbarium. Whenever an examination is required, the object, being already dry-mounted, may at once be placed under the microscope. In this manner the mode of attachment of the spores can be seen, but if mounted in fluid they are at once detached; and if the moulds are only preserved in boxes, in the course of a short time nearly every spore will have fallen from its support.

Two or three accessories to a good herbarium may be named. For fleshy fungi, especially Agarics, faithfully coloured drawings, side by side with the dried specimens, will compensate for loss or change of colour which most species undergo in the process of drying. For minute species, camera lucida drawings of the spores, together with their measurements, will add greatly to the practical value of a collection. In mounting specimens, whether on leaves, bark, or wood, it will be of advantage to have one specimen glued down to the paper so as to be seen at once, and a duplicate loose in a small envelope beside it, so that the latter may at any time be removed and examined under the microscope.

In arranging specimens for the herbarium, a diversity of taste and opinion exists as to the best size for the herbarium paper. It is generally admitted that a small size is preferable to the large one usually employed for phanerogamous plants. Probably the size of foolscap is the most convenient, each sheet being confined to a single species. In public herbaria, the advantage of a uniform size for all plants supersedes all other advantages, but in a private herbarium, consisting entirely of fungi, the smaller size is better.

The microscopic examination of minute species is an absolute necessity to ensure accurate identification. Little special remark is called for here, since the methods adopted for other objects will be available. Specimens which have become dry may be placed in water previous to examination, a process which will be found essential in such genera as *Peziza*, *Sphæria*, etc. For moulds, which must be examined as opaque objects, if all their beauties and peculiarities are to be made out, a half-inch objective is recommended, with the nozzle bevelled as much to a point as possible, so that no light be obstructed.*

In examining the sporidia of minute *Pezizæ* and some others, the aid of some reagent will be found necessary. When th

* Bubbles of air are often very tiresome in the examination of moulds. A little alcohol will remove them.

sporidia are very delicate and hyaline, the septa cannot readily be seen if present; to aid in the examination, a drop of tincture of iodine will be of considerable advantage. In many cases sporidia, which are very indistinct in glycerine, are much more distinct when the fluid is water.

The following hints to travellers, as regards the collection of fungi, drawn up some years since by the Rev. M. J. Berkeley, have been widely circulated, and may be usefully inserted here, though at the risk of repetition:—

"It is frequently complained that in collections of exotic plants, no tribe is so much neglected as that of fungi; this arises partly from the supposed difficulty of preserving good specimens, partly from their being less generally studied than other vegetable productions. As, however, in no department of botany, there is a greater probability of meeting with new forms, and the difficulties, though confessedly great in one or two genera, are far less than is often imagined, the following hints are respectfully submitted to such collectors as may desire to neglect no part of the vegetable kingdom.

"The greater proportion, especially of tropical fungi, are dried, simply by light pressure, with as much ease as phœnogamous plants; indeed, a single change of the paper in which they are placed is generally sufficient, and many, if wrapped up in soft paper when gathered, and submitted to light pressure, require no further attention. Such as are of a tough leathery nature, if the paper be changed a few hours after the specimens have been laid in, preserve all their characters admirably; and if in the course of a few weeks there is an opportunity of washing them with a solution of turpentine and corrosive sublimate, submitting them again to pressure for a few hours merely to prevent their shrinking, there will be no fear of their suffering from the attacks of insects.

"Many of the mushroom tribe are so soft and watery that it is very difficult to make good specimens without a degree of labour which is quite out of the question with travellers. By changing, however, the papers in which they are dried two or three times the first day, if practicable, useful specimens may be prepared, especially if a few notes be made as to colour, etc. The more important notes are as to the colour of the stem and pileus, together with any peculiarities of the surface, *e.g.*, whether it be dry, viscid, downy, scaly, etc., and whether the flesh of the pileus be thin or otherwise; as to the stem, whether hollow or solid; as to the gills, whether they are attached to the stem or free; and especially what is their colour and that of the spores. It is not in general expedient to preserve specimens in spirits, except others are dried by pressure, or copious notes be made; except, indeed, in some fungi of a gelatinous nature, which can scarcely be dried at all by pressure.

"The large woody fungi, the puff-balls, and a great number of those which grow on wood, etc., are best preserved, after ascertaining that they are dry and free from larvæ, by simply wrapping them in paper or placing them in chip-boxes, taking care that they are so closely packed as not to rub. As in other tribes of plants, it is very requisite to have specimens in different stages of growth, and notes as to precise habitats are always interesting.

"The attention of the traveller can scarcely be directed to any more interesting branch, or one more likely to produce novelty, than the puff-ball tribe; and he is particularly requested to collect these in every stage of growth, especially in the earliest, and, if possible, to preserve some of the younger specimens in spirits. One or two species are produced on ant-hills, the knowledge of the early state of which is very desirable.

"The fungi which grow on leaves in tropical climates are scarcely less abundant than in our own country, though belonging to a different type. Many of these must constantly come under the eye of the collector of phœnogams, and would be most acceptable to the mycologist. But the attention of the collector should also be directed to the lichen-like fungi, which are so abundant in some countries on fallen sticks. Hundreds of species of the utmost interest would reward active research, and they are amongst the easiest to dry; indeed, in tropical countries, the greater proportion of the species are easy to preserve, but they will not strike the eye which is not on the watch for them. The number of fleshy species is but few, and far less likely to furnish novelty."

In conclusion, we may urge upon all those who have followed us thus far to adopt this branch of botany as their speciality. Hitherto it has been very much neglected, and a wide field is open for investigation and research. The life-history of the majority of species has still to be read, and the prospects of new discoveries for the industrious and persevering student are great. All who have as yet devoted themselves with assiduity have been in this manner rewarded. The objects are easily obtainable, and there is a constantly increasing infatuation in the study. Where so much is unknown, not a few difficulties have to be encountered, and here the race is not to the swift so much as to the untiring. May our efforts to supply this introduction to the study receive their most welcome reward in an accession to the number of the students and investigators of the nature, uses, and influences of fungi.

INDEX.

August, 1876.

AN ALPHABETICAL LIST

OF

HENRY S. KING & CO.'S

PUBLICATIONS.

65 Cornhill, and 1 Paternoster Square, London,
August, 1876.

A LIST OF

HENRY S. KING & CO.'S

PUBLICATIONS.

ABBEY (Henry).

BALLADS OF GOOD DEEDS, AND OTHER VERSES. Fcap. 8vo. Cloth gilt, price 5*s*.

ABDULLA (The Hakayit).

AUTOBIOGRAPHY OF A MALAY MUNSHI. Translated by J. T. Thomson, F.R.G.S. With Photo-lithograph Page of Abdulla's Manuscript. Post 8vo. Cloth, price 12*s*.

ADAMS (A. L.), M.A., M.B., F.R.S., F.G.S.

FIELD AND FOREST RAMBLES OF A NATURALIST IN NEW BRUNSWICK. With Notes and Observations on the Natural History of Eastern Canada. Illustrated. 8vo. Cloth, price 14*s*.

ADAMS (F. O.), F.R.G.S., H.B.M.'s Secretary of Embassy at Paris, formerly H.B.M.'s Chargé d'Affaires, and Secretary of Legation at Yedo.

THE HISTORY OF JAPAN. From the Earliest Period to the Present Time. New Edition, revised. 2 volumes. With Maps and Plans. Demy 8vo. Cloth, price 21*s*. each.

ADAMS (W. Davenport, Jun.)

LYRICS OF LOVE, from Shakespeare to Tennyson. Selected and arranged by. Fcap. 8vo. Cloth extra, gilt edges, price 3*s*. 6*d*.

ADON.

THROUGH STORM AND SUNSHINE. Illustrated by M. E. Edwards, A. T. H. Paterson, and the Author. Crown 8vo. Cloth, price 7*s.* 6*d.*

A. K. H. B.

A SCOTCH COMMUNION SUNDAY, to which are added Certain Discourses from a University City. By the Author of "The Recreations of a Country Parson." Second Edition. Crown 8vo. Cloth, price 5*s.*

ALLEN (Rev. R.), M.A.

ABRAHAM: HIS LIFE, TIMES, AND TRAVELS, as told by a Contemporary 3800 years ago. With Map. Post 8vo. Cloth, price 10*s.* 6*d.*

AMOS (Professor Sheldon).

THE SCIENCE OF LAW. Second Edition. Crown 8vo. Cloth, price 5*s.*

Volume X. of the International Scientific Series.

ANDERSON (Rev. Charles), M.A.

NEW READINGS OF OLD PARABLES. Demy 8vo. Cloth, price 4*s.* 6*d.*

CHURCH THOUGHT AND CHURCH WORK. Edited by. Containing articles by the Revs. J. M. Capes, Professor Cheetham, J. Ll. Davis, Harry Jones, Brooke, Lambert, A. J. Ross, the Editor, and others. Second Edition. Demy 8vo. Cloth, price 7*s.* 6*d.*

WORDS AND WORKS IN A LONDON PARISH. Edited by. Second Edition. Demy 8vo. Cloth, price 6*s.*

THE CURATE OF SHYRE. Second Edition. 8vo. Cloth, price 7*s.* 6*d.*

ANDERSON (Colonel R. P.)

VICTORIES AND DEFEATS. An Attempt to explain the Causes which have led to them. An Officer's Manual. Demy 8vo. Cloth, price 14*s.*

ANDERSON (R. C.), C.E.

TABLES FOR FACILITATING THE CALCULATION OF EVERY DETAIL IN CONNECTION WITH EARTHEN AND MASONRY DAMS. Royal 8vo. Cloth, price £2 2*s.*

ANSON (Lieut.-Col. The Hon. A.), V.C., M.P.

THE ABOLITION OF PURCHASE AND THE ARMY REGULATION BILL OF 1871. Crown 8vo. Sewed, price 1*s*.

ARMY RESERVES AND MILITIA REFORMS. Crown 8vo. Sewed, price 1*s*.

THE STORY OF THE SUPERSESSIONS. Crown 8vo. Sewed, price 6*d*.

ARCHER (Thomas).

ABOUT MY FATHER'S BUSINESS. Work amidst the Sick, the Sad, and the Sorrowing. Crown 8vo. Cloth, price 5*s*.

ARGYLE (Duke of).

SPEECHES ON THE SECOND READING OF THE CHURCH PATRONAGE (SCOTLAND) BILL IN THE HOUSE OF LORDS, June 2, 1874; and Earl of Camperdown's Amendment, June 9, 1874, placing the Election of Ministers in the hands of Ratepayers. Crown 8vo. Sewed, price 1*s*.

ARMY OF THE NORTH GERMAN CONFEDERATION.

A Brief Description of its Organization, of the Different Branches of the Service and their *rôle* in War, of its Mode of Fighting, etc., etc. Translated from the Corrected Edition, by permission of the Author, by Colonel Edward Newdegate. Demy 8vo. Cloth, price 5*s*.

ASHANTEE WAR (The).

A Popular Narrative. By the Special Correspondent of the Daily News. Crown 8vo. Cloth, price 6s.

ASHTON (John).

ROUGH NOTES OF A VISIT TO BELGIUM, SEDAN, AND PARIS, in September, 1870-71. Crown 8vo. Cloth, price 3*s*. 6*d*.

AUNT MARY'S BRAN PIE.

By the author of "St. Olave's," "When I was a Little Girl," etc. Illustrated. Cloth, price 3*s*. 6*d*.

SUNNYLAND STORIES. Illustrated. Small 8vo. Cloth, price 3*s*. 6*d*.

AURORA.

A Volume of Verse. Fcap. 8vo. Cloth, price 5*s*.

AYRTON (J. C.)

A SCOTCH WOOING. 2 vols. Crown 8vo. Cloth.

BAGEHOT (Walter).

PHYSICS AND POLITICS; or, Thoughts on the Application of the Principles of "Natural Selection" and "Inheritance" to Political Society. Third Edition. Crown 8vo. Cloth, price 4*s*. Volume II. of the International Scientific Series.

THE ENGLISH CONSTITUTION. A New Edition, Revised and Corrected, with an Introductory Dissertation on Recent Changes and Events. Crown 8vo. Cloth, price 7*s*. 6*d*.

LOMBARD STREET. A Description of the Money Market. Sixth Edition. Crown 8vo. Cloth, price 7*s*. 6*d*.

BAIN (Alexander), LL.D.

MIND AND BODY: the Theories of their Relation. Fifth Edition. Crown 8vo. Cloth, price 4*s*. Volume IV. of the International Scientific Series.

BANKS (Mrs. G. Linnæus).

GOD'S PROVIDENCE HOUSE. New Edition. Crown 8vo. Cloth, price 3*s*. 6*d*.

BARING (T. C.), M.A., M.P., late Fellow of Brasenose College, Oxford.

PINDAR IN ENGLISH RHYME. Being an Attempt to render the Epinikian Odes with the principal remaining Fragments of Pindar into English Rhymed Verse. Small quarto. Cloth, price 7*s*.

BARLEE (Ellen).

LOCKED OUT: a Tale of the Strike. With a Frontispiece. Cloth, price 1*s*. 6*d*.

BAYNES (Rev. Canon R. H.), M.A., Editor of "Lyra Anglicana," etc.

HOME SONGS FOR QUIET HOURS. Third Edition. Fcap. 8vo. Cloth extra, price 3*s*. 6*d*.

*** *This may also be had handsomely bound in Morocco with gilt edges.*

BECKER (Bernard H.)

THE SCIENTIFIC SOCIETIES OF LONDON. Crown 8vo. Cloth, price 5*s*.

BENNETT (Dr. W. C.)

SONGS FOR SAILORS. Dedicated by Special Request to H.R.H. the Duke of Edinburgh. With Steel Portrait and Illustrations. Crown 8vo. Cloth, price 3*s*. 6*d*. An Edition in Illustrated Paper Covers, price 1*s*.

BENNETT (Dr. W. C.)

BABY MAY. HOME POEMS AND BALLADS. With Frontispiece. Crown 8vo. Cloth elegant, price 6*s*.

BABY MAY AND HOME POEMS. Fcap. 8vo. Sewed in Coloured Wrapper, price 1*s*.

NARRATIVE POEMS AND BALLADS. Fcap. 8vo. Sewed in Coloured Wrapper, price 1*s*.

BENNIE (Rev. Jas. Noble), M.A.

THE ETERNAL LIFE. Sermons preached during the last twelve years. Crown 8vo. Cloth, price 6*s*.

BERNARD (Bayle).

SAMUEL LOVER, THE LIFE AND UNPUBLISHED WORKS OF. In 2 vols. With a Steel Portrait. Post 8vo. Cloth, price 21*s*.

BERNSTEIN (Professor), of the University of Halle.

THE FIVE SENSES OF MAN. With 91 Illustrations. Second Edition. Crown 8vo. Cloth, price 5*s*.
Volume XXI. of the International Scientific Series.

BETHAM-EDWARDS (Miss M.)

KITTY. With a Frontispiece. Crown 8vo. Cloth, price 3*s*. 6*d*.

MADEMOISELLE JOSEPHINE'S FRIDAYS, AND OTHER STORIES. Crown 8vo. Cloth, price 7*s*. 6*d*.

BISCOE (A. C.)

THE EARLS OF MIDDLETON, Lords of Clermont and of Fettercairn, and the Middleton Family. Crown 8vo. Cloth, price 10*s*. 6*d*.

BLANC (Henry), M.D.

CHOLERA: HOW TO AVOID AND TREAT IT. Popular and Practical Notes. Crown 8vo. Cloth, price 4*s*. 6*d*.

BLUME (Major William).

THE OPERATIONS OF THE GERMAN ARMIES IN FRANCE, from Sedan to the end of the war of 1870–71. With Map. From the Journals of the Head-quarters Staff. Translated by the late E. M. Jones, Maj. 20th Foot, Prof. of Mil. Hist., Sandhurst. Demy 8vo. Cloth, price 9*s*.

Boguslawski (Captain A. von).

TACTICAL DEDUCTIONS FROM THE WAR OF 1870-71. Translated by Colonel Sir Lumley Graham, Bart., late 18th (Royal Irish) Regiment. Third Edition, Revised and Corrected. Demy 8vo. Cloth, price 7*s.*

Bonwick (James), F.R.G.S.

THE TASMANIAN LILY. With Frontispiece. Crown 8vo. Cloth, price 5*s.*

MIKE HOWE, THE BUSHRANGER OF VAN DIEMEN'S LAND. With Frontispiece. Crown 8vo. Cloth, price 5*s.*

Boswell (R. B.), M.A., Oxon.

METRICAL TRANSLATIONS FROM THE GREEK AND LATIN POETS, and other Poems. Crown 8vo. Cloth, price 5*s.*

Bothmer (Countess Von).

CRUEL AS THE GRAVE. A Novel. 3 vols. Cloth.

Bowen (H. C.), M.A., Headmaster of the Grocers Company's Middle-Class School at Hackney.

STUDIES IN ENGLISH, for the use of Modern Schools. Small Crown 8vo. Cloth, price 1*s.* 6*d.*

Bowring (L.), C.S.I., Lord Canning's Private Secretary, and for many years Chief Commissioner of Mysore and Coorg.

EASTERN EXPERIENCES. Illustrated with Maps and Diagrams. Demy 8vo. Cloth, price 16*s.*

Bradley (F. H.), Fellow of Merton College, Oxford.

ETHICAL STUDIES. Critical Essays in Moral Philosophy. Large post 8vo. Cloth, price 9*s.*

Brave Men's Footsteps.

By the Editor of "Men who have Risen." A Book of Example and Anecdote for Young People. With Four Illustrations by C. Doyle. Third Edition. Crown 8vo. Cloth, price 3*s.* 6*d.*

Brialmont (Colonel A.)

HASTY INTRENCHMENTS. Translated by Lieut. Charles A. Empsom, R.A. With nine Plates. Demy 8vo. Cloth, price 6*s.*

Briefs and Papers.

Being Sketches of the Bar and the Press. By Two Idle Apprentices. Second Edition. Crown 8vo. Cloth, price 7*s.* 6*d.*

BROOKE (Rev. James M. S.), M. A.

HEART, BE STILL. A Sermon preached in Holy Trinity Church, Southall. Imp. 32mo. Sewed, price 6*d*.

BROOKE (Rev. Stopford A.), M.A., Chaplain in Ordinary to Her Majesty the Queen.

THE LATE REV. F. W. ROBERTSON, M.A., LIFE AND LETTERS OF. Edited by Stopford Brooke, M.A.

I. Uniform with the Sermons. 2 vols. With Steel Portrait. Price 7*s*. 6*d*.

II. Library Edition. 8vo. With Two Steel Portraits. Price 12*s*.

III. A Popular Edition, in 1 vol. 8vo. Price 6*s*.

THEOLOGY IN THE ENGLISH POETS.—COWPER, COLERIDGE, WORDSWORTH, and BURNS. Second Edition. Post 8vo. Cloth, price 9*s*.

CHRIST IN MODERN LIFE. Ninth Edition. Crown 8vo. Cloth, price 7*s*. 6*d*.

FREEDOM IN THE CHURCH OF ENGLAND. Six Sermons suggested by the Voysey Judgment. Second Edition. Crown 8vo. Cloth, price 3*s*. 6*d*.

SERMONS. First Series. Ninth Edition. Crown 8vo. Cloth, price 6*s*.

SERMONS. Second Series. Third Edition. Crown 8vo. Cloth, price 7*s*.

FREDERICK DENISON MAURICE: The Life and Work of. A Memorial Sermon. Crown 8vo. Sewed, price 1*s*.

BROOKE (W. G.), M.A., Barrister-at-Law.

THE PUBLIC WORSHIP REGULATION ACT. With a Classified Statement of its Provisions, Notes, and Index. Third Edition, revised and corrected. Crown 8vo. Cloth, price 3*s*. 6*d*.

SIX PRIVY COUNCIL JUDGMENTS—1850-1872. Annotated by. Third Edition. Crown 8vo. Cloth, price 9*s*.

BROWN (J. A.)

MAGNETIC OBSERVATIONS AT TREVANDRUM AND AUGUSTIA MALLEY. Vol. I. 4to. Cloth, price 63*s*.

The Report from above, separately sewed, price 21*s*.

BROWN (Rev. J. Baldwin), B.A.

THE HIGHER LIFE. Its Reality, Experience, and Destiny. Fourth Edition. Crown 8vo. Cloth, price 7*s*. 6*d*.

THE DOCTRINE OF ANNIHILATION IN THE LIGHT OF THE GOSPEL OF LOVE. Five Discourses. Second Edition. Crown 8vo. Cloth, price 2*s*. 6*d*.

BROWN (John Croumbie), LL.D., etc.

REBOISEMENT IN FRANCE; or, Records of the Replanting of the Alps, the Cevennes, and the Pyrenees with Trees, Herbage, and Bush. Demy 8vo. Cloth, price 12*s*. 6*d*.

THE HYDROLOGY OF SOUTHERN AFRICA. Demy 8vo. Cloth, price 10*s*. 6*d*.

BROWNE (Rev. Marmaduke E.)

UNTIL THE DAY DAWN. Four Advent Lectures. Crown 8vo. Cloth, price 2*s*. 6*d*.

BRYANT (William Cullen).

POEMS. Red-line Edition. With 24 Illustrations and Portrait of the Author. Post 8vo. Cloth extra, price 7*s*. 6*d*.

A Cheaper Edition, with Frontispiece. Post 8vo. Cloth, price 3*s*. 6*d*.

BUCHANAN (Robert).

POETICAL WORKS. Collected Edition, in 3 Vols., with Portrait. Price 6*s*. each.

CONTENTS OF THE VOLUMES.

I. "BALLADS AND ROMANCES." II. "BALLADS AND POEMS OF LIFE."
III. "CRUISKEEN SONNETS;" AND "BOOK OF ORM."

MASTER-SPIRITS. Post 8vo. Cloth, price 10*s*. 6*d*.

BULKELEY (Rev. Henry J.)

WALLED IN, and other Poems. Crown 8vo. Cloth, price 5*s*.

BUNNÈTT (F. E.)

LEONORA CHRISTINA, MEMOIRS OF, Daughter of Christian IV. of Denmark; Written during her Imprisonment in the Blue Tower of the Royal Palace at Copenhagen, 1663-1685. Translated by F. E. Bunnètt. With an Autotype Portrait of the Princess. A New and Cheaper Edition. Medium 8vo. Cloth, price 5*s*.

LINKED AT LAST. 1 vol. Crown 8vo. Cloth.

UNDER A CLOUD; OR, JOHANNES OLAF. By E. D. Wille. Translated by F. E. Bunnètt. 3 vols. Crown 8vo. Cloth.

BURTON (Mrs. Richard).

THE INNER LIFE OF SYRIA, PALESTINE, AND THE HOLY LAND. With Maps, Photographs, and Coloured Plates. 2 vols. Second Edition. Demy 8vo. Cloth, price 24*s*.

BUTLER (Josephine E.)

JOHN GREY (of Dilston): MEMOIRS. By his Daughter. New and Cheaper Edition. Crown 8vo. Cloth, price 3*s*. 6*d*.

CADELL (Mrs. H. M.)

IDA CRAVEN: A Novel. 2 vols. Crown 8vo. Cloth.

CALDERON.

CALDERON'S DRAMAS: The Wonder-Working Magician—Life is a Dream—The Purgatory of St. Patrick. Translated by Denis Florence MacCarthy. Post 8vo. Cloth, price 10*s*.

CAMERON (Julia M.)

PHOTOGRAPHIC ILLUSTRATIONS TO ALFRED TENNYSON'S IDYLLS OF THE KING, AND OTHER POEMS. Folio. Half bound, morocco, gilt edges, price £6 6*s*.

Second Series. Half bound, morocco, gilt edges, price £6 6*s*.

CAMPBELL-MACLACHLAN (A. W.)

A SKETCH OF THE MILITARY LIFE AND CHARACTER OF WILLIAM AUGUSTUS, DUKE OF CUMBERLAND. With Three Illustrations. Post 8vo. Cloth, price 15*s*.

CARLISLE (A. D.), B.A., Trin. Coll., Camb.

ROUND THE WORLD IN 1870. A Volume of Travels, with Maps. New and Cheaper Edition. Demy 8vo. Cloth, price 6*s*.

CARNE (Miss E. T.)

THE REALM OF TRUTH. Crown 8vo. Cloth, price 5*s*. 6*d*.

CARPENTER (E.)

NARCISSUS AND OTHER POEMS. Fcap. 8vo. Cloth, price 5*s*.

CARPENTER (W. B.), LL.D., M.D., F.R.S., etc.

THE PRINCIPLES OF MENTAL PHYSIOLOGY. With their Applications to the Training and Discipline of the Mind, and the Study of its Morbid Conditions. Illustrated. 8vo. Fourth Edition. Cloth, price 12*s*.

CARR (Lisle).

JUDITH GWYNNE. 3 vols. Second Edition. Crown 8vo. Cloth.

CHRISTOPHERSON (The late Rev. Henry), M.A., Assistant Minister at Trinity Church, Brighton.

SERMONS. With an Introduction by John Rae, LL.D., F.S.A. First Series. Crown 8vo. Cloth, price 7*s.* 6*d.*

SERMONS. With an introduction by John Rae, LL.D., F.S.A. Second Series. Crown 8vo. Cloth, price 6s.

CLAYTON (Cecil).

EFFIE'S GAME; HOW SHE LOST AND HOW SHE WON. A Novel. 2 vols. Cloth.

CLERK (Mrs. Godfrey), Author of "The Antipodes and Round the World."

'ILAM EN NAS. Historical Tales and Anecdotes of the Times of the Early Khalifahs. Translated from the Arabic Originals. Illustrated with Historical and Explanatory Notes. Crown 8vo. Cloth, price 7*s.*

CLERY (C.), Captain.

MINOR TACTICS. With 26 Maps and Plans. Second Edition. Demy 8vo. Cloth, price 16s.

CLODD (Edward), F.R.A.S.

THE CHILDHOOD OF THE WORLD: a Simple Account of Man in Early Times. Third Edition. Crown 8vo. Cloth, price 3s.

A Special Edition for Schools. Price 1*s.*

THE CHILDHOOD OF RELIGIONS. Including a Simple Account of the Birth and Growth of Myths and Legends. Crown 8vo. Cloth, price 5s.

COLERIDGE (Sara).

PRETTY LESSONS IN VERSE FOR GOOD CHILDREN, with some Lessons in Latin, in Easy Rhyme. A New Edition. Illustrated. Cloth, price 3*s.* 6*d.*

PHANTASMION. A Fairy Tale. With an Introductory Preface by the Right Hon. Lord Coleridge, of Ottery St. Mary. A New Edition. Illustrated. Cloth, price 7*s.* 6*d.*

MEMOIR AND LETTERS OF SARA COLERIDGE. Edited by her Daughter. With Index. 2 vols. With Two Portraits. Third Edition, Revised and Corrected. Crown 8vo. Cloth, price 24*s.*

Cheap Edition. With one Portrait. Cloth, price 7*s.* 6*d.*

COLLINS (Mortimer).

THE PRINCESS CLARICE. A Story of 1871. 2 vols. Cloth.

SQUIRE SILCHESTER'S WHIM. 3 vols. Cloth.

MIRANDA. A Midsummer Madness. 3 vols. Cloth.

THE INN OF STRANGE MEETINGS, AND OTHER POEMS. Crown 8vo. Cloth, price 5*s*.

THE SECRET OF LONG LIFE. Dedicated by special permission to Lord St. Leonards. Fourth Edition. Large crown 8vo. Price 5*s*.

COLLINS (Rev. Richard), M.A.

MISSIONARY ENTERPRISE IN THE EAST. With special reference to the Syrian Christians of Malabar, and the results of modern Missions. With Four Illustrations. Crown 8vo. Cloth, price 6*s*.

CONGREVE (Richard), M.A., M.R.C.P.L.

HUMAN CATHOLICISM. Two Sermons delivered at the Positivist School on the Festival of Humanity, 87 and 88, January 1, 1875 and 1876. Demy 8vo. Sewed, price 1*s*.

CONWAY (Moncure D.)

REPUBLICAN SUPERSTITIONS. Illustrated by the Political History of the United States. Including a Correspondence with M. Louis Blanc. Crown 8vo. Cloth, price 5*s*.

CONYERS (Ansley).

CHESTERLEIGH. 3 vols. Crown 8vo. Cloth.

COOKE (M. C.), M.A., LL.D.

FUNGI; their Nature, Influences, Uses, etc. Edited by the Rev. M. J. Berkeley, M.A., F.L.S. With Illustrations. Second Edition. Crown 8vo. Cloth, price 5*s*.
Volume XIV. of the International Scientific Series.

COOKE (Professor Josiah P.), of the Harvard University.

THE NEW CHEMISTRY. With Thirty-one Illustrations. Third Edition. Crown 8vo. Cloth, price 5*s*.
Volume IX. of the International Scientific Series.

SCIENTIFIC CULTURE. Crown 8vo. Cloth, price 1*s*.

COOPER (T. T.), F.R.G.S.

THE MISHMEE HILLS: an Account of a Journey made in an Attempt to Penetrate Thibet from Assam, to open New Routes for Commerce. Second Edition. With Four Illustrations and Map. Demy 8vo. Crown 8vo. Cloth, price 10*s*. 6*d*.

CORNHILL LIBRARY OF FICTION (The). Crown 8vo. Cloth, price 3*s*. 6*d*. per Volume.

HALF-A-DOZEN DAUGHTERS. By J. Masterman.

THE HOUSE OF RABY. By Mrs. G. Hooper.

A FIGHT FOR LIFE. By Moy Thomas.

ROBIN GRAY. By Charles Gibbon.

KITTY. By Miss M. Betham-Edwards.

HIRELL. By John Saunders.

ONE OF TWO; OR, THE LEFT-HANDED BRIDE. By J. Hain Friswell.

READY-MONEY MORTIBOY. A Matter-of-Fact Story.

GOD'S PROVIDENCE HOUSE. By Mrs. G. L. Banks.

FOR LACK OF GOLD. By Charles Gibbon.

ABEL DRAKE'S WIFE. By John Saunders.

CORY (Lieutenant-Colonel Arthur).

THE EASTERN MENACE; OR, SHADOWS OF COMING EVENTS. Crown 8vo. Cloth, price 5*s*.

COSMOS.

A Poem. Fcap. 8vo. Cloth, price 3*s*. 6*d*.

SUBJECTS.—Nature in the Past and in the Present—Man in the Past and in the Present—The Future.

COTTON (Robert Turner).

MR. CARINGTON. A Tale of Love and Conspiracy. 3 vols. Crown 8vo. Cloth.

CUMMINS (Henry Irwin), M.A.

PAROCHIAL CHARITIES OF THE CITY OF LONDON. Sewed, price 1*s*.

CURWEN (Henry).

SORROW AND SONG: Studies of Literary Struggle. Henry Mürger—Novalis—Alexander Petöfi—Honoré de Balzac—Edgar Allan Poe—André Chénier. 2 vols. Crown 8vo. Cloth, price 15*s*.

DAVIDSON (Samuel), D.D., LL.D.

THE NEW TESTAMENT, TRANSLATED FROM THE LATEST GREEK TEXT OF TISCHENDORF. A new and thoroughly revised Edition. Post 8vo. Cloth, price 10*s*. 6*d*.

DAVIES (G. Christopher).

MOUNTAIN, MEADOW, AND MERE: a Series of Outdoor Sketches of Sport, Scenery, Adventures, and Natural History. With Sixteen Illustrations by Bosworth W. Harcourt. Crown 8vo. Cloth, price 6*s.*

RAMBLES AND ADVENTURES OF OUR SCHOOL FIELD CLUB. With Four Illustrations. Crown 8vo. Cloth, price 5*s.*

DAVIES (Rev. J. Llewelyn), M.A.

THEOLOGY AND MORALITY. Essays on Questions of Belief and Practice. Crown 8vo. Cloth, price 7*s.* 6*d.*

D'ANVERS (N. R.)

THE SUEZ CANAL: Letters and Documents descriptive of its Rise and Progress in 1854-1856. By Ferdinand de Lesseps. Translated by N. D'Anvers. Demy 8vo. Cloth, price 10*s.* 6*d.*

LITTLE MINNIE'S TROUBLES. An Every-day Chronicle. With Four Illustrations by W. H. Hughes. Fcap. Cloth, price 3*s.* 6*d.*

DANCE (Rev. Charles Daniel).

RECOLLECTIONS OF FOUR YEARS IN VENEZUELA. With Three Illustrations and a Map. Crown 8vo. Cloth, price 7*s.* 6*d.*

DE KERKADEC (Vicomtesse Solange).

A CHEQUERED LIFE, being Memoirs of the Vicomtesse de Leoville Meilhan. Edited by. Crown 8vo. Cloth, price 7*s.* 6*d.*

Containing many recollections of the First Emperor Napoleon and his Court.

DE L'HOSTE (Colonel E. P).

THE DESERT PASTOR, JEAN JAROUSSEAU. Translated from the French of Eugène Pelletan. With a Frontispiece. New Edition. Fcap. 8vo. Cloth, price 3*s.* 6*d.*

DE REDCLIFFE (Viscount Stratford), P.C., K.G., G.C.B.

WHY AM I A CHRISTIAN? Fifth Edition. Crown 8vo. Cloth, price 3*s.*

DE TOCQUEVILLE (Alexis).

CORRESPONDENCE AND CONVERSATIONS OF, WITH NASSAU WILLIAM SENIOR, FROM 1834 TO 1859. Edited by M. C. M. Simpson. 2 vols. Post 8vo. Cloth, price 21*s.*

DE VERE (Aubrey).

ALEXANDER THE GREAT. A Dramatic Poem. Small crown 8vo. Cloth, price 5*s.*

THE INFANT BRIDAL, AND OTHER POEMS. A New and Enlarged Edition. Fcap. 8vo. Cloth, price 7*s.* 6*d.*

THE LEGENDS OF ST. PATRICK, AND OTHER POEMS. Small crown 8vo. Cloth, price 5*s.*

ST. THOMAS OF CANTERBURY. A Dramatic Poem. Large fcap 8vo. Cloth, price 5*s.*

DE WILLE (E.)

UNDER A CLOUD; OR, JOHANNES OLAF. A Novel. Translated by F. E. Bunnètt. 3 vols. Crown 8vo. Cloth.

DENNIS (John).

ENGLISH SONNETS. Collected and Arranged. Elegantly bound. Fcap. 8vo. Cloth, price 3*s.* 6*d.*

DOBSON (Austin).

VIGNETTES IN RHYME AND VERS DE SOCIÉTÉ. Second Edition. Fcap. 8vo. Cloth, price 5*s.*

DONNÉ (Alphonse), M.D.

CHANGE OF AIR AND SCENE. A Physician's Hints about Doctors, Patients, Hygiene, and Society; with Notes of Excursions for Health in the Pyrenees, and amongst the Watering-places of France (Inland and Seaward), Switzerland, Corsica, and the Mediterranean. Second Edition. Large post 8vo. Cloth, price 9*s.*

DOWDEN (Edward), LL.D.

SHAKSPERE: a Critical Study of his Mind and Art. Second Edition. Post 8vo. Cloth, price 12*s.*

DOWNTON (Rev. Henry), M.A.

HYMNS AND VERSES. Original and Translated. Small crown 8vo. Cloth, price 3*s.* 6*d.*

DRAPER (John William), M.D., LL.D. Professor in the University of New York; Author of "A Treatise on Human Physiology."

HISTORY OF THE CONFLICT BETWEEN RELIGION AND SCIENCE. Seventh Edition. Crown 8vo. Cloth, price 5*s.*
Volume XIII. of the International Scientific Series.

DREW (Rev. G. S.), M.A., Vicar of Trinity, Lambeth.

SCRIPTURE LANDS IN CONNECTION WITH THEIR HISTORY. Second Edition. 8vo. Cloth, price 10*s.* 6*d.*

NAZARETH: ITS LIFE AND LESSONS. Third Edition. Crown 8vo. Cloth, price 5*s.*

THE DIVINE KINGDOM ON EARTH AS IT IS IN HEAVEN. 8vo. Cloth, price 10*s.* 6*d.*

THE SON OF MAN: His Life and Ministry. Crown 8vo. Cloth, price 7*s.* 6*d.*

DREWRY (G. Overend), M.D.

THE COMMON-SENSE MANAGEMENT OF THE STOMACH. Third Edition. Fcap. 8vo. Cloth, price 2*s.* 6*d.*

—— and BARTLETT (H. C.), Ph.D., F.C.S.

CUP AND PLATTER; or, Notes on Food and its Effects. Small 8vo. Cloth, price 2*s.* 6*d.*

DURAND (Lady).

IMITATIONS FROM THE GERMAN OF SPITTA AND TERSTEGEN. Fcap. 8vo. Cloth, price 4*s.*

DU VERNOIS (Colonel von Verdy).

STUDIES IN LEADING TROOPS. An authorized and accurate Translation by Lieutenant H. J. T. Hildyard, 71st Foot. Parts I. and II. Demy 8vo. Cloth, price 7*s.*

E. A. V.

JOSEPH MAZZINI: A Memoir. With Two Essays by Mazzini. Dedicated to the Working Classes by P. H. Taylor, M.P. With Two Portraits. Crown 8vo. Cloth, price 3*s.* 6*d.*

EDEN (Frederic).

THE NILE WITHOUT A DRAGOMAN. Second Edition. Crown 8vo. Cloth, price 7*s.* 6*d.*

EDWARDS (Rev. Basil).

MINOR CHORDS; OR, SONGS FOR THE SUFFERING: a Volume of Verse. Fcap. 8vo. Cloth, price 3*s.* 6*d.*; paper, price 2*s.* 6*d.*

EILOART (Mrs.)

LADY MORETOUN'S DAUGHTER. 3 vols. Crown 8vo.

ENGLISH CLERGYMAN.

AN ESSAY ON THE RULE OF FAITH AND CREED OF ATHANASIUS. Shall the Rubric preceding the Creed be removed from the Prayer-book? Sewed. 8vo. Price 1*s.*

EPIC OF HADES (The).

By a New Writer. Author of "Songs of Two Worlds." Fcap. 8vo. Cloth, price 5*s.*

EROS AGONISTES.

Poems. By E. B. D. Fcap. 8vo. Cloth, price 3*s.* 6*d.*

ESSAYS ON THE ENDOWMENT OF RESEARCH.

By Various Writers.

LIST OF CONTRIBUTORS.

MARK PATTISON, B.D.
JAMES S. COTTON, B.A.
CHARLES E. APPLETON, D.C.L.
ARCHIBALD H. SAYCE, M.A.
HENRY CLIFTON SORBY, F.R.S.
THOMAS K. CHEYNE, M.A.
W. T. THISTELTON DYER, M.A.
HENRY NETTLESHIP, M.A.

Square crown octavo. Cloth, price 10*s.* 6*d.*

EVANS (Mark).

THE STORY OF OUR FATHER'S LOVE, told to Children; being a New and Enlarged Edition of THEOLOGY FOR CHILDREN. With Four Illustrations. Fcap. 8vo. Cloth, price 3*s.* 6*d.*

A BOOK OF COMMON PRAYER AND WORSHIP FOR HOUSEHOLD USE, compiled exclusively from the Holy Scriptures. Fcap. 8vo. Cloth, price 2*s.* 6*d.*

EYRE (Maj.-Gen. Sir Vincent), C.B., K.C.S.I., etc.

LAYS OF A KNIGHT-ERRANT IN MANY LANDS. Square crown 8vo. With Six Illustrations. Cloth, price 7*s.* 6*d.*

FAITHFULL (Mrs. Francis G.)

LOVE ME, OR LOVE ME NOT. 3 vols. Crown 8vo. Cloth.

FARQUHARSON (Martha).

I. **ELSIE DINSMORE.** Crown 8vo. Cloth, price 3*s.* 6*d.*

II. **ELSIE'S GIRLHOOD.** Crown 8vo. Cloth, price 3*s.* 6*d.*

III. **ELSIE'S HOLIDAYS AT ROSELANDS.** Crown 8vo. Cloth, price 3*s.* 6*d.*

FAVRE (Mons. Jules).

THE GOVERNMENT OF THE NATIONAL DEFENCE. From the 30th June to the 31st October, 1870. Translated by H. Clark. Demy 8vo. Cloth, price 10*s.* 6*d.*

FISHER (Alice).

HIS QUEEN. 3 vols. Crown 8vo. Cloth.

FOOTMAN (Rev. Henry), M.A.

FROM HOME AND BACK; or, Some Aspects of Sin as seen in the Light of the Parable of the Prodigal. Crown 8vo. Cloth, price 5*s.*

FORBES (Archibald).

SOLDIERING AND SCRIBBLING. A Series of Sketches. Crown 8vo. Cloth, price 7*s.* 6*d.*

FOTHERGILL (Jessie).

HEALEY. A Romance. 3 vols. Crown 8vo. Cloth.

FOWLE (Rev. T. W.), M.A.

THE RECONCILIATION OF RELIGION AND SCIENCE. Being Essays on Immortality, Inspiration, Miracles, and the Being of Christ. Demy 8vo. Cloth, price 10*s.* 6*d.*

FOX-BOURNE (H. R.)

THE LIFE OF JOHN LOCKE, 1632—1704. 2 vols. Demy 8vo. Cloth, price 28*s.*

FRASER (Donald), Accountant to the British-Indian Steam Navigation Company, Limited.

EXCHANGE TABLES OF STERLING AND INDIAN RUPEE CURRENCY, upon a new and extended system, embracing Values from One Farthing to One Hundred Thousand Pounds, and at Rates progressing, in Sixteenths of a Penny, from 1*s.* 9*d.* to 2*s.* 3*d.* per Rupee. Royal 8vo. Cloth, price 10*s.* 6*d.*

FRERE (Sir H. Bartle E.), G.C.S.I., K.C.B., etc.

THE THREATENED FAMINE IN BENGAL: How it may be Met, and the Recurrence of Famines in India Prevented. Being No. 1 of "Occasional Notes on Indian Affairs." With 3 Maps. Crown 8vo. Cloth, price 5*s.*

FRISWELL (J. Hain).

THE BETTER SELF. Essays for Home Life. Crown 8vo. Cloth, price 6*s.*

Contents:—Beginning at Home—The Girls at Home—The Wife's Mother—Pride in the Family—Discontent and Grumbling—Domestic Economy—On Keeping People Down—Likes and Dislikes—On Falling Out—Peace.

ONE OF TWO; OR, THE LEFT-HANDED BRIDE. With a Frontispiece. Crown 8vo. Cloth, price 3*s.* 6*d.*

GARDNER (John), M.D.

LONGEVITY; THE MEANS OF PROLONGING LIFE AFTER MIDDLE AGE. Third Edition, revised and enlarged. Small crown 8vo. Cloth, price 4*s*.

GARDNER (Herbert).

SUNFLOWERS. A Book of Verses. Fcap. 8vo. Cloth, price 5*s*.

GARRETT (Edward).

BY STILL WATERS. A Story for Quiet Hours. With Seven Illustrations. Crown 8vo. Cloth, price 6*s*.

GIBBON (Charles).

FOR LACK OF GOLD. With a Frontispiece. Crown 8vo. Cloth, price 3*s*. 6*d*.

ROBIN GRAY. With a Frontispiece. Crown 8vo. Cloth, price 3*s*. 6*d*.

GILBERT (Mrs.), formerly Ann Taylor.

AUTOBIOGRAPHY AND OTHER MEMORIALS. Edited by Josiah Gilbert. Second Edition. In 2 vols. With 2 Steel Portraits and several Wood Engravings. Post 8vo. Cloth, price 24*s*.

GILL (Rev. W. W.), B.A.

MYTHS AND SONGS FROM THE SOUTH PACIFIC. With a Preface by F. Max Müller, M.A., Professor of Comparative Philology at Oxford. Post 8vo. Cloth, price 9*s*.

GODKIN (James).

THE RELIGIOUS HISTORY OF IRELAND: Primitive, Papal, and Protestant. Including the Evangelical Missions, Catholic Agitations, and Church Progress of the last half Century. 8vo. Cloth, price 12*s*.

GODWIN (William).

WILLIAM GODWIN: HIS FRIENDS AND CONTEMPORARIES. With Portraits and Facsimiles of the handwriting of Godwin and his Wife. By C. Kegan Paul. 2 vols. Demy 8vo. Cloth, price 28*s*.

THE GENIUS OF CHRISTIANITY UNVEILED. Being Essays never before published. Edited, with a Preface, by C. Kegan Paul. Crown 8vo. Cloth, price 7*s*. 6*d*.

GOETZE (Capt. A. von), Captain of the Prussian Corps of Engineers.

OPERATIONS OF THE GERMAN ENGINEERS DURING THE WAR OF 1870-1871. Published by Authority, and in accordance with Official Documents. Translated from the German by Colonel G. Graham, V.C., C.B., R.E. With 6 large Maps. Demy 8vo. Cloth, price 21*s.*

GOODENOUGH (Commodore J. G.), Royal Navy, C.B., C.M.G.

JOURNALS OF, during his Last Command as Senior Officer on the Australian Station, 1873–1875. Edited, with a Memoir, by his Widow. With Maps, Woodcuts, and Steel Engraved Portrait. Square post 8vo. Cloth, price 14*s.*

GOODMAN (Walter).

CUBA, THE PEARL OF THE ANTILLES. Crown 8vo. Cloth, price 7*s.* 6*d.*

GOULD (Rev. S. Baring).

THE VICAR OF MORWENSTOW: a Memoir of the Rev. R. S. Hawker. With Portrait. Third Edition, revised. Post 8vo. Cloth, price 10*s.* 6*d.*

GRANVILLE (A. B.), M.D., F.R.S., etc.

AUTOBIOGRAPHY OF A. B. GRANVILLE, F.R.S., etc. Edited, with a brief account of the concluding years of his life, by his youngest Daughter, Paulina B. Granville. 2 vols. With a Portrait. Second Edition. Demy 8vo. Cloth, price 32*s.*

GRAY (Mrs. Russell).

LISETTE'S VENTURE. A Novel. 2 vols. Crown 8vo. Cloth.

GREEN (T. Bowden).

FRAGMENTS OF THOUGHT. Dedicated by permission to the Poet Laureate. Crown 8vo. Cloth, price 7*s.* 6*d.*

GREENWOOD (James), "The Amateur Casual."

IN STRANGE COMPANY; or, The Note Book of a Roving Correspondent. Second Edition. Crown 8vo. Cloth, price 6*s.*

GREY (John), of Dilston.

JOHN GREY (of Dilston): MEMOIRS. By Josephine E. Butler. New and Revised Edition. Crown 8vo. Cloth, price 3*s.* 6*d.*

GRIFFITH (Rev. T.), A.M.

STUDIES OF THE DIVINE MASTER. Demy 8vo. Cloth, price 12*s*.

GRIFFITHS (Captain Arthur).

MEMORIALS OF MILLBANK, AND CHAPTERS IN PRISON HISTORY. With Illustrations by R. Goff and the Author. 2 vols. Post 8vo. Cloth, price 21*s*.

THE QUEEN'S SHILLING. A Novel. 2 vols. Cloth.

GRIMLEY (Rev. H. N.), M.A., Professor of Mathematics in the University of Wales, and Chaplain of Tremadoc Church.

TREMADOC SERMONS, chiefly on the SPIRITUAL BODY, the UNSEEN WORLD, and the DIVINE HUMANITY. Crown 8vo. Cloth, price 7*s*. 6*d*.

GRUNER (M. L.)

STUDIES OF BLAST FURNACE PHENOMENA. Translated by L. D. B. Gordon, F.R.S.E., F.G.S. Demy 8vo. Cloth, price 7*s*. 6*d*.

GURNEY (Rev. Archer Thompson).

WORDS OF FAITH AND CHEER. A Mission of Instruction and Suggestion. Crown 8vo. Cloth, price 6*s*.

FIRST PRINCIPLES IN CHURCH AND STATE. Demy 8vo. Sewed, price 1*s*. 6*d*.

HAECKEL (Professor Ernst), of the University of Jena.

THE HISTORY OF CREATION. A Popular Account of the Development of the Earth and its Inhabitants, according to the Theories of Kant, Laplace, Lamarck, and Darwin. The Translation revised by Professor E. Ray Lankester, M.A., F.R.S. With Coloured Plates and Genealogical Trees of the various groups of both plants and animals. 2 vols. Post 8vo. Cloth, price 32*s*.

HARCOURT (Capt. A. F. P.)

THE SHAKESPEARE ARGOSY: Containing much of the wealth of Shakespeare's Wisdom and Wit, alphabetically arranged and classified. Crown 8vo. Cloth, price 6*s*.

HAWEIS (Rev. H. R.), M.A.

SPEECH IN SEASON. Third Edition. Crown 8vo. Cloth, price 9*s*.

THOUGHTS FOR THE TIMES. Ninth Edition. Crown 8vo. Cloth, price 7*s*. 6*d*.

HAWEIS (Rev. H. R.), M.A.

UNSECTARIAN FAMILY PRAYERS, for Morning and Evening for a Week, with short selected passages from the Bible. Square crown 8vo. Cloth, price 3*s*. 6*d*.

HAWTHORNE (Julian).

BRESSANT. A Romance. 2 vols. Crown 8vo. Cloth.

IDOLATRY. A Romance. 2 vols. Crown 8vo. Cloth.

HAWTHORNE (Nathaniel).

NATHANIEL HAWTHORNE. A Memoir, with Stories now first published in this country. By H. A. Page. Post 8vo. Cloth, price 7*s*. 6*d*.

SEPTIMIUS. A Romance. Second Edition. Crown 8vo. Cloth, price 9*s*.

HAYMAN (Henry), D.D., late Head Master of Rugby School.

RUGBY SCHOOL SERMONS. With an Introductory Essay on the Indwelling of the Holy Spirit. Crown 8vo. Cloth, price 7*s*. 6*d*.

HEATHERGATE.

A Story of Scottish Life and Character. By a New Author. 2 vols. Crown 8vo. Cloth.

HELLWALD (Baron F. Von).

THE RUSSIANS IN CENTRAL ASIA. A Critical Examination, down to the present time, of the Geography and History of Central Asia. Translated by Lieut.-Col. Theodore Wirgman, LL.B. Large post 8vo. With Map. Cloth, price 12*s*.

HELVIG (Captain Hugo).

THE OPERATIONS OF THE BAVARIAN ARMY CORPS. Translated by Captain G. S. Schwabe. With Five large Maps. In 2 vols. Demy 8vo. Cloth, price 24*s*.

HINTON (James), late Aural Surgeon to Guy's Hospital.

THE PLACE OF THE PHYSICIAN. To which is added ESSAYS ON THE LAW OF HUMAN LIFE, AND ON THE RELATION BETWEEN ORGANIC AND INORGANIC WORLDS. Second Edition. Crown 8vo. Cloth, price 3*s*. 6*d*.

PHYSIOLOGY FOR PRACTICAL USE. By various Writers. With 50 Illustrations. 2 vols. Second Edition. Crown 8vo. Cloth, price 12*s*. 6*d*.

HINTON (James), late Aural Surgeon to Guy's Hospital.

AN ATLAS OF DISEASES OF THE MEMBRANA TYMPANI. With Descriptive Text. Post 8vo. Price £6 6*s*.

THE QUESTIONS OF AURAL SURGERY. With Illustrations. 2 vols. Post 8vo. Cloth, price 12*s*. 6*d*.

H. J. C.

THE ART OF FURNISHING. A Popular Treatise on the Principles of Furnishing, based on the Laws of Common Sense, Requirement, and Picturesque Effect. Small crown 8vo. Cloth, price 3*s*. 6*d*.

HOCKLEY (W. B.)

TALES OF THE ZENANA; or, A Nuwab's Leisure Hours. By the Author of "Pandurang Hari." With a Preface by Lord Stanley of Alderley. 2 vols. Crown 8vo. Cloth, price 21*s*.

PANDURANG HARI; or, Memoirs of a Hindoo. A Tale of Mahratta Life sixty years ago. With a Preface by Sir H. Bartle E. Frere, G.C.S.I., etc. 2 vols. Crown 8vo. Cloth, price 21*s*.

HOFFBAUER (Captain).

THE GERMAN ARTILLERY IN THE BATTLES NEAR METZ. Based on the official reports of the German Artillery. Translated by Capt. E. O. Hollist. With Map and Plans. Demy 8vo. Cloth, price 21*s*.

HOGAN, M.P.

A Novel. 3 vols. Crown 8vo. Cloth.

HOLMES (Edmond G. A.)

POEMS. Fcap. 8vo. Cloth, price 5*s*.

HOLROYD (Major W. R. M.)

TAS-HIL UL KĀLĀM; or, Hindustani made Easy. Crown 8vo. Cloth, price 5*s*.

HOPE (Lieut. James).

IN QUEST OF COOLIES. With Illustrations. Crown 8vo. Cloth, price 6*s*.

HOOPER (Mary).

LITTLE DINNERS: HOW TO SERVE THEM WITH ELEGANCE AND ECONOMY. Tenth Edition. Crown 8vo. Cloth, price 5*s*.

COOKERY FOR INVALIDS, PERSONS OF DELICATE DIGESTION, AND CHILDREN. Crown 8vo. Cloth, price 3*s*. 6*d*.

HOOPER (Mrs. G.)

THE HOUSE OF RABY. With a Frontispiece. Crown 8vo. Cloth, price 3*s.* 6*d.*

HOPKINS (Manley).

THE PORT OF REFUGE; or, Counsel and Aid to Shipmasters in Difficulty, Doubt, or Distress. Crown 8vo. Cloth, price 6*s.*

HOWARD (Mary M.), Author of "Brampton Rectory."

BEATRICE AYLMER, AND OTHER TALES. Crown 8vo. Cloth, price 6*s.*

HOWARD (Rev. G. B.)

AN OLD LEGEND OF ST. PAUL'S. Fcap. 8vo. Cloth, price 4*s.* 6*d.*

HOWELL (James).

A TALE OF THE SEA, SONNETS, AND OTHER POEMS. Fcap. 8vo. Cloth, price 5*s.*

HUGHES (Allison).

PENELOPE, AND OTHER POEMS. Fcap. 8vo. Cloth, price 4*s.* 6*d.*

HULL (Edmund C. P.)

THE EUROPEAN IN INDIA. A Handbook of Practical Information for those proceeding to, or residing in, the East Indies. With a MEDICAL GUIDE FOR ANGLO-INDIANS. By R. R. S. Mair, M.D., F.R.C.S.E. Second Edition, Revised and Corrected. Post 8vo. Cloth, price 6*s.*

HUMPHREY (Rev. W.), of the Congregation of the Oblates of St. Charles.

MR. FITZJAMES STEPHEN AND CARDINAL BELLARMINE. Demy 8vo. Sewed, price 1*s.*

HUTTON (James).

MISSIONARY LIFE IN THE SOUTHERN SEAS. With Illustrations. Crown 8vo. Cloth, price 7*s.* 6*d.*

IGNOTUS.

CULMSHIRE FOLK. A Novel. New and Cheaper Edition. Crown 8vo. Cloth, price 6*s.*

International Scientific Series (The).

I. **THE FORMS OF WATER IN CLOUDS AND RIVERS, ICE AND GLACIERS.** By J. Tyndall, LL.D., F.R.S. With 25 Illustrations. Sixth Edition. 5*s*.

II. **PHYSICS AND POLITICS**; or, Thoughts on the Application of the Principles of "Natural Selection" and "Inheritance" to Political Society. By Walter Bagehot. Third Edition. 4*s*.

III. **FOODS.** By Edward Smith, M.D., LL.B., F.R.S. Profusely Illustrated. Fourth Edition. 5*s*.

IV. **MIND AND BODY**: The Theories of their Relation. By Alexander Bain, LL.D. With Four Illustrations. Fifth Edition. 4*s*.

V. **THE STUDY OF SOCIOLOGY.** By Herbert Spencer. Fifth Edition. 5*s*.

VI. **ON THE CONSERVATION OF ENERGY.** By Balfour Stewart, M.A., LL.D., F.R.S. With 14 Illustrations. Third Edition. 5*s*.

VII. **ANIMAL LOCOMOTION**; or, Walking, Swimming, and Flying. By J. B. Pettigrew, M.D., F.R.S., etc. With 130 Illustrations. Second Edition. 5*s*.

VIII. **RESPONSIBILITY IN MENTAL DISEASE.** By Henry Maudsley, M.D. Second Edition. 5*s*.

IX. **THE NEW CHEMISTRY.** By Professor J. P. Cooke, of the Harvard University. With 31 Illustrations. Third Edition. 5*s*.

X. **THE SCIENCE OF LAW.** By Professor Sheldon Amos. Second Edition. 5*s*.

XI. **ANIMAL MECHANISM.** A Treatise on Terrestrial and Aerial Locomotion. By Professor E. J. Marey. With 117 Illustrations. Second Edition. 5*s*.

INTERNATIONAL SCIENTIFIC SERIES (The).—*Continued.*

XII. **THE DOCTRINE OF DESCENT AND DARWINISM.** By Professor Oscar Schmidt (Strasburg University). With 26 Illustrations. Third Edition. 5*s.*

XIII. **THE HISTORY OF THE CONFLICT BETWEEN RELIGION AND SCIENCE.** By Professor J. W. Draper, M.D., LL.D. Seventh Edition. 5*s.*

XIV. **FUNGI**; their Nature, Influences, Uses, etc. By M. C. Cooke, M.A., LL.D. Edited by the Rev. M. J. Berkeley, M.A., F.L.S. With numerous Illustrations. Second Edition. 5*s.*

XV. **THE CHEMICAL EFFECTS OF LIGHT AND PHOTOGRAPHY.** By Dr. Hermann Vogel (Polytechnic Academy of Berlin). Translation thoroughly revised. With 100 Illustrations. Third Edition. 5*s.*

XVI. **THE LIFE AND GROWTH OF LANGUAGE.** By William Dwight Whitney, Professor of Sanskrit and Comparative Philology in Yale College, New Haven. Second Edition. 5*s.*

XVII. **MONEY AND THE MECHANISM OF EXCHANGE.** By W. Stanley Jevons, M.A., F.R.S. Third Edition. 5*s.*

XVIII. **THE NATURE OF LIGHT**: With a General Account of Physical Optics. By Dr. Eugene Lommel, Professor of Physics in the University of Erlangen. With 188 Illustrations and a table of Spectra in Chromolithography. Second Edition. 5*s.*

XIX. **ANIMAL PARASITES AND MESSMATES.** By Monsieur Van Beneden, Professor of the University of Louvain, Correspondent of the Institute of France. With 83 Illustrations. Second Edition. 5*s.*

XX. **FERMENTATION.** By Professor Schützenberger, Director of the Chemical Laboratory at the Sorbonne. With 28 Illustrations. 5*s.*

XXI. **THE FIVE SENSES OF MAN.** By Professor Bernstein, of the University of Halle. With 91 Illustrations. Second Edition. 5*s.*

International Scientific Series (The).

Forthcoming Volumes.

Prof. W. Kingdon Clifford, M.A. The First Principles of the Exact Sciences explained to the Non-mathematical.

Prof. T. H. Huxley, LL.D., F.R.S. Bodily Motion and Consciousness.

Dr. W. B. Carpenter, LL.D., F.R.S. The Physical Geography of the Sea.

Prof. William Odling, F.R.S. The Old Chemistry viewed from the New Standpoint.

W. Lauder Lindsay, M.D., F.R.S.E. Mind in the Lower Animals.

Sir John Lubbock, Bart., F.R.S. On Ants and Bees.

Prof. W. T. Thiselton Dyer, B.A., B.Sc. Form and Habit in Flowering Plants.

Mr. J. N. Lockyer, F.R.S. Spectrum Analysis.

Prof. Michael Foster, M.D. Protoplasm and the Cell Theory.

H. Charlton Bastian, M.D., F.R.S. The Brain as an Organ of Mind.

Prof. A. C. Ramsay, LL.D., F.R.S. Earth Sculpture: Hills, Valleys, Mountains, Plains, Rivers, Lakes; how they were Produced, and how they have been Destroyed.

Prof. Rudolph Virchow (Berlin Univ.) Morbid Physiological Action.

Prof. Claude Bernard. History of the Theories of Life.

Prof. H. Sainte-Claire Deville. An Introduction to General Chemistry.

Prof. Wurtz. Atoms and the Atomic Theory.

Prof. Lacaze-Duthiers. Zoology since Cuvier.

Prof. Berthelot. Chemical Synthesis.

INTERNATIONAL SCIENTIFIC SERIES (The).—*Continued.*
(*Forthcoming Volumes.*)

Prof. J. ROSENTHAL. General Physiology of Muscles and Nerves.

Prof. JAMES D. DANA, M.A., LL.D. On Cephalization; or, Head-Characters in the Gradation and Progress of Life.

Prof. S. W. JOHNSON, M.A. On the Nutrition of Plants.

Prof. AUSTIN FLINT, Jr. M.D. The Nervous System, and its Relation to the Bodily Functions.

Prof. FERDINAND COHN (Breslau Univ.) Thallophytes (Algæ, Lichens, Fungi).

Prof. HERMANN (University of Zurich). Respiration.

Prof. LEUCKART (University of Leipsic). Outlines of Animal Organization.

Prof. LIEBREICH (University of Berlin). Outlines of Toxicology.

Prof. KUNDT (University of Strasburg). On Sound.

Prof. REES (University of Erlangen). On Parasitic Plants.

Prof. STEINTHAL (University of Berlin). Outlines of the Science of Language.

P. BERT (Professor of Physiology, Paris). Forms of Life and other Cosmical Conditions.

E. ALGLAVE (Professor of Constitutional and Administrative Law at Douai, and of Political Economy at Lille). The Primitive Elements of Political Constitutions.

P. LORAIN (Professor of Medicine, Paris). Modern Epidemics.

Mons. FREIDEL. The Functions of Organic Chemistry.

Mons. DEBRAY. Precious Metals.

Prof. CORFIELD, M.A., M.D. (Oxon.) Air in its relation to Health.

Prof. A. GIARD. General Embryology.

INGELOW (Jean).

THE LITTLE WONDER-HORN. A Second Series of "Stories Told to a Child." With Fifteen Illustrations. Square 24mo. Cloth, price 3*s.* 6*d.*

OFF THE SKELLIGS. (Her First Romance.) 4 vols. Crown 8vo. Cloth, price 42*s.*

JACKSON (T. G.)

MODERN GOTHIC ARCHITECTURE. Crown 8vo. Cloth, price 5*s.*

JACOB (Maj.-Gen. Sir G. Le Grand), K.C.S.I., C.B.

WESTERN INDIA BEFORE AND DURING THE MUTINIES. Pictures drawn from life. Second Edition. Crown 8vo. Cloth, price 7*s.* 6*d.*

JENKINS (E.) and RAYMOND (J.), Esqs.

A LEGAL HANDBOOK FOR ARCHITECTS, BUILDERS, AND BUILDING OWNERS. Second Edition Revised. Crown 8vo. Cloth, price 6*s.*

JENKINS (Rev. R. C.), M.A.

THE PRIVILEGE OF PETER and the Claims of the Roman Church confronted with the Scriptures, the Councils, and the Testimony of the Popes themselves. Fcap. 8vo. Cloth, price 3*s.* 6*d.*

JEVONS (W. Stanley), M.A., F.R.S.

MONEY AND THE MECHANISM OF EXCHANGE. Second Edition. Crown 8vo. Cloth, price 5*s.*

Volume XVII. of the International Scientific Series.

KAUFMANN (Rev. M.), B.A.

SOCIALISM: Its Nature, its Dangers, and its Remedies considered. Crown 8vo. Cloth, price 7*s.* 6*d.*

KEATINGE (Mrs.)

HONOR BLAKE: The Story of a Plain Woman. 2 vols. Crown 8vo. Cloth.

KER (David).

ON THE ROAD TO KHIVA. Illustrated with Photographs of the Country and its Inhabitants, and a copy of the Official Map in use during the Campaign, from the Survey of Captain Leusilin. Post 8vo. Cloth, price 12*s.*

THE BOY SLAVE IN BOKHARA. A Tale of Central Asia. With Illustrations. Crown 8vo. Cloth, price 5*s.*

KER (David).

THE WILD HORSEMAN OF THE PAMPAS. Illustrated. Crown 8vo. Cloth, price 5*s*.

KING (Alice).

A CLUSTER OF LIVES. Crown 8vo. Cloth, price 7*s*. 6*d*.

KING (Mrs. Hamilton).

THE DISCIPLES. A New Poem. Second Edition, with some Notes. Crown 8vo. Cloth, price 7*s*. 6*d*.

ASPROMONTE, AND OTHER POEMS. Second Edition. Fcap. 8vo. Cloth, price 4*s*. 6*d*.

KINGSFORD (Rev. F. W.), M.A., Vicar of St. Thomas's, Stamford Hill; late Chaplain H. E. I. C. (Bengal Presidency).

HARTHAM CONFERENCES; or, Discussions upon some of the Religious Topics of the Day. "Audi alteram partem." Crown 8vo. Cloth, price 3*s*. 6*d*.

KINGSMAN (A.)

OVER VOLCANOES; or, Through France and Spain in 1871. Crown 8vo. Cloth, price 10*s*. 6*d*.

KNIGHT (Annette F. C.)

POEMS. Fcap. 8vo. Cloth, price 5*s*.

LACORDAIRE (Rev. Père).

LIFE: Conferences delivered at Toulouse. A New and Cheaper Edition. Crown 8vo. Cloth, price 3*s*. 6*d*.

LADY OF LIPARI (The).

A Poem in Three Cantos. Fcap. 8vo. Cloth, price 5*s*.

LAURIE (J. S.), of the Inner Temple, Barrister-at-Law; formerly H.M. Inspector of Schools, England; Assistant Royal Commissioner, Ireland; Special Commissioner, African Settlement; Director of Public Instruction, Ceylon.

EDUCATIONAL COURSE OF SECULAR SCHOOL BOOKS FOR INDIA.

The following Works are now ready:—

THE FIRST HINDUSTANI READER. Stiff linen wrapper, price 6*d*.

THE SECOND HINDUSTANI READER. Stiff linen wrapper, price 6*d*.

GEOGRAPHY OF INDIA; with Maps and Historical Appendix, tracing the growth of the British Empire in Hindustan. Fcap. 8vo. Cloth, price 1*s*. 6*d*.

LAYMANN (Captain), Instructor of Tactics at the Military College, Neisse.

THE FRONTAL ATTACK OF INFANTRY. Translated by Colonel Edward Newdigate. Crown 8vo. Cloth, price 2*s.* 6*d.*

L. D. S.

LETTERS FROM CHINA AND JAPAN. With Illustrated Title-page. Crown 8vo. Cloth, price 7*s.* 6*d.*

LEANDER (Richard).

FANTASTIC STORIES. Translated from the German by Paulina B. Granville. With Eight full-page Illustrations by M. E. Fraser-Tytler. Crown 8vo. Cloth, price 5*s.*

LEATHES (Rev. Stanley), M.A.

THE GOSPEL ITS OWN WITNESS. Crown 8vo. Cloth, price 5*s.*

LEE (Rev. Frederick George), D.C.L.

THE OTHER WORLD; or, Glimpses of the Supernatural. Being Facts, Records, and Traditions, relating to Dreams, Omens, Miraculous Occurrences, Apparitions, Wraiths, Warnings, Second-sight, Necromancy, Witchcraft, etc. 2 vols. A New Edition. Crown 8vo. Cloth, price 15*s.*

LEE (Holme).

HER TITLE OF HONOUR. A Book for Girls. New Edition. With a Frontispiece. Crown 8vo. Cloth, price 5*s.*

LENOIR (J).

FAYOUM; or, Artists in Egypt. A Tour with M. Gérome and others. With 13 Illustrations. A New and Cheaper Edition. Crown 8vo. Cloth, price 3*s.* 6*d.*

LEWIS (Mary A.)

A RAT WITH THREE TALES. With Four Illustrations by Catherine F. Frere. Cloth, price 5*s.*

LISTADO (J. T.)

CIVIL SERVICE. A Novel. 2 vols. Crown 8vo. Cloth.

LOCKER (Frederick).

LONDON LYRICS. A New and Revised Edition, with Additions and a Portrait of the Author. Crown 8vo. Cloth, elegant, price 7*s.* 6*d.*

LOMMEL (Dr. Eugene), Professor of Physics in the University of Erlangen.

THE NATURE OF LIGHT: With a General Account of Physical Optics. Second Edition. With 188 Illustrations and a table of Spectra in Chromolithography. Crown 8vo. Cloth, price 5*s*.

Volume XVIII. of the International Scientific Series.

LORIMER (Peter), D.D.

JOHN KNOX AND THE CHURCH OF ENGLAND: His work in her Pulpit and his influence upon her Liturgy, Articles, and Parties. Demy 8vo. Cloth, price 12*s*.

LOVER (Samuel), R.H.A.

THE LIFE OF SAMUEL LOVER, R.H.A.; Artistic, Literary, and Musical. With Selections from his Unpublished Papers and Correspondence. By Bayle Bernard. 2 vols. With a Portrait. Post 8vo. Cloth, price 21*s*.

LOWER (Mark Antony), M.A., F.S.A.

WAYSIDE NOTES IN SCANDINAVIA. Being Notes of Travel in the North of Europe. Crown 8vo. Cloth, price 9*s*.

LYONS (R. T.), Surgeon-Major, Bengal Army.

A TREATISE ON RELAPSING FEVER. Post 8vo. Cloth, price 7*s*. 6*d*.

MACAULAY (James), M.A., M.D., Edin.

THE TRUTH ABOUT IRELAND: Tours of Observation in 1872 and 1875. With Remarks on Irish Public Questions. Being a Second Edition of "Ireland in 1872," with a New and Supplementary Preface. Crown 8vo. Cloth, price 3*s*. 6*d*.

MAC CARTHY (Denis Florence).

CALDERON'S DRAMAS. Translated from the Spanish. Post 8vo. Cloth, gilt edges, price 10*s*.

MAC DONALD (George).

MALCOLM. A Novel. 3 vols. Second Edition. Crown 8vo. Cloth.

ST. GEORGE AND ST. MICHAEL. 3 vols. Crown 8vo. Cloth.

MACLACHLAN (Archibald Neil Campbell), M.A.

WILLIAM AUGUSTUS, DUKE OF CUMBERLAND: being a Sketch of his Military Life and Character, chiefly as exhibited in the General Orders of his Royal Highness, 1745—1747. With Illustrations. Post 8vo. Cloth, price 15*s*.

MAC KENNA (Stephen J.)

PLUCKY FELLOWS. A Book for Boys. With Six Illustrations. Second Edition. Crown 8vo. Cloth, price 3*s*. 6*d*.

AT SCHOOL WITH AN OLD DRAGOON. With Six Illustrations. Second Edition. Crown 8vo. Cloth, price 5*s*.

MAIR (R. S.), M.D., F.R.C.S.E., late Deputy Coroner of Madras.

THE MEDICAL GUIDE FOR ANGLO-INDIANS. Being a Compendium of Advice to Europeans in India, relating to the Preservation and Regulation of Health. With a Supplement on the Management of Children in India. Crown 8vo. Limp cloth, price 3*s*. 6*d*.

MANNING (His Eminence Cardinal).

ESSAYS ON RELIGION AND LITERATURE. By various Writers. Third Series. Demy 8vo. Cloth, price 10*s*. 6*d*.

Contents:—The Philosophy of Christianity—Mystic Elements of Religion—Controversy with the Agnostics—A Reasoning Thought—Darwinism brought to Book—Mr. Mill on Liberty of the Press—Christianity in Relation to Society—The Religious Condition of Germany—The Philosophy of Bacon—Catholic Laymen and Scholastic Philosophy.

MAREY (E. J.)

ANIMAL MECHANICS. A Treatise on Terrestrial and Aerial Locomotion. With 117 Illustrations. Second Edition. Crown 8vo. Cloth, price 5*s*.

Volume XI. of the International Scientific Series.

MARKEWITCH (B.)

THE NEGLECTED QUESTION. Translated from the Russian, by the Princess Ourousoff, and dedicated by Express Permission to Her Imperial and Royal Highness Marie Alexandrovna, the Duchess of Edinburgh. 2 vols. Crown 8vo. Cloth, price 14*s*.

MARRIOTT (Maj.-Gen. W. F.), C.S.I.

A GRAMMAR OF POLITICAL ECONOMY. Crown 8vo. Cloth, price 6*s*.

MARSHALL (Hamilton).

THE STORY OF SIR EDWARD'S WIFE. A Novel. Crown 8vo. Cloth, price 10*s*. 6*d*.

MASTERMAN (J.)

HALF-A-DOZEN DAUGHTERS. With a Frontispiece. Crown 8vo. Cloth, price 3*s*. 6*d*.

MAUDSLEY (Dr. Henry).

RESPONSIBILITY IN MENTAL DISEASE. Second Edition. Crown 8vo. Cloth, price 5*s*.

Volume VIII. of the International Scientific Series.

MAUGHAN (William Charles).

THE ALPS OF ARABIA; or, Travels through Egypt, Sinai, Arabia, and the Holy Land. With Map. Second Edition. Demy 8vo. Cloth, price 5*s*.

MAURICE (C. Edmund).

LIVES OF ENGLISH POPULAR LEADERS. No. 1.—STEPHEN LANGTON. Crown 8vo. Cloth, price 7*s*. 6*d*.

No. 2.—TYLER, BALL, and OLDCASTLE. Crown 8vo. Price 7*s*. 6*d*.

MAZZINI (Joseph).

A Memoir. By E. A. V. Two Photographic Portraits. Crown 8vo Cloth, price 3*s*. 6*d*.

MEDLEY (Lieut.-Col. J. G.), Royal Engineers.

AN AUTUMN TOUR IN THE UNITED STATES AND CANADA. Crown 8vo. Cloth, price 5*s*.

MENZIES (Sutherland).

MEMOIRS OF DISTINGUISHED WOMEN. 2 vols. Post 8vo. Cloth, price 10*s*. 6*d*.

ANNE DE BOURBON.
THE DUCHESS DE LONGUEVILLE.
THE DUCHESS DE CHEVREUSE.
PRINCESS PALATINE.
MADEMOISELLE DE MONTPENSIER.
MADAME DE MONTBAZON.
THE DUCHESS OF PORTSMOUTH.
SARAH JENNINGS.
SARAH, DUCHESS OF MARLBOROUH.

MICKLETHWAITE (J. T.), F.S.A.

MODERN PARISH CHURCHES: Their Plan, Design, and Furniture. Crown 8vo. Cloth, price 7*s*. 6*d*.

MILNE (James).

TABLES OF EXCHANGE for the Conversion of Sterling Money into Indian and Ceylon Currency, at Rates from 1*s*. 8*d*. to 2*s*. 3*d*. per Rupee. Second Edition. Demy 8vo. Cloth, price £2 2*s*.

MIRUS (Major-General von).

CAVALRY FIELD DUTY. Translated by Major Frank S. Russell, 14th (King's) Hussars. Crown 8vo. Cloth limp, price 7*s*. 6*d*.

MIVART (St. George), F.R.S.

CONTEMPORARY EVOLUTION: An Essay on some recent Social Changes. Post 8vo. Cloth, price 7*s*. 6*d*.

MOORE (Rev. Daniel), M.A.

CHRIST AND HIS CHURCH. By the author of "The Age and the Gospel: Hulsean Lectures," etc. Crown 8vo. Cloth, price 3*s*. 6*d*.

MOORE (Rev. Thomas), Vicar of Christ Church, Chesham.

SERMONETTES: on Synonymous Texts, taken from the Bible and Book of Common Prayer, for the Study, Family Reading, and Private Devotion. Small Crown 8vo. Cloth, price 4*s*. 6*d*.

MORELL (J. R.)

EUCLID SIMPLIFIED IN METHOD AND LANGUAGE. Being a Manual of Geometry. Compiled from the most important French Works, approved by the University of Paris and the Minister of Public Instruction. Fcap. 8vo. Cloth, price 2*s*. 6*d*.

MORICE (Rev. F. D.), M.A., Fellow of Queen's College, Oxford.

THE OLYMPIAN AND PYTHIAN ODES OF PINDAR. A New Translation in English Verse. Crown 8vo. Cloth, price 7*s*. 6*d*.

MORLEY (Susan).

AILEEN FERRERS. A Novel. 2 vols. Crown 8vo. Cloth.

THROSTLETHWAITE. A Novel. 3 vols. Crown 8vo. Cloth.

MORSE (Edward S.), Ph.D., late Professor of Comparative Anatomy and Zoology in Bowdoin College.

FIRST BOOK OF ZOOLOGY. With numerous Illustrations. Crown 8vo. Cloth, price 5*s*.

MOSTYN (Sydney).

PERPLEXITY. A Novel. 3 vols. Crown 8vo. Cloth.

MUSGRAVE (Anthony).

STUDIES IN POLITICAL ECONOMY. Crown 8vo. Cloth, 6*s*.

MY SISTER ROSALIND.

A Novel. By the Author of "Christiana North," and "Under the Limes." 2 vols. Cloth.

NAAKÈ (John T.), of the British Museum.

SLAVONIC FAIRY TALES. From Russian, Servian, Polish, and Bohemian Sources. With Four Illustrations. Crown 8vo. Cloth, price 5*s*.

NEWMAN (John Henry), D.D.

CHARACTERISTICS FROM THE WRITINGS OF DR. J. H. NEWMAN. Being Selections, Personal, Historical, Philosophical, and Religious, from his various Works. Arranged with the Author's personal approval. Second Edition. With Portrait. Crown 8vo. Cloth, price 6*s*.

*** A Portrait of the Rev. Dr. J. H. Newman, mounted for framing, can be had, price 2*s*. 6*d*.

NEWMAN (Mrs.)

TOO LATE. A Novel. 2 vols. Crown 8vo. Cloth.

NOBLE (James Ashcroft).

THE PELICAN PAPERS. Reminiscences and Remains of a Dweller in the Wilderness. Crown 8vo. Cloth, price 6*s*.

NORMAN PEOPLE (The).

THE NORMAN PEOPLE, and their Existing Descendants in the British Dominions and the United States of America. Demy 8vo. Cloth, price 21*s*.

NORRIS (Rev. A.)

THE INNER AND OUTER LIFE POEMS. Fcap. 8vo. Cloth, price 6*s*.

NOTREGE (John), A.M.

THE SPIRITUAL FUNCTION OF A PRESBYTER IN THE CHURCH OF ENGLAND. Crown 8vo. Cloth, red edges, price 3*s*. 6*d*.

ORIENTAL SPORTING MAGAZINE (The).

A Reprint of the first 5 Volumes, in 2 Volumes. Demy 8vo. Cloth, price 28*s*.

OUR INCREASING MILITARY DIFFICULTY, and one Way of Meeting it.

Demy 8vo. Stitched, price 1*s*.

PAGE (H. A.)

NATHANIEL HAWTHORNE, A MEMOIR OF, with Stories now first published in this country. Large post 8vo. Cloth, price 7*s*. 6*d*.

PAGE (Capt. S. Flood).

DISCIPLINE AND DRILL. Cheaper Edition. Crown 8vo. Price 1*s*.

PALGRAVE (W. Gifford).

HERMANN AGHA. An Eastern Narrative. 2 vols. Crown 8vo. Cloth, extra gilt, price 18*s.*

PANDURANG HARI;

OR MEMOIRS OF A HINDOO. With an Introductory Preface by Sir H. Bartle E. Frere, G.C.S.I., K.C.B., D.C.L. 2 vols. Crown 8vo. Cloth, price 21*s.*

TALES OF THE ZENANA. 2 vols. Crown 8vo. Cloth, price 21*s.*

PARKER (Joseph), D.D.

THE PARACLETE: An Essay on the Personality and Ministry of the Holy Ghost, with some reference to current discussions. Second Edition. Demy 8vo. Cloth, price 12*s.*

PARR (Harriett).

ECHOES OF A FAMOUS YEAR. Crown 8vo. Cloth, price 8*s.* 6*d.*

PAUL (C. Kegan).

GOETHE'S FAUST. A New Translation in Rime. Crown 8vo. Cloth, price 6*s.*

WILLIAM GODWIN: HIS FRIENDS AND CONTEMPORARIES. With Portraits and Facsimiles of the Handwriting of Godwin and his Wife. 2 vols. Demy 8vo. Cloth, price 28*s.*

THE GENIUS OF CHRISTIANITY UNVEILED. Being Essays never before published. Edited, with a Preface, by C. Kegan Paul. Crown 8vo. Cloth, price 7*s.* 6*d.*

PAYNE (John).

SONGS OF LIFE AND DEATH. Crown 8vo. Cloth, price 5*s.*

PAYNE (Professor).

LECTURES ON EDUCATION. Price 6*d.* each.

I. Pestalozzi: the Influence of His Principles and Practice.
II. Fröbel and the Kindergarten System. Second Edition.
III. The Science and Art of Education.
IV. The True Foundation of Science Teaching.

PELLETAN (Eugène).

THE DESERT PASTOR, JEAN JAROUSSEAU. Translated from the French. By Colonel E. P. De L'Hoste. With a Frontispiece. New Edition. Fcap. 8vo. Cloth, price 3*s.* 6*d.*

PENRICE (Major J.), B.A.

A DICTIONARY AND GLOSSARY OF THE KO-RAN. With copious Grammatical References and Explanations of the Text. 4to. Cloth, price 21*s.*

PERCEVAL (Rev. P.)

TAMIL PROVERBS, WITH THEIR ENGLISH TRANSLATION. Containing upwards of Six Thousand Proverbs. Third Edition. Demy 8vo. Sewed, price 9*s.*

PERRIER (Amelia).

A WINTER IN MOROCCO. With Four Illustrations. A New and Cheaper Edition. Crown 8vo. Cloth, price 3*s.* 6*d.*

A GOOD MATCH. A Novel. 2 vols. Crown 8vo. Cloth.

PERRY (Rev. S. J.), F.R.S.

NOTES OF A VOYAGE TO KERGUELEN ISLAND, to observe the Transit of Venus. Demy 8vo. Sewed, price 2*s.*

PETTIGREW (J. B.), M.D., F.R.S.

ANIMAL LOCOMOTION; or, Walking, Swimming, and Flying. With 130 Illustrations. Second Edition. Crown 8vo. Cloth, price 5*s.*

Volume VII. of the International Scientific Series.

PIGGOT (John), F.S.A, F.R.G.S.

PERSIA—ANCIENT AND MODERN. Post 8vo. Cloth, price 10*s.* 6*d.*

POUSHKIN (Alexander Serguevitch).

RUSSIAN ROMANCE. Translated from the Tales of Belkin, etc. By Mrs. J. Buchan Telfer (*née* Mouravieff). Crown 8vo. Cloth, price 7*s.* 6*d.*

POWER (Harriet).

OUR INVALIDS: HOW SHALL WE EMPLOY AND AMUSE THEM? Fcap 8vo. Cloth, price 2*s.* 6*d.*

POWLETT (Lieut. Norton), Royal Artillery.

EASTERN LEGENDS AND STORIES IN ENGLISH VERSE. Crown 8vo. Cloth, price 5*s.*

PRESBYTER.

UNFOLDINGS OF CHRISTIAN HOPE. An Essay showing that the Doctrine contained in the Damnatory Clauses of the Creed commonly called Athanasian is unscriptural. Small crown 8vo. Cloth, price 4*s.* 6*d.*

PRICE (Prof. Bonamy).

CURRENCY AND BANKING. Crown 8vo. Cloth, price 6*s.*

PROCTOR (Richard A.), B.A.

OUR PLACE AMONG INFINITIES. A Series of Essays contrasting our little abode in space and time with the Infinities around us. To which are added Essays on "Astrology," and "The Jewish Sabbath." Second Edition. Crown 8vo. Cloth, price 6*s*.

THE EXPANSE OF HEAVEN. A Series of Essays on the Wonders of the Firmament. With a Frontispiece. Second Edition. Crown 8vo. Cloth, price 6*s*.

RANKING (B. Montgomerie).

STREAMS FROM HIDDEN SOURCES. Crown 8vo. Cloth, price 6*s*.

READY-MONEY MORTIBOY.

A Matter-of-Fact Story. With Frontispiece. Crown 8vo. Cloth, price 3*s*. 6*d*.

REANEY (Mrs. G. S.)

WAKING AND WORKING; OR, FROM GIRLHOOD TO WOMANHOOD. With a Frontispiece. Crown 8vo. Cloth, price 5*s*.

SUNBEAM WILLIE, AND OTHER STORIES. Three Illustrations. Square crown, uniform with "Lost Gip," etc. Cloth, price 1*s*. 6*d*.

REGINALD BRAMBLE.

A Cynic of the Nineteenth Century. An Autobiography. Crown 8vo. Cloth, price 10*s*. 6*d*.

REID (T. Wemyss).

CABINET PORTRAITS. Biographical Sketches of Statesmen of the Day. Crown 8vo. Cloth, price 7*s*. 6*d*.

RHOADES (James).

TIMOLEON. A Dramatic Poem. Fcap. 8vo. Cloth, price 5*s*.

RIBOT (Professor Th.)

CONTEMPORARY ENGLISH PSYCHOLOGY. Second Edition. A revised and corrected translation from the latest French Edition. Large post 8vo. Cloth, price 9*s*.

An analysis of the views and opinions of the following metaphysicians, as expressed in their writings:—James Mill Alexander Bain, John Stuart Mill, George H. Lewes, Herbert Spencer, Samuel Bailey.

HEREDITY: A Psychological Study on its Phenomena, its Laws, its Causes, and its Consequences. Large crown 8vo. Cloth, price 9*s*.

ROBERTSON (The Late Rev. F. W.), M.A.

THE LATE REV. F. W. ROBERTSON, M.A., LIFE AND LETTERS OF. Edited by the Rev. Stopford Brooke, M.A., Chaplain in Ordinary to the Queen.

I. 2 vols., uniform with the Sermons. With Steel Portrait. Crown 8vo. Cloth, price 7*s* 6*d*

II. Library Edition, in Demy 8vo. with Two Steel Portraits. Cloth, price 12*s*.

III. A Popular Edition, in 1 vol. Crown 8vo. Cloth, price 6*s*.

New and Cheaper Editions :—

SERMONS.

First Series. Small crown 8vo. Cloth, price 3*s*. 6*d*.
Second Series. Small crown 8vo. Cloth, price 3*s*. 6*d*.
Third Series. Small crown 8vo. Cloth, price 3*s*. 6*d*.
Fourth Series. Small crown 8vo. Cloth, price 3*s*. 6*d*.

EXPOSITORY LECTURES ON ST. PAUL'S EPISTLES TO THE CORINTHIANS. A New Edition. Small crown 8vo. Cloth, price 5*s*.

LECTURES AND ADDRESSES, with other literary remains. A New Edition. Crown 8vo. Cloth, price 5*s*.

AN ANALYSIS OF MR. TENNYSON'S "IN MEMORIAM." (Dedicated by Permission to the Poet-Laureate.) Fcap. 8vo. Cloth, price 2*s*.

THE EDUCATION OF THE HUMAN RACE. Translated from the German of Gotthold Ephraim Lessing. Fcap. 8vo. Cloth, price 2*s*. 6*d*.

The above Works can also be had bound in half-morocco.

*** A Portrait of the late Rev. F. W. Robertson, mounted for framing, can be had, price 2*s*. 6*d*.

ROSS (Mrs. Ellen), ("Nelsie Brook.")

DADDY'S PET. A Sketch from Humble Life. Uniform with "Lost Gip." With Six Illustrations. Square crown 8vo. Cloth, price 1*s*.

ROXBURGHE LOTHIAN.

DANTE AND BEATRICE FROM 1282 TO 1290. A Romance. 2 vols. Post 8vo. Cloth, price 24*s*.

RUSSELL (William Clark).

MEMOIRS OF MRS. LÆTITIA BOOTHBY. Crown 8vo. Cloth, price 7*s*. 6*d*.

RUSSELL (E. R.)

IRVING AS HAMLET. Second Edition. Demy 8vo. Sewed, price 1*s.*

SADLER (S. W.), R.N.

THE AFRICAN CRUISER. A Midshipman's Adventures on the West Coast. With Three Illustrations. Second Edition. Crown 8vo. Cloth, price 3*s.* 6*d.*

SAMAROW (Gregor).

FOR SCEPTRE AND CROWN. A Romance of the Present Time. Translated by Fanny Wormald. 2 vols. Crown 8vo. Cloth, price 15*s.*

SAUNDERS (Katherine).

THE HIGH MILLS. A Novel. 3 vols. Crown 8vo. Cloth.

GIDEON'S ROCK, and other Stories. Crown 8vo. Cloth, price 6*s.*

JOAN MERRYWEATHER, and other Stories. Crown 8vo. Cloth, price 6*s.*

MARGARET AND ELIZABETH. A Story of the Sea. Crown 8vo. Cloth, price 6*s.*

SAUNDERS (John).

ISRAEL MORT, OVERMAN. A Story of the Mine. 3 vols. Crown 8vo.

HIRELL. With Frontispiece. Crown 8vo. Cloth, price 3*s.* 6*d.*

ABEL DRAKE'S WIFE. With Frontispiece. Crown 8vo. Cloth, price 3*s.* 6*d.*

SCHELL (Major von).

THE OPERATIONS OF THE FIRST ARMY UNDER GEN. VON GOEBEN. Translated by Col. C. H. von Wright. Four Maps. Demy 8vo. Cloth, price 9*s.*

THE OPERATIONS OF THE FIRST ARMY UNDER GEN. VON STEINMETZ. Translated by Captain E. O. Hollist. Demy 8vo. Cloth, price 10*s.* 6*d.*

SCHERFF (Major W. von).

STUDIES IN THE NEW INFANTRY TACTICS. Parts I. and II. Translated from the German by Colonel Lumley Graham. Demy 8vo. Cloth, price 7*s.* 6*d.*

SCHMIDT (Prof. Oscar), Strasburg University.

THE DOCTRINE OF DESCENT AND DARWINISM. With 26 Illustrations. Third Edition. Crown 8vo. Cloth, price 5*s.*

Volume XII. of the International Scientific Series.

SCHÜTZENBERGER (Prof. F.), Director of the Chemical Laboratory at the Sorbonne.

FERMENTATION. With numerous Illustrations. Crown 8vo. Cloth, price 5*s.*

Volume XX. of the International Scientific Series.

SCOTT (Patrick).

THE DREAM AND THE DEED, and other Poems. Fcap. 8vo. Cloth, price 5*s.*

SCOTT (W. T.)

ANTIQUITIES OF AN ESSEX PARISH; or, Pages from the History of Great Dunmow. Crown 8vo. Cloth, price 5*s.* Sewed, 4*s.*

SCOTT (Robert H.)

WEATHER CHARTS AND STORM WARNINGS. Illustrated. Crown 8vo. Cloth, price 3*s.* 6*d.*

SEEKING HIS FORTUNE, and other Stories.

With Four Illustrations. Crown 8vo. Cloth, price 3*s.* 6*d.*

SENIOR (Nassau William).

ALEXIS DE TOCQUEVILLE. Correspondence and Conversations with Nassau W. Senior, from 1833 to 1859. Edited by M. C. M. Simpson. 2 vols. Large post 8vo. Cloth, price 21*s.*

JOURNALS KEPT IN FRANCE AND ITALY. From 1848 to 1852. With a Sketch of the Revolution of 1848. Edited by his Daughter, M. C. M. Simpson. 2 vols. Post 8vo. Cloth, price 24*s.*

SEVEN AUTUMN LEAVES FROM FAIRYLAND.

Illustrated with Nine Etchings. Square crown 8vo. Cloth, price 3*s.* 6*d.*

SEYD (Ernest), F.S.S.

THE FALL IN THE PRICE OF SILVER. Its Causes, its Consequences, and their Possible Avoidance, with Special Reference to India. Demy 8vo. Sewed, price 2*s.* 6*d.*

SHADWELL (Major-General), C.B.

MOUNTAIN WARFARE. Illustrated by the Campaign of 1799 in Switzerland. Being a Translation of the Swiss Narrative compiled from the Works of the Archduke Charles, Jomini, and others. Also of Notes by General H. Dufour on the Campaign of the Valtelline in 1635. With Appendix, Maps, and Introductory Remarks. Demy 8vo. Cloth, price 16*s*.

SHELDON (Philip).

WOMAN'S A RIDDLE; or, Baby Warmstrey. A Novel. 3 vols. Crown 8vo. Cloth.

SHERMAN (Gen. W. T.)

MEMOIRS OF GEN. W. T. SHERMAN, Commander of the Federal Forces in the American Civil War. By Himself. 2 vols. With Map. Demy 8vo. Cloth, price 24*s*. *Copyright English Edition.*

SHELLEY (Lady).

SHELLEY MEMORIALS FROM AUTHENTIC SOURCES. With (now first printed) an Essay on Christianity by Percy Bysshe Shelley. With Portrait. Third Edition. Crown 8vo. Cloth, price 5*s*.

SHIPLEY (Rev. Orby), M.A.

STUDIES IN MODERN PROBLEMS. By various Writers. 2 vols. Crown 8vo. Cloth, price 5s. each.

CONTENTS.—VOL. I.

Sacramental Confession.
Abolition of the Thirty-nine Articles. Part I.
The Sanctity of Marriage.
Creation and Modern Science.
Retreats for Persons Living in the World.
Catholic and Protestant.
The Bishops on Confession in the Church of England.

CONTENTS.—VOL. II.

Some Principles of Christian Ceremonial.
A Layman's View of Confession of Sin to a Priest. Parts I. and II.
Reservation of the Blessed Sacrament.
Missions and Preaching Orders.
Abolition of the Thirty nine Articles. Part II.
The First Liturgy of Edward VI. and our own office contrasted and compared.

SMEDLEY (M. B.)

BOARDING-OUT AND PAUPER SCHOOLS FOR GIRLS. Crown 8vo. Cloth, price 3*s*. 6*d*.

Smith (Edward), M.D., LL.B., F.R.S.

HEALTH AND DISEASE, as influenced by the Daily, Seasonal, and other Cyclical Changes in the Human System. A New Edition. Post 8vo. Cloth, price 7*s*. 6*d*.

FOODS. Profusely Illustrated. Fourth Edition. Crown 8vo. Cloth, price 5*s*.

Volume III. of the International Scientific Series.

PRACTICAL DIETARY FOR FAMILIES, SCHOOLS, AND THE LABOURING CLASSES. A New Edition. Post 8vo. Cloth, price 3*s*. 6*d*.

TUBERCULAR CONSUMPTION IN ITS EARLY AND REMEDIABLE STAGES. Second Edition. Crown 8vo. Cloth, price 6*s*.

Smith (Hubert).

TENT LIFE WITH ENGLISH GIPSIES IN NORWAY. With Five full-page Engravings and Thirty-one smaller Illustrations by Whymper and others, and Map of the Country showing Routes. Third Edition. Revised and Corrected. Post 8vo. Cloth, price 21*s*.

Songs for Music.

By Four Friends. Square crown 8vo. Cloth, price 5*s*.

Containing Songs by Reginald A. Gatty, Stephen H. Gatty, Greville J. Chester, and Juliana H. Ewing.

Some Time in Ireland.

A Recollection. Crown 8vo. Cloth, price 7*s*. 6*d*.

Songs of Two Worlds.

SONGS OF TWO WORLDS. By a New Writer. Third Series. Second Edition. Fcap. 8vo. Cloth, price 5*s*.

THE EPIC OF HADES. By the Author of "Songs of Two Worlds." Fcap. 8vo. Cloth, price 5*s*.

Spencer (Herbert).

THE STUDY OF SOCIOLOGY. Fifth Edition. Crown 8vo. Cloth, price 5*s*.

Vol. V. of the International Scientific Series.

Spicer (Henry).

OTHO'S DEATH WAGER. A Dark Page of History Illustrated. In Five Acts. Fcap. 8vo. Cloth, price 5*s*.

STEVENSON (Rev. W. Fleming).

HYMNS FOR THE CHURCH AND HOME. Selected and Edited by the Rev. W. Fleming Stevenson.

The most complete Hymn Book published.

The Hymn Book consists of Three Parts:—I. For Public Worship.—II. For Family and Private Worship.—III. For Children.

*** *Published in various forms and prices, the latter ranging from 8d. to 6s. Lists and full particulars will be furnished on application to the Publishers.*

STEWART (Professor Balfour), M.A., LL.D., F.R.S.

ON THE CONSERVATION OF ENERGY. Third Edition. With Fourteen Engravings. Crown 8vo. Cloth, price 5*s.*

Volume VI. of the International Scientific Series.

STONEHEWER (Agnes).

MONACELLA: A Legend of North Wales. A Poem. Fcap. 8vo. Cloth, price 3*s.* 6*d.*

STRETTON (Hesba). Author of "Jessica's First Prayer."

THE CREW OF THE DOLPHIN. Illustrated. Sixth Thousand. Square crown 8vo. Cloth, price 1*s.* 6*d.*

CASSY. Twenty-eighth Thousand. With Six Illustrations. Square crown 8vo. Cloth, price 1*s.* 6*d.*

THE KING'S SERVANTS. Thirty-third Thousand. With Eight Illustrations. Square crown 8vo. Cloth, price 1*s.* 6*d.*

LOST GIP. Forty-seventh Thousand. With Six Illustrations. Square crown 8vo. Cloth, price 1*s.* 6*d.*

*** *Also a handsomely bound Edition, with Twelve Illustrations, price* 2*s.* 6*d.*

THE WONDERFUL LIFE. Ninth Thousand. Fcap. 8vo. Cloth, price 2*s.* 6*d.*

FRIENDS TILL DEATH. With Frontispiece. Fourteenth Thousand. Limp cloth, price 6*d.*

TWO CHRISTMAS STORIES. With Frontispiece. Eleventh Thousand. Limp cloth, price 6*d.*

MICHEL LORIO'S CROSS, AND LEFT ALONE. With Frontispiece. Seventh Thousand. Limp cloth, price 6*d.*

OLD TRANSOME. With Frontispiece. Ninth Thousand. Limp cloth, price 6*d.*

THE WORTH OF A BABY, AND HOW APPLE-TREE COURT WAS WON. With Frontispiece. Ninth Thousand. Limp cloth, price 6d.

HESTER MORLEY'S PROMISE. 3 vols. Crown 8vo. Cloth.

THE DOCTOR'S DILEMMA. 3 vols. Crown 8vo. Cloth.

STUMM (Lieut. Hugo).

RUSSIA'S ADVANCE EASTWARD. With Map. Crown 8vo. Cloth, price 6*s.*

SULLY (James), M.A..

SENSATION AND INTUITION. Demy 8vo. Cloth, price 10*s.* 6*d.*

SUNNYLAND STORIES.

By the Author of "Aunt Mary's Bran Pie." Illustrated. Small 8vo. Cloth, price 3*s.* 6*d.*

TALES OF THE ZENANA.

By the Author of "Pandurang Hari." 2 vols. Crown 8vo. Cloth, price 21*s.*

TAYLOR (Rev. J. W. Augustus), M.A.

POEMS. Fcap. 8vo. Cloth, price 5*s.*

TAYLOR (Sir Henry).

EDWIN THE FAIR AND ISAAC COMNENUS. A New Edition. Fcap. 8vo. Cloth, price 3*s.* 6*d.*

A SICILIAN SUMMER AND OTHER POEMS. A New Edition. Fcap. 8vo. Cloth, price 3*s.* 6*d.*

PHILIP VAN ARTEVELDE. A Dramatic Poem. A New Edition. Fcap. 8vo. Cloth, price 5*s.*

TAYLOR (Colonel Meadows), C.S.I., M.R.I.A.

SEETA. A Novel. 3 vols. Crown 8vo. Cloth.

THE CONFESSIONS OF A THUG. Crown 8vo. Cloth, price 6*s.*

TARA: a Mahratta Tale. Crown 8vo. Cloth, price 6*s.*

TELFER (J. Buchan), F.R.G.S., Commander R.N.

THE CRIMEA AND TRANSCAUCASIA. Being the Narrative of a Journey in the Tauric Range, and in the Kouban, Gouria, Georgia, Armenia, Ossety, Imeritia, Letchgoumm, Swannety, and Mingrelia. With numerous Illustrations and Maps. 2 vols. Medium 8vo. Cloth, price 36*s.*

THOMAS (Moy).

A FIGHT FOR LIFE. With Frontispiece. Crown 8vo. Cloth, price 3*s.* 6*d.*

THOMASINA.

A Novel. 2 vols. Crown 8vo.

TENNYSON (Alfred).

QUEEN MARY. A Drama. New Edition. Crown 8vo. Cloth, price 6*s*.

TENNYSON'S (Alfred) Works. Cabinet Edition. Ten Volumes. Each with Frontispiece. Fcap. 8vo. Cloth, price 2*s*. 6*d*.

CABINET EDITION. 10 vols. Complete in handsome Ornamental Case. Price 28*s*.

TENNYSON'S (Alfred) Works. Author's Edition. Complete in Five Volumes. Post 8vo. Cloth gilt; or half-morocco, Roxburgh style.

VOL. I. **EARLY POEMS, and ENGLISH IDYLLS.** Price 6*s*.; Roxburgh, 7*s*. 6*d*.

VOL. II. **LOCKSLEY HALL, LUCRETIUS, and other Poems.** Price 6*s*.; Roxburgh, 7*s*. 6*d*.

VOL. III. **THE IDYLLS OF THE KING** (*Complete*). Price 7*s*. 6*d*.; Roxburgh, 9*s*.

VOL. IV. **THE PRINCESS, and MAUD.** Price 6*s*.; Roxburgh, 7*s*. 6*d*.

VOL. V. **ENOCH ARDEN, and IN MEMORIAM.** Price 6*s*.; Roxburgh, 7*s*. 6*d*.

TENNYSON'S IDYLLS OF THE KING, and other Poems. Illustrated by Julia Margaret Cameron. 2 vols. Folio. Half-bound morocco, cloth sides, £6 6*s*. each.

TENNYSON'S (Alfred) Works. Original Editions.

POEMS. Small 8vo. Cloth, price 6*s*.

MAUD, and other Poems. Small 8vo. Cloth, price 3*s*. 6*d*.

THE PRINCESS. Small 8vo. Cloth, price 3*s*. 6*d*.

IDYLLS OF THE KING. Small 8vo. Cloth, price 5*s*.

IDYLLS OF THE KING. Collected. Small 8vo. Cloth, price 6*s*.

THE HOLY GRAIL, and other Poems. Small 8vo. Cloth, price 4*s*. 6*d*.

GARETH AND LYNETTE. Small 8vo. Cloth, price 3*s*.

ENOCH ARDEN, etc. Small 8vo. Cloth, price 3*s*. 6*d*.

SELECTIONS FROM THE ABOVE WORKS. Square 8vo. Cloth, price 3*s*. 6*d*. Cloth gilt, extra, price 4*s*.

SONGS FROM THE ABOVE WORKS. Square 8vo. Cloth extra, price 3*s*. 6*d*.

IN MEMORIAM. Small 8vo. Cloth, price 4*s*.

LIBRARY EDITION. In 6 vols. Demy 8vo. Cloth, price 10*s*. 6*d*. each.

POCKET VOLUME EDITION. 11 vols. In neat case, 31*s*. 6*d*.
Ditto, ditto. Extra cloth gilt, in case, 35*s*.

POEMS. Illustrated Edition. 4to. Cloth, price 25*s*.

THOMPSON (A. C.)

PRELUDES. A Volume of Poems. Illustrated by Elizabeth Thompson (Painter of "The Roll Call"). 8vo. Cloth, price 7*s.* 6*d.*

THOMSON (J. T.), F.R.G.S.

HAKAYIT ABDULLA. The Autobiography of a Malay Munshi, between the years 1808 and 1843. Demy 8vo. Cloth, price 12*s.*

THOMPSON (Rev. A. S.), British Chaplain at St. Petersburg.

HOME WORDS FOR WANDERERS. A Volume of Sermons. Crown 8vo. Cloth, price 6*s.*

THOUGHTS IN VERSE.

Small crown 8vo. Cloth, price 1*s.* 6*d.*

THRING (Rev. Godfrey), B.A.

HYMNS AND SACRED LYRICS. Fcap. 8vo. Cloth, price 5*s.*

TODD (Herbert), M.A.

ARVAN; or, The Story of the Sword. A Poem. Crown 8vo. Cloth, price 7*s.* 6*d.*

TRAHERNE (Mrs. Arthur).

THE ROMANTIC ANNALS OF A NAVAL FAMILY. A New and Cheaper Edition. Crown 8vo. Cloth, price 5*s.*

TRAVERS (Mar.)

THE SPINSTERS OF BLATCHINGTON. A Novel. 2 vols. Crown 8vo. Cloth.

TREVANDRUM OBSERVATIONS.

OBSERVATIONS OF MAGNETIC DECLINATION MADE AT TREVANDRUM AND AGUSTIA MALLEY in the Observatories of his Highness the Maharajah of Travancore, G.C.S.I., in the Years 1852 to 1860. Being Trevandrum Magnetical Observations, Volume I. Discussed and Edited by John Allan Brown, F.R.S., late Director of the Observatories. With an Appendix. Imp. 4to. Cloth, price £3 3*s.*

*** *The Appendix, containing Reports on the Observatories and on the Public Museum, Public Park, and Gardens at Trevandrum, pp.* xii.-116, *may be had separately, price* 21*s.*

TURNER (Rev. Charles).

SONNETS, LYRICS, AND TRANSLATIONS. Crown 8vo. Cloth, price 4*s.* 6*d.*

TYNDALL (J.), LL.D., F.R.S.

THE FORMS OF WATER IN CLOUDS AND RIVERS, ICE AND GLACIERS. With Twenty-six Illustrations. Sixth Edition. Crown 8vo. Cloth, price 5*s.*

Volume I. of the International Scientific Series.

UMBRA OXONIENSIS.

RESULTS OF THE EXPOSTULATION OF THE RIGHT HONOURABLE W. E. GLADSTONE, in their Relation to the Unity of Roman Catholicism. Large fcap. 8vo. Cloth, price 5*s.*

UPTON (Roger D.), Captain late 9th Royal Lancers.

NEWMARKET AND ARABIA. An Examination of the Descent of Racers and Coursers. With Pedigrees and Frontispiece. Post 8vo. Cloth, price 9*s.*

VAMBERY (Prof. Arminius), of the University of Pesth.

BOKHARA: Its History and Conquest. Second Edition. Demy 8vo. Cloth, price 18*s.*

VAN BENEDEN (Monsieur), Professor of the University of Louvain, Correspondent of the Institute of France.

ANIMAL PARASITES AND MESSMATES. With 83 Illustrations. Second Edition. Cloth, price 5*s.*

Volume XIX. of the International Scientific Series.

VANESSA.

By the Author of "Thomasina," etc. A Novel. 2 vols. Second Edition. Crown 8vo. Cloth.

VAUGHAN (Rev. C. J.), D.D.

WORDS OF HOPE FROM THE PULPIT OF THE TEMPLE CHURCH. Third Edition. Crown 8vo. Cloth, price 5*s.*

THE SOLIDITY OF TRUE RELIGION, and other Sermons Preached in London during the Election and Mission Week, February, 1874. Crown 8vo. Cloth, price 3*s.* 6*d.*

FORGET THINE OWN PEOPLE. An Appeal for Missions. Crown 8vo. Cloth, price 3*s.* 6*d.*

THE YOUNG LIFE EQUIPPING ITSELF FOR GOD'S SERVICE. Being Four Sermons Preached before the University of Cambridge, in November, 1872. Fourth Edition. Crown 8vo. Cloth, price 3*s.* 6*d.*

VERNOIS (Col. Von Verdy du).

STUDIES IN LEADING TROOPS. Translated by Lieutenant H. J. S. Hildyard. Parts I. and II. Demy 8vo. Cloth, price 7*s.*

VINCENT (Capt. C. E. H.), late Royal Welsh Fusiliers.

ELEMENTARY MILITARY GEOGRAPHY, RECONNOITRING, AND SKETCHING. Compiled for Non-Commissioned Officers and Soldiers of all Arms. Square crown 8vo. Cloth, price 2*s.* 6*d.*

RUSSIA'S ADVANCE EASTWARD. Based on the Official Reports of Lieutenant Hugo Stumm, German Military Attaché to the Khivan Expedition. With Map. Crown 8vo. Cloth, price 6*s.*

VIZCAYA; or, Life in the Land of the Carlists at the Outbreak of the Insurrection, with some Account of the Iron Mines and other Characteristics of the Country. With a Map and Eight Illustrations. Crown 8vo. Cloth, price 9*s.*

VOGEL (Prof.), Polytechnic Academy of Berlin.

THE CHEMICAL EFFECTS OF LIGHT AND PHOTOGRAPHY, in their application to Art, Science, and Industry. The translation thoroughly revised. With 100 Illustrations, including some beautiful Specimens of Photography. Third Edition. Crown 8vo. Cloth, price 5*s.*

Volume XV. of the International Scientific Series.

VOLUNTEER (The), THE MILITIAMAN, AND THE REGULAR SOLDIER.

By a Public Schoolboy. Crown 8vo. Cloth, price 5*s.*

VYNER (Lady Mary).

EVERY DAY A PORTION. Adapted from the Bible and the Prayer Book, for the Private Devotions of those living in Widowhood. Collected and Edited by Lady Mary Vyner. Square crown 8vo. Cloth extra, price 5*s.*

WAITING FOR TIDINGS.

By the Author of "White and Black." 3 vols. Crown 8vo. Cloth.

WARTENSLEBEN (Count Hermann von), Colonel in the Prussian General Staff.

THE OPERATIONS OF THE SOUTH ARMY IN JANUARY AND FEBRUARY, 1871. Compiled from the Official War Documents of the Head-quarters of the Southern Army. Translated by Colonel C. H. von Wright. With Maps. Demy 8vo. Cloth, price 6*s.*

THE OPERATIONS OF THE FIRST ARMY UNDER GEN. VON MANTEUFFEL. Translated by Colonel C. H. von Wright. Uniform with the above. Demy 8vo. Cloth, price 9*s.*

WAY (Arthur), M.A.,

THE ODES OF HORACE LITERALLY TRANSLATED IN METRE. Fcap. 8vo. Cloth, price 2s.

WEDMORE (Frederick).

TWO GIRLS. 2 vols. Crown 8vo. Cloth.

WELLS (Captain John C.), R.N.

SPITZBERGEN—THE GATEWAY TO THE POLYNIA; or, A Voyage to Spitzbergen. With numerous Illustrations by Whymper and others, and Map. New and Cheaper Edition. Demy 8vo. Cloth, price 6*s*.

WETMORE (W. S.).

COMMERCIAL TELEGRAPHIC CODE. Post 4to. Boards, price 42*s*.

WHAT 'TIS TO LOVE.

By the Author of "Flora Adair," "The Value of Fostertown." 3 vols. Crown 8vo. Cloth.

WHITAKER (Florence).

CHRISTY'S INHERITANCE: A London Story. Illustrated. Royal 32mo. Cloth, price 1*s*. 6*d*.

WHITE (A. D.), L.L.D.

WARFARE OF SCIENCE. With Prefatory Note by Professor Tyndall. Crown 8vo. Cloth, price 3*s*. 6*d*.

WHITE (Captain F. B. P.)

THE SUBSTANTIVE SENIORITY ARMY LIST—MAJORS AND CAPTAINS. 8vo. Sewed, price 2*s*. 6*d*.

WHITNEY (William Dwight), Professor of Sanskrit and Comparative Philology in Yale College, New Haven.

THE LIFE AND GROWTH OF LANGUAGE. Second Edition. Crown 8vo. Cloth, price 5*s*. *Copyright Edition.*

Volume XVI. of the International Scientific Series.

WHITTLE (J. Lowry), A.M., Trin. Coll., Dublin.

CATHOLICISM AND THE VATICAN. With a Narrative of the Old Catholic Congress at Munich. Second Edition. Crown 8vo. Cloth, price 4*s*. 6*d*.

WILBERFORCE (Henry W.)

THE CHURCH AND THE EMPIRES. Historical Periods. Preceded by a Memoir of the Author by John Henry Newman, D.D., of the Oratory. With Portrait. Post 8vo. Cloth, price 10*s*. 6*d*.

WILKINSON (T. Lean).

SHORT LECTURES ON THE LAND LAWS. Delivered before the Working Men's College. Crown 8vo. Limp cloth, price 2*s*.

WILLIAMS (A. Lukyn), Jesus College, Cambridge.

FAMINES IN INDIA; their Causes and Possible Prevention. The Essay for the Le Bas Prize, 1875. Demy 8vo. Cloth, price 5*s*.

WILLIAMS (Rev. Rowland), D.D.

LIFE AND LETTERS OF ROWLAND WILLIAMS, D.D., with Extracts from his Note-books. Edited by Mrs. Rowland Williams. With a Photographic Portrait. 2 vols. Large post 8vo. Cloth, price 24*s*.

THE PSALMS, LITANIES, COUNSELS, AND COLLECTS FOR DEVOUT PERSONS. Edited by his Widow. New and Popular Edition. Crown 8vo. Cloth, price 3*s*. 6*d*.

WILLOUGHBY (The Hon. Mrs.)

ON THE NORTH WIND—THISTLEDOWN. A Volume of Poems. Elegantly bound. Small crown 8vo. Cloth, price 7*s*. 6*d*.

WILSON (H. Schütz).

STUDIES AND ROMANCES. Crown 8vo. Cloth, price 7*s*. 6*d*.

WILSON (Lieutenant-Colonel C. Townshend).

JAMES THE SECOND AND THE DUKE OF BERWICK. Demy 8vo. Cloth, price 12*s*. 6*d*.

WINTERBOTHAM (Rev. R.), M.A., B.Sc.

SERMONS AND EXPOSITIONS. Crown 8vo. Cloth, price 7*s*. 6*d*.

WOINOVITS (Captain Illia).

AUSTRIAN CAVALRY EXERCISE. Translated by Captain W. S. Cooke. Crown 8vo. Cloth, price 7*s*.

WOOD (C. F.)

A YACHTING CRUISE IN THE SOUTH SEAS. With Six Photographic Illustrations. Demy 8vo. Cloth, price 7*s*. 6*d*.

WRIGHT (Rev. D.), M.A.

MAN AND ANIMALS: A Sermon. Crown 8vo. Stitched in wrapper, price 1s.

WAITING FOR THE LIGHT, AND OTHER SERMONS. Crown 8vo. Cloth, price 6s.

WYLD (R. S.), F.R.S.E.

THE PHYSICS AND PHILOSOPHY OF THE SENSES; or, The Mental and the Physical in their Mutual Relation. Illustrated by several Plates. Demy 8vo. Cloth, price 16s.

YONGE (C. D.), Regius Professor, Queen's College, Belfast.

HISTORY OF THE ENGLISH REVOLUTION OF 1688. Crown 8vo. Cloth, price 6s.

YORKE (Stephen), Author of "Tales of the North Riding."

CLEVEDEN. A Novel. 2 vols. Crown 8vo. Cloth.

YOUMANS (Eliza A.)

AN ESSAY ON THE CULTURE OF THE OBSERVING POWERS OF CHILDREN, especially in connection with the Study of Botany. Edited, with Notes and a Supplement, by Joseph Payne, F.C.P., Author of "Lectures on the Science and Art of Education," etc. Crown 8vo. Cloth, price 2s. 6d.

FIRST BOOK OF BOTANY. Designed to cultivate the Observing Powers of Children. With 300 Engravings. New and Enlarged Edition. Crown 8vo. Cloth, price 5s.

YOUMANS (Edward L.), M.D.

A CLASS BOOK OF CHEMISTRY, on the Basis of the new System. With 200 Illustrations. Crown 8vo. Cloth, price 5s.

ZIMMERN (Helen).

STORIES IN PRECIOUS STONES. With Six Illustrations. Third Edition. Crown 8vo. Cloth, price 5s.